FORMS OF
ASSOCIATION

Forms of Association

MAKING PUBLICS IN EARLY MODERN EUROPE

EDITED BY

Paul Yachnin

AND

Marlene Eberhart

University of Massachusetts Press
Amherst and Boston

ISBN 978-1-62534-167-9 (paper); 166-2 (hardcover)

Designed by Jack Harrison

Set in Adobe Garamon Pro

Printed and bound by The Maple-Vail Book Manufacturing Group

Library of Congress Cataloging-in-Publication Data

Forms of association : making publics in early modern Europe /
edited by Paul Yachnin and Marlene Eberhart.
pages cm. — (Massachusetts studies in early modern culture)
Includes bibliographical references and index.
ISBN 978-1-62534-167-9 (pbk. : alk. paper) — ISBN 978-1-62534-166-2 (hardcover : alk. paper)
1. European literature—Renaissance, 1450–1600—History and criticism.
2. European literature—17th century—History and criticism.
3. Europe—Intellectual life—16th century. 4. Europe—Intellectual life—17th century.
5. Literature and society—Europe—History. 6. Communities—Europe—History.
7. Civil society—Europe—History—16th century.
8. Civil society—Europe—History—17th century.
I. Yachnin, Paul Edward, 1953– editor. II. Eberhart, Marlene, 1964– editor.
PN721.F67 2015
809'.93355—dc23
2014050136

British Library Cataloguing-in-Publication Data
A catalogue record for this book is available from the British Library.

Contents

Acknowledgments

THIS VOLUME is one of several to emerge from the Making Publics (MaPs) project (2005–10). We are grateful to the Social Sciences and Humanities Research Council of Canada (SSHRC) and its Major Collaborative Research Initiatives (MCRI) program for exemplary support of MaPs. The present book celebrates the work of a beloved colleague and mentor, Richard Helgerson, and reevaluates the avenues that his work has opened up onto the current landscape of early modern studies. We are above all grateful that Richard challenged us with compelling questions raised by his own exemplary scholarly exploration. We owe the elaboration of multiple forms of association presented here, especially those of early modern publics, not only to our volume's authors, but also to those members of the MaPs project, students, and colleagues who attended a two-day workshop at McGill University in August 2009. They generously contributed their insights to this discussion.

We would particularly like to recognize the magnanimity of a workshop grant from the Social Science and Humanities Research Council of Canada and the support of McGill University's Vice President of Research that together enabled the realization of the workshop itself and the preparatory work necessary to bring this volume to press. We are also especially grateful to David Cayley, retired producer of CBC Radio's IDEAS, for the program *The Origins of the Modern Public* (2010). A conversation with Richard Helgerson was one of the first he undertook; he subsequently interviewed a number of the MaPs team members and workshop contributors, as well as other notable public intellectuals in the course of producing the fourteen-episode program. Over the five active years of the project, David was our embedded reporter: he attended our annual research meetings as one of the team and has helped to make our work on publics, and our questions about them, more public. For all of it, we are deeply grateful.

Roland Greene and Edward (Mac) Test shared workshop papers with us that we would have happily included here but for the fact they were already spoken for elsewhere. Our contributors offer their specific acknowledgments at the end of their chapters. In addition, the editors would like to thank Meredith Donaldson Clark and Amy Britton Scott, both contributors to the volume who, before completing their PhDs at McGill, offered us their excellent assistance with grant writing, the workshop, and the initial stages of the volume. Finally, we must acknowledge the saintly patience of our editors at University of Massachusetts Press.

FORMS OF
ASSOCIATION

Introduction

MARLENE EBERHART, AMY SCOTT,
AND PAUL YACHNIN

I guess I didn't know it, but I was writing about publics before we
started the MaPs project.

RICHARD HELGERSON

IN THE SUMMER OF 2005, on what would be his last visit to Montreal,
Richard Helgerson remarked to a group of colleagues that he had been
writing about publics long before the creation of the Making Publics project. The project, "Making Publics: Media, Markets, and Association in
Early Modern Europe," which ended up being called "MaPs," was in its
inaugural year. Funded by the Social Sciences and Humanities Research
Council of Canada as well as by McGill University and other participating institutions, MaPs was an interdisciplinary research undertaking that,
over the course of its life from 2005 to 2010, developed a transformative
account of the cultural and social life of early modern Europe. The international research team studied the formation of "publics"—forms of
association built on the shared interests, tastes, and desires of individuals,
most of them ordinary "private" people. The project argued that public
making was enabled by new media and new cultural forms and was nested
in an emerging market in cultural goods. The team concluded that publics
were a highly significant feature of early modernity; the project's account
of public making has enabled a new way of understanding the social and
political dimensions of artistic and intellectual works and has opened the
path toward a new understanding of the political culture of modernity
itself. Helgerson's remark that he had already been writing about publics
and had been doing so for some time was surprising, even strikingly so. It
was also certainly true, but true in a complicated and telling way.

The truth of his observation is well demonstrated by the introduction to his book, *Forms of Nationhood: The Elizabethan Writing of England,* published in 1992, thirteen years before the beginning of MaPs. In it Helgerson explains that the artistic and intellectual nation building of early modern England—the writing of English nationhood—was not a monolithic operation but rather a many-sided initiative carried forward by a number of individuals as well as by a gathering of what he calls "discursive communities."[1]

The men who are the protagonists in the stories the book recounts were not just members of a single generation or merely representatives of particular social classes. They were always and freely on the move: "the men who wrote England shared an unusual social, economic, and psychic mobility. They were . . . men uprooted by education and ambition from familiar associations and local structures, men who were free—and compelled by their freedom—to imagine a new identity based on the kingdom or nation" (13). Unmoored from class and locality, the men who would go on to author English nationhood joined and thereby helped to form communities gathered around particular areas of interest and forms of discourse—poetry, law, theology, chorography, and so on. So, Helgerson tells us, "[t]he younger Elizabethans may have been partially uprooted from traditional associations . . . but they did nevertheless enter into a wide variety of new or newly reformed discursive communities, and it was often on behalf of those communities that they represented England" (14).

Discursive communities, like publics, are mobile and changeful, capable of overlapping one with another, and able to speak formatively about the whole nation from particular sectoral positions. However, the term is also problematic and even the source of misdirection in Helgerson's account of how England became England. Its particular limitation as a term is its remarkable lack of political content. Communities tend by definition to be inward-looking and closed to others; they are not bent on expansion, inclusiveness, and publicity, they are not friendly toward strangers, and they are not oriented toward the future, as publics are. (Publics are future-oriented because they aspire to greater and greater inclusiveness—they seek to grow up to be *the public*.) The very word "community" is sometimes used to name a kind of collective relationship bracketed off from the stress, struggle, and changeability of the political world. There is nothing in the term "discursive community," then, that connects strongly with the political character of the nation, a quality of "shared participation and possession" (2) that they are said to have created.

What Helgerson's thinking was tending toward, therefore, was a history of early modern English publics. Publics are able to grow, change, move in social space, and induct merely "private" people into public discourse, debate, and judgment. They create new forms of private–public association; they are oriented toward a national politics of shared participation, or at least toward the creation of an active ideal of democratic participation and publicity.[2]

On this account, David Sacks, whose essay focuses on the first chapter of *Forms of Nationhood,* is exactly right when he says that "[i]mplicit [in Helgerson's book] is a narrative of the history of public life and its publics in Europe before the modern age of nation-state and nationhood." Sacks tells us that publics and publicity were key factors in the emergence of the nation-state. Ancient and medieval empires and the pre-Reformation Church were marked by secrecy, members of the ruling elite were " 'public' in some ways" but remained cloistered in practice, in their courts and inner sanctums, whereas the vast majority of the population was relegated to the status of private persons subject to the authority of the sovereign rather than taking their place as citizens with rights and responsibilities within the polity. Public making was thus necessarily integral to the emergence of political modernity.

In his critique of the last chapter of *Forms of Nationhood,* Torrance Kirby develops Sacks's insight further by focusing on the publics that are implicit in Helgerson's argument. Where Helgerson develops a contrastive account of Foxe's *Actes and Monuments* (1563) and Hooker's *Of the Lawes of the Ecclesiastical Polity* (1593), treating the two as if they were embroiled in a debate within an already constituted public sphere, Kirby asks if we can understand the "mysterious genesis" of early modern public life by reconsidering the relationship between the two texts. "My purpose," Kirby says, "is to carry Helgerson's argument back a step, with a view to exploring further the religious preconditions underlying the formation of the modern nation in the context of the formation of publics."

We shall have more to say about the chapters by Sacks and Kirby (and the other chapters), but first we want to say something about how Richard Helgerson came to be one of the founders of Making Publics. The fact is that, at the start, he didn't want to join the project. He had his own work, his teaching, his family life. Paul Yachnin told him that the "best heads" were needed to begin to rethink the emergence of a "public sphere" in early modern Europe (Yachnin deliberately used the Habermasian term) and assured him he would not be obligating himself to take on the work of the project itself. And so Helgerson agreed to come to Montreal in summer 2003 just to lend a hand in the thinking toward a major project. But something happened on the first day of the meeting that changed his mind.

What happened, we think, was that the nascent research team shifted from a focus on "the public sphere," which, as it turned out, none of the team thought existed in early modern Europe, to a newly invented focus on "making publics." We believe that "publics" caught his attention in a very substantial way. If one considers what Helgerson had written by 2003 in comparison with other major contemporary scholars of early modern literature and culture, especially in comparison with the New Historicists, it will come as no great surprise that "making publics" began immediately to work on his imagination. The New Historicists had taken as their abiding theme the relationship between the individual subject and the social formation. Helgerson had certainly not ignored the individual artist or the social world, but from the very start of his publishing career he had written about groups of artists and intellectuals. Collectivity rather than subjectivity was at the center of his thinking. That is why it makes sense for Anne Lake Prescott, in this volume, to redescribe *Forms of Nationhood* as a study of the formation of publics: "The rational evolution of English law, the thoughtful desire for a national literature, the creation of more accurate maps of the British Isles . . . created *publics* that eventually overlapped with and helped constitute a *nation* as a whole, whatever the divisions that would remain or even grow" (italics in original). Helgerson's long-term scholarly focus on collectivities and forms of association evidently made an emerging collaborative study of something called publics irresistible to him. It was, as he said, just what he had been writing about all his life.

It was on account of his long-standing interest in socially and artistically creative collectivity, not to mention because of his drive toward the organized analysis of complex cultural phenomena, that Helgerson insisted that we work toward a definition of publics. What kind of social things were they? Were they forms of association just like other forms? What are their most salient characteristics? The chapters in this volume continue to address Helgerson's questions about publics even as they engage critically with his work.

This book is a memorial Festschrift, but not a memorial of the usual kind: it is a celebration of an esteemed and loved scholar. Indeed, the volume takes its inspiration from Helgerson's large and original body of work, especially his multidisciplinary exploration of the interrelationships between the private and public domains as they formed and reformed throughout the early modern period. But it is also a book that honors him by developing a multifaceted, sustained, and critical dialogue with his work. The very title of our book, *Forms of Association: Making Publics in Early Modern Europe*, pays critical tribute to Helgerson's central, pathbreaking book *Forms of Nationhood: The Elizabethan Writing of England*, with "association" taking the place of "nationhood" (nationhood being unthinkable without the foundational forms of association among people of different kinds), and the more various, more socially diverse activities of public making supplanting the more elite practices of writing.

The chapters in this book, then, are part of a sustained conversation with Helgerson's scholarship, initially presented at a workshop held in Montreal in August 2009. In what follows, colleagues, friends, and former students take up the currents of publics and public making that run just below the surface throughout Helgerson's work, offering a critical examination of his arguments, a more expansive treatment of the forms of association they involve, and a consideration of the social and political agency of early modern publics. The diversity of the group of scholars contributing to this volume is a testament to the wide-ranging curiosity and intellectual reach and rigor of Helgerson's scholarship and teaching.

The argument of Jürgen Habermas's book, *The Structural Transformation of the Public Sphere*, was a large presence at the start of what would become the MaPs project. When the nascent team, including Helgerson, gathered in Montreal in August 2003, they were handed a carefully organized agenda for three days of work. Their task would be to design a large-scale study of how the emergence of a "culture industry"—including the proliferation of new forms or reproduction and dissemination such as commercial theater, print publication, and the early news business—had created a popular "public sphere" in early modern Europe distinct from the sovereignty and public visibility of the social and political elite. The agenda stuck closely to Habermas's characterization of the public sphere as "the sphere of private people come together as a public," where that newly constituted public sphere was able to confront "the public authorities themselves" and where the form of this confrontation was "peculiar and without historical precedent: people's public use of their reason."[3] The proposal for the research project, which was more or less handed to the scholars gathered in Montreal, did not seek to put in question Habermas's basic idea about the emergence of a public sphere, or to undertake a new theoretical exploration of how societies change (how they generate new forms and domains of publicity and privacy) or aspire to develop a new research methodology. The proposed project sought simply to push back "the structural transformation of the public sphere" from the eighteenth century, where Habermas had located it, to the sixteenth and seventeenth centuries.

What happened was that, on the morning of the first day of the meeting, the assembled scholars balked at the agenda that had been presented to them and began an unplanned and very lively discussion of the central claim about an early modern public sphere, a claim that had been intended to drive forward the whole research enterprise. They were not persuaded that there had been a structural transformation in the strongly hierarchical society of early modernity, a political order, after all, where sovereignty and publicity belonged almost exclusively to the monarch and the nobility. They did not believe that the sixteenth and seventeenth centuries had seen the emergence of a popular public sphere, a political space of rational-critical debate (to use Habermas's term) open to people regardless of their vocation or social rank.

Of course, such a categorical rejection of the foundational hypothesis might have proved fatal to the infant project. However, instead of breaking up the meeting and all of them going home, the team members agreed to move forward toward a new understanding of the relationship between early modern works of art and intellect on the one hand and transformations in public and private life on the other. They were from the start a hardworking, critical, and collegial group.

Toward the end of the first day the team somehow conjured into existence the phrase "making publics." The plural form alleviated the problem that had confronted the group at the start of the day. With "publics" as the guiding idea, they did not have to assume the emergence of a popular public sphere, an idea they had already rejected. "Publics" suggested not a total transformation of early modern society but rather the emergence of a congeries of artistically, intellectually, and socially creative undertakings on the part of particular groupings of people. "Making" foregrounded the active, processual, and local—a model of hands-on association building and of change happening on a small scale rather than anything like a structural transformation across the whole social landscape. The problem that had confronted the project in the morning seemed by the end of the day to have been quite miraculously solved.

As is often the case with these kinds of acts of collective invention, those who do the inventing often find themselves happy, even vindicated, but not entirely sure about the meaning of their new idea, not to mention the concomitant new idea of themselves. In the event, it took another year and a half before the project secured the necessary grant from the Canadian funding agency and at least another year and a half to begin fully to come to terms with the meaning of the phrase "making publics." The work that issued over time in a coherent account of early modernity as an age characterized by the massive expansion of public-making practices drew on Habermas, of course. He continued and continues to be an important source for anyone interested in how the domains of the private and public change and interact over time. The team also learned a great deal from political thinkers such as Craig Calhoun and Nancy Fraser, who themselves recognized both the value and the limitations of Habermas's theory of the public sphere.[4] Hannah Arendt's rethinking of the space of the polity as a place where people become public to each other and with each other was influential for many members of the team.[5] And among the very many other thinkers with whom the team engaged (such as Michel de Certeau, Bruno Latour, and Charles Taylor), Michael Warner emerged as one of the most important. His ideas about how publics are made ("[a] public is a space of discourse organized by nothing other than discourse itself") exercised a powerful, positive influence on the team's thinking.[6]

Throughout this period of intensive, collaborative thinking, reading, discussing, arguing, presenting, and writing, Helgerson exercised extraordinary leadership in two respects. His own practices of precise and evidence-based historical analysis and argument set a high standard for his fellow researchers. At the 2005 team meeting, where nine collaborative case-study groups were presenting their findings, he broke the flow of reporting and called on the leaders of the nine groups to define publics (in something like twenty-five words or less!) and to frame their definitions according to what each group had gleaned from its case study. The leaders could not refuse his summons. They came back from a coffee break and duly offered their succinct, case-based definitions of publics. From these, Helgerson compiled a list of core attributes of publics; the list came to be known as "Richard's Twelve."

"Richard's Twelve" advanced the project's work on the burgeoning questions about publics and public making, both by virtue of the list's inherent power of organization and by how it served as an incitement to further thinking. What developed over the next half-year was a sixty-eight-page "Compendium of Responses to the Provisional 'Definition' of Publics" that included essays by eighteen members of the research team. Together, "Richard's Twelve" and his colleagues' responses moved the project forward decisively. The team recognized that publics were far from uniform one with another but came to understand that they shared a certain family resemblance. In her introduction to the Compendium, then

Graduate Student Associate Yael Margalit, quoting Wittgenstein, commented, "the publics that the MaPs team studies exhibit 'a complicated network of similarities, overlapping and criss-crossing: sometimes overall similarities, sometimes similarities of detail,' rather than an exactness of form."[7] The work of the Compendium also redirected the team's attention back to the word "making" and to the processual, made character of publics—the ways in which early modern artists, thinkers, printers, readers, and so on created new forms of association that are well described as publics. "Making" emphasized the dynamic capacity of publics to grow, change, sometimes to disappear altogether (like the "cartographic public" described by Lesley Cormack in this volume) and sometimes to morph from loose, fluid forms of association into full-fledged institutions (as early modern "natural history" changed into the Royal Academy and then into professional science).

We learned that publics develop in untrammeled ways because they are separate from the grand world of publicity, the world of the court, the social elite, the Church, and so on. They are significant because of their potential ability to enter and influence the broader public sphere and the centers of power and authority. However, once they become identified with the institutions of power or with the public on a grand scale, and once they shift from informal and flexible conditions of participation to formal membership and rule-boundedness, they change into other kinds of association—their life cycle as publics has run its course. Then other publics or counterpublics arise, bringing new vitality and inventiveness to the social landscape.

Helgerson's second area of leadership was of a piece with the first. From the beginning of the work, he insisted that we not be selective or prescriptive in our study of the historical archive and that we test theories of publics and public making against historical cases. This mixing of historical cases and theoretical work became one of the hallmarks of the MaPs project. It made the work more difficult. It would have been easier, say, simply to apply Warner's theory of publics to early modern Europe, trimming away any recalcitrant historical details in order to produce a theoretically smooth and untroubled account of how commoners made a public life for themselves and achieved a kind of public voice by creating publics. But where Warner claimed that all that is needed for public making is sheer attention to discourse, the team discovered many instances of deep investment and creative participation in publics on the part of individuals and groups; where he had little to say about the long-term temporality of publics, the project found that, for early moderns, publicity was never far away from the classical ideal of fame, an attribute of a well-lived life that afforded people an *afterlife* in the world rather than, and in preference to, an actual life of public visibility and influence. Under the creative pressure of Helgerson's insistence on testing theory against real historical cases, the project moved forward toward more complex, more specific theorizing about the political dimensions of works of art and intellect and the associations of people that constellate around them.

The chapters that follow are exemplary of Helgerson's insistence on testing theory against history and history against theory. Each of them develops a well-defined case study of the formation of new kinds of association in early modernity. In each, both the history of early modernity and the theoretical understanding of how societies change are at stake and are in productive dialogue with each other. Of course, each chapter is in dialogue with Helgerson as well. Each also works toward some kind of definition of the particular form or forms of association under examination. The result is certainly not a smooth or untroubled account of early modern forms of association and public making. The chapters speak to each other, but they also jostle against one another (see the Afterword for an account of how the chapters both inform and critique each other). They focus very differently on the broader questions revolving around art, ideas, the social formation, and social change, and they tell different stories about the political dimensions of early modern works of art and intellect. For instance, theater has a protodemocratic bent for Jean Howard but is complexly elitist for Jeffrey Knapp; the production and movement of texts create publics that contribute to nation building for Stephen Deng or Meredith Donaldson Clark; for Vera Keller or David Sacks, the publication and circulation of texts anchors the formation of international publics. The chapters in this volume advance our understanding of the social creativity of works of art and intellect on the firm ground of what can justly be called a Helgersonian methodology, and they do so even as they engage in a critical rethinking of Helgerson's work.

Part I: Writing Publics (Publics and Nation)

The opening group of chapters attends to three specific concerns that Helgerson elaborates in *Forms of Nationhood*. They trace the development of the conception of the early modern state as a critical counterpart to the development of publics. The relationship between the state and the emerging congeries of publics plays out in this section in terms of language, law, and religion—specifically. in relation to linguistic, legal, and religious kinds of knowledge, the authority those forms of knowledge were able to aggregate to themselves, and the expanding gatherings of people who became critically engaged with questions about forms of knowledge and the shifting centers of power and authority.

In "States, Nations, and Publics: The Politics of Language Reform in Renaissance England," David Sacks examines what, in practice, would be the impact of an intentionally and rigorously re-formed English language capable of the eloquence and erudition understood at the time to be inherent in Latin and Greek. He examines Edmund Spenser's 1580 call to his friend Gabriel Harvey for a "kingdome of our own language" against the backdrop of shifting definitions of "nation" and "state" and in relation to Helgerson's discussion of the same exchange. Through his investigation of the changing modes of discourse and interaction, Sacks describes the connection between a relatively closed circle of discourse and the much wider international debate on the question of language as crucial to the identity of nations.

Stephen Deng is interested in the seeds of a "juridical public" that were sown in the debates pitting the primacy of the common law and its fierce advocate, Sir Edward Coke, against the principles of monarchical supremacy and royal prerogative espoused by King James I. To be effective, and for subjects to understand the knowledge the common law comprehends, it must be rendered in a common language, simplified and transparent enough that subjects may appreciate their rights and responsibilities free from infringement by monarchical authority. As Spenser sought to create "a kingdome of our own language" in order to foster the cultural identity of England, so, Deng suggests, did Coke seek to establish the nation's legal identity as English through and through—rooted in the history of English judicial practice. Throughout, both the king and Justice Coke felt a need to appeal to "the public" or "the people." On this account, an English juridical public was created in large measure by arguments in print, and especially by the rhetorical addresses to "the public" or "the commonwealth" that were characteristic of the disputes among the legal theorists of Jacobean England.

Torrance Kirby explores Helgerson's chapter "Apocalyptics and Apologetics." Kirby's focus is the distinction between "the private realm of individual conscience and the public demand for institutional order" as this distinction was worked out in Foxe's *Actes and Monuments* and Richard Hooker's *Lawes*. Kirby contrasts the dialogue between Paul's Cross and the situatedness of sermons there with the "un-situated" discourse of works like Foxe's *Actes* and Hooker's *Lawes;* the movement of ideas and arguments between these two spaces, the situated and the virtual, exemplifies the back-and-forth mobility of discourse that is integral to the formation of early modern publics and an emerging public sphere.

Part II: Forming Social Identities and Publics

The second section discusses the forms of social identity that emerged from publics and public making. Helgerson's work sought to account for early modern writings as part of the shaping of a social identity related to nation building. These chapters maintain that public identities are often formed in relation to the private sphere, and that private identities are usually shaped in relation to the public sphere. Social identities are also reshaped when a private person joins a network of people with shared interests who do not see themselves as a cohesive group.

Anne Lake Prescott identifies an early modern English public that was hungry for sensational news and gossip about France. She shifts the scope of Helgerson's discussion of nation and identity onto the muddy territory of anti-French gossipy news, scurrilous report, and polemical pamphleteering. Woven into the fabric of this sensational art is the cultivation of conversation and debate as well as the added pleasure of joining an imagined patriotic readership. On this account, even scandalous publications could unite an English readership around the perverse delights of sensational news and the conversation that news aroused.

Lena Cowen Orlin elaborates on Helgerson's attention to the "interpenetration" of the private and public spheres. Where Helgerson identified an *invasion* of the private by the public, Orlin sees instead a dynamic of *display* between the public and the private, marked by the presence of women in a window (or indeed, the withdrawal of a woman from a window) in early modern drama and art. Orlin's vital contribution to this volume is the claim that the relationship between private and public is not always adversarial, and that the state (figured by the man who views the woman in the window) is not always in the dominant position, not always the figure of public power able to invade and thereby despoil the space of everyday work and domestic life.

Angela Vanhaelen attends to the tension between the grand public gestures of large-scale history painting and the private-public hybridity of genre painting in Dutch art of the 1650s and 1660s. It is a study, she acknowledges, that begins with Helgerson's claim that Dutch genre paintings, far from evading political and historical meanings, in fact exhibit the intrusion of the state into the space of the domestic and private. She argues that conversation about paintings turns even a private space into one of debate about the nation and its politics, and that such debates crafted a social identity for private people.

Reading Helgerson's final book, *A Sonnet from Carthage,* as well as his penultimate volume, *Adulterous Alliances,* Javier Castro-Ibaseta takes us from the Castilian poet Garcilaso de la Vega (ca. 1498–1536) and the exclusive genre of the sonnet in mid-sixteenth-century Spain to popular and entertaining genres of the early 1600s, particularly the popular balladic poetry of *romance* and its subgenre, the *jácaras.* While the sonnet remained the province of the elite, the *jácaras,* with their outlaw protagonists and their parodies of more erudite genres, enjoyed wide circulation in print as well as in public theatrical performances appealing to elite and common audience members alike. His chapter explores the role of entertainment in forming early modern publics and in crafting social identities. Castro-Ibaseta urges us to evaluate how public-making art unmakes socially given class identities in order to remake participants as members of publics, affording people altogether new kinds of identity for as least as long as they remain within the zone of participation in the artworks.

Part III: Networks and Publics

In Part III, four essays consider the mobility of knowledge, information, and discourse in and between publics. Taking up Helgerson's attention to the early modern shaping of the nation through the mapping of its land and the sharing of knowledge, each contributor identifies the collaborative nature of public making as it appeared in works of chorography, historiography and ballad making. These chapters reveal how personal experiences and specialized projects became absorbed into larger networks that were populated by people who did not necessarily have a uniform understanding of the group to which they belonged, but who did recognize how they shared key interests with many others, many of them complete strangers.

Lesley Cormack argues that the chorographic work Helgerson described first in his seminal 1986 article, "The Land Speaks," and later in *Forms of Nationhood,* offers an excellent testing ground to examine the growth of publics. Following a brief examination of the works discussed by Helgerson, Cormack turns to William Camden's *Britannia,* which she suggests is a better model of the formation of publics throughout their life cycle. She traces an ever-growing group of people interested in issues of antiquity, loyalty, and legitimacy. This group transforms into a public by virtue of manuscript correspondence among scholars across a broad research network, and also and more importantly, by dependence on the strength of the publication, circulation, uptake, revision, and republication of texts among a very large and widely distributed readership.

Meredith Donaldson-Clark also examines Camden's *Britannia* as a pivotal text and chorography as a critical genre in public making. She is particularly interested in the individual's experience as a member of a public. Her chapter uncovers the "rare glimpse" available to us of John Shrimpton and his *Antiquities of Verulam* bound up in the intertextual crossings of *Britannia* with a number of other texts at the turn of the seventeenth century, including those of Edmund Spenser, Michael Drayton, and John Weever. Shrimpton's particular sensitivity to his immediate surroundings reveals an awareness of belonging to a broader national discourse. Donaldson-Clark examines ideas of monumentality and the role of common placing as practices of collaborative thinking as she leads us through the intricate process of participating as both a partaker and a maker in an early modern public.

Patricia Fumerton reflects on generation as a principal theme in her exploration of networks and publics interested in the early modern ballad—its production, dissemination, and collection. She describes expanding networks of collectors that spurred the growth of a ballad public, a process she describes as "protean." It was the dynamism of the debate over preferred forms of ballad production and the successive generations of production and consumption that called into being a significant public for the early modern broadside ballad, one that extended well beyond circles of privilege and the networks of collectors.

Vera Keller argues that "forms of association became new objects of study" in the seventeenth century motivated by the growth of empirical interest in the nature of the public and the state. She points out that publics could disturb traditional notions of the state and its containment within prescribed borders precisely because they emerged and operated beyond institutional power and its myth of "wholeness and immediate belonging." In particular, she considers how "methodical travel," and the various genres that travelers relied on to guide their observations and to organize newly acquired knowledge about states and publics, contributed to the tension between the national and international spheres. By producing, exchanging, and studying these genres (including stock images and inscriptions like the epigram), early modern travelers were able to move toward an understanding of where they fit into the social matrix as well as to describe the character of the social matrix itself.

Part IV: Theatrical Publicity

The final group of chapters engages with Helgerson's claim that Shakespeare's histories excluded popular audiences and sought to speak only to the social elite. They consider how a theatrical public can bind playwright and playgoers in a shared project that puts aside distinctions based on social rank. Theatrical publicity emerges when the audiences observe staged material from a critical distance even while immersing themselves in its fictions.

Jeffrey Knapp's "Shakespeare's Pains to Please" challenges the apparent protodemocratic character of the theater. He tends to side with Helgerson, but he does so in a complex way. Knapp shows us that in *Macbeth,* and indeed in many other plays by Shakespeare, the tension between civility and barbarity is more complex than previous critics have allowed. He observes the burden of civility at work not only in the events dramatized in *Macbeth* but also in prologues of the early modern theater, and he explains how the early modern playwright's ambivalent attitude toward his audience is produced by the conflict between his need to please the audience and his resentment at having to pander to crowds of commoners. According to Knapp, we can understand theatrical publicity by considering how playwrights and audiences conceived of themselves and each other in terms of this strained relationship. The relationship may be unsettling, but it is also productive, because in a play like *Macbeth* the audience—and the playwright himself—can observe the social conditions that motivate both politeness and the desire to do violence.

In "The Voice of Caesar's Wounds," David Lee Miller takes up Helgerson's suggestion that a sense of public space emerges from the opposition of the domestic and the imperial. Miller identifies the mobility of place, voice, and the past in Shakespeare's *Julius Caesar* and asserts that a theatrical performance transforms a crowd into an audience bound by "variable moments of engagement" that both establish and challenge the "fantasy of shared space." He links this dynamic to the dislocation of voice, the powerful effects of rhetoric, and Shakespeare's adaptation of the gospel story source. According to Miller, the play's often uncomfortable mirroring of Caesar's death to that of Christ recalls the horrors of the Marian martyrdoms; this mirroring effects a kind of distancing from the turmoil of recent religious history. The play's strategic dislocations of place and voice enable a perspective that stands apart from history; it affords playgoers a place from which they can understand critically the socially traumatic events of their own recent past rather than simply reviving and augmenting the trauma.

Jean Howard takes up the Robin Hood legend in order to argue against Helgerson's notion that Shakespeare's histories, unlike Henslowe's, excluded the popular. She describes publics that formed around the Robin Hood material composed of audiences and playwrights who participated together to reconsider Robin Hood's masculinity and its relationship to political commentary. The Robin Hood story could be adapted to endorse monarchial authority or to subvert it; in either case, these adaptations of the legend reworked, often to ambivalent effects, the complex relationship between the monarch and his or her subjects, the elite and the popular. The various stories and differing ways of representing the matter of Robin Hood created what could be described as a popular, public conversation about political matters, a conversation that unfolded across the multiple playhouses, playing companies, and performances in early modern London.

The discursive communities explored in Richard Helgerson's work responded to and advanced the dialectical relationships between the private and public domains, popular and elite, and kingdom and nation. Helgerson insisted that the separation between these domains was not always absolute. In *Forms of Nationhood,* he saw a need, in writing about early modern Europe, especially from the point of view of our own times, for a "freer, more permeable world, a world of dotted instead of solid lines" (18). As exemplified by the chapters in this volume, the lines between different forms of association in the early modern world, as in our own, are frequently not solid and not impermeable. Public making, we might say, delivers a creative permeability that enables the interplay of people across the social spectrum and fosters dialogue among differing forms of knowledge. Because of this, as Richard Helgerson understood well, works of art and intellect and the forms of public association that grow up around them can serve to break open the traditional social formation, create new spaces for transformation of deeply engrained principles of social distinction, and contribute formatively to the growth and vitality of social and political life.

NOTES

1. Richard Helgerson, *Forms of Nationhood: The Elizabethan Writing of England* (Chicago: University of Chicago Press, 1992), 13. For all subsequent references to this work, page numbers are given parenthetically in the text.
2. The primary meaning of "publicity" is simply the condition of being public.

3. Jürgen Habermas, *The Structural Transformation of the Public Sphere: An Inquiry into a Category of Bourgeois Society,* trans. Thomas Burger (Cambridge: MIT Press, 1991), 27.

4. See the essays in *Habermas and the Public Sphere,* ed. Craig Calhoun (Cambridge: MIT Press, 1992).

5. Hannah Arendt, *The Human Condition,* 2nd ed. (Chicago: University of Chicago Press, 1998).

6. Michael Warner, *Publics and Counterpublics* (New York: Zone Books, 2002), 67.

7. Ludwig Wittgenstein, *Philosophical Investigations,* trans. G. E. M. Anscombe (Oxford: Blackwell, 2001), 27.

PART ONE

Writing Publics
(Publics and Nation)

CHAPTER ONE

States, Nations, and Publics

The Politics of Language Reform in Renaissance England

DAVID HARRIS SACKS

Prolegomena: Empires, Nation-States, and Publics

AMONG STUDENTS of early modern English and British history and culture, Richard Helgerson is best known for his *Forms of Nationhood: The Elizabethan Writing of England,* published in 1992.[1] One of the book's central claims—illustrated in a series of stimulating chapters arguing for the distinctive Englishness of the nation's epic poetry, common law, chorography, travel literature, theatrical writing, and ecclesiastical history—is that to Elizabethans "things English came to matter with a special intensity both because England itself came to matter more than it had and because other sources of identity and cultural authority mattered less."[2] Implicit is a narrative of the history of public life and its publics in Europe before the modern age of the nation-state and nationhood whose beginnings the book explored. In that earlier era, political order consisted mainly of very large, territorially diffuse forms of organization, such as the Roman Empire or the Catholic Church, and small localized ones—lineages and tribes, village and town or religious communities, city-states, petty fiefdoms or principalities. Neither the state nor the nation, or their associated publics, occupied the middle ground in recognizably modern forms.

Although empires may be said to have been "public" in some ways, and their rulers "public" figures, they were largely governed from behind the walls of imperial households and lived their "public" lives cloistered in their courts, served by courtiers with privileged access to the imperial inner sanctum and the *arcana imperii.* Secrecy was their watchword, even when the courtiers were exercising their public roles as counselors. Everyone else was a "subject," whether they lived in rural or urban communities, or whether those communities enjoyed a degree of self-government. From the perspective of the ruling regime, their inhabitants were private persons who owed obedience to those who ruled. Similar points can be made for the universal Church through most of its history until the Reformation. However, since most ancient and medieval empires lacked well-developed socioeconomic infrastructures and possessed only limited institutional resources, rule over them covered only a restricted range of activities—mainly the extraction of revenues, the maintenance of institutional authority, and the suppression of threats to the regime. For the Church in the West, centralized rule also was limited in its scope and often intermittent in its application. In both church and state, therefore, power rarely penetrated very deeply or consistently into the everyday affairs of subject communities, even when rulers claimed dominion over them.

Ancient and medieval empires and the Western Church were not global in strict geographical terms, but in their form they shared structural features with what Fernand Braudel called "a world-economy." Although each of them represented only a "fragment of the world," like the various Braudelian world-economies they resembled, they "bestrode the political and cultural frontiers which . . . in its own way quartered and differentiated" the region in question.[3] Within them, groups contested with one another across ethnic or cultural lines or over great distances on behalf of competing philosophical schools, hero cults, or religious communities and sects. We might call these groups or entities "publics," that is, groups or entities that transcended the private or local and yet were not states or statelike things. Each of these might be said to have, or to constitute, its own "public." The itinerant ancient philosophers who moved from city to city in the Mediterranean world to spread their teachings and the scholars who traveled among the medieval universities represent such groups. Facilitated by the use of a common language—Latin in the Roman Empire and its successors in the Christian West—and by common sets of structures, symbols, and ideals, these publics formed networks of communication that were cosmopolitan in character and based on universal philosophical, religious, cultural, and aesthetic values.

Modern nation-states are different. Compared to empires, they are far more integrated; more open to the exchange of information as well as goods and services in their territories; more centralized in their governance; and therefore better able to impose a "monopoly of the legitimate use of physical force" within their borders.[4] These facts not only make them more effective in rule but, by specifying the person or body responsible for particular decisions, also advance the principle of accountability and open room to criticize or amend policies. The inhabitants of a nation-state, therefore, are not just subjects of the ruling regime; they are also members of a national community to which they owe duties of service or citizenship as well as loyalty and obedience. Such nation-states also possess national markets, dependent on organized urban hierarchies and networks of exchange and communication, as well as common systems of property rights and regulation, common price mechanisms, and common regimes for the maintenance of public order and enforcement of private obligations. The "publics" that have emerged within them are, in significant measure, inward-looking. They depend on the use of common national languages, inculcated by national systems of education, and they focus on the institutions of the nation-state, the political controversies and policy questions that affected them, and the cultural forms and practices prevalent within their respective national communities.

Under the aegis of modern nationhood and nationality, therefore, an intimate relationship links states, nations, and publics together. This trinity—in which publics play the role of Holy Ghost—became Helgerson's subject in *Forms of Nationhood* and continued to occupy him productively thereafter.[5] However, as I hope to show, rather than eliminating a focus on universal ideals and norm, in the early modern era these new conditions added forms of publicness to the existing picture, which in the process was transformed into a new regime of transnational ideological and cultural publics. These are the topics I propose to discuss.

The Kingdom of Our Own Language

As Helgerson explained, he was first drawn to his study of *Forms of Nationhood* by a remark Edmund Spenser made in a letter written in 1580 to his friend Gabriel Harvey, then a Fellow of Trinity Hall, Cambridge.[6] Spenser's comment to Harvey reads, in full: "For why a God's name may not we, as else the Greekes, haue the kingdome of our owne Language, and measure our Accentes, by the sounde, reseruing the Quantitie to the Verse?"[7] Helgerson connected this sentence with "a tension," as he put it, that he had first observed in his earlier books on Elizabethan England's young poets, who had found it necessary (and difficult) to reconcile "their literary undertaking" with "the claims of the state to whose service both their humanist upbringing and the exigencies of the 'new monarchy' had directed them."[8]

Characteristically, Helgerson saw more than *literary* implications in Spenser's words. For example, to him the word "kingdom" conveyed "an essentially dynastic conception of communal identity," while the phrase "our own language" represented, contradictorily, "one of the bases of post-dynastic nationalism." As he put it, a "kingdom whose boundaries are determined by the language of its inhabitants is no longer a kingdom in the purely dynastic sense." As long as it identifies itself "with the person of an hereditary monarch" it is also, he says, not "quite a nation" either. The interposition of "our," "with its suggestion of shared participation and possession," further complicates the picture. "King, people, and language," Helgerson asks, "[w]hich, if any, is to be given priority? From this formulation it is impossible to tell. But even a small acquaintance with the history of England" in the seventeenth century "will remind us that conflict was to develop along precisely the lines suggested by those few words: between royal prerogative, subjects' rights, and the cultural system."[9]

In Spenser's reference to "the kingdome of our own language," therefore, Helgerson saw an anticipation of what many early modern English historians have called "the English Revolution," here conceived as a battle between rival conceptions of legitimate government. In the classic formulation, this battle pitted views of the state as ruled by the "absolute," meaning the sole or exclusive authority of a single ruler—the form that Sir John Fortescue had classified as *dominium regale*—against conceptions of it as ruled with the consent and participation of its people, either in a pure republic, a *dominium politicum* in Fortescue's terms, or in a mixed polity—a *dominium politicum et regale* in his paradigm.[10] The central issue, as Helgerson recognized, concerns where, or in whom, in a body politic the right of rule resides. As Helgerson also emphasized, the English state had already achieved a high degree of "monarchic consolidation" in the Middle Ages,[11] which he also suggested, citing G. R. Elton, had been transformed into a "modern sovereign state" in the course of the sixteenth century.[12]

Political states had been part of Western history in its ancient past, of course. However, by the time Spenser and Harvey exchanged their letters, the word "state" in most European languages no longer referred only to the condition in which a ruler or a realm found itself. Instead, as Quentin Skinner among others has emphasized, writers on politics and the law had begun "to think of the State as a locus of power distinct from either the ruler or the body of the people"—what the French theorist Guillaume Budé called the "politic state" or the "public state"—and to claim "that the duties of subjects were owed to the state, rather than the person of the ruler."[13] This momentous change opened up the possibility for public discourse about public things. Among the issues debated, the nature of the state and the structure of its institutions were perhaps the most important.

Although theorists had long recognized that the state enjoyed *Imperium,* commonly translated as "sovereignty," the meaning of this concept was by no means a settled matter by 1600, or indeed by 1700. "Sovereignty" had long been used to refer to "supremacy" of the kind enjoyed, for example, by a lord over his vassals or a prior over his priory or a master over his servants. But even when applied to the ruler of a state, it conveyed the idea that he or she owed obedience or deference to no superior on earth and did not necessarily carry the implication that rule was "absolute," in the sense of being indivisible and unlimited or unrestrained. Instead, as applied to the state, its meaning, scope, and application were formed, as Skinner suggests, in the course of rivalry between a "theory of politics . . . at once absolutist and secular-minded in its ideological allegiances" and a theory of "popular sovereignty" and political resistance developed in the course of Europe's religious wars.[14] As such, the constitution of the state and the character of its putative sovereignty became subjects for public debate, with rival viewpoints each having their own advocates and publics.

Nevertheless, Spenser's call for the English to emulate the Greeks by having the kingdom of their own language was not about the state, dynastic or otherwise, as ancient Greece was not a unified territorial polity, let alone a kingdom ruled by a single hereditary monarch. As Spenser knew, ancient Greece was made up of a number of city-states with diverse governing structures and constitutions, only some of which were kingdoms. Instead, as Helgerson emphasized, Spenser was calling for the authority— seemingly similar to that exercised by Homer among the Hellenes—to govern the "linguistic system, and perhaps more generally the whole cultural system" by which English "identity" and English "consciousness were constituted."[15]

Was Spenser, then, referring to nationality or nationhood, to use modern expressions? These words derive from *natio,* the Latin word for "birth" and the root of the English word "nation." A nation, in these terms, is a group of people claiming a common descent, typically connected with a foundation myth and often associated with possession of a common language. While "nations" understood in these terms often also occupy a common territory, they need not. It was enough to call them nations if they shared a common ancestry, heritage, and culture, especially a common tongue, as was true for Greek speakers in the Mediterranean and Asia Minor in the postclassical age. The open-endedness of this conception can also be seen in the case of foreigners in medieval universities, where the so-called nations were made up primarily of students or masters who originated from the same birthplace and were conceived therefore as members of the same *gens* or people with common cultural traditions. But even this designation could be murky and bear little relation to any modern idea of ethnic identity.[16] What counted was shared engagement in study under the rules and protection of one of the university's recognized "nations" in whatever manner these were structured. Indeed, the linkage of nation to the territorial state in the form of the "nation-state" is a nineteenth-century conception—Skinner calls it "post-Enlightenment"—while the term itself entered into English usage only in the 1890s.[17]

Although the English certainly possessed a sense of national identity in the sixteenth century,[18] confessional differences introduced during the Reformation greatly complicated its character, even as they shattered the unity of Christendom. In addition, there were wide regional differences not just of custom and social practice but also of dialect, pronunciation, and orthography evident within England itself. Indeed, in many instances people from one region would have had difficulty grasping the sounds, the idioms, and the sense of the English spoken by those from elsewhere in the kingdom.[19] Although there were programs of "linguistic colonialism" in such places as Wales and Ireland,[20] these efforts entailed that English would be spoken by people lacking English ethnicity. Ireland and Scotland, moreover, had their own distinct forms of English in the early modern era: Hiberno-English, which was used in the Irish Pale and in the plantations;[21] and Scots, a distinct form of English with its own norms, which was used in the Lowlands. The latter had become the lingua franca there well before 1500, as was recognized by the scholastic philosopher and historian John Mair.[22] Scots was the language used by King James VI and I in composing many of his writings such as *Basilikon Doron*[23] as well as in speaking. On first meeting the king in 1603, for example, Francis Bacon said he spoke "the full dialect of his country."[24]

Equally important is the fact that educated English men and women commonly used Latin not just in addressing readers or correspondents on the continent but in their written communications with each other and in making marginal notes in texts.[25] Although a number of authors in the sixteenth century sought to advance the claims of English as "a learned and literary language,"[26] Harvey, a graduate of Cambridge University and sometime Cambridge don, not only carefully studied and heavily annotated in Latin the classical texts in his possession such as his copy of Livy's history, but also published some of his own works exclusively in Latin. In doing so, he was participating as an Englishman in a discourse that transcended nationhood.[27]

Was Spenser, then, seeking to counter these conditions by anticipating the demands of latter-day linguistic nationalism? That is, was he endeavoring to erase or level regional, ethnic, and class differences in the British Isles by imposing a common form of English grammar, spelling, idiom, syntax, and pronunciation on its inhabitants in what, in effect, would have been an early modern version of "proper English"?[28] In his *A View of the Present State of Ireland* (ca. 1596), completed more than fifteen years after his exchanges with Harvey about language, Spenser does allow that "it hathe bene the vse of the Conquerour to despise the Language of the Conquered and to force him by all means to learne his."[29] In this passage, Spenser surely seems to have been endorsing a view of language as "the companion of empire" that saw the imposition of English on newly conquered or colonized territories as emulating the mutually reinforcing spread of Latin, civility, and the law achieved by the ancient Romans in their empire. However, as I shall argue in what follows, when Spenser wrote to Harvey in 1580 calling for the English to have a kingdom of their own language, he had something a bit different in mind.

The Athenian Tribe

Although we can accept that Spenser's larger aim was "to remake the very cultural matrix in which his own identity had been formed,"[30] the poet's immediate goal in language reform, as he put it, was to measure English "Accentes, by the sounde," while "reseruing the Quantitie to the Verse." He wished, that is, to subdue "rough words" to order and discipline by making their pronunciation and appearance in poetry consistent with each other, as he believed was true for the Greeks. Success would then allow him to pursue what Helgerson calls "the comically misguided effort to base English prosody on the rules of ancient quantitative meters"—hexameters, pentameters, and so on.[31] Harvey, who also employed quantitative meters in his poetry, would have none of it. "Is there no other Pollicie to pull downe Ryming, and set vppe Versifying," he asked, but to correct the established pronunciations and "forcibly vsurpe, and tyrannize vppon a quiet companye of wordes, that so farre beyond the memorie of man, haue so peaceably enioyed their seuerall Priuileges and Liberties, without any disturbance, or the least controlement?" He saw Spenser's proposal, therefore, as made "in despite of Custome."[32] Responding, as Helgerson suggests, in terms derived from resistance to monarchical usurpation, he "locates authority" for the form of the English language instead in " 'God and his English people,' " who together over time providentially have made the language what it has become.[33] The issue between Spenser and Harvey turns playfully, then, on differences in political understanding—ones that would be heavily debated in the seventeenth century—about what can be imposed by a sovereign act as a matter of policy, the unique responsibility of the monarch and state officials, and what is established by convention or custom, which is the product of reason tested by experience, whose legitimacy is derived from consent, especially as expressed in the form of practice.[34]

However, elsewhere in the exchange, Harvey also made another critical point to his friend: He was "of Opinion," he said, that the way to bring an "assured and infallible Certaintie" to English poetry or, more generally, "to bring our Language into Arte," was "first of all vniversally to agree vpon *one and the same Ortographie . . .* conformable and proportionate to *our Common Natural Prosodye.*" Here he thought Sir Thomas Smith's efforts "in that respect [to] be the most perfit" or at least "very good."[35] Harvey refers to Sir Thomas Smith's *De recta & emendata Lingvae Anglicae Scritione, Dialogus* (Dialogue of the Correct and Improved Writing of English), written in 1542 and published in Paris in 1568. This work sought to standardize English spelling according to phonetics primarily by following the practices of the "original Anglo-Saxons"—whom he called "our ancestors"—as he believed they had "looked much more closely into the nature of letters, and wrote more correctly than we do to-day." Rather than employing a linguistic theory derived from the study of the classical languages, therefore, his aim was to restore English to its ancient forms, which would thereby reestablish its regularity and make it easier for the illiterate at home or non-English-speakers in Wales, Cornwall, Scotland, and Ireland, or on the continent to acquire a reading knowledge.[36] John Cheke took a similar position in seeking a "clean and pure" form of English, "unmixt and unmangled with other tongues."[37]

Although Harvey acknowledged that Smith's program had some "wantes," which he thought someone of "profounder Learning, and longer Experience" might "by necessarie demonstration . . . supplie," he was content, he said, to accept Smith's version until he saw "something or other, too, or fro, publickely and autentically established, as it were by a generall Counsel, or acte of Parliament."[38] In other words, no matter how profound the learning and long experience of the language reformer, Smith (a family friend) or someone else, his authority would not be enough by itself to produce acceptance of his views because the question concerned what was the correct custom. Also required would be the consent of the public—or at least of a public composed of scholars and poets—after an open debate.

In making this argument, Harvey was joining, of course, in just such a public debate. This is manifested not only by the publication of his letter alongside Spenser's, but by the two of them addressing issues that had achieved a high degree of "publicness" within a wide national and international community. At its center was a scholarly effort to regularize the pronunciation of the classical languages, Latin and Greek. Smith, appointed Regius Professor of Civil Law at Cambridge in 1540, addressed the latter in his *De recta & emendata Lingvae Graecae Pronvnciatione* (On the Correct and Improved Pronunciation of the Greek), which was also written in 1542 and published in Paris in 1568.[39] Harvey also possessed a presentation copy; his assiduous markings in the text and his occasional marginal notes reveal him to have read it quite closely. In the work, Smith defended the view that each letter in ancient Greek represented a different sound and argued in favor of the reform of Greek pronunciation, which Smith, along with Cheke, had introduced into Cambridge in the 1530s. (In 1540, Cheke himself had been appointed Regius Professor of Greek in Cambridge.)[40] Another prominent backer, more senior in age than Smith and Cheke, was John Redman—twice the Lady Margaret Professor of Divinity, sometime Fellow of St. John's College, the last warden of King's Hall and the first Master of Trinity College, and, as Patrick Collinson says, "in reality the true founder of Trinity."[41]

These figures based their teaching of the Greek language on ideas advocated by Erasmus, who had taught Greek in Cambridge between 1511 and 1514, and who in 1528 had published influentially on its proper pronunciation.[42] As Hadfield has emphasized, their immediate aim was to advance the teaching of the Greek language and its literature and make their study according to humanist standards more effective.[43] By the early 1540s, Cambridge's Chancellor, Stephen Gardiner, Bishop of Winchester—an arch-conservative on educational and religious matters who in 1539 had replaced the ousted Thomas Cromwell as Cambridge's chancellor—turned his attention to these innovations, which he endeavored to suppress by enforcing modern practice, based on the pronunciation in use in the Byzantine Empire.[44]

Gardiner's opening move had challenged Cheke, the principal advocate of Erasmus's position, on the grounds of his reform's "unwary rashness," the fact that it cut off communications with those among the learned using the modern form, and the anger that it had caused. When this effort failed, Gardiner, now acting with his "authority as a magistrate," imposed

the modern pronunciation by a decree carrying harsh penalties to all resist-
ers whatever their university status. Violators among the regents were to be
excluded from the Senate, candidates for degrees were to be barred from
graduation, undergraduates on scholarships were to be denied their ben-
efits, and the rest were to be birched.[45] To counter these draconian measures, Smith presented a learned and witty response to Gardiner's orders in
the form of a letter, which the Chancellor, learned himself in the ancient
languages, met in turn in a cogently framed letter of his own defending
the modern custom. To enforce compliance, Gardiner then issued further
harsh, but ultimately unsuccessful, measures.[46]

Although Harvey makes no reference to Smith's commentaries on Greek
pronunciation, Spenser appears to have relied on them, and on writings
related to Smith's, in implying—as did Smith and Cheke following Erasmus's lead—that the ancient Greeks, unlike the English, were able to measure their accents "by the sound." Spenser, moreover, would have been well
aware that, for their devotion to the study of Greek, Smith and Cheke were
singled out while at Cambridge as leaders of what John Leland had called
its "tribe of Crecopia," its "Athenian tribe."[47] That is, they were leaders of
a party of scholars who, like Erasmus and the grammarians he mentions
in his dialogue on Latin and Greek pronunciation, supported a regime of
education devoted to rhetoric and the classical languages.[48] Such figures
were sometimes referred to in learned circles as "the Greeks" or, as Francis
Bacon put it in disparaging them for their reliance on rhetoric, "the Grecians."[49] In this light, Spenser's reference to "the Greeks" associates him not
only with the ancients and their practices but, as Harvey appears to have
recognized, with Smith and Cheke and other contemporary humanists
who wished to restore them.

Cheke and Smith's debate with Gardiner was, to quote Winthrop Hudson, no "tempest in a teapot."[50] Like Erasmus himself, the Cambridge
Athenians were associating their actions with a long-standing scholarly
tradition regarding the role of language in educational reform, traceable back before the Common Era, given new impetus among the early
Christian fathers, and renewed during the Renaissance. Erasmus's work
on pronunciation imparted added momentum to this movement and
prompted further efforts by sixteenth-century philologists, grammarians,
and phoneticists. These figures treated alteration in the sounds of letters
and syllables alongside the corruption of texts as undermining eloquence
and good letters and sought to restore the moral force of texts through acts
of purification. For Erasmus and his followers like Redman, Smith, and
Cheke, the purification of language—the correction of error—was critical

to the purification of religion and the curing of the soul. These language reformers sought to do this in part by restoring ancient texts—most especially scripture—to their original states so far as this was possible, so that they could speak clearly to those who read them or heard them read and expounded. They also believed that the mind and soul could be cleansed by removing corruptions from the language in which thought is expressed, an approach that Smith and Cheke followed in their Greek lectures. Like Erasmus himself, Smith and Cheke viewed Greek, along with Latin, as setting permanent standards of excellence.[51]

Although in Cambridge the reform of Greek pronunciation was backed by religious conservatives like Redman as well as by early Protestants like Smith and Cheke, this Erasmian project received new impetus under the Royal Injunctions of 1535, and its renovation of pedagogy, and in this way, also became intertwined with the period's movement for religious reform. Taken together, the injunctions stressed a return to sources in all aspects of education. The study of divinity, for example, was to be based solely on scripture, and students were to be permitted to study the Bible in private. The injunctions also required the creation at the expense of the colleges of "two daily public lectures, one in Greek and one in Latin." For students in logic, rhetoric, arithmetic, geography, music, and philosophy, which remained dependent on the study of Aristotle, these same injunctions instructed the adoption of modern interpretations and the abandonment of what was called "the frivolous questions and obscure glosses" of the scholastics. Subsequently, an order issued under the authority of Thomas Cromwell, then the university's chancellor, also established an additional lecture either in Greek or Hebrew to be supported at the expense of the university.[52]

Gardiner greeted these ideas with growing anxiety, however, not only for the way they challenged pedagogical conventions but also for the threat they represented to authority in the aftermath of Henry VIII's break from Rome. To be sure, Protestantism held no monopoly among Cambridge's humanists. There were significant numbers of humanists in the university who, like Redman, the principal author of the "conservative Henricianism" embodied in the King's Book of 1543, remained loyal to the traditions of theology and liturgy inherited from the medieval Church.[53] To Gardiner, however, the language reformers, regardless of their religious convictions, represented a threat both to political stability and to orthodox belief. As he put it, what especially concerned him were "the tendencies of the age, the lack of discipline and the uncontrolled licence to which people are prone." Although the pronunciation of Greek had once been different,

the changes, he insisted, had resulted not from willful ignorance but from
the "passage of time," which works "slowly and tranquilly, with the co-
operation of usage," to alter "the character of things." "[T]he distance of
time and space separates us," he said, from the ancient Greeks and makes
it impossible even "to attempt a restoration of the sounds" of their letters
and words "with certainty in every detail." He was willing to allow Smith
to use the word "error" in describing the shortcomings of modern pronunciation. "But it is a collective error," he insisted, "an established error,
an error accepted and approved everywhere, by every living being except
the two of you, an error held in honor among scholars." Against Smith's
claim that the ancient way of pronouncing Greek was the only true way,
and that they therefore had a duty to restore it as best they could, Gardiner
contended, on analogy with "legal usage," that the modern pronunciation
had become correct through convention and use and in consequence was
now "the correct thing to do." In thus arguing, Gardiner adopted a view
of an "ancient constitution" or its literary and linguistic equivalent, similar
to the one Harvey would later use to answer Spenser. But backing it as he
did with the fiat of his magisterial authority as chancellor also involved
an admixture of authority with convention that reveals the depth of his
concern.[54]

For the poets of Spenser's and Harvey's generation, Roger Ascham—
sometime Fellow of Cambridge's St. Johns College and tutor to the Princess Elizabeth—was the most important member of Cambridge's Athenian
tribe. He had been deeply affected as a student in St. John's by the teaching
of Smith and especially Cheke, and was the most influential Englishman
in applying the Athenian tribe's humanist program to poetry. His views,
expressed in *The Schoolmaster* (1570), represent, as Helgerson suggested,
the bridge leading from the world of Cheke and his fellow Cambridge
Athenians in Henry VIII's reign to the Elizabethans. Cheke, Ascham said,
had found Plautus and Terence as poets to be "verie mean and not to be
followed," but had demonstrated that Virgil and Horace "by right *Imitation* of the perfit Grecians, had brought Poetrie to perfitness also in the
Latin tong." Ascham hoped that the same would happen to the English,
whose "rude beggarly ryming" resulted, he said, from the bad influence
of "Gothes and Hunnes" who had destroyed "all good verses and all good
learning." Now, however, "when men know the difference, and haue the
examples, both of the best, and of the worste, surelie, to follow rather
the *Gothes* in Rymng, than the Greekes in trew versifying, were euen to
eat ackornes with swine, when we may freely eate wheate bread emonges
men." When the English came to know better, then, they, like Virgil and

Horace, would reject the barbarous customs of their predecessors and join in transforming English into a language capable of eloquence and suited to civil discourse and learning.[55]

Spenser's aims in his exchange with Harvey were similar. Hence, when he uttered his wish for the English to emulate the Greeks in having the kingdom of their own language, he was not only engaged in the "writing of England" but also participating as a member of England's community of humanist scholars and poets in a discussion about the role of language in culture that, under the influence of Erasmus and his followers, had, since circa 1530 if not earlier, engaged the interests of an international scholarly public. The members of this wider network of learning formed a self-professed aristocracy, which by the early fifteenth century had begun to be called the Republic of Letters (*respublica literaria*).[56] The phrase, resonant with meaning for students of classical civilization, emphasized its members' citizenship in a community in which they enjoyed moral freedom in identifying models of excellence and conforming to them. Such a view had underpinned Cheke's own defense of himself in his exchange of letters with Gardiner, which Smith also endorsed.[57] Unconnected to any single institution, the Republic transcended the nationality and, to a degree, also the religious affiliations of its members. It existed primarily in their shared commitments to learning and their associations and communications with one another, and Catholics as well as Protestants were active members.[58]

As in medieval universities where scholars pursued the same religious and philosophical truths although organized in separate "nations," the goals of the members of this republic, wherever they originated, were universal—a fact that Ascham captured by frequently using the concept of perfection in his commentary. To "perfect" in this case means more than simply to "complete" or "accomplish"; it also conveys the idea of "fulfillment," that is, of achieving a final end and bringing things to an ideal condition. In this meaning, one could speak, as did Archbishop Edwin Sandys, of a man "perfiting himselfe in Godlinesse," which implies, of course, his striving to return himself to mankind's original untainted state.[59] The members of the Republic of Letters—pursuing their goals in their native countries—sought fulfillment in this same sense by restoring universal ideals through the recovery of ultimate truths and common standards of excellence.

The desire to reform English, a language little known and even less used outside the British Isles, had a similar purpose. Standardizing and simplifying English orthography, and with it its pronunciation, would not only make learning to read English easier among the English themselves—and consequently aid in spreading divine truths through the reading of the

Bible in the vernacular—but would also help bring English into the orbit of humanist culture, as Smith wished to do. In this, he and his English colleagues shared a good deal with Joachim du Bellay in France and others who wished to improve the characteristics of the vernacular languages in the mid-sixteenth century. By doing so, these languages could be used in the study of the arts and sciences as instruments, comparable to Greek and Latin, not only of "good letters and erudition," but also "of Philosophy."[60] Imposing a system of metrical order on English poetry based on Greek paradigms, as Ascham and Spenser desired, would have a similar effect. For them, the introduction of quantitative verse would advance national identity by providing English poetry with a form capable of perfection, thereby drawing it into the circle of excellence exemplified by the ancient poets and elevating it in value. The effect would be to enhance the honor of English letters in light of universal standards. In calling for the English to have the kingdom of their own language, therefore, Spenser was "writing the English nation" by representing it as a constitutive part of a larger whole, to which its poets as good citizens would contribute their works.

Respublica Anglorum

We can now return to Spenser's reference to the word "kingdome" in his playful commentary. Unlike ancient Greece, sixteenth-century England was one, of course. But as Sir Thomas Smith had emphasized, it was widely conceived as the *respublica Anglorum,* the "commonwealth of England," which Patrick Collinson and others have called a "monarchical republic."[61] For Smith, as for Sir John Fortescue before him, the authority exercised in different states over their respective lands and peoples was equal.[62] Fortescue in particular stressed that, insofar as the laws of a particular place such as England are sanctioned "by reason of the law of nature," they "are neither better nor worse in their judgements than all the laws of other nations in like cases."[63] However, their constitutions differed, as Smith put it, "according to the nature of the people."[64] England, Smith argued (again following Fortescue), was especially distinctive not only in its reliance on Parliament in the making of laws and granting of taxes but in its form of administering justice under the common law.[65] As Helgerson emphasizes, these views, especially as regards the distinctiveness of English law, were given force in the later Elizabethan and early Stuart era by Sir Edward Coke, who is widely seen as exemplifying what J. G. A. Pocock calls the English "common-law mind."[66] But, as Helgerson also acknowledges, Coke represents only one side in his era's debate about the virtues of English common law, which a number of legal thinkers, Sir Francis Bacon prominent among them, wished to reform along lines derived from the civilians. In addition, Coke, in his *Institutes of the Laws of England,* had himself sought to bring English law into a form that would allow for its comparison to Roman law. Although this massive work was meant in part to show the superiority of the former over the latter, it also demonstrates that Coke accepted that there was but one standard against which to measure the excellences of legal systems. In this respect, Coke's project had a similar goal to what Ascham and Spenser had desired from the reform of English poetry aims.[67]

The concept of "commonwealth" captures the complexities of this understanding. In the early modern era, the word itself carried two different if related meanings: it could be used, on the one hand, to refer to public welfare or the general good and, on the other, to a body politic in which the good is achieved or enjoyed. In this latter meaning, it was also frequently used to describe not only kingdoms but other kinds of social bodies of both greater and lesser scope and scale—from the *res publica Christiana,* which still represented an ideal, perhaps most especially among Erasmians,[68] to corporate towns,[69] to craft guilds and trading companies,[70] and to the family, which was itself conceived as "a little common-wealth," as William Gouge put it.[71] Like the English state itself, each was a body politic composed of a head and members.[72]

All commonwealths, small and large, were understood to pursue the same ultimate end, "the good life," to quote Aristotle—namely, a life lived in complete fulfillment of the inherent nature of human beings as political animals.[73] "Every state," the philosopher says in *The Politics,* "is a community of some kind, and every community is established with a view to some good," with the state, the polis, "aiming at good in a greater degree than any other, and at the highest good" and therefore embracing all the rest.[74] In this model, contained in a text that according to Harvey everyone in his day "had by rote,"[75] larger commonwealths contain the smaller ones, and the smaller provide support to the larger. In consequence, there was no *necessary* competition between the state or the nation and other forms of association, including those we call "publics," whether the latter were primarily popular and local, or elite and national, or learned and transnational, as was the *respublica literaria,* the Republic of Letters. This view of the mutually supportive character of commonwealths, which was embodied in the organization of the Roman Catholic Church, also was manifest among the publics promoting Protestant reform or international Calvinism based in different regions.[76] It contrasts with modern conceptions of "sovereignty," in which, to quote Thomas Hobbes, "lesser Common-wealths" inhabit "the bowels of a greater, like wormes in the entrayles of a naturall man," sapping their power.[77]

Among the English language reformers, a focus on the relationship of the state and the nation to the international public for scholarly learning—the *respublica literaria*—was the primary concern. Although these figures, particularly Smith, manifested their national identities through their participation in discussions of state policies and public affairs,[78] most of them understood their roles to coexist with, and even to spring from, their calling as "men of letters." This is true whether they wrote in Latin, which they frequently did even when commenting on purely English problems, or in the vernacular.[79] When they exchanged their views on proper spelling, pronunciation, or prosody, they were associating themselves with scholars and literary figures at home and abroad with whom they shared commitments to the Republic's ideals and goals.

In other words, the Republic of Letters, which found its starting places at the writing desks or in the studies and libraries of its scholar-members, took in an ever-widening web of participation not only through the operation of interlocking networks of patronage and association with fellow countrymen and foreign correspondents but also, and perhaps more importantly, through the activity of the imagination. Imagination allowed the Republic's citizens to identify themselves as friends of learning with whoever shared their ideals and aspirations, wherever they were located, whether living or dead or indeed yet to be born, and regardless of personal acquaintance. Like the modern nation, therefore, the Republic was an "imagined community,"[80] but one that transcended linguistic differences among its members as well as national boundaries. Seen in this light, the English linguistic reformers, Spenser included, manifested their patriotism—for such we can call it—in their desire to bring their country's language and literature into line with the standards of the classics and thereby write England into the universal history of literary and cultural value and make it part of the public for the progress of learning.[81]

The citizens of sixteenth-century Europe's Republic of Letters lived in a world buffeted by cultural and religious storms engendered by the new discoveries in cosmography, ethnography, and natural philosophy, and by the onset of the Reformation. They responded by creating a "world made with words," to use Anthony Grafton's suggestive phrase, whose inhabitants dedicated themselves to the pursuit of civility, eloquence, decorum, critical judgment, and the advancement of knowledge. This world, as its citizens imagined it, "had no borders, no government, and no capital" and transcended differences in religious outlook and social rank as well as ethnic or national origin. Its goal was to rise through reason and debate above the conditions of divisive and violent disagreement about matters beyond resolution. It never was quite the Arcadia of learning that it imagined itself, and in any case what it was is no more.[82] But it still offers us models of conduct with which we can negotiate our own ways through the confusion and turmoil of our own stormy cultural environment. We need look no further than to Richard Helgerson's life of learning for how to begin.

NOTES

This essay was originally presented to the Workshop on "Richard Helgerson and Making Publics in Early Modern Europe" held at McGill University from August 21 to August 22, 2009. A second version was delivered on December 8, 2009, to the Arts, Society, and Humanities seminar at Clare Hall, University of Cambridge. I want to thank the audiences on both occasions for their thoughtful questions and comments.

1. Richard Helgerson, *Forms of Nationhood: The Elizabethan Writing of England* (Chicago: University of Chicago Press, 1992).

2. Ibid., 3.

3. See Fernand Braudel, *Civilization and Capitalism,* trans. Siân Reynold, 3 vols. (New York: Harper & Row Publishers, 1982), 3: 22.

4. See Max Weber, "Politics as a Vocation," in *From Max Weber: Essays in Sociology,* ed. and trans. H. H. Gerth and C. Wright Mills (New York: Oxford University Press, 1946), 78.

5. See esp. Richard Helgerson, *Adulterous Alliances: Home, State, and Early Modern European Drama and Painting* (Chicago: University of Chicago Press, 2000). Related themes are addressed in Joachim du Bellay, *The Regrets: With the Antiquities of Rome, Three Latin Elegies, and The Defense and Enrichment of the French Language,* ed. and trans. Richard Helgerson (Philadelphia: University of Pennsylvania Press, 2006); and Richard Helgerson, *A Sonnet from Carthage: Garcilaso de la Vega and the New Poetry of Sixteenth-Century Europe* (Philadelphia: University of Pennsylvania Press, 2007).

6. On Harvey's and Spenser's friendship and letters, see Virginia F. Stern, *Gabriel Harvey: His Life, Marginalia and Library* (Oxford: Clarendon Press, 1979), 15–16, 49, 55, 56, 62–63, 66–67, 77, 77n97, 108, 203, 226, 228, 240.

7. Helgerson, *Forms of Nationhood,* 1; Immerito [Edmund Spenser], "To my long approoued and singular good frende, Master *G. H.,*" in [Edmund Spenser and Gabriel Harvey], *Three proper, and wittie, familiar letters: lately passed betvveene tvvo vniversitie men: touching the earthquake in Aprill last, and our English refourmed versifying With the preface of a wellwiller to them both* (London, 1580; STC 23095), 6. Helgerson cites *The Works of Edmund Spenser: A Variorum Edition,* ed. Edwin Greenlaw, Charles Grosvenor Osgood, Frederick Morgan Padelford, and Ray Heffner, 10 vols. in 11 (Baltimore: Johns Hopkins Press, 1932–57), 10:16.

8. Helgerson, *Forms of Nationhood,* 1–2; see also Richard Helgerson, "Language Lessons: Linguistic Colonialism, Linguistic Postcolonialism, and the Early Modern English Nation," *The Yale Journal of Criticism* 11.1 (Spring 1998): 290–93 and 289–99 passim.

9. Helgerson, *Forms of Nationhood,* 2.

10. Sir John Fortescue, *De Laudibus Legum Anglie,* ed. and trans. S. B. Chrimes (Cambridge: Cambridge University Press, 1949), 24–37, 79–91; see also Sir John Fortescue, *On*

the Laws and Governance of England, ed. and trans. Shelley Lockwood (Cambridge: Cambridge University Press, 1997), 17–25, 48–54.

11. Helgerson, *Forms of Nationhood,* 9.

12. Ibid., 4, quoting G. R. Elton, *The Tudor Revolution in Government: Administrative Changes in the Reign of Henry VIII* (Cambridge: Cambridge University Press 1953), 3.

13. Quentin Skinner, *The Foundations of Modern Political Thought* (Cambridge: Cambridge University Press, 1978), 2:355 and 352–58 passim; Quentin Skinner, "The State," in *Political Innovation and Conceptual Change,* ed. Terence Ball, James Farr, and Russell L. Hanson (Cambridge: Cambridge University Press, 1989), 90, 121 and 90–131 passim.

14. Skinner, "The State," 121.

15. Helgerson, *Forms of Nationhood,* 3.

16. For the characteristics of the "nations" in different medieval European universities, see Pearl Kibre, *The Nations in the Medieval Universities* (Cambridge, Mass.: Medieval Academy of America, 1948), 3–5, 19, 160–67.

17. Skinner, *Foundations,* 1: ixni.

18. See Cathy Shrank, *Writing the Nation in Reformation England, 1530–1580* (Oxford: Oxford University Press, 2004), 1–7.

19. See Vivian Salmon, "Language Politics of the 16th and 17th Century English Church," in Salmon, *Language and Society in Early Modern England: Selected Essays, 1981–1994,* ed. Konrad Koerner (Amsterdam: John Benjamins Publishing Company, 1996), 77–82.

20. Shrank, *Writing the Nation,* 3.

21. Raymond Hickey, *Irish English: History and Present-day Forms* (Cambridge: Cambridge University Press, 2007); see also Vivian Salmon, "Missionary Linguistics in 17th-Century Ireland and a North American Analogy," in *Language and Society,* 212–38.

22. See Colin Kidd, *Union and Unionisms: Political Thought in Scotland, 1500–2000* (Cambridge: Cambridge University Press, 2008), 45.

23. Neil Rhodes et al., "Preface" and "Introduction," in *King James VI and I, Selected Writings,* ed. Neil Rhodes, Jennifer Richards, and Joseph Marshall (Aldershot: Ashgate, 2003), ix, 2.

24. Francis Bacon to Earl of Northumberland, April–May 1603 (BL Add MSS 5503, fol. 24), in James Spedding, *The Letters and Life of Francis Bacon* (London: Longmans, Green, Reader and Dyer, 1868), 3:77, in Francis Bacon, *The Works of Francis Bacon,* ed. James Spedding, Robert Leslie Ellis, and Douglas Denon Heath (London: Longmans, Green, Reader, and Dyer, 1868), 10:77; cited in David Harris Willson, *King James VI and I* (London: Jonathan Cape, 1956), 116.

25. On the use of Latin in marginalia, see Gabriel Harvey, *Gabriel Harvey's Marginalia,* ed. G. C. Moore Smith (Stratford-upon-Avon: Shakespeare Head Press, 1913); Stern, *Gabriel Harvey,* 146, 156n23; and, more generally, William H. Sherman, *John Dee: The Politics of Reading and Writing in the English Renaissance* (Amherst: University of Massachusetts Press, 1995), esp. 65–75; William H. Sherman, *Used Books: Marking Readers in Renaissance England* (Philadelphia: University of Pennsylvania Press, 2008).

26. Shrank, *Writing the Nation,* 104–45.

27. Lisa Jardine and Anthony Grafton, "'Studied for Action': How Gabriel Harvey Read His Livy," *Past and Present* 129 (November 1990): 30–78; more generally, see Harvey, *Gabriel Harvey's Marginalia,* 80–310 passim; Stern, *Gabriel Harvey,* 134–271 passim. For Harvey's writings in Latin see STC 12899 (1577), STC 12901 (1578), STC 12902.5 (1575), STC 12904.5 (1577), STC 12905 (1578); on Spenser's evolving friendship with Harvey, see Andrew Hadfield, *Edmund Spenser: A Life* (Oxford: Oxford University Press, 2012), 51–82, 88–89, 101, 105–6, 191.

28. See Elie Kedourie, *Nationalism* (London: Hutchinson, 1960), 9; Patrick J. Geary, *The Myth of Nations: The Medieval Origins of Europe* (Princeton: Princeton University Press, 2002), 26–34; Benedict Anderson, *Imagined Communities: Reflections on the Origins and*

Spread of Nationalism, rev. ed. (London: Verso, 1991), 42; Shrank, *Writing the Nation,* 2–3; Anthony D. Smith, *The Ethnic Origins of Nations* (Oxford: Blackwell, 1986), 133.

29. E[dmund] S[penser], *A vewe of the present state of Irelande discoursed by way of a dialogue betweene* Eudoxus *and* Irenius, Huntington Library, Ellesmere Ms 7041, f. 38ᵛ; Spenser, *Works,* 118–19. Spenser's *View* was entered into the Stationers' Register in 1598, but its publication was suppressed at the time and it did not appear in print until 1633, long after Spenser's death in 1599.

30. Helgerson, *Forms of Nationhood,* 25.

31. Immerito, "To my long approoued and singular good frende, Master *G. H.,*" in [Spenser and Harvey,] *Three . . . letters,* 6; Helgerson, *Forms of Nationhood,* 25. On this point see also [Spenser and Harvey,] *Tvvo Other very commendable Letters, of the same menss vvriting: both touching the foresaid Artificiall Versifying, and certain other Particulars* (London, 1580; printed with *Three . . . letters,* STC 23095), 53–69. Spenser's letter to Harvey at Trinity Hall is dated from Leicester House on October 5, 1579; Harvey's response is dated from Trinity Hall on October 23, 1579. These letters, written before those published in *Three . . . letters,* were published afterward with a separate title page as an appendix to the others. Note, however, that Spenser as well as Harvey eventually abandoned the "quantitative verse project"; see Hadfield, *Edmund Spenser,* 109.

32. [Harvey,] "A Gallant familiar Letter, containing an Ansvvere to that of M. Immerito, vvith sundry proper examples, and some Precepts of our Englishe reforming Versifying," ibid., 43 [mismarked "44"].

33. Helgerson, *Forms of Nationhood,* 28, citing [Harvey,] "A Gallant familiar Letter," in [Spenser and Harvey,] *Three . . . letters,* 43.

34. See J. G. A. Pocock, *The Ancient Constitution and the Feudal Law: A Study of English Historical Thought in the Seventeenth Century; A Reissue with a Retrospect* (Cambridge: Cambridge University Press, 1987); Alan Cromartie, *The Constitutionalist Revolution: An Essay in the History of England, 1450–1642* (Cambridge: Cambridge University Press, 2005).

35. [Harvey,] "A Gallant familiar Letter," in [Spenser and Harvey,] *Three . . . letters,* 32.

36. Sir Thomas Smith, *De recta & emendata Lingvae Anglicae Scritione, Dialogus* (Paris: Ex officina Roberti Stephani Typographi Regii, 1568), quote at fols. 32v–33r; Shrank, *Writing the Nation,* 145–46; Mary Dewar, *Sir Thomas Smith: A Tudor Intellectual in Office* (London: The Athlone Press, 1964), 19–20, 88–121. A facsimile of Harvey's copy, with an English translation, makes up volume 3 in Bror Danielsson, ed., *Sir Thomas Smith: Literary and Linguistic Works [1542. 1549. 1568]* (Stockholm: Almqvist & Wiksell International, 1963–81), quote at 3:40–41. This copy was a gift from Smith himself.

37. Quoted in Peter Burke, *Languages and Communities in Early Modern Europe* (Cambridge: Cambridge University Press, 2004), 149; see also 158. For Cheke's views on English spelling, see E. J. Dobson, *English Pronunciation, 1500–1700,* 2nd ed. (Oxford: Clarendon Press, 1968), 1:43–46. This theme subsequently was taken up in print by Richard Mulcaster, who as headmaster of the Merchant Taylor's School, played a major role in educating Spenser while he was a student there; see Richard Mulcaster, *The first part of the elementary vvhich entreateth chefelie of the right writing of our English tung* (London, 1582: STC 18250); see Hadfield, *Edmund Spenser,* 38.

38. [Harvey,] "A Gallant familiar Letter," in [Spenser and Harvey,] *Three . . . letters,* 32.

39. Sir Thomas Smith, *De recta & emendata Lingvae Graecae Pronvnciatione, Thomae Smithin Angli, tunc in Academia Cantabrigiensi publici praelctoris, ad Vintoniensem Episcopum Espistola* (Paris: Ex officina Roberti Stephani Typographi Regii, 1968); a facsimile of Harvey's copy, a gift from Smith, is published with an English translation as volume 2 in *Smith: Literary and Linguistic Works,* ed. Danielsson. Smith's views on Greek pronunciation are described in Dobson, *English Pronunciation,* 1:46–50. For commentary on Smith's position, see Shrank, *Writing the Nation,* 143–81, esp. 144–54.

40. John Cheke, *Ioannis Cheki Angli Pronuntiatione Graecae potissimum linguae disputa-*

tions cum Stephano Vuintoniensi Episcopo, septem contrarijs epostolis comprehensae, magna quadam & elegantia & eruditione refertae. (Basileae: Per N. Episcopium iuniorem, 1555); a facsimile edition was published under the title *De pronuntiatione Graecae linguae, 1555* (Menston, England: Scolar Press, 1968). His views on Greek pronunciation are described in Dobson, *English Pronunciation,* 1:41–43.

41. Patrick Collinson, "Andrew Perne and His Times," in *Andrew Perne: Quartercentenary studies,* ed. David McKitterick (Cambridge: Cambridge Bibliographical Society, 1991), 3; *A History of the University of Cambridge,* 4 vols., gen. ed. Christopher Brooke, vol. 2: Victor Morgan with Christopher Brooke, *1546–1750,* (Cambridge: Cambridge University Press, 2004), 8; Richard Rex, "Lady Margaret Beaufort and her Professorship, 1502–1559," in Patrick Collinson, Richard Rex, and Graham Stanton, *Lady Margaret Beaufort and her Professors of Divinity at Cambridge, 1502–1649* (Cambridge: Cambridge University Press, 2003), 41–42. On the founding of Trinity College, see *A History of the University of Cambridge,* vol. 1: Damian Riehl Leader, *The University to 1546* (Cambridge: Cambridge University Press, 1988), 341–48.

42. See Desiderius Erasmus, *De recta latini graeique semonis pronunciatione . . . dialogus* (Basel: In Officina Frobeniana, 1528); Desiderius Erasmus, *The Right Way of Speaking Latin and Greek: A Dialogue,* ed. and trans. Maurice Pope, in *Collected Works of Erasmus: Literary and Educational Writings,* ed. J. K. Sowards (Toronto: University of Toronto Press, 1978–86), 4:347–475 (this is vol. 26 in *Collected Works*). By the end of the sixteenth century, this work had appeared seventeen times in one version or another, see Pope, "Introductory Note," ibid., 4:358–59; on Erasmus in Cambridge, see H. C. Porter, *Reformation and Reaction in Tudor Cambridge* (Cambridge: Cambridge University Press, 1958), 21–40; H. C. Porter, "Fisher and Erasmus," in *Humanism, Reform and the Reformation: The Career of Bishop John Fisher,* ed. Brendan Bradshaw and Eamon Duffy (Cambridge: Cambridge University Press, 1989), 81–102; Rex, "Lady Margaret Beaufort and Her Professorship, 1502–1559," 29–31.

43. Hadfield, *Edmund Spenser,* 71.

44. See John Strype, *The Life of the Learned Sir John Cheke, K*, new ed. (Oxford: Clarendon Press, 1821), 14, 18; John Strype, *The Life of the Learned Sir Thomas Smith, Kt. D. C. L,* new ed. (Oxford: Clarendon Press, 1820), 10–12; James Arthur Muller, *Stephen Gardiner and the Tudor Reaction* (London: Society for Promoting Christian Knowledge, 1926), 121; see also Winthrop S. Hudson, *The Cambridge Connection and the Elizabethan Settlement of 1559* (Durham, N.C.: Duke University Press, 1980), 44n1, 54–55.

45. See Cheke, *Pronuciatione Graecae,* 1–21; Strype, *Life of . . . Cheke,* 15–18; Muller, *Stephen Gardiner,* 122; Hudson, *Cambridge Connection,* 43–60. The exchange is described in detail in Dobson, *English Pronunciation,* 1:39–40.

46. Stephen Gardiner to Thomas Smith, September 18, [1542], in *The Letters of Stephen Gardiner,* ed. James Arthur Muller (Cambridge: Cambridge University Press, 1933), 100–120, and in *Smith: Literary and Linguistic Works,* ed. Danielsson, 2:204–14 (App.).

47. John Leland, "Ad D. Guilielmum Seisillium," in *Principum ac illustrium aliquot & eruditorrum in Anglia virorum, encomia, trophaea, genethliaca, & epithalamia* (London, 1589; STC 15447), 106. Leland identified Cheke as the chief of the Athenian tribe; for additional references to Crecopia, see ibid., 7, 46, 72. Leland also offered separate epigrams to Smith and to Cheke, ibid., 87, 88. See also, Strype, *Life of . . . Cheke,* 7, 20; Hudson, *Cambridge Connection,* 43, 54–55 and 43–60 passim. I thank Dr. Richard Serjeantson of Trinity College, Cambridge, for his assistance with this subject.

48. See Roger Ascham, *The Scholemaster, Or plaine and perfitie way of teaching children, to vnderstand, write, and speake the Latin tong* (London, 1570; STC 832), fols. 16v–17v; Roger Ascham, *The Schoolmaster (1570),* ed. Lawrence V. Ryan (Ithaca, N.Y.: Cornell University Press, 1967), 46–49.

49. Francis Bacon, "Of Tribute; or giving that which is due," in *Francis Bacon,* ed. Brian Vickers (Oxford: Oxford University Press, 1996), 35.

50. Hudson, *Cambridge Connection,* 43.

51. See James Bass Mullinger, *The University of Cambridge from the Earliest Times to the Royal Injunctions of 1535* (Cambridge: Cambridge University Press, 1873), 629–32; James Bass Mullinger, *The University of Cambridge from the Royal Injunctions of 1535 to the Accession of Charles the First* (Cambridge: Cambridge University Press, 1884), 7–11; *History of the University of Cambridge,* 1:332–41; Hudson, *Cambridge Connection,* 49; Strype, *Life of. . . Smith,* 10–11; Muller, *Stephen Gardiner,* 121; Dewar, *Sir Thomas Smith,* 17; Pope, "Introductory Note," in Erasmus, *The Right Way of Speaking Latin and Greek,* 4:349–50, 352–56.

52. Mullinger, *The University of Cambridge from Earliest Times,* 629–32; Leader, *History of the University of Cambridge,* 1:332–41.

53. Collinson, "Andrew Perne," 4; Richard Rex, "The Role of English Humanists in the Reformation up to 1559," in *The Education of a Christian Society: Humanism and the Reformation in Britain and the Netherlands,* ed. N. Scott Amos, Andrew Pettegree, and Henk van Nierop (Aldershot: Ashgate, 1999), 19–40; Richard Rex, "St. John's College and the Reformation, 1534–1574," paper delivered to the Early Modern British and Irish History Seminar, University of Cambridge, January 27, 2010. Materials from the latter have now been incorporated into Richard Rex, "The Sixteenth Century," in *St. John's College: A History,* ed. Peter Linehan (Woodbridge, England: Boydell Press, 2011), 30–57. I am grateful to Dr. Rex for sharing a copy of his seminar paper and his book chapter with me.

54. Stephen Gardiner to Thomas Smith, September 18, [1542], in *Letters of . . . Gardiner,* 100–120. Gardiner here argues for a form of ancient constitutionalism as read through the lens of an Edmund Burke–like romantic conservatism; see Helgerson, *Forms of Nationhood,* 7–104; Pocock, *Ancient Constitution,* 30–69, 255–305.

55. Ascham, *Scholemaster,* fols. 59v–60r; Ascham, *Schoolmaster,* ed. Ryan, 144–45; see Helgerson, *Forms of Nationhood,* 29. Ascham commented at length on poetry in the final section of *The Schoolmaster;* see Ascham, *Scholemaster,* fols. 57r–63v; Ascham, *Schoolmaster,* ed. Ryan, 141–53.

56. F. Schalk, "Erasmus und die *Res Publica Literaria,*" *Actes du Congrès Érasme: Rotterdam, 27–29 Octobre 1969* (Amsterdam and London: North Holland Publishing Company, 1971), 14–28; Lisa Jardine, *Erasmus, Man of Letters: The Construction of Charisma in Print* (Princeton: Princeton University Press, 1993), 14–20, 147–74 and passim.

57. For Cheke's letters to Gardiner, see Cheke, *Pronuntiatione Graecae,* 22–162, 218–325, 339–45; for Smith's account, see Smith, *De recta & emendata lingvae Graecae,* bk. 3, fols. 39v–48v, in *Literary and Linguistic Works,* ed. Danielsson, 166–203; Dobson, *English Pronunciation,* 1:39–40, 47–48.

58. See Anthony Grafton, *Worlds Made by Words: Scholarship and Community in the Modern West* (Cambridge: Harvard University Press, 2009), 1–2 and 9–34; Anne Goldgar, *Impolite Learning: Conduct and Community in the Republic of Letters, 1680–1750* (New Haven, Conn.: Yale University Press, 1995), 2–3, 6; Elizabeth L. Eisenstein, *The Printing Press as an Agent of Change: Communications and Cultural Transformations in Early-Modern Europe* (Cambridge: Cambridge University Press, 1979), 1:137n287; Françoise Waquet, "Qu'est-ce que la République des Lettres? Essai de la sémantique historique," *Bibliothèque de l'École des chartes* 147 (1989): 473–502; Marc Fumaroli, "The Republic of Letters," *Diogenes* 143 (Fall 1983): 134–39; Paul Dibon, "Les échanges épistolaires dans l'Europe savante du XVIIIe siècle," *Revue de Synthèse,* 3rd ser., 81–82 (May–June 1976): 32–33.

59. Edwin Sandys, "The two and twentieth Sermon: A Sermon preached at Paul's Crosse at his remouing to Yorke," in *Sermons made by the most reuerende Father in God, Edwin, Archbishop of Yorke, primate of England and metropolitane* (London, 1585; STC 21713), 379.

60. See Joachim du Bellay, *La Deffence, et Illustratione de la Langue Francoyse* (Paris:

Arnoul l'Angelier, 1549), sigs. a4v, b[8]r–c4r; Joachim du Bellay, *The Defense & Illustration of the French Language,* trans. Glady M. Turquet (London: J. M. Dent & Sons, 1939), 22, 45–52; see also Helgerson, "Introduction," *Joachim du Bellay,* 1–2, 4–6, 26–32, text at 346–55; Shrank, *Writing the Nation,* 145–46; Burke, *Languages and Communities,* 89; Hadfield, *Edmund Spenser,* 38–39.

61. Sir Thomas Smith, *De Republica Anglorum,* ed. Mary Dewar (Cambridge: Cambridge University Press, 1982), 57. Smith drafted this work ca. 1565 and revised it shortly before he died in 1577. It was first published in 1583 (STC 22857). For commentary on Smith's political and social thought, see David Harris Sacks, "The Prudence of Thrasymachus: Sir Thomas Smith and the Commonwealth of England," in *Historians and Ideologues,* ed. Anthony Grafton and J. H. M. Salmon (Rochester, N.Y.: University of Rochester Press, 2001), 89–122. Collinson first introduced the term "monarchical republic" in "The Monarchical Republic of Queen Elizabeth I," *Bulletin of the John Rylands University Library of Manchester* 69.2 (Spring 1987): 394–424.

62. Smith, *De Republica Anglorum,* 88; Fortescue, *De Laudibus,* 26–29; see also Fortescue, *On the Laws . . . of England,* 18–19, and App. A, 133–36.

63. Fortescue, *De Laudibus,* 38–39; see also Fortescue, *On the Laws . . . of England,* 25–26.

64. Smith, *De Republica Anglorum,* 62–64.

65. Ibid., 88 and 88–144 passim; see David Harris Sacks, "The Paradox of Taxation: Fiscal Crises, Parliament, and Liberty in England, 1450–1640," in *Fiscal Crises, Liberty, and Representative Government, 1450–1789,* ed. Philip T. Hoffman and Kathryn Norberg (Stanford, Calif.: Stanford University Press, 1994), 9–13.

66. Helgerson, *Forms of Nationhood,* 70–104; Pocock, *Ancient Constitution,* 30–69; for related views to Pocock's, see Donald R. Kelley, *Foundations of Modern Historical Scholarship: Language, Law, and History in the French Renaissance* (New York: Columbia University Press, 1970); Donald R. Kelley, "History, English Law, and the Renaissance," *Past and Present* 65 (November 1974): 24–51.

67. Helgerson, *Forms of Nationhood,* 70–71, 88–104; see also Christopher Brooks and Kevin Sharpe, "History, English Law, and the Renaissance," *Past and Present* 72 (August 1976): 134–36, and 133–41 passim.

68. See Denys Hay, *Europe: The Emergence of an Idea,* rev. ed. (Edinburgh: University of Edinburgh Press, 1968), 16–36; Garrett Mattingly, *Renaissance Diplomacy* (London: Jonathan Cape, 1955), 17–25. See also St. Augustine, *The City of God against the Pagans,* ed. and trans. R. W. Dyson (Cambridge: Cambridge University Press, 1998), e.g., bk. 14, chap. 28; bk. 15, chaps. 1–2; and bk. 19, 632–37, 909–64.

69. Thomas Wilson, *The State of England, Anno Dom. 1600,* ed. F. J. Fisher, *Camden Miscellany* XVI, Camden Society, 3rd ser., 52 (1936): 20–21.

70. See Phil Withington, *The Politics of Commonwealth: Citizens and Freemen in Early Modern England* (Cambridge: Cambridge University Press, 2005), 51–84.

71. William Gouge, *Of domesticall duties eight treatises* (London, 1622; STC 12119), 17–20.

72. Whether Christ or a mortal human being served as head of the *res publica Christiana* was in dispute.

73. *Pol.* 1.1.1252b29–30, in Aristotle, *The Complete Works of Aristotle: The Revised Oxford Translation,* ed. Jonathan Barnes (Princeton: Princeton University Press, 1984), 2:1987.

74. *Pol.* 1.1.1252a1–6, ibid., 2:1686; see also *Nic. Eth.* 9.8.1168a28–1169b2 in 2:1846–48.

75. Gabriel Harvey to Edmund Spenser (1579) in *Letter-Book of Gabriel Harvey, A. D. 1573–1580,* ed. Edward J. L. Scott, Camden Society, new ser., 33 (1884): 79.

76. See Menna Prestwich, *International Calvinism, 1541–1714* (Oxford: Oxford University Press, 1987); *Calvinism in Europe, 1540–1620,* ed. Andrew Pettegree, Alastair Duke, and Gillian Lewis (Cambridge: Cambridge University Press, 1996); Philip Benedict, *Christ's Church Purely Reformed: A Social History of Calvinism* (New Haven, Conn.: Yale University Press, 2004).

77. Thomas Hobbes, *Leviathan,* ed. Richard Tuck (Cambridge: Cambridge University Press, 1996), 230.

78. See, e.g., Whitney R. D. Jones, *The Tudor Commonwealth, 1529–1559: A Study of the Impact of the Social and Economic Developments of mid-Tudor England upon Contemporary Concepts of the Nature and Duties of the Commonwealth* (London: Athlone, 1970); Whitney R. D. Jones, *The Tree of Commonwealth, 1450–1793* (Madison, N.J.: Fairleigh Dickinson University Press, 2000), 13–118.

79. On the Latinate culture of early modern England, see J. W. Binns, *Intellectual Culture in Elizabethan and Jacobean England: The Latin Writings of the Age* (Leeds: Francis Cairns, 1990). On manuscript publication, see Harold Love, *Scribal Publication in Seventeenth-Century England* (Oxford: Clarendon Press, 1993).

80. Benedict Anderson, *Imagined Communities.*

81. For evidence of Spenser's participation in the culture of the *Respublica litteria,* on his own and through the influence of Harvey, see Hadfield, *Edmund Spenser,* 95–110, 120.

82. Grafton, *Worlds Made by Words,* 1–2, 9–34.

CHAPTER TWO

Translating the Law

Sir Edward Coke and the Formation of a Juristic Public

STEPHEN DENG

IN HIS INFLUENTIAL BOOK *Forms of Nationhood,* Richard Helgerson argues that a group of men from the same generation during the Elizabethan period—a group that includes Edmund Spenser, Sir Edward Coke, William Camden, John Speed, Michael Drayton, Richard Hakluyt, William Shakespeare, and Richard Hooker—undertook the ambitious project of "writing" the English nation. Sir Edward Coke's own contribution entailed the diligent recording and codification of "unwritten" English common law, which had been in competition with a Roman civil law influential on the Continent to become what Sir John Davies would describe as the "soule" of the "body politike of a common wealth."[1] According to Helgerson, Coke's *Reports* and *Institutes* represent the culmination of an attempt to avoid the experience of continental nations, which because of their reliance on civil law tended to be "doubly foreign: foreign to themselves as well as to the English."[2] But Helgerson points out that Justinian's *Corpus iuris civilis* maintained one key influence on Coke. Although it was never displaced by Roman law, English common law as represented in the *Institutes* did "receive a Roman idea of the law, or rather a Roman idea of the form in which the law should present itself."[3] Nevertheless, Coke composed his *Institutes* in a form that Justinian would not have appreciated or even understood. While legal scholars have been critical of Coke's method, which seems idiosyncratic and often meanders from the specific topic at hand, Helgerson argues that the form of the *Institutes* remains true to the political cause of English common law: "Not merely the product of a disorderly mind, Coke's lack of method was both politically motivated and politically effective. It allowed him to write the law without weakening its oppositional prerogative, allowed him to produce what was in effect a writing against the written, a writing against the Roman imperial tradition and all that it stood for."[4]

But Coke's political motivation extended beyond a desire to keep England free from Roman influence; he also intended to keep the law out of the hands of the king. The form of the *Institutes,* then, could be construed as an attempt to make "the law's fundamental coherence, its reason, reside only in the mind of the diligent and experienced *artifex,* the well-trained lawyer."[5] Therefore, like the *Reports,* which other than the prefaces were written in "law-French" and thus were only comprehensible to those trained in the particular language of the common law, in the *Institutes* Coke utilized a complex form in order to serve only dedicated professional lawyers, those who had the capacity to employ "artificial reason" for a privileged grasp of English law.

However, an important distinction remains between the *Reports* and the *Institutes:* whereas Coke published the main body of the *Reports* only in the professional language of law-French, he translated the legal texts of the *Institutes* into English and also included extensive commentaries in English. Despite the complex form Coke used, Helgerson's assertion that he composed the *Institutes* to be accessible only to the *artifex* invites the question of why translate them at all, as the well-trained lawyer would presumably have a working knowledge of law-French, and even law students would be expected to learn the language of their profession.

In this chapter, I shall argue that the body of the *Reports* was indeed intended for a particular audience of professional common lawyers, but that in the *Institutes,* ostensibly an introduction to common law for Inns of Court students, Coke also had in mind a more general audience, a "juristic public" consisting not just of professional lawyers and law students but of learned individuals who had a political interest and political stake in understanding the law. And indeed, the seeds of this juristic public may be found prior to the publication of the *Institutes* during an implicit debate between Coke and King James I over how best to simplify the law. In this debate James and Coke, respectively, invoked the "people" and the "commonwealth" as sources of authority—James to promote translation, consolidation, and public codification of the law in order to grant the king legal representation of the common interest, and Coke to warn against such actions in order to maintain the integrity of a law based in custom and the wisdom of common-law judges. But James also adopted a Reformation argument to associate the mystification of common law by Coke and other lawyers, especially their insistence on publishing reports in law-French, with "Papist" attempts to withhold God's word from worshippers.

In what seems to be capitulation to the king, Coke decided to translate the common law into English with his publication of the *Institutes*. However, in composing them Coke realized the limitations of his earlier approach and the need to unfold the mysteries of the common law to a broader segment of the English nation, who by understanding their rights under the law could serve as another check on absolutist ambitions. Whereas the *Reports* were intended to defend the law against the king's appropriation by emphasizing the professional legal skills and linguistic knowledge necessary to interpret common law, the *Institutes* instead conjured a public consisting of informal students and competent defenders of their "birthright," the legal heritage of England. Therefore, in response to Helgerson's claims about exclusivity among the professional legal community in "writing" the nation, I argue that the common law of the *Institutes* was *more* common than that of the *Reports* and opened up the project of legal nation making from common lawyers alone to a broader juristic public, offering an example of the potential contribution of such publics to nation formation in general.

The clearest indication that Coke intended his *Reports* for a specialized audience is that he published the main text only in law-French. Helgerson describes the works as "writing that in English and Latin prefaces addresses those unlearned in the law only to tell them of that which they cannot understand, the impenetrably written/unwritten law-French reports that fill the greater part of the volume they hold in their hands. As such, this writing preserves the special prerogative of the professional community in whose collective memory the unwritten law resides, making that community 'connatural,' as Davies says of the law itself, 'to the nation.'"[6] As with other writers of law reports, Coke employed the professional jargon that King James described as "an old, mixt, and corrupt Language, onely vnderstood by Lawyers."[7] According to Helgerson, Coke's prefaces in English and Latin seduced a more general readership into this privileged realm of the common law only to frustrate their efforts once they had reached the main body of the text. This means, moreover, that only a select few would be able to contribute to that entity that Davies describes as "connatural to the nation," and therefore only an elite group would be able to partake in this dimension of the "making" of England. The legal formation of England and Englishness, Helgerson suggests, was a privileged project. Though Coke's *Reports* were necessary resources for lawyers to consult on a regular basis, they were also "ideal figurations of the legal community and the nation—books that told not only how the law functioned and what the courts had decided but also what England was and what part lawyers had in the making of its identity."[8]

This early exclusionary strategy was perhaps a necessary response to absolutist ambitions of James I, as Helgerson argues.[9] The king's desire to become involved in the codification of English common law was of particular concern. After assuming the throne, James somewhat softened his earlier absolutist rhetoric in *The Trew Law of Free Monarchies* ("the King is aboue the law, as both the author and giuer of strength thereto") to include the advisory function of Parliament in modifications of law.[10] For example, he concedes in a March 1609 speech to Parliament that any actions he might make in regard to the codification of English law—"things specially to be purged & cleared in the Common Law"—would be "always by the aduise of Parliament: For the King with his Parliament here are absolute, (as I vnderstand) in making or forming of any sort of Lawes."[11]

And yet this desire to "purge" and "clear" the common law by the king-in-parliament would be tantamount to the codification of all common law through statute, a point Helgerson makes with regard to Francis Bacon's "proposed registering and recompiling of the common law."[12] This plan to allow statute to replace judicial decisions recorded in reports becomes evident soon after in James's speech: "since the very Reports themselues are not alwayes so binding, but that diuers times Iudges doe disclaime them, and recede from the iudgment of their predecessors; it were good, that vpon a mature deliberation, the exposition of the Law were set downe by Acte of Parliament, and such reports therein confirmed, as were thought fit to serue for Law in all times hereafter, and so the people should not depend vpon the bare opinions of Iudges, and vncertaine Reports."[13] Here, James proposes to give solidity, consistency, and substance to the common law by replacing the "bare opinions of Iudges and vncertaine Reports" with a formal "Exposition of the Law . . . by Acte of Parliament"; in other words, he intends to use the parliamentary right to make law in order to appropriate legislative power from common-law judges. For this reason, Helgerson notes that some royal supporters like Bacon "imagined the writing (or rewriting) of the law as belonging essentially to the monarch," following the model of the emperor Justinian, who had in effect "written" Roman law.[14] Such an opening would provide James with the power to interpret and even transform English law for his own benefit.

In order to uphold the authority of common-law judges, Coke pushed to maintain a common law in judicial acts distinct from statute law. In the preface to the fourth part of the *Reports*, he acknowledges that reformation of statutes, which "his majesty out of his great wisdom and care to the commonwealth, hath commanded to be done," would be welcome "so as each man may clearly know what and how much is of them in force, and how to obey them." However, he cautions that "there be certain statutes concerning the administration of justice, that are in effect so woven into the common law, and so well approved by experience, as it will be no small danger to alter or change them."[15] In his admonition, Coke implies that statute reform, rather than merely clarifying or effectively codifying the common law, might instead manipulate and transform a law that should be based in custom and judicial reason. He therefore offers his own *Reports*, "the true sense and exposition of the laws in divers and many cases," which he considers "a part of my great duty that I owe to the commonwealth not to keep . . . private, but being withal both encouraged, and in manner thereunto inforced, to publish and communicate them to all.[16] That is, Coke answers James's proposed simplification of the law by *increasing* the circulating body of law reports still in their specialized language, in effect offering a purportedly clarifying document to all that can only be understood by a select few.

And yet the rhetorical strategies both James and he employ create the conditions for an early modern public to weigh in on the matter of the law. While Coke appeals to the authority of the "commonwealth," to which he feels a "great duty . . . to publish and communicate" his "true sense and exposition of the laws," James invokes the "people," who "should not depend vpon the bare opinions of Iudges, and vncertaine Reports." Peter Lake and Steve Pincus have recently shown that such rhetorical strategies were not uncommon in the period. They describe a "post-Reformation public sphere and mode of political maneuver and public politics" from the 1530s to the 1630s—therefore predating Jürgen Habermas's "bourgeois" public sphere of the eighteenth century—which constituted "a series of exchanges not so much between the rulers and the ruled as between elements within the regime and their allies, clients, and connections." They point in particular to "sophisticated attempts to appeal to and mobilize various publics emanat[ing] from the center of the regime itself," for example in the Elizabethan parliaments' "transmutation of a variety of local, private, and conciliar complaints and concerns into legislation about *commonwealth* matters."[17] Lake and Pincus focus mostly on religious controversies during the period, but a similar case may be made for legal matters. As with the religious debates, two central figures of authority appealed to the "people" and the "commonwealth"—that is, insisted they were speaking on behalf of the "public" interest—in order to argue respectively for and against statute-based consolidation of the common law. As a result of such "communicative strategies," the historians argue, central authorities "notionally at least called into being . . . an adjudicating public or publics able to judge or determine the truth of the matter in hand on the basis of the information and argument placed before them."[18]

In their discussion of early modern publics, Lake and Pincus seem to focus more on the subsequent emergence of a "public sphere"—that is, they place the post-Reformation "communicative strategies" within a longer historical narrative—rather than analyzing the strategies themselves as localized discursive phenomena, as does Michael Warner. Warner calls a public "a space of discourse organized by nothing other than discourse itself. . . . It exists *by virtue of being addressed*," and though it "might be real and efficacious, . . . its reality lies in just this reflexivity by which an addressable object is conjured into being in order to enable the very discourse that gives it existence."[19] In this sense, writing to a public is performative "world making," in that "the object of address is brought into being partly by postulating and characterizing it." However, Warner does concede the necessity of this object of address being a "real path for the circulation of this discourse," a receptive body of addressees who recognize they are being addressed, which therefore constitutes a real "social entity."[20] In order for a public to be successfully conjured, there must be an actual group of people (readers, viewers, auditors, etc.) paying attention to the act of conjuration, and therefore paradoxically observing themselves *being* conjured.

The success of such public conjuration, as well as the *type* of public being conjured through the address, depends on the language (or imagery) used to conjure it. I note this qualification because Coke seems careful not to invoke "the people" in his prefaces to the *Reports* but rather "the commonwealth," despite the fact that there was a widespread "fiction" among common lawyers of the period that "the people" are the source of law.[21] Davies, for example, expresses the impossibility of ever recording the common law, because "in vse & practise, it can bee recorded and registred no where, but in the memory of the people."[22] Coke, on the other hand, never identifies "the people" as the source of the law. In the preface to the eighth part of the *Reports,* he answers a question raised as to "what the body or text of the common law is, and consequently where a man may find it?" by concluding that "the grounds of our common laws at this day were beyond the memory or register of any beginning."[23] Later, in the first part of the *Institutes,* Coke describes the common law as "nothing else but reason, which is to be vnderstood of an artificiall perfection of reason."[24] While at various points in his career he seems to emphasize an origin for the common law more in the mists of history or more in the "artificial reason" of common law judges across history, he never attributes the source of the law to "the people."

Coke's choice of "commonwealth" over "people" in his appeal to "public" authority allows him to maintain the argument that he has the interests of the entire social body in mind even if not all individual people are allowed direct access to the law. Indeed, a particular episode from 1608 described in the twelfth part of the *Reports,* which was compiled after Coke's death, emphasizes his belief that not all English people would have developed the "artificial reason" necessary to understand the complexities of the common law. According to the account, Coke in effect overruled a legal decision made by King James regarding a case involving land rights:

> A controversy of land between parties was heard by the King, and sentence given, which was repealed, for this, that it did belong to the common law: then the King said, that he thought the law was founded upon reason, and that he and others had reason, as well as the Judges: to which it was answered by me, that true it was, that God had endowed his Majesty with excellent science, and great endowments of nature; but his Majesty was not learned in the laws of his realm of England, and causes which concern the life, or inheritance, or goods, or fortunes of his subjects, are not to be decided by natural reason but by the artificial reason and judgment of law, which law is an act which requires long study and experience, before that a man can attain to the cognizance of it.[25]

Legal historians have questioned whether this incident ever in fact took place, but it is nevertheless consistent with Coke's frequent challenges to the royal prerogative with respect to the law. He upholds the notion of "artificial reason" in order to challenge the king in matters of the law, to wrest legal authority from the king. Moreover, by linking the common law to those issues that "concern the life, or inheritance or goods, or fortunes of his subjects," he suggests that through his knowledge of the law he knows what is better for the king's subjects in certain matters than the king himself. So, in addition to wresting legal authority from the monarch, Coke also wrests the right of legal representation, meaning both the right to represent the interests of the people through the law, and also the right to represent the law through his and other common lawyers' interpretations. All, however, is done in the interest of the "commonwealth."

James clearly understood that a key strategy of Coke and other common-law judges was to maintain their reports in law-French, which would make knowledge of the law inaccessible to nonprofessionals, and he therefore called them out on it. In the 1609 speech, he appeals to Reformation logic (and again to "the people") by comparing common-law judges to secretive "Papists":

> For since it is our plea against the Papists, that the language in GODS Seruice ought not to be in an vnknowne tongue, according to the rule in the law of *Moyses*, That the Law should be written in the fringes of the Priests garment, and should be publikely read in the eares of all the people: so mee thinkes ought our Law to be made as plaine as can be to the people, that the excuse of ignorance may be taken from them, for conforming themselues thereunto.

He therefore declares his desire that the common law "were written in our vulgar Language" because "euery Subiect ought to vnderstand the Law vnder which he liues."[26] In a peculiar intersection between Reformation-based and law-based publics, James contends that common-law judges preserving the use of law-French in common-law reports are equivalent to priests withholding from worshippers access to the word of God (that is, *divine* law) by delivering sermons only in Latin and preventing translation of scripture.

With the publication of the *Institutes,* Coke came to terms with the difficulty of claiming that one is working in the common interest while publishing the law in a highly specialized language, the difficulty in not representing what he would describe as the "birthright" of English subjects in their native language. Denying access to any but trained lawyers could leave common-law practitioners vulnerable to "priestly" associations, as in James's remark, and perhaps even to marginalization as English subjects began to seek alternative avenues of justice through prerogative courts within the commonwealth. Moreover, he understood that granting public access to the common law through the English language was in the law's own interest, because it would serve as an important check on monarchical power and its attempt to control representation of the English nation. Therefore, though Coke's 1608 confrontation with King James described in the *Reports* suggested his desire to wrest away the right to represent the interests of the people, the subsequent publication of his *Institutes,* with their English translations and extensive English commentaries, indicated a desire to empower more of these subjects to become involved in their own, as well as the nation's, representation.

A key step in reaching a broader public, in creating a "real path for the circulation" of the common law to conjure a juristic public, would be to translate it into the language of the nation. Although Coke had published the main text of the *Reports* in law-French, it is not clear that he thought this choice of language mandatory. Davies did believe so, asserting in his own *Reports* that "the proper & peculiar phrase of the common lawe cannot bee so well exprest, nor any case in lawe bee so succinctly, sensibly, & whithall so fully reported, as in this speech."[27] He offers a historical rationale for the use of this "*mixt* kinde of speech which wee call the *lawe French,*" an odd composite of English, Latin, and French that differed from contemporary French because lawyers had retained specialized "*Tearmes* of the lawe" from previous generations as well as "many other old words & Phrases of speech which . . . are growne by long & continuall vse so apt, so naturall, & so proper for the matter & subiect of these *Reports,* as no other language is significant enough to expresse the same."[28] In addition to emphasizing the historic significance of law-French, he refutes any suggestions that common lawyers intentionally mystified their practice, even claiming "how easie the *Lawe french* is to bee learned: in somuch that the meanest witt that euer came to the study of the lawe, doth come to vnderstand it almost perfectly within ten dayes without a Reader."[29] Davies suggests that the common law is entirely open and available to any who would like to know it, provided they are willing to spend a few days learning the language. But in order for the common law to be accurately represented, it must remain in its "naturall" form.

Coke, on the other hand, emphasizes the "matter" of the law over the particular language used for it.[30] In the preface to the third part of the *Reports,* he claims that common lawyers continued to use law-French only because the "former reports of the law, and the rest of the authors of the law," other than Christopher St. German in his *Doctor and Student,* "are written in French."[31] But this was by no means the "natural" or original language of English law, the latter of which, if anything, was *Greek.* In order to prove that English common law predated Roman occupation, Coke points to legends about the Trojan Brutus who, when he settled the land, "wrote a book in the Greek tongue, calling it the Laws of the Britons, and he collected the same out of the laws of the Trojans."[32]

Moreover, the Norman influence on legal language entailed merely an appropriation and translation of English common-law ideas into their own language. According to Coke, William the Conqueror, "finding the excellency and equity of the laws of England, did transport some of them into Normandy, and taught the former laws, written, as they say, in Greek, Latin, British, and Saxon tongues (for the better use of Normans) in the Norman lang.," which remain as the present "customs of Normandy." Even before the Norman influence, the common law was apparently already in a mixed language form. But though the terms were reintroduced using the Norman language, the matter of the law remained the same, just as while the English employed Norman terms for "hunting, hawking, and, in effect, of all other plays and pastimes . . . no man maketh question but these recreations and disports were used within this realm before the Conqueror's time."[33] In order to establish historic continuity in the common law, Coke argues that the matter of the law persisted untransformed despite a long history of appropriation and translation.

If only the matter matters, why then not use the native language of England to represent English common law? Coke decided to do just that when he published the *Institutes,* defending his decision by noting that the works "are an introduction to the knowledge of the nationall Lawes of the Realme"; he calls his translation "a worke necessarie, and yet heeretofore not vndertaken by any, albeit in all other professions there are the like." Such statements suggest Coke's belief that "nationall" laws ought to be represented in the language of the nation, and he even feigns surprise that it has not been done so already. Following a logic similar to that of Davies, he does maintain the use of key "Termes and Words drawne from that legall French" because they are "so apt and significant to expresse the true sence of the Laws, and are so wouen into the Laws themselues, as it is in a manner impossible to change them, neither ought legall Termes to be changed."[34] This explanation belies the claim that the "matter" is more important than the "language" of the law. Nevertheless, the bulk of the text would be in English prose, which, along with the English commentaries accompanying the legal texts, would help to shed light on the specific meanings of these legal terms, opening up the mysteries of the profession and the professional language to all English speakers. In effect, the legal terms would be merely appended to the English language, as with other technical terms and foreign borrowings, so the entirety of the legal texts would be presented in this newly expanded version of English.

Ironically, to further support his decision of translating common law into English, Coke invokes the "Wisdome of a Parliament" in a statute of 35 Eliz., which states that *"the Lawes and Customes of this Realme the rather should bee reasonably perceiued and knowne, and better vnderstood by the tongue vsed in this Realme, and by so much euery man might the better gouerne himselfe without offending of the Law, and the better keepe, saue, and defend his heritage and possessions."*[35] In citing this statute, Coke appears to be responding to James's 1609 speech to Parliament, which had been published soon after the event and was included among five key speeches in the king's *Works.* Recall that in this speech James had promoted the same idea of translating the common law into "our vulgar Language" so that "the excuse of ignorance may be taken from them, for conforming themselues thereunto."[36] The king argues that subjects need to see the laws in their own language in order to follow them appropriately, to know how to be good subjects of the realm.

Coke instead cites the statute from an earlier parliament of Elizabeth—whom he frequently refers to as a "just" monarch in his prefaces to *Reports* published during her reign—which includes both the need for the subject to "*better gouerne himself*" and the ability to "*better keepe, saue, and defend his heritage and possessions.*" While James's rationale mentions only the *duties* of subjects, the Elizabethan statute also invokes subjects' *rights.* Moreover, Coke appends as commentary to this statute a legal commonplace he cites elsewhere as a defense against the royal prerogative: "*Et neminem oportet esse sapientorem Legibus,* No man ought to bee wiser than the Law."[37] While the context alludes primarily to the obedience of subjects to the law, the statement also implies the king's own subservience to the law, to those particular rights that English subjects have under the law.

Furthermore, Coke's emphasis on the common law as the "birthright" of all English subjects makes explicit the law's role in nation formation. In the first part of the *Institutes,* he calls the English common law "the best and most common birth-right that the subject hath for the safegard and defence not onely of goods, lands, and reuenues, but of his wife & children, his body, fame, and life also."[38] While this "safegard and defence" could serve individuals in all private matters of land dispute, and so on, the rhetoric of this statement, especially the use of the term "subject," also intimates concerns about political menaces, threats from the state, and particularly from the monarch. Following Helgerson's model of early modern English nationhood as a series of writings that "rivals the monarch as the fundamental source of national identity," the writing of the nation embodied in the common law as birthright stands firm against infringements and attempts at appropriation and manipulation by monarchical authority.[39] Nevertheless, Coke realized that such a birthright would be useless without knowledge of what this right entails, and he therefore hoped in the *Institutes* to shed light on it for a general group of readers, who as subjects of the Crown had a clear political motivation to understand the law, and especially to understand their legal position in various situations that might arise. So, rather than just a privileged project among common law judges, the writing and especially the English translation of the common law entailed the discursive revocation of a juristic public that would contribute to the process of English nation formation.

Earlier in the *Reports,* Coke had envisioned just such a community in England's glorified past. In his preface to the eighth part of the *Reports,* he wistfully mentions a time when not only professional lawyers but clerics and nobles as well had acquired a working knowledge of the law. He describes "divers Bishops and other ecclesiastical persons in ancient time, [who] did studiously read over the laws of England, and thereby attained to great and perfect knowledge of the same."[40] He also describes "many noblemen [who] have been excellently learned in the laws of England," and especially a group under Henry III, whose adamant refusal to change the law in a particular matter of inheritance demonstrated "the inward and affectionate love and reverence they bear unto the common laws of their dear country."[41] The contemporary version of these learned nobles are the "young Gentlemen about the number of eight or nine score" at each of the Inns of Court, "who there spend their time in study of law, and in commendable exercises fit for gentlemen."[42] He acknowledges that there exists a certain group already at the Inns who would obtain exposure to English law despite the fact that they would not pursue it as a professional career. They would help to promote the common law, but the publication of the *Institutes* would introduce English law to other gentlemen and any other literate people who would appreciate knowledge of their "birthright."

The translation of legal language in the *Institutes* therefore introduced the common law to an even broader potential readership. Indeed, Coke appears to have cultivated this extended readership by addressing them in his prefaces apart from law students. In the preface to the first part of the *Institutes,* he explains why he chose to include both the "original" of Littleton's *Tenures,* in order to leave "our Author to speake his owne language," and an English translation, "to the end that any of the Nobilitie, or Gentrie of this Realme, *or of any other estate, or profession whatsoeuer,* that will be pleased to read him and these Institutes, may vnderstand the language wherein they are written."[43] Therefore, in addition to providing an introductory textbook for students studying law at the Inns, Coke hoped to reach a more inclusive readership including a number of informal students of the law from a wide spectrum of estates and professions. In fact, this latter expression of desire to reach a wider audience is also included in the 1628 preface, whereas an address to students in the 1629 version is not, suggesting that, from the very start, Coke was hoping to establish a broad audience for his work.

In the preface to the third part of the *Institutes,* Coke places special emphasis on a more general audience because of its particular subject matter:

This, as other parts of the *Institutes,* wee have set forth in our English tongue, not onely for the reasons in the Preface to the first Part of the *Institutes* alledged, which wee presume may satisfie any indifferent and prudent reader: but specially this Treatise of the *Pleas of the Crowne,* because, as it appeareth by that which hath been said, it concerneth all the subjects of the realme more neerly by many degrees, then any of the other.[44]

Rather than suggesting that the law would be incomprehensible to a general readership devoid of the "artificial reason" developed only through diligent legal study over a long period, Coke insists that knowledge of the law is in the interest of "all of the subjects of the realme." Moreover, he again cites the statute of 35 *Eliz.* in order to defend his decision to translate the text into English, especially against edicts by William the Conqueror, as reported by Robert Holcoth during the reign of Edward III, intended "to destroy" (*destruere*) the Anglo-Saxon language while promoting the use of "Gallic" in the *curia regis* and the teaching of the same to all students. Elizabeth's statute, Coke notes, has "given due honour to our English language, which is as copious and significant, and as able to expresse any thing in as few and apt words, as any other native language, that is spoken at this day. And (to speake what we think) we would derive from the Conqueror as little as we could."[45]

In a clear expression of linguistic nationalism—not unlike Spenser's "kingdome of our own language" with which Helgerson begins *Forms of Nationhood*—Coke defends the right of English to represent the law and even suggests rejecting all Norman influence, which would of course include the important linguistic influence on law-French that had dominated common law discourse over the past five hundred years.[46] This statement signifies the culmination in Coke's transformed attitude toward representation of the common law as the privileged and specialized prerogative of a professional community to a national "birthright" that should be made accessible to all English subjects.

However, in order to prevent manipulation and appropriation of the law, and to retain a special place for the expertise of common-law judges, Coke was still careful to maintain an emphasis on the "artificial reason" embodied in the law. He most clearly distinguishes between "naturall" and "artificiall" reason in the first part of the *Institutes:*

> reason is the life of the Law, nay the common Law it selfe is nothing else but reason, which is to be vnderstood of an artificiall perfection of reason, gotten by long study, obseruation, and experience, and not of euery mans naturall reason, for, *Nemo nascitur artifex* [No one is born a craftsman/expert]. This legall reason, *est summa ratio.* And therefore if all the reason that is dispersed

into so many seuerall heads were vnited into one, yet could he not make such a law as the Law of England is, because by many succession of ages it hath beene fined and refined by an infinite number of graue and learned men, and by long experience growne to such a perfection, for the government of this Realme, as the old rule may be iustly verified of it, *Neminem oportet esse sapientiorem legibus:* No man (out of his owne priuate reason) ought to be wiser than the Law, which is the perfection of reason.[47]

Helgerson cites this passage first to emphasize the one man Coke had in mind, as Thomas Hobbes understood, whose private reason ought not to be wiser than the Law: the king.[48] But he subsequently alludes to the "*summa ratio*" of this passage in order to make his case for a privileged project of nation writing among common-law judges.[49] Indeed, this passage does give common lawyers a special place in upholding the laws of the nation as those most studied in the law, those who have cultivated "artificial reason" through "long study, obseruation, and experience." However, the passage and other allusions to "artificial reason" in Coke have a more urgent purpose: to preserve the common law from manipulation and appropriation by any individual. It emphasizes that the perfection of the common law stems primarily from the collective wisdom that has been accumulated in England both synchronically and diachronically. The diachronic dimension is indeed more important, because it is the law's antiquity, the tried and tested reason across generations, that allows for the process of perfection through experience. Although it does give learned common-law judges a privileged place in understanding the law, it represents more of an attempt at preventing transformation of the law by individual "priuate" reason than an attempt to foreclose access to the law to a broader public.

While Coke's *summa ratio* should be distinguished from Jürgen Habermas's emphasis on *ratio* within the bourgeois public sphere, it does not imply continued mystification of the law. Habermas contrasts the "secrecy" implicit in the *arcana imperii* (what James would refer to as "mysteries of state") that "was supposed to serve the maintenance of sovereignty based on *voluntas*," the personal will of the monarch, to the "publicity" that "was supposed to serve the promotion of legislation based on *ratio*."[50] Coke's *summa ratio* is clearly not a device for public debate that would lead to transformation in legislation; rather, he invokes the idea to uphold the long tradition of learned reason that has gone into making the law, thereby warning against any arbitrary transformations in the law.

Coke did not want the law to be subject to fickle changes made by either the king or public opinion. And professional common lawyers would still be a privileged class, in that they alone would have cultivated the "artificial reason" necessary in order to pass judgment in particular legal cases. But this does not mean that Coke continued to represent in the common law "its own *arcana*" as a mechanism of exclusion, as Helgerson argues.[51] Rather, by publishing and translating the *Institutes* into English and by cultivating a public of readers with interest in understanding their "birthright," Coke made public what had previously been arcane, an exclusive entity available only to those who had knowledge of law-French. More than just a select group of common lawyers would thereby be able to understand the nature of their Englishness according to the dimension of the law. England could in effect become *more* English through the publication, promotion, and expanded comprehension of its native law by members of a newly fashioned juristic public.

NOTES

1. Sir John Davies, *Le Primer Report des Cases* (Dublin, 1615), sig. *8v.

2. Richard Helgerson, *Forms of Nationhood: The Elizabethan Writing of England* (Chicago: University of Chicago Press, 1992), 67.

3. Ibid., 69.

4. Ibid., 100.

5. Ibid., 99.

6. Ibid., 88.

7. James VI and I, "A Speach to the Lords and Commons of the Parliament at White-Hall, on Wednesday the XXI. of March. Anno 1609," *Political Writings*, ed. Johann P. Sommerville (Cambridge: Cambridge University Press, 1994), 186. In referring to the speech throughout, I use the "old-style" date of 1609 in the title, rather than 1610, as according to the new system.

8. Helgerson, *Forms of Nationhood*, 86.

9. See ibid., 73–77, 82–85, 98–101. In addition to debates over the source of the law, there were jurisdictional conflicts between common-law courts and "equity" courts like Chancery. See Brian C. Lockey, *Law and Empire in English Renaissance Literature* (Cambridge: Cambridge University Press, 2006), 145–73.

10. James VI and I, "The Trew Law of Free Monarchies," in *Political Writings,* ed. Johann P. Sommerville (Cambridge: Cambridge University Press, 1994), 75.

11. James VI and I, "A Speach to the Lords and Commons," 186.

12. Helgerson, *Forms of Nationhood*, 76–77.

13. James VI and I, "A Speach to the Lords and Commons," 187.

14. Helgerson, *Forms of Nationhood*, 75.

15. Sir Edward Coke, *The Reports of Sir Edward Coke, Knt. [1572–1617]: In English in Thirteen Parts Complete,* 7 vols. (London, 1777), 2: sig. N1v.

16. Ibid., 2: sig. N2r–v.

17. Peter Lake and Steve Pincus, "Rethinking the Public Sphere in Early Modern England," *Journal of British Studies* 45 (April 2006): 273, 275, 274, 275 (emphasis added).

18. Ibid., 277.

19. Michael Warner, *Publics and Counterpublics* (New York: Zone Books, 2005), 67.

20. Ibid., 91–92.

21. J. W. Tubbs, *The Common Law Mind: Medieval and Early Modern Conceptions* (Baltimore: Johns Hopkins University Press, 2000), 131.

22. Davies, *Le Primer Report,* sig. *2r. Tubbs notes that Davies here literalizes what was commonly taken for a mere "fiction." *Common Law Mind,* 131.

23. Coke, *Reports,* 4: sig. L3r, L3v.

24. Sir Edward Coke, *The first part of the Institutes of the lawes of England* (London, 1629), sig. Bb1v.

25. Coke, *Reports,* 7: sig. G8r.

26. James VI and I, "A Speach to the Lords and Commons," 186. Davies had acknowledged this complaint, stating in his preface that some believe common lawyers maintain their reports in law-French so that "the people, being kept in ignorance of the lawe, may the more admire their skill & knowledge, & esteeme & value it at a higher price." *Le Primer Report,* sig. *3v.

27. Davies, *Le Primer Report,* sig. *3v.

28. Ibid., sig. *3r–v.

29. Ibid., sig. *3v.

30. On Coke's distinction between the "language" and "matter" of the law, see *Reports,* 2: sig. C7v.

31. Coke, *Reports,* 2: sig. C6r. *Doctor and Student* was first published in Latin and then translated into English.

32. Ibid., 2: sig. B1r. See also ibid., 2: sig. B1v–B2r, on Caesar's commentaries about the Druids employing Greek in the "dispatching and deciding of causes, as well public as private."

33. Ibid., 2: sig. C6v–C7r. Davies tells a similar history: *Le Primer Report,* sig. *3r.

34. Sir Edward Coke, *The first part of the Institutes of the lawes of England* (London, 1628), sig. ¶¶v.

35. Ibid.

36. James VI and I, "A Speach to the Lords and Commons," 187.

37. Ibid. On other uses of the phrase, see especially Sir Edward Coke, *The first part of the Institutes of the lawes of England* (London, 1629), sig. Bb1v.

38. Coke, *The first part of the Institutes* (1629), sig. Nn2r. See also Coke, *Reports,* 3: sig. A4r.

39. Helgerson, *Forms of Nationhood,* 10.

40. Coke, *Reports,* 5: sig. M1v.

41. Ibid., 5: sig. M2r–M2v.

42. Ibid., 2: sig. C5r.

43. Coke, *The first part of the Institutes* (1628), sig. ¶¶v (emphasis added).

44. Sir Edward Coke, *The third part of the Institutes of the laws of England* (London, 1644), sig. B1v.

45. Ibid.

46. Helgerson, *Forms of Nationhood,* 1.

47. Coke, *The first part of the Institutes* (1629), sig. Bb1v.

48. Helgerson, *Forms of Nationhood,* 98.

49. Ibid., 100.

50. Jürgen Habermas, *The Structural Transformation of the Public Sphere: An Inquiry into a Category of Bourgeois Society,* trans. Thomas Burger (Cambridge: MIT Press, 1991), 53.

51. Helgerson, *Forms of Nationhood,* 100.

CHAPTER THREE

Apocalyptics and Apologetics

Richard Helgerson on Elizabethan England's Religious
Identity and the Formation of the Public Sphere

TORRANCE KIRBY

"In early modern England the language of politics was most often the language of religion." So Richard Helgerson claims in *Forms of Nationhood.*[1] Brian Cummings makes the point even more forcefully: "without reference to religion," he states, "the study of early modern writing is incomprehensible."[2]

As a number of recent studies have shown, religious discourse played a critical role in shaping the contours of an emerging civil society in Elizabethan England, to such an extent that religious assumptions can be credited with the momentous role of fostering a nascent early modern "public sphere."[3] At Paul's Cross, the open-air pulpit situated in the cathedral churchyard, a radical reshaping of religious identity in the Tudor period, was achieved through a determined displacement of the primacy of a traditional, late-medieval "sacramental culture" by a new "culture of persuasion" centered on the medium of the public sermon; a cultural shift, moreover, that manifested itself in the consequent growth and flourishing of conditions conducive to the formation of the modern forms of association usually identified as "publics."[4]

In addressing this process of transformation from a ritually focused, late-medieval "representative publicity" to early modern publics in the sense of "voluntary forms of association," some scholars have tended to ascribe primary importance to the medium of print in comparison with the spoken word.[5] At one extreme Alexandra Halasz has treated the early modern public sphere in England as an "unsituated" or "virtual" discourse, conducted principally by means of a public "marketplace of print" operating almost entirely through pamphlets, newsbooks, and so on, with authors, printers, booksellers, and readers as the meaningfully engaged participants.[6] On the other side, Andrew Pettegree has cautioned that any account of how Protestantism could become a mass movement in an age before mass literacy must be careful to "relocate the role of the book, as part of a broader range of modes of persuasion," and that preaching in particular should be "restored to its central place as the 'bedrock' around which the churches harnessed other communication media."[7] Natalie Mears proposes that the most plausible model lies somewhere between these extremes of the "un-situated," imaginary construct of print, and the physically determinate, "situated" gathering for the purposes of actual communication and debate, as at the Inns of Court, for example, or at Paul's Cross. For Mears, "the Elizabethan public sphere and the concept of the public sphere itself, therefore, have to be seen as a combination of both" modes.[8] Elizabethan popular debate, especially on questions of religious reform, was characterized on one level by an "unsituated discourse"—printed sermons, admonitions, scholarly polemics, the scurrilous screed of Martin Marprelate—while at the same time, the subject matter of this printed conversation was discussed locally, thus meeting a basic requirement conceived by Habermas, namely that publics embody an activity typically experienced in a determinate physical locality—for example, in the vicinity of pulpits, in ale houses, workshops, markets, and parish churches—and most important, in the company of other flesh-and-blood participants.[9]

Certainly none of the sixteenth-century Reformers themselves underestimated the critical importance of orality to their religious task; the evangelical avant-garde placed enormous emphasis on the claim that faith comes through hearing, to the point that the formula *fides ex auditu* came to be universally regarded as a primary axiom of the Reformation.[10] The most palpable presence of this axiom was manifest in public utterance from the pulpit; and as I have argued elsewhere, one particular pulpit in Paul's churchyard arguably counts among the most influential of all venues for public discourse between rulers and ruled from the outset of the Henrician Reformation in the early 1530s up to the final years of the reign of Elizabeth.[11]

So, having written already on the radical "situatedness" of the pulpit at Paul's Cross, and in the interest of striking the sensible balance proposed by Natalie Mears between real and virtual publics, I would like to explore the conditions underlying the formation of early modern publics in Elizabethan England from the religious discourse of two churchmen, John Foxe and Richard Hooker—the one a historian, the other a philosopher and theologian—and propose to do so with due acknowledgment of my debt to the discernment and very considerable erudition of Richard Helgerson.

In a substantial concluding chapter in *Forms of Nationhood* titled "Apocalyptic and Apologetic," Helgerson begins with the arresting observation that "no books, with the obvious exception of the English Bible and the *Book of Common Prayer*, have had a greater part in shaping England's religious self-understanding than Foxe's *Acts* and Hooker's *Laws*."[12] Among all the enormous production of the so-called unsituated discourse of print issuing from the Elizabethan publishing houses, these are, for Helgerson, the two decisive works in the formation of modern English nationhood—after Tyndale's and Cranmer's great contributions, of course. Combined with Helgerson's claim that in Elizabethan England "the language of politics was most often the language of religion," and assuming that this choice of representative texts has been well made, we may perhaps entertain some hope of penetrating the mysterious genesis of early modern publics by attending to these two outstanding achievements of religious reflection.

In order to ensure that there is no misapprehension here, the connection I am aiming to draw between Elizabethan theology and church history, on the one hand, and the formation of early modern publics, on the other, was not explicitly Helgerson's concern. Helgerson's main claim is more general in scope, namely that these two enormous books—Foxe's *Actes and Monuments* (1563) and Hooker's *Of the Lawes of Ecclesiasticall Politie* (1593), published exactly thirty years apart, one at the beginning and the other toward the end of Elizabeth's reign—provide a key to understanding the reshaping of England's religious and political identity, and by extension an early modern sense of English nationhood. My purpose is to carry Helgerson's argument back a step, with a view to exploring further the religious preconditions underlying the formation of the modern nation in the context of the formation of publics. Such an exploration depends on recognition of the crucial role of religious self-understanding in the formulation of what Charles Taylor terms the new "moral ontology" of modernity—the metaphysical bridge, as it were, that connects the discourse of religion with the political assumptions necessary to the formation of civil society.[13] In short, England's early modern sense of nationhood is inextricably bound up with deep religious assumptions that have shaped the emergence of early modern publics. This link, however, remains to a large extent implicit in Helgerson's argument, and the task of our present inquiry is to seek to make this connection more explicit.

The Hermeneutics of Apocalyptic and Apologetic

According to Helgerson, Foxe and Hooker are united in their common endeavor to defend and reinforce the Elizabethan religious and political settlement. While their religious assumptions are closely related and in broad agreement, they nonetheless pursue their respective arguments from radically different polemical perspectives and with almost diametrically opposed methods.[14] Both Foxe and Hooker unequivocally support the proto-Erastian principles of the religious settlement of 1559—namely, ecclesiastical separation from Rome, provincial autonomy in the form of the royal headship of the Church, and retention of the hierarchical constitution of episcopacy.[15] Both defend the Act of Uniformity with its prescriptive national liturgy of the *Book of Common Prayer,* although Foxe does so somewhat less enthusiastically than Hooker. Yet their respective works differ markedly in terms of both genre and hermeneutical presupposition as well as in their respective longer-term historical effects: Foxe's book is historically narrative and anecdotal in structure, while Hooker's is a carefully constructed philosophical and theological argument. Helgerson summarizes this difference of genre by noting that Hooker contributes principally to the nation's "thought" whereas Foxe attends to its "story."[16]

Published respectively near the beginning and near the end of Elizabeth's long reign, the two books were composed under dramatically different circumstances and historical conditions and also differ markedly in the manner of their reception. Foxe's polemic is addressed almost entirely against the perceived menace emanating from Rome in the context of a reign still young and fragile. Hooker, on the other hand, was writing after the watershed of 1588, when the struggle being faced by the reformed Church of England proceeded more from the internal dissent of the so-called hotter sort of Protestants seeking "further Reformation" than from the agents of the Church of Rome. According to Helgerson, these major differences of polemical context, genre, and reception contributed to "radically differing constructions of England's religious identity."[17]

Despite his claim that Hooker and Foxe are closely allied in their underlying religious assumptions, as his argument unfolds Helgerson appears largely content to allow the perception of their basic opposition to stand. His tendency to rest content with the contrariety of the "apocalyptic" and the "apologetic" visions can be considered his argument's chief shortcoming. In the best traditions of Whig historiography, Helgerson portrays Foxe, in the company of his host of Puritan admirers, as the hopeful, progressive, forward-looking liberal, whereas Hooker's traditionalist apology comes across as all anxiety and wistful longing for a fast-fading dream of cosmic order, and he the proverbial conservative stick-in-the-mud.[18] Yet, as I hope to show, it is precisely through the dynamic interaction of these two distinct approaches—the apocalyptic and the apologetic—that the formation of early modern publics in England is rendered intelligible. Whereas Helgerson's analysis emphasizes the differences and conflict between the apocalyptic and apologetic genres, my proposal is that the generation of the public sphere transpires in the context of a dynamic interplay between these two distinct modes of religious self-understanding. In order to apprehend the full significance of this interaction, however, it would be helpful first to explore more closely the salient differences *and* common presuppositions of these two approaches to the formulation of England's Protestant religious identity.

Apocalyptic narrative is characterized by vigorous affirmation of an unremitting struggle between potent opposites—between Christ and Antichrist, Jerusalem and Babylon, God and Satan, and ecclesiastically, between the true church, as an invisible community of the godly, and the false church, for Foxe an oppressive institutional hierarchy emanating from the papacy at Rome and portrayed by him as the historical embodiment of the Antichrist.[19] The ecclesiological manifestation of this narrative is heavily dependent on the eschatological dialectic of Augustine's "two cities," namely, the earthly city (*civitas terrena*) and the heavenly city (*civitas Dei*).[20] Foxe's apocalyptic narrative places a heavy, scripturally inspired emphasis on the negative impact on the scattered and invisible community of the godly by coercive power wielded by religious and political institutions; the *Book of Martyrs* represents the religious conscience as standing in continuous conflict with respect to these oppressive "higher powers." It is through the oppressive regime of these powers that martyrs are made, and hence the focus of Foxe's narrative is overwhelmingly on the sufferings of the godly at the hands of institutional religious authority. In his apocalyptic narrative the authority of scripture is set in opposition to human power, the vernacular and universal accessibility of the Bible in opposition to the exclusivity of Latin learning and clericalism, and a levelling equality of universal priesthood against sacerdotal hierarchy. John Pocock once observed that "apocalyptic, which sacralizes secular time, must always in an opposite sense secularize the sacred, by drawing the process of salvation into that time which is known as the *sæculum*."[21] Consistent with this view, the religious heroes of Foxe's story are commoners—simple, ordinary folk, laborers and craftsmen, whom the religious elites fear as profane spreaders of heresy and insubordination. Through a process of evangelical "level-ling," common folk are "seen to die with the same fortitude as their bet-ters; bible-reading labourers defeat university educated men; poverty and simplicity join martyrdom as signs of the true church."[22] The phenomenon of the sacralizing of the secular and secularizing of the sacred is important to keep in mind with respect to the question of the dynamic interaction between the two rhetorics of apocalyptic and apologetic.

On the other side of the coin, Hooker the philosophical theologian seeks to explain and to justify the hierarchical structures of the established church with a view to securing conscientious obedience to the authority of government. He states that the chief purpose of his apologetic is to address those who are disgruntled and seek further reformation of the Elizabethan Church[23] in order to persuade them toward a conscientious embrace of the institutions and practices of the religious settlement of 1559: *"my whole endeavour is to resolve the conscience, and to shewe as neere as I can what in this controversie the hart is to thinke, if it follow the light of sound and sincere judgement, without clowd of prejudice, or mist of passionate affection."*[24] In sharp contrast to Foxe, order, hierarchy, and obedience—the entire exter-nal, visible, and coercive apparatus of the church—are to be celebrated and embraced as the institutionalizing and necessary normalizing of the Reformation in England. Systematic defense of the church's institutional structures is the burden of Hooker's apologetic discourse, and in a very palpable sense it stands at odds with the extreme polarization of the vis-ible and invisible communities presupposed by Foxe's apocalyptic ecclesi-ology. Over against the apocalyptic insistence upon a clear-cut opposition of the revealed authority of scripture to corrupt human authority, Hooker grounds his defense of the structures of ecclesiastical order constituted by the Act of Uniformity of 1559 in a complex account of a cosmic hierarchy of laws—eternal, natural, angelic, human, positive, and revealed, to name just a few of the principal generic divisions.[25] Every aspect of Hooker's defense of the complex structures of the Elizabethan settlement—all the way from the royal supremacy, through the hierarchy of bishops and other ministers, down to the most minute details of the liturgical forms of com-mon prayer—can be viewed as posing a direct challenge to the apocalyptic emphasis on the sharply defined eschatological duality of the visible and the invisible church, true and the false religion, corrupt human reason and the light of divine revelation, Christ and Antichrist.

Hooker's apology of the ecclesiastical order of the Church of England rests on overturning apocalyptically inspired Puritan claims on behalf of the prescriptive authority of the Bible in matters of polity, discipline, and order.[26] For Hooker there is an important epistemological principle at stake in these religious polemics. In the *Lawes* he responds at length to the Disciplinarian Puritan Thomas Cartwright's apocalyptic insistence that scripture alone (*sola scriptura*) constitutes a universal rule of human action, and that whatever is not done in strict accord with the divinely revealed word is sinful, corrupt, and therefore the work of the Antichrist.[27] The substance of Hooker's apologetic is to appeal to the necessary authority of a diversity of sources of religious knowledge, with particular emphasis on the weight of secular reason. That he does so by grounding his apologetic appeal on the express authority of scripture adds an element of irony to the controversy:

> Whatsoever either men on earth, or the Angels of heaven do know, it is as a drop of that unemptiable fountaine of Wisdom, which wisdom hath diversly imparted her treasures unto the world. As her waies are of sundry kinds, so her maner of teaching is not meerely one and the same. Some things she openeth by the sacred bookes of Scripture; some things by the glorious works of nature: with some things she inspireth them from above by spirituall influence, in some thinges she leadeth and trayneth them onely by worldly experience and practise. We may not so in any one speciall kind admire her that we disgrace her in any other, but let all her wayes be according unto their place and degree adored.[28]

An apt summary of the epistemological premise of Hooker's apologetic orientation is contained in his concluding observation: "let all [Wisdom's] wayes be according unto their place and degree adored."

Taking their cue from a Foxeian apocalyptic frame of reference, the anonymous Puritan authors of *A Christian Letter of certayne Englishe Protestantes* (1599) interpret the philosophical assumptions of Hooker's apologetic as a direct challenge to the foundational claim of the Reformation concerning the sufficiency of the holy scripture (*sola scriptura*).[29] Hooker's appeal to a diversity of sources of the divine wisdom—a complex variety of modes of access ordered according to "place and degree"—reveals that the hermeneutics of his apologetic depend on strong affirmation of the "light of nature" manifest in human reason and experience. His Puritan opponents, arguing from an apocalyptic premise, interpret this defense of a "natural" knowledge of God, of natural law as a supplement to the revealed law of scripture, and of a hierarchical *dispositio* of the laws and modes of knowing, as fundamentally at odds with the first principles of reformation.[30] For Hooker the apologist, ecclesiastical jurisdiction, discipline, and worship are matters to be determined largely by a worldly reason—by prudence, legal tradition, and human judgment contextualized from the study of the practices of the early church, and indeed so far as the papacy and the Church of Rome herself "follow reason and truth, we fear not to tread the self same steps wherein they have gone and to be their follower."[31]

Here we can discern a deep divergence between the apologetic and apocalyptic perspectives. In his apologetic mode, Hooker has moved sharply away from the apocalyptic insistence upon the polarity of Jerusalem and Babylon, the heavenly and the earthly cities, the true and the false church. As Helgerson astutely points out, for Hooker the historical contingency of "things indifferent" (*adiaphora*) touches all but a few noncontroversial articles of faith and order that are deemed to be necessary for salvation, namely, those things belonging to the *esse* or substance of religious identity.[32] Hooker's apologetic hermeneutic was interpreted by his Puritan opponents as the very antithesis of the evangelical narrative epitomized by Foxe and consequently earned him accusations of undermining the Reformed formularies of the Elizabethan religious settlement to the extent that

> almost all the principall pointes of our English creed [are] greatlie shaken and contradicted. Shall wee doe you wronge to suspect you as a privie and subtill enemie to the whole state of the Englishe Church, and that you would have men to deeme her Majestie to have done ill in abolishing the Romish religion, and banishing the Popes authoritie; and that you would bee glad to see the backesliding of all reformed churches to bee made conformable to that wicked synagogue of Rome . . . and that you esteeme . . . the bookes of holy scripture to bee at the least of no greater moment then Aristotle and the Schoolemen?[33]

The level of Puritan discomfort with Hooker's apologetic purpose is framed in explicitly apocalyptic terms. The passage continues with the following pointed remark: "doe you meane to bring in a confusion of all thinges, to reconcile heaven and earth, and to make all religions equall: Will you bring us to Atheisme, or to Poperie?" The apocalyptic assumptions of Hooker's Puritan critics cannot tolerate any muting of the clarity of the eschatological contraries.

Helgerson identifies a thread that holds out the possibility of disclosing a path leading out of this hermeneutical labyrinth. Unlikely as it might seem, the thread is Helgerson's allusion to Foxe's narrative of the martyrdom of Alice Driver, who was burnt at the stake in Ipswich on November 4, 1558, just two weeks before the death of Queen Mary and the accession of Queen Elizabeth.[34] On being questioned about the "real presence" of Christ in the sacrament, Driver responded in genuinely apocalyptic form by appealing to the authority of scripture *against* tradition and the *magisterium* of the church.[35] That she was a woman of little education engaged in debate with learned theologians underlines the subversive social reality of a Reformed church as an "imagined community of the saints" who are members by virtue of being committed readers and hearers of the scriptures. When asked by John Spencer, Chancellor of Norwich, whether the host was "a sign of a holy thing," Driver responded, "You have said the truth, sir, it is a sign indeed, and I must needs grant it; and therefore seeing it is a sign, it cannot be the thing signified also. Thus far we agree."

Driver's insistent distinction between the sacramental "sign" and the "thing signified" is of the utmost significance in the unfolding debate over the formulation of religious identity. Spencer, of course, could not have agreed with her direct challenge to the official dogma concerning transubstantiation. Nonetheless, just a few months later, shortly after the accession of Elizabeth I in November 1558, John Jewel, soon to be appointed bishop of Salisbury, put the question of sacramental presence in almost identical terms in his celebrated "Challenge Sermon" preached at Paul's Cross.[36] In the context of a learned critique of the received scholastic doctrine of transubstantiation, Jewel adopted Alice Driver's assertion as the principal axiom of his own *apologia:* "first we put a *difference* between the sign and the thing itself that is signified."[37] In the course of the 1560s and 1570s, formulations of such a sharp distinction between a literal and a figurative interpretation of sacramental "presence" came to be of profound significance for the development of a distinctively Protestant Elizabethan hermeneutics. Indeed, for Jewel the central issue of the Reformation, and thus of the substantive disagreement between the churches of England and Rome, was ultimately reducible to one of hermeneutical method, namely how to interpret sacramental signs and their relation to things signified. The unprecedented attention received by his Challenge Sermon throughout the 1560s testifies to the importance of his formulation of what can be fairly described as the central semiotic problem of the sixteenth-century reshaping of England's religious identity. Jewel's and Driver's common formulation of the question of sacramental presence offers a valuable clue to assist in our grappling with the tension and interaction between the apocalyptic and apologetic formulations of religious identity.

Viewed through the lens of his narrative of Alice Driver's interrogation, Foxe's apocalyptic approach to the definition of religious identity in *Actes and Monuments* can be read as a deconstruction of the primary hermeneutical assumptions of a traditional "sacramental culture," chiefly the "essential" identification of the sign with the thing signified. With its marked Augustinian emphasis on a sharp eschatological distinction between the visible and the invisible churches, between the earthly and the heavenly cities, closely analogous to that between sign and thing signified, apocalyptic hermeneutics can be read as a deconstruction of the semiotics of transubstantiation, and hence as a move in the direction of "disenchantment." Alice Driver's and John Jewel's insistence upon the sharp distinction between the visible sacramental sign and the invisible divine reality signified encapsulates what we might term "the apocalyptic premise," whereby the visible and invisible worlds, the finite and the infinite, the temporal and eternal orders of reality, are to be kept thoroughly discrete.

Apocalyptics, Apologetics, and Emerging Modern Publics

Where, then, in this analysis of the hermeneutics of apocalyptic and apologetic are we to look for the principle of the conditions for emerging modern publics? The political assumptions of the later sixteenth century would seem to be quite remote from such arcane questions as the precise locus of sacramental presence. In what manner does interplay between the respective rhetorics of apocalyptic and apologetic shed light on our preliminary question concerning the genesis of the early modern publics? As Helgerson makes plain, despite their radically divergent approaches, Foxe the apocalyptic historian and Hooker the apologetic historicist nonetheless share an acute sense of the demarcation between the inner subjective "forum of the conscience" and the external "political forum" of common, institutional life (both religious and civil).[38] It is precisely in the definition of this liminal space between the internal and the external forums and of their interaction with one another that the conditions for a radical transformation of the forms of civil association are revealed. It is specifically through re-formation of the terms of the relation between the forum of the conscience and the external political forum that the hermeneutics of the sacrament sheds light on the conditions for the emergence of new forms of civil association—that is, "publics."

According to Timothy Rosendale, the contrasting assumptions of traditional and evangelical hermeneutics in the sixteenth century are most clearly manifest in their divergent accounts of sacramental theology.[39] Whereas the doctrine of the Mass and transubstantiation tended to collapse the distinction between signifier and signified in their assertion of an objectified "real presence," the doctrine implicit in the liturgy of Thomas Cranmer's *Book of Common Prayer* upholds the clear distinction between the two. According to Jewel's defense of this doctrine in the section on "Real Presence" in his *Defense of the Apologie*, "To conclude, three things herein we must consider: first, that we put a difference between the sign and the thing itself that is signified. Secondly, that we seek Christ above in heaven, and imagine not Him to be present bodily upon the earth. Thirdly, that the body of Christ is to be eaten by faith only, and none other wise."[40] Such a distinction between literal and figurative interpretation of sacramental presence is, according to Rosendale, of crucial significance in the development of a distinctively Protestant Elizabethan hermeneutics.

The revised liturgy of the second prayer book of Edward VI in 1552 shifts the locus of presence decisively away from the physical elements of the sacrament and transfers it to the inner, subjective experience of the worshipper.[41] Consequently, "presence" is interpreted in Cranmer's liturgy of 1552 as "figural," a conceptual synthesis of word and elements performed in the subjective forum of the minds of the worshippers and thus inseparable from an internal, spiritual "reception" of the consecrated host.[42] In Cranmer's reformed liturgy, the gap between sign and signified is thus no longer bridged primarily by means of an external, theurgical act as is implied by the ritual of the mass and the doctrine of transubstantiation, but rather, "presence" depends on an inward, subjective act of remembrance—that is, through an acknowledgment of "presence" in and through the conscience. As Rosendale points out, "the internalization of this figural sacrament is necessarily an interpretative act; though it takes place in a communal context, it ultimately requires a highly individual mode of understanding the elements as metaphors whose effectuality is dependent on faithful personal reading."[43]

The opening up of the breach between sign and thing signified in the apocalyptic discourse is the hermeneutical condition for the deconstruction of the primacy of a sacramental culture—a process of "disenchantment."[44] This disenchantment of sacramental culture constitutes a central motif in the narrative of Foxe's martyrology as it is also of the Protestant Reformation more generally. However, with the exception of a handful of religious extremists—for example, Anabaptists, the Family of Love, and various English Separatists—once the break with Rome had been accomplished, the magisterial reformers were intent on reconstruction of a visible, institutional, hierarchical, and liturgical church order. And in doing so they were compelled to adopt, in one way or another, the main assumptions of an apologetic frame of reference. The reconstruction of Reformed religious institutions was to be on a distinctly different foundation from that assumed by late-medieval Christianity.[45] Nonetheless, the reformers' reconstruction of a visible, institutional church presupposed the apocalyptic premise of the contrast between the historical and the imagined community of the saints, between visible and invisible church, and of course the hermeneutics of the necessary distinction between sign and signified. The sign was still connected to the thing signified but was now linked by means of a redefined principle of presence and of mediation, namely by means of "persuasion."

As an "apologist" of the newly reformed ecclesiastical and civil order, Hooker takes great pains to persuade his audience of the existence of a necessary bond between sign and signified, but such a bond as can no longer subsist "magically," that is, purely in an external, theurgically created reality *ex opere operato.*[46] In effect, the apologetics of Elizabethan religious reform redefine the nature of the "sacramental" itself. In the liturgy Hooker claims that there is indeed a sacramental change or conversion of substance, but this transubstantiation is not to be found outwardly in the physical elements of the sacrament, but rather in the conscience of the participant in the liturgical action. In this sense Hooker affirms the apocalyptic premise of the distinction between sign and thing signified yet nonetheless asserts with apologetic intention the necessity for their real connection.

On the one hand, sacramental signs and the things signified are *distinct;* yet, the truth or "substance" of the sign is not ultimately *separated* from the sign. This is the force of Hooker's use of the language of sacramental "instrumentality," a language whose main purpose is to bridge the distance between apocalyptic and apologetic hermeneutics.[47] While from an apocalyptic frame of reference the signs are not in any way to be confused with the things signified thereby, nonetheless the apologist insists that the former continue to be connected to the latter in such a manner that enables a sacramental offering and a reception of the gift signified through the means of the sign. Thus, for Hooker, "The Real Presence of Christs most Blessed Body and Blood is not therefore to be sought for in the [external] Sacrament, but in the worthy Receiver of the Sacrament. . . . As for the Sacraments, they really exhibite; but, for ought we can gather out of that which is written of them, they are not really, nor do really contain in themselves, that Grace, which with them, or by them, it pleaseth God to bestow."[48]

Real presence, therefore, in the sacraments presupposes the faithful worshipper who is able to interpret the unity of the three things that "make the substance of the sacrament," namely recognition of the gift offered, that is the thing signified; the elements that depict the gift, that is the signs; and the word of scripture that articulates the link between the two.[49] Thus viewed, sacraments become necessarily dynamic events where the instrumentality of signs works through the act of interpretation on the part of the receiver. "Whereupon," Hooker concludes, "there ensueth a kinde of

Transubstantiation in us, a true change, both of Soul and Body, an alteration from death to life."[50] This subtle but telling redefinition of the hermeneutics of presence cautiously avoids the extremes of either separating or
confusing sign and thing signified.

For Hooker, the sharp demarcation between the inner, private realm
of individual conscience and the outer, public demands of institutional
order thus calls forth an arena of *persuasion*—in effect a public sphere—as
the necessary means of mediation between the seemingly opposed and
incommensurable demands of two opposed realms of existence and religious identity. John Calvin had earlier explicitly referred to this opposition
of subjective and external realms by employing the distinction between
the *forum conscientiae* and the *forum politicum*.[51] Building upon this new
hermeneutics, all of the persuasive devices of apologetic are employed as
instruments to bridge the very gulf opened up by the apocalyptic narrative—namely, that between the sign and the thing signified. Thus the
primary function of the apocalyptic narrative is to fashion a new religious
identity based upon a deconstruction or "dis-enchantment" of the premises of a "sacramental culture," while the apologetic discourse, on the other
side, aims to reconstitute a place for religious identity within a reconstruct-
ed institutional order by way of a positive "re-enchantment": the former
emphasizes the disparity of sign and thing signified, while the latter seeks
to restore the link between the two.

Thus, according to Helgerson's account of the narrative of "Apocalyptic
and Apologetic," John Foxe and Richard Hooker contribute in complementary ways to a distinctively early modern reformulation of negotiating
the space between the inner private realm of individual conscience and
the external public realm of institutional order and political community
with all of its hierarchical institutions, structures, and coercive demands.
In this distinctively early modern problematic of religious identity, one
of the principal instruments of mediation between individual and community would prove to be the emerging "public" of religious persuasion.

By way of conclusion, a dialogue of sorts between the unsituated world
of theological semiotics and the more concrete, situated space of public religious teaching—between print and practice as it were—can be discerned
in the distinction evident in the two prominent genres of later Elizabethan
sermons at Paul's Cross, namely the so-called Jeremiads and the "exhorta-
tions to charity," the former with their emphasis on the gulf separating the
fallen and derelict church in history from the splendor of the heavenly city,
and the latter encouraging the faithful to labor toward a fullfilment of the
heavenly promises in a process of habitual sanctification.[52] Although the

earthly sign must be clearly distinguished from the mystical reality signified in the Jeremiad, nonetheless the union of sign with thing signified is an object of striving; both the clarity of distinction and the possibility of mediation are proposed by means of the revised ontology of presence such as that outlined by Hooker, namely through an inner "persuasion" of the conscience. It was through pursuit of a common persuasion in both pulpit and press that a public sphere came to be formed in Elizabethan England.

NOTES

1. Richard Helgerson, *Forms of Nationhood: The Elizabethan Writing of England* (Chicago: University of Chicago Press, 1992), 252.

2. Brian Cummings, *The Literary Culture of the Reformation: Grammar and Grace* (Oxford: Oxford University Press, 2002), 6.

3. See Patrick Collinson, *The Birthpangs of Protestant England* (New York: St Martin's Press, 1988). In *Liturgy and Literature in the Making of Protestant England* (Cambridge: Cambridge University Press, 2007), Timothy Rosendale claims: "English history from the mid-sixteenth through the late-seventeenth centuries centres on the *Book of Common Prayer*" (25).

4. Torrance Kirby, "The Public Sermon: Paul's Cross and the Culture of Persuasion in England, 1534–1570," *Renaissance and Reformation* 31.1 (2008): 3–29. See Andrew Pettegree, *Reformation and the Culture of Persuasion* (Cambridge: Cambridge University Press, 2005).

5. Jürgen Habermas, *The Structural Transformation of the Public Sphere: An Inquiry into a Category of Bourgeois Society,* trans. Thomas Burger (Cambridge: MIT Press, 1991), 14–26.

6. Alexandra Halasz, *The Marketplace of Print: Pamphlets and the Public Sphere in Early Modern England* (Cambridge: Cambridge University Press, 1997), 115–16, 23–34. For a critical view of this approach, see Natalie Mears, *Queenship and Political Discourse in the Elizabethan Realms* (Cambridge: Cambridge University Press, 2005), 26, 184.

7. Pettegree, *Reformation and the Culture of Persuasion,* 39.

8. Mears, *Queenship and Political Discourse,* 268.

9. See Mears's chapter on "The Elizabethan Public Sphere," in *Queenship and Political Discourse,* 182–216.

10. Hughes Oliphant Old, *The Reading and Preaching of the Scriptures in the Worship of the Christian Church* (Grand Rapids, Mich.: Eerdmans, 1998), 183–84.

11. Kirby, "The Public Sermon."

12. Helgerson, *Forms of Nationhood,* 253.

13. Charles Taylor, *Sources of the Self* (1989; repr., Cambridge: Cambridge University Press, 2006), 5–8, 9, 10, 41.

14. Helgerson, *Forms of Nationhood,* 249–94.

15. Ibid., 253. In the Act of Supremacy of 1559 (1 *Eliz.* c. 1, *Statutes of the Realm,* 4:350–55), the queen is styled "the only Supreme Governor of this realm . . . as well in all ecclesiastical things or causes as temporal."

16. Helgerson, *Forms of Nationhood,* 253.

17. Ibid., 254.

18. Ibid., 269, 270.

19. See Andrew Escobedo, *Nationalism and Historical Loss in Renaissance England: Foxe, Dee, Spenser, Milton* (Ithaca, N.Y.: Cornell University Press, 2004), and Katharine R. Firth,

The Apocalyptic Tradition in Reformation Britain, 1530–1645 (New York: Oxford University Press, 1979).

20. See Augustine, *De civitate Dei* 14.28.

21. J. G. A. Pocock, "England," in *National Consciousness, History and Political Culture in Early Modern Europe,* ed. Orest Ranum (Baltimore: Johns Hopkins University Press, 1975), 109.

22. Helgerson, *Forms of Nationhood,* 265.

23. See John Field and Thomas Wilcox, *An Admonition to the Parliament* ([Hemel Hempstead?: J. Stroud?], 1572), in *Puritan Manifestoes,* ed. W. H. Frere and C. E. Douglas (London: Church History Society, 1907), 19; (repr., New York: Franklin, 1972).

24. Hooker, *Lawes,* Pref.7.1; 1:34.20–23.

25. Hooker, *Lawes,* Book I.

26. Hooker, *Lawes,* Book II.

27. Thomas Cartwright, *A Replye to an Answere made of M. doctor Whitgifte . . . Agaynste the Admonition* ([Hemel Hempstead?: J. Stroud?], 1575), 26–27, cited in *Lawes* II.1.3; 1:146.1, II.2.1; 1:148.7, II.3.1; 1:150.19 and II.4.1; 1:151.18.

28. Hooker, *Lawes* II.1.4; 1:147.23–148.6. *The Wisdom of Solomon* 11:4. Compare Calvin, *Inst.* 1.1.1: "Those blessings which unceasingly distill to us from heaven, are like streams conducting us to the fountain."

29. See [Andrew Willett?], *A Christian Letter* (Middelburg: R. Schilders, 1599) [*STC* 13721], the only attack on the *Lawes* published in Hooker's lifetime. See *FLE* 4, ed. John Booty (1982), 1–79.

30. See *ACL* §3. *The Holye Scripture contayneth all thinges necessarie to salvation. FLE* 4:11.1–14.9.

31. Hooker, *Lawes,* V.28.1.

32. Helgerson, *Forms of Nationhood,* 274, 275.

33. *ACL* §20. *Schoolemen, Philosophie, and Poperie. FLE* 4:65.16–68.19: "yet in all your discourse, for the most parte, Aristotle the patriarch of Philosophers (with divers other human writers) and the ingenuous [*sic*!] schoolemen, almost in all pointes have some finger; Reason is highlie sett up against holie scripture, and reading against preaching; the church of Rome favourablie admitted to bee of the house of God."

34. Foxe, *Actes and Monuments,* 8:494.

35. Driver was interrogated by one Dr. Spenser, Chancellor of the Diocese of Norwich.

> *Spenser:* "What sayest thou to the Blessed Sacrament of the altar? Dost thou believe that it is very flesh and blood after the words be spoken of consecration?" Alice Driver stood with her lips deliberately sealed. A priest who stood by told her, "Answer the Chancellor, woman!"
>
> *Driver:* "Why, priest, I came not to talk with thee, but I came to talk with thy master, but if thou wilt I shall talk with thee, command thy master to hold his peace." With that the priest put his nose in his cap and spake never a word again.

36. "To conclude, three things herein we must consider: first, that we put a difference between the sign and the thing itself that is signified. Secondly, that we seek Christ above in heaven, and imagine not Him to be present bodily upon the earth. Thirdly, that the body of Christ is to be eaten by faith only, and none other wise." John Jewel, *The copie of a sermon pronounced by the Byshop of Salisburie at Paules Crosse* (London: John Day, 1560). *Jewel's Works,* 1:448.

37. *Jewel's Works,* 1:448.

38. Helgerson, *Forms of Nationhood,* 274.

39. Rosendale, *Liturgy and Literature,* 96.

40. John Jewel, "Of Real Presence," *A defense of the Apologie of the Churche of Englande* (London: Henry Wykes, 1570). See *Jewel's Works,* 1:448.

41. The "realist" words of 1549—"this is my body"—are replaced in 1552 with "eat this

in remembrance that Christ died for thee, and feed on him in thy heart, by faith, with thanksgiving."

42. It is interesting in this connection to note that in the BCP of 1552, as well as in the subsequent revisions of 1559 and 1662, administration of the communion occurs at precisely the stage in the liturgy at which the elevation of the host had previously occurred—i.e., the moment of transubstantiation—thus serving to underline vividly the difference between the two divergent liturgical accounts of presence.

43. Rosendale, *Liturgy and Literature,* 96.

44. For this connection see Alexandra Walsham, "The Reformation and the 'Disenchantment of the World' Reassessed," *The Historical Journal* 51.2 (2008): 497–528.

45. For a fuller account of the apologetic reestablishment of a semiotic linkage between *signum* and *res significata,* see my article *"Of Musique with Psalms:* The Hermeneutics of Richard Hooker's Defence of the 'Sensible Excellencie' of Public Worship," in *Lutheran and Anglican: Essays in honour of Egil Grisli,* ed. John Stafford (Winnipeg: University of Manitoba Press, 2009), 127–51.

46. Hooker, *Lawes* V.57.4; 2:246.20–30. "Seinge therefore that grace is a consequent of the Sacramentes, a thinge which accompanieth them as theire ende, a benefit which he that hath receyveth from God him selfe the author of sacramentes and not from anie other naturall or supernaturall qualitie in them, it may be hereby both understood that sacramentes are necessarie, and that the manner of theire necessitie to life supernaturall is not in all respected as foode unto naturall life, because they conteine *in them selves* no vitall force or efficacie, they are not physicall but *morall instrumentes* of salvation, duties of service and worship, which unlesse wee performe as the author of grace requireth, they are unprofitable."

47. Hooker, *Lawes* V.67.5; 2:334.17–33. "The Bread and Cup are his Body and Blood, because they are causes instrumental, upon the receit whereof, the Participation of his Body and Blood ensueth. For that which produceth any certain effect, is not vainly nor improperly said to be, that very effect whereunto it tendeth. Every cause is in the effect which groweth from it. Our Souls and Bodies quickned to Eternal Life, are effects; the cause whereof, is the Person of Christ: His Body and Blood are the true Well-spring, out of which, this Life floweth. . . . The Real Presence of Christs most Blessed Body and Blood, is not therefore to be sought for in the Sacrament, but in the worthy Receiver of the Sacrament. . . . As for the Sacraments, they really exhibite; but, for ought we can gather out of that which is written of them, they are not really, nor do really contain in themselves, that Grace, which with them, or by them, it pleaseth God to bestow."

48. Hooker, *Lawes* V.67.5; 2:334.17–33.

49. See Hooker, *Lawes* V.58.2; 2:249.161–250.3.

50. Hooker, *Lawes* V.67.11; 2:338.13–340.1.

51. John Calvin, *Institutes of the Christian Religion,* 3:19.15; 847. See my essay "Negotiating the *'forum politicum'* and the *'forum conscientiæ'*: John Calvin and the Religious Origins of the Early-Modern Public Sphere," in *Making Space Public in Early Modern Europe: Geography, Performance, Privacy,* ed. Angela Vanhaelen and Joseph Ward (New York: Routledge, 2013).

52. See Mary Morrissey, "Ideal Communities and Early Modern London in the Paul's Cross Sermons," paper presented at the meeting of the Renaissance Society of America in Venice, Italy, April 2010.

PART TWO

Forming Social Identities
and Publics

CHAPTER FOUR

Perverse Delights
Cross Channel Trash Talk and Identity Publics

ANNE LAKE PRESCOTT

In memoriam Richardi

WE KNOW that "it takes a village" to build up a child. But what does it take to build up a village? The village in which I am interested, and hardly the only one to which readers could belong, is the one created by the late sixteenth-century crowd of English readers attentive to the often horrifying news from France and, presumably, by the somewhat larger consequent crowd of gossiping or otherwise talkative ale drinkers at the Mitre or Mermaid, courtiers falling quiet when they saw someone likely to be offended come into view, merchants exclaiming over what the goings-on across the Channel might mean for trade, and university scholars jointly punning in Latin and eventually in print over the sight of a France ill thanks to drugs of a bad *medicus* (Latin grammar can give us "Medicis") and the need for someone to cure—*navar[r]e*—the nation.[1]

The publics created by news and polemics, particularly news of a neighbor nation and even more particularly by published satire and slander appealing to what some would call our baser instincts, may not be as "national" as those explored by Richard Helgerson's wonderful *Forms of Nationhood*, but I believe they contribute to a sense of shared cultural space, even if that space is not fully national. And yet the texts I will describe are indeed "national" in a primitive but significant sense: they encouraged, through the promotion of fear or through providing examples of wicked behavior, the satisfied feeling that the misdeeds they describe are committed by those *others*, the *not us*—in this case the French.

In a sense, then, this chapter is an addendum to Helgerson's work, a reminder that building both publics and nations can involve texts, aims, and particularities that *Forms of Nationhood,* for all its many contributions to understanding such matters, ignores. The rational evolution of English law, the thoughtful desire for a national literature, and the creation of more accurate maps of the British Isles (to take examples from Helgerson's book) created *publics* that eventually overlapped with and helped constitute a *nation* as a whole, whatever the divisions that would remain or even grow. Wholes have parts—publics in the plural or even minipublics that can contribute, through overlapping conversations, to an interconnected larger public and, eventually, to a nation—even to an empire. In the texts I examine, a largely literate public, even if not yet a largely literate nation, was encouraged, sometimes by quiet governmental support of printed materials, to look across the water to war-torn France with both a fear of being like it as well as a relief at being different from it—so far. John of Gaunt's "This earth, this realm, this England" is the not-France.

To understand that nation and those publics, we need, then, to remember that both publics and nations can be partly constituted, when print is involved, by minor and even disreputable genres that encourage not rational discourse or elite emulation but shared scorn and a related taste for polemics and satire. Paul Yachnin argues that "classic liberal theory" ignores "the passions, playfulness, and private personhood as legitimate attributes to public speech and action" and that many associations are "both public and not public."[2] Indeed so. And to this I would add the muddy social cement of scandal and even slime. As Antónia Szabari says, if Saturn as Father Time can reveal the truth, it is not surprising to find Renaissance images of a Satyr doing so or to find "polemics" that in appealing to readers also "organize, imagine, and project communities of readers."[3] I agree, and that the slander and denigration I shall describe doubtless passed from print to semiprivate conversation over ale in public houses only sustains his point.

That such a public was in part created by the influx of news pamphlets is not itself news, and that in turn such a reading public influenced or helped construct a space for political discussion, if usually a cautiously expressed discussion, likewise seems clear, although the date at which one can say that yes, the public square (or coffeehouse) is now open for political and public business may be debated. Recent books on such matters, many of which take issue with Habermas and his claims for the eighteenth century and public space for rational or quasi-rational conversation, give various dates as an alternative to his positing a public in the eighteenth century. As Peter Lake and Steve Pincus wittily note, "The 'public sphere has been moving backward in time' " (a retrograde motion temporally, one might add, but also one likely to move us forward in understanding).[4] Thus Paul Voss's fine study, *Elizabethan News Pamphlets,* locates a discursive community in the late sixteenth century formed by praise of English soldiers and blame of the ultra-Catholic enemy.[5] Others, such as Richard Hillman or Andrew Kirk, have shown that news from France figures in or affects texts such as Marlowe's *Edward II* and his *Massacre at Paris* and Shakespeare's *Love's Labors Lost.*[6] Hillman's preface, for example, has some interesting readings of France as an "other" to which "neither colonialism nor exoticism is really at issue" but that helped produce "subjectivities" that are "collective."[7] Alexandra Halasz, who also engages with Habermas, explains that her "argument that a public sphere indeed emerges in and around pamphlets in the late sixteenth century as they articulate a variety of intersecting and conflicting interests challenges not the concept of the public sphere but . . . the universalizing claims to a general interest and a national consensus."[8] Sensible, even if this valuable book largely ignores the tidal wave of French news.

On the other hand, David Zaret's *Origins of Democratic Culture,* a book with some subtle criticisms of earlier theorizing, asserts that "A political public sphere first appeared in the English Revolution" because "restrictive norms of secrecy and privilege in prerevolutionary England precluded a public sphere in politics."[9] This makes good sense in its own terms, but what is "public" and what is "private" is itself debatable. Is gossip at the Mitre or government propaganda distributed all over England public? Must a public sphere be free to be public? Deep waters. When the speaker of Donne's "Satyre IV" fears that one of the "giant statues" might "ope its mouth," he knows that at the worst there might be a very "public" execution. Do hangings and beheadings make publics? Temporarily, maybe. Certainly Elizabethan censorship and exploitation of the press created a different *sort* of public discourse than the political clubs of Burke, Sheridan, and Fox, even if England had censorship then too (contemporary commentary about English trials in the 1790s occasionally includes the remark that a government allowing Thomas More's *Utopia* to see print should not balk at Tom Paine's *Rights of Man*).[10]

What I would like to offer in this chapter is one way to connect recent work by scholars who explore cross-Channel ties or the impact of French events on the English to that focusing on the public-making impact of printing—a group to which one should add John Staines's book on public-making cultural energies that include empathy.[11] My suggestion is that in the 1580s and 1590s this print-created proto-public space had even more building blocks, or more clearing away of feudal blocks, than can be accounted for by studying the evolution of space for rational or quasi-rational discourse, polemics over the roles of monarchy, parliaments, and bishops, news of battles on the Continent, or reports of monsters or murders, although both Henri III and the Guise figured—in France often and in England sometimes—as monsters (problematic) and murderers (which in fact they were).[12] The growing public for news from France, that is, enjoyed, or was thought by printers to enjoy, not just reasoned argument (however defined), not just the spectacle of horror that might stir compassion, not just heroic military news to encourage support of Elizabeth's support of Navarre or even Henri III, but slime, particularly polemics and satire exploiting slime.

Yes, we now have a public space for discussion—too much of it, and often demented, some might say. But it can be no accident that one popular—is there such a word as "subpopular"?—journal of celebrity gossip is called . . . *US.* Not just "United States" but *us,* the "us" that likes to gossip, to hear the latest, to report, which primatologists say is the equivalent of simian or pongid grooming. Apes eat the ticks they pull off; we "dish." When dishing takes the form of polemics with an urgent political or religious point, there is, even for the ideologically engaged, a degree of *spectacle,* of performance, and that suggests an audience. As Jesse Lander says in his fine book on polemic, religion, and print, our own distinction between literature and fighting is modern: "In the sixteenth and seventeenth centuries, English writers and readers seemed to have assumed" that books "were, more often than not, understood to be engaged in battle."[13] Yes, and battles can have observers who cheer or hiss. When the battle is fought in print the observer usually observes by reading in private, but the ensuing conversation with friends or even enemies is in some degree public. It seems right, if anachronistic, to mention here that the cover of Michael Warner's 2005 *Publics and Counterpublics* shows a small crowd of photographers in a "camera club" snapping—each other. Making publics can feed off narcissism's paradoxical I and US.

For some years I have been examining the impact on England of a spill-over into England of French texts, or texts describing France, that involve the largely but not entirely undeserved sliming both of the Sainte Ligue, headed by the Guise family, and of King Henri III of France, the son of Catherine de' Medici whose assassination on August 1, 1589 (about a year after the Armada and seven months after he had ordered the murder of Henri, duc de Guise) left the still Protestant Henri de Navarre—at least in the opinion of his supporters—king of France. It is against this background, I have argued in several essays, that we can profitably set Book V of *The Faerie Queene* and Mary Sidney's translation of Robert Garnier's *Marc Antoine*.[14] The situation as seen from England was both fluid and complex. One of Navarre's supporters, of course, was Elizabeth, but then, in the three-sided French civil war—"the war of the three Henries"—she had also, ambivalently and intermittently, supported his cousin Henri III.[15]

After the Valois family lost effective control of the printing press and eventually of the capital itself, The Holy League, headed by the Guise family, issued a flood of pamphlets, parodies, and pictures attacking the childless king not only for his policies, including his declaration that Navarre was his heir, but for what was widely thought to be his "sodomitical" behavior with his *mignons* (favorites, moreover, lacking in noble ancestry). No wonder he had no heirs. As one angry sonnet had it, he was putting the nation's *"semence"* (seed) in bad soil where, we are to understand, it could do France no good.[16] No wonder that one of the League's sympathizers, Jean Boucher, wrote an *Histoire tragique et memorable de Pierre de Gaverston, Gentil-homme Gascon jadis le mignon d'Edoüard 2 . . . Dédiée à Monseigneur le duc d'Espernon* (1588, based on a late medieval chronicle by Thomas Walsingham). Boucher snarkily dedicates it to the king's chief *"mignon,"* the Gascon duc d'Épernon. A prefatory sonnet to Henri suggests that he and the duke take turns being king—first one of them could be on top and then the other. I suspect there is more than political posture being exchanged here, and the text itself is explicit about Edward II's sodomy.

Marlowe seems to have known this work, as Hillman argues,[17] but the worst attacks on Henri III of course never made it into English print, and perhaps only a few came into English hands; English ears is another matter. The League's antiroyalist propaganda called the king a ravisher of nuns (*La Vie et faits notables de Henry de Valois* [1589, G3], further evidence that early modern Europeans could call a man a sodomite in the modern sense yet still think him capable of heterosexual sins), a heretic too fond of Elizabeth, and a demon. One picture of him furnishes his brow with little devilish horns.[18] As an example of what anti-League counterpropaganda was up against, at least in France, one might take *Le Testament de Henry de Valoys, Recommandé à son amy Jean d'Espernon* (Blois, 1589), a mock will in which the king leaves his beard to wipe baby bottoms, his remaining teeth to old women, and his *"cul"* (ass) as a flute for the citizens of La Rochelle (A 4ff.); a bastard conceived behind a great bush, "frere Henry" was "nothing but a Sodomite, a Ravisher of nuns, and a Machiavellian" who gave himself to a demon for the love of Epernon and had a portable devil to take with him on the road, a man who has "kissed" (*baisé*) Satan on the "*poitron*" ["bumme," says Randle Cotgrave's 1611 dictionary], and to whom the heretical whore of England gave the Garter (B1). Henry really was a murderer, unless one excuses—as did his supporters in some pamphlets translated into English—the assassination at Blois of the two Guise leaders by arguing that the safety of the realm was truly at stake. That he abused nuns seems unlikely, whatever his supposed cavorting with Veronica Franco as he returned from Poland to France by way of Venice. That he made love to his *mignons* nobody really knows. That he was a heretic is a matter of opinion. That he was a demon few scholars are competent to judge.

Some of this wave of slime reached English shores, its sliminess much diminished, however, by government censorship or various forms of hesitancy. Many texts are news reports, but many others are polemics, and if most of the dirt about Henri's supposed love-life or his truck with Satan did not reach English print, there is still dirt enough, although directed in not unprecedented ways against the League, sexualized into a monster, a whore—and later a regicidal one. Printers, even when not encouraged or paid by the authorities, knew that there was a growing public anxious about and fascinated by the events in France—events that far too many of us in English departments keep separate from those of the conflict with Spain, the Dutch revolution, and even the suppression of Irish rebels. The fact of the flood and its impact on *political* thinking has not of course gone unnoticed, as witness Lisa Parmelee's useful *Good Newes from Fraunce: French Anti-League Propaganda in Late Elizabethan England;* and indeed some who write about Spenser and Ireland, or drama and the Armada, do widen their view and see how such policies or events made part of a larger Europe-wide set of conflicts.[19] And because the news from France came to England not just through diplomats' or agents' reports but through a tsunami of printed pamphlets, poems, and polemics, much of it apparently encouraged or commissioned by the government, some who have written about this surge of newsy or aggressive texts have mentioned, at least in passing, that one result was the creation or solidification of a public, a reading public but also—as Paul Voss perceptively notes—a self-consciously *English* reading public.[20] After all, some of these texts breathe deep sighs of relief that England is not like France. France had long been, as we say nowadays, "othered." Such relief at not being French is, needless to say, sometimes accompanied by warnings that if we English are not careful—careful to execute our Jesuits, for example, or to protect the queen, or to avoid civil dissension—we could indeed become like *them.*

We probably need to pay more attention to the role of scandal, pruri-
ence, and hence of morally dubious pleasure in the creation of this public,
or rather these publics—publics for which I confess we have only indirect evidence. Let me be disreputable: like modern breaking news about
United States senators not in fact on the Appalachian Trail or sliding their
feet suggestively in Minneapolis airport men's rooms, or taking bribes from
FBI agents posing as Arab sheiks, these texts are not just about political
theory, keeping up with events, or a public-generating nationalism; they
are often *funny* in a cruel way, and their humor can involve sex, risible
clerical ignorance, mean puns or cheerful verse, parodies, rhetorical cavorting, and reports of ridiculous goings-on that edge into farce. Those in
the book trade knew that such matter sells, of course, as witness the very
funny scene in the anonymous *Returne from Parnassus* (1601) in which the
printer Danter tells the clever if hardly elite writer Ingenioso (seemingly
modeled on the real Danter's friend Tom Nashe) that his latest book has
not sold well and that he has doubts about publishing any new project by
him. Not to worry, says Ingenioso, his manuscript, "A Chronicle of Cambridge Cuckolds," indecently and punningly described as telling "what day
of the moneth such a mans commons were inclosed, and when throwne
upon, and when any entayled some odde crownes upon the heirs of their
bodies unlawfully begotten," will sell briskly when "all these bookes of ex-
hortations and Catechismes, lie moulding on thy shopboard." Impressed,
Danter invites Ingenioso to "sit over a cup of wine and agree on it."[21]

Exactly, and still true. Which is why, if Elizabeth's government wanted
to keep support for its support of Navarre high, both before and even after
his conversion to Catholicism in 1593, or for that matter its on-again, off-
again support for Henri III and his brother Anjou, it was wise to adopt
the same tactic it also used against Martin Marprelate when it hired Nashe
and John Lyly: to encourage sermons, yes, and even some serious political
or religious argument, but also help readers come together as Protestant or
loyal Catholics through shared laughter. Even an Alpha chimp—for my
point is that this collectivity is deep in our instincts and is only reinforced,
not in fact created, by print—knows that he can humiliate upstart Betas so
as to keep them in their place.

Let me now take a few pages to show how what I have said about building a village with bricks of slime and slander works in a few of the texts I
have been studying and, God forgive me, enjoying; after all, even if women
derive from a rib, the men who made these bricks were composed of earthly slime, or so Genesis suggests, and dirt is in our very being. I offer several
sorts of such bricks, with the reminder that these do *not* come from jest

books, popular fiction, or proto-porn but from texts meant to shape public opinion concerning national foreign policy and religious and national community. My point is that the many fine scholars who examine popular print and the many others, equally fine, who look at the impact of French events and news on the English literature might notice yet more than they have done so far the synergy between these two in the creation of a public space for talk, government sponsored or not, and recognize even further the utility for village-making bricks of eye-catching theatricality, of laugh-producing and sometimes indecent narratives, and of amusing rhetorical cavortings with puns and scoffs.

True, this does not exhaust the generic or economic range of cheaply printed largely anti-League or at least anti-Catholic satire and slander (overtly obscene anti–Henri III texts could not easily have seen print, whatever the rumors and jests that crossed the Channel by word of mouth—or perhaps in smuggled texts). Nor do scoffing and defamation appear only in cheap print. George North's *Stage of popish toyes* (1581), translated from Henri Estienne's vividly satirical *Apologie pour Hérodote* (1566 ff.), is a very elite production with, says the title page, "both Tragicall and Comicall partes." The "Comicall" parts include one story about clerical ignorance that parallels jest 17 in *A C. Mery Talys* (1526): thanks to false analogy, a would-be priest confuses the name of Amon's sons' father with that of the father of his dog's four pups (B3), and another that tells of a Dutch priest who looks at an almanac, sees "Sol in Cancro"—on June 11, presumably—and leafs desperately through his breviary to see who this unknown saint might be, muttering that whoever it was didn't seem to be either a virgin or a martyr (H2v).[22] And the long *Legendarie, conteining an ample discourse of the life and behaviour of Charles Cardinal of Lorraine . . . of the House of Guise* (London, 1577, translated from Louis Régnier de La Planche), although more serious in its many accusatory pages, despite the parodic title, at least offers the quasi-theatrical pleasure of seeing a loathed Catholic leader skulking though his treasonable paces, Catherine de' Medici occasionally vilified as an atheist, and a learned sonnet in *vers rapportés* (M6).

I turn now to some texts that combine foreign policy (explicit or implied), efforts to strengthen religious and national community, and eye-catching slander or the report of secrets in vivid and entertaining ways, or at least entertaining for those of us who are deficient in charity or who share the writers' opinions. Not surprisingly, many such writers assume—often with a touch of satire or parody—that the reader believes in devils and will prick up his . . . ears . . . when hearing about even allegorical sex.

To read actions as theater, a common and ancient trope going back at least to Lucian's claim in his *Menippos* that all the world's a stage, invites the reader to imagine him or herself as belonging to an audience. After all, as noted by *The Contre-League* after the deaths of the Guise brothers, "France is the Theater of the world: every one seeth what is done: the Muscovite heareth of it: the Turke is astonished: the Tartarian is abashed: the Persian marveileth, and the Indian rejoyceth: for his fleets do saile thither" (and an American might almost say that here France is a city on a hill). The Guise themselves, we read, these parvenu giants newly "sprong from some obscure race, like mushroomes" and without true descent from Hercules, have set their "seditious preachers" against Henri III so that they leave their texts behind and get so tired that "the sweate hath runne downe their cheekes" (F2–F2v; C2). The more restrained author of *Remonstrances to the Duke de Mayne,* translated by Anthony Chute (London, 1593), adopts the same metaphor, referring to "the unfortunate Theater of Fraunce" (A2v).

Assassinations are themselves, moreover, and almost by definition theatrical—if the victim is a mere nobody we just call the crime "murder"—and the presence of the supernatural adds *energia* and *enargia,* as witness the *Whole and true Discourse of the Enterprises and secrete Conspiracies that have bene made against the person of Henry de Valois, most Christian king of Fraunce & Poland* (1589). This is a description of how Jacques Clément, suborned by Satan himself as he went about the realm roaring like a lion and seeking whom he might devour, and after a long "verie secret practising against the king" (A3v) in a France where even the supporters of a king now as isolated as Roboam was in Israel, felt forced to cry, "God save the League, God save the League (B1), killed Henri, was himself stabbed more than a hundred times. And then, "which is worthy the marvayling at, it is reported that the sayd Monks flesh became as blacke as a very raven, which ys easie to be beleeved, because Sathan dwelt wythin hum, and then the Judgement of god that appeareth to men in diverse sorts: behold here a pytyfull tragedy" (B3v). As if in a theater, we are invited to look collectively, although the black flesh might need modern special effects.

Less explicitly imagining a theater but still moving the reader to laugh in community-reinforcing ways are sexualized narratives, something that, if they were more respectable, classical rhetoricians would call a "pathetic," not a "logical" proof. One pamphlet could do well as a tale from the *Heptaméron* or Tudor jest book (no wonder it tells of friars—one trouble with the League, many thought, was its crowd of such clerics). Jest books are not entirely private read-by-yourself texts, and indeed, as any teacher or public speaker knows, many have long served as scripts for performance, stories the reader can recycle with his or her own embellishments.[23] One short anti-League pamphlet from 1590 gives the entire plot in the title, and without a spoiler alert: *A Subtill practise, wrought in Paris by Fryer Fraun-cis, who to deceive Fryer Donnet of a sweet skind Nun which he secretly kept, procured him to go to Rome, where he tolde the Pope a notable lie concerning the taking of the king of France prisoner by the Duke de Mayne: For which, they whipt each other so greevously in Rome, that they died thereof within two dayes after.*[24] These few black-letter pages, which affect to be a letter home from the expedition led by Lord Willoughby to aid "the invincible Henry of Burbon," fill in the details—the "dastard traytor" duke's overfed "chuffe-headed Chaplaine" and "baudy ghostly father," the nineteen-year-old nun whom one of them has "in shrift betweene the sheets," the flight to Rome with false news of Navarre, the friars' walloping each other like mechani-cal figures in a clockhouse, and the deaths that close this supposedly true "cometragicall historie," a tale "laughed at here, and so much moned else-where." So, says the writer "be merry with this." To be merry is to join the merriment of the English camp abroad and, now that the story is in print, the anti-League English at home.

The merriment, needless to say, had long greeted the sight of clerics breaking every vow they could remember. For some decades, indeed, and this too is hardly news in our own time, the anti-Catholic rhetoric that sustains much anti-League propaganda or diatribe had sexualized the en-emy—in allegorical as well as jest-book terms. To call the Roman Church a whore is not subtle theology, but it can promote a sort of bonding (a complex matter involving gender issues still with us in rap music, for ex-ample, or relying on a shared sense of threatened domination in some racist humor, or an energizing expression of mutually experienced vic-timhood). It was probably impossible to overgo earlier Tudor polemic in this regard—what could, or indeed should, outdo the image created by Pietro P. Vergerio of the deceased Pope Paul III proceeding to Hell and there bleeding menstrual blood into a communion chalice to be used in an infernal Mass?[25] That is both over the top and beneath contempt. Some anti-League narratives can compete, however—this is foreign policy en-couraged by community prejudice and, to repeat, a human taste for slime and slander.

One short account by "T.L.," *A True and perfect description of a straunge Monstar borne in the Citty of Rome in Italy* (London, 1590), parodies the broadsides announcing the birth of such monsters as a two-headed calf or hirsute baby. This creature is conceived when Satan, having boasted of his magical powers, gives Pope Sixtus the Fifth, strumpet queen of Babylon, a loving kiss and retires with "hir holiness" to bed. She (the pope) does not "show" until 1588, when the king of Spain gets drunk with the contents of this harlot's golden chalice. Soon the double-headed, blaspheming, and multilanguaged monster is born: Philip II is literally the creature's imperialist right arm, described at length and with much resort to the anti-Spanish "black legend"; the French-speaking left arm is red with blood. The guts are friars and Jesuits, and the legs are princes of the Church. From the double tail grow many heads, a few of them noble, but most "the scumme and outcast of the world," and the creature is baptized "The Holy League." This is not the end of the story, though, for the League scuttles off to France and the Low Countries with its "lubbers" and the courtesans who follow the Spanish "mungrells." Despite the Armada's defeat, the League lives on.

The pamphlet ends with pages of verse on recent events and a prayer for Henri IV; a note remarks that the Spanish prefer sodomites and dogs to "us." Such preferences jibe with other versions of the "black legend" that can make "us" (although in this case more French than English) glad not to be Spanish, a nation mongrelized by its Jews, Moslems, and "negroes"—or so says Antoine Arnauld's *Copie of the Anti-Spaniard, . . . made by a French Gentleman a Catholique* (1590), aimed at stopping the claims of the half-Valois Spanish infanta. Why would the manly French allow themselves to be dominated by "a yong woman, a Wench. What? Shall Fraunce be subject unto a Distaffe, as a member and dependance of Spaine?" (C3) The English censor must have been dozing as he read this attack on female rule.

Even when not theatrical or narrative, some anti-League pamphlets could deploy rhetorical dance steps that appeal to or help create a sense of community through "othering" the League on the one hand but on the other hand uniting us through an implicitly shared laughter at or pleasure in the parody, the metaphors, the strutting around. One of the most startling of such texts is *A Letter written by a Catholicke Gentleman, to the Lady Jane Clement, the haulting Princesse of the League,* translated anonymously in 1590 and printed in London. The "halting" princess is the lame Cathérine, duchesse de Montpensier and Guise's powerful sister, whose limp the king had mocked. She is Jane Clement because she incestuously loves Jacques Clément, the "brother" who killed the king. The twelve pages are a pastiche of accusation, snatches of verse (a bit of Petrarch, a bit of Sophocles, an injunction to go ahead and be a Moor's whore) allusions to sorcery, and indecent jokes: a mini-Menippean satire, but angry—with a little real grief, or the performance of such grief—over a king "of happy but pittifull memory" (B3). Most likely to elicit the communal feelings generated by witty indecency, and in addition to the reminder that Paris cannot truly be starving while her flesh is so available, is the self-mocking dismay that the author has just quoted Latin to a woman. But no, all is well, "for the Friers and Monks, with whom most part thou hast to doe, have put so oftentimes their latin tongue into thy mouth, that it cannot be, but that it is as familiar unto thee as thy naturall and countrey speech"[26]— French kissing as Latin 101.

Theater, narrative, rhetorical flash: to these and to such popular forms as jests and reports of monsters we can add the semipopular "legend"—not just the long "legend" of the duc de Guise that I have quoted but also texts such as a brief *Divels Legend or A Learned Cachehochysme containing the Confession of the Leaguers Fayth* (London, 1595), an anonymous dialogue supposedly translated from the French of Juvenall Borget (after the conversion and coronation of Henri IV) between Pantaloon and his Zanie—the names are taken, obviously, from the Italian commedia dell'arte. The author relies on such bad puns as the "holy (O lie) league" and risky allusions to the Trinity ("the Father of Spaine, the sonne of Savoy," and the Holy Ghost that "grand divell of Loraine"). There is a parody of the creed of the "league or Spanish Synagogue" and, in a parallel to the queen of Spenser's House of Pride in *The Faerie Queene*'s "Legend of Holinesse," the Holy League is the daughter of Lucifer and Proserpine. More striking is the addition of commentary on the traditional almanac by the master astrologer "Harlequin." The signs have changed, for the League's wolves have banished mutton (Aries, presumably, and possibly an allusion to Gregory XIII's new calendar, rejected by the English, which put New Year's Day on January 1, not March 25), and of course the pope concerns himself with Taurus—papal bulls. Yes, feeble. The goats and archers butt and shoot in vain against Navarre; and so on through other changes to the traditional almanac's components. But Harlequin, a "good Burbonian," will lick the fat from the League's trenchers. And, of course, by 1595 Henri was doing just that—if at the price of a Mass.

I end this discussion with a text that shows how anti-Catholic propaganda sometimes combined with explicit appeals to English nationhood, but I would also spell out the role in this public making of *pleasure* in vivid rhetoric, not just of a shared hatred of pope or Spain or of a relief that England is not France. The title page of J. L.'s *Birth, Purpose, and mortall Wound of the Romish holie League* (1589) quotes Psalm 2: "The kings of the earth band themselves, and the Princes come together against the Lord"— all the more need, then, for our own banding together.[27] Written after the

Armada (the "wound") and the murders of the cardinal and duc de Guise at Blois but before the assassination of Henri III, there is a splendid bit on the Armada as a crescent moon or crocodile with jaws agape for the little "Israel" of England (A3). There is also a story, for Satan visits Rome to chat up the pope and talk tactics against Elizabeth and Navarre. There he finds the "purple Whore sitting on the Beast with seaven heads, or rather . . . on the Citie with seaven hills" (A2). Now the "spirit of malignitie" begets the "Holie League," who holds a "superstitious cup of Romish abhominations" (A2v) and seeks to destroy Navarre and Elizabeth, although, being merely lunar, such forces are outshone by God. Now follow six pages of verse that poignantly (poignantly because fear of Spain and anxiety over France had not subsided despite the defeat of the crocodilian Armada and some victories by Henri IV) suggest the "us" that the propaganda I have been describing was meant to create—"For England yet both is, and shall be English still; / And English Brutes [the Trojan kind, not the League kind] do bravely keepe the same: / Though bastard Britaines boast and bragge their fill, / And leave their Land and skorne the English name." Let us, then, "be true in one, let us together holde" (B2). There is little slime, unless one counts crocodiles, but there is vividness and drama of the sort Spenser exploits in Book I of *The Faerie Queene*.

In 1589, despite what we now know about the effects of the Armada, the fates of the Spanish and British empires, the conversion and triumph of Henri IV—whose smiling statue would survive the Revolution—and England's own survival of civil war, the "public" that anti-League propaganda and cheaper print combined to help create may have felt, subjectively, and at the time, like a huddle against the carnivorous dark.

Allow me an appended and too brief tribute to Richard, to whom I myself am particularly grateful not only for the early books that helped structure my thinking about the Elizabethans but also about the French (du Bellay was not a prodigal, but only because a successfully self-crowned laureate who helped create a new public through an expansion of the French language in his present and the exclusion of too many French poets in his past). I deeply admire Richard's translations of du Bellay and am grateful to him for helping build one more line through the much-needed Chunnel between England and the Continent. And I miss him.

NOTES

1. On "navare" see *De Caede et Interitu Gallorum Regis Henrici Tertii* by the pseudonymous "Stellatus" (Oxford: Barnes, 1589), sig. A3; there is an English translation (I would quarrel with one or two details) posted by Dana Sutton on his Web-based "Philological Museum." For other puns and further discussion, see my "Mary Sidney's *Antonius* and the Ambiguities of French History," *Yearbook of English Studies* 38 (2008): 216–33. That same year Barnes published *A Skeltonicall Salutation* on the recent defeat of the Armada that in macaronic Skeltonics, not academic Latin, warns us away from bad "medicis," the Roman "meretrice," and the "factione Guisiana" (A4v).

2. Paul Yachnin, "Performing Publicity," *Shakespeare Bulletin* 28.2 (2010): 201–19; 201, 212.

3. Antonia Szabari, *Less Rightly Said: Scandals and Readers in Sixteenth Century France* (Stanford, Calif.: Stanford University Press, 2010), 1–2.

4. Peter Lake and Steve Pincus, "Rethinking the Public Sphere in Early Modern England," *Journal of British Studies* 45 (April 2006): 270–92; 270.

5. Paul Voss, *Elizabethan News Pamphlets: Shakespeare, Spenser, Marlowe & the Birth of Journalism* (Pittsburgh, Pa.: Duquesne University Press, 2001), 119, 157, and chapter 5, "The News Quarterly and National Identity." Voss may sometimes oversimplify English foreign policy, for Elizabeth had to contend not only with the Spanish-connected "Holy League" but also with tensions between Henri III and his brother Anjou (her former suitor), and sometimes with *three* parties: the Guise, the Huguenots, and the moderate Catholic royalists ("politiques"), some of whose writings were printed in England.

6. Richard Hillman, *Shakespeare, Marlowe and the Politics of France* (Houndmills, Basingstoke, UK: Palgrave, 2002); see also my "Mary Sidney's French Sophocles: The Countess of Pembroke reads Robert Garnier," in *Representing France and the French in Early Modern English Drama,* ed. Jean-Christophe Mayer (Newark: University of Delaware Press, 2008), 68–89, a collection of essays on topics ranging from Shakespeare to the French pox. Andrew M. Kirk's preface to his *Mirror of Confusion: The Representation of French History in English Renaissance Drama* (New York: Garland, 1996) comments on France as England's and effeminate "other"; although he ignores some extreme slander, Kirk quotes (204) the reported scene in Chapman's *The Revenge of Bussy d'Ambois* (1613) in which "Hee had the foure and twenty ways of Venerie / Done all before him" (IV.ii.8–9). This sounds like a staging of Aretino's athletic but heterosexual images, "I Positi." Alastair Bellany's introduction to his *Politics of Court Scandal in Early Modern England: News Culture and the Overbury Affair, 1603–1660* (Cambridge: Cambridge University Press, 2002) discusses how rumors did or did not delegitimize the monarchy. When thinking about Habermas and the public sphere, he also argues, we should broaden our definition of "political."

7. Hillman, *Shakespeare, Marlowe and the Politics of France,* 14.

8. Alexandra Halasz, *The Marketplace of Print: Pamphlets and the Public Sphere in Early Modern England* (Cambridge: Cambridge University Press, 1997), 163.

9. David Zaret, *Origins of Democratic Culture: Printing, Petitions, and the Public Sphere in Early-Modern England* (Princeton: Princeton University Press, 2000), 174, 133. On France's pre-Revolutionary flood of print see, of course, the work of Robert Darnton.

10. E.g., the anonymous *Trial of Thomas Muir . . . before the High Court of Justicary, at Edinburgh* (1793), 82.

11. John D. Staines, *The Tragic Histories of Mary Queen of Scots* (Burlington, Vt.: Ashgate, 2009), looks at French propaganda concerning Mary Stuart; cf. Alexander Wilkinson, *Mary Queen of Scots and French Public Opinion, 1542–1600* (Basingstoke: Palgrave, 2004).

12. The League exploited the execution of Mary Stuart, a Guise on her mother's side, accusing Henri III of being close to the murderous Jezebel, Elizabeth. Philip Benedict, "Of Marmites and Martyrs: Images and Polemics in the Wars of Religion," in *The French*

Renaissance in Prints from the Bibliothèque Nationale de France, ed. Karen Jacobson (Los Angeles: University of California Press, 1994), 109–37, points out (125) that with Anjou's death in 1584 French Catholics dismayed by English persecution of Catholics could now fear what a Protestant Henri IV might do. Benedict reprints a demonically horned Henri from *Le Faux muffle* (1589).

13. Jesse Lander, *Inventing Polemic* (Cambridge: Cambridge University Press, 2006), 54. Lander ignores news and polemics related to events abroad. Joad Raymond, *Pamphlets and Pamphleteering in Early Modern Britain* (Cambridge: Cambridge University Press, 2003), examines the surge of news pamphlets, including those related to France, and also the taste for sensation, but does not mention the overlap. My own point is that French news and polemic did not just help create an interested public for political or military information but also appealed to a public with a human taste for lively imagery and scandalous denigration.

14. Mayer's introduction to *Representing France and the French* theorizes the sometimes paradoxical Anglo-French relations. On Spenser, see my "Foreign Policy in Fairyland: Henry IV and Spenser's Burbon," *Spenser Studies* 14 (2000): 189–214.

15. Printed claims that Henri III was a heretic and "sodomite" were common where the Guise had control, but in England censorship ensured that they appeared only indirectly in print and that similar accusations against James I appeared not at all. Latin and a foreign press could get around this: *Coronia Regia* (Louvain, 1615; ascribed to Isaac Casaubon but by Corneille de Breda or less probably Kaspar Schoppe) applies the words of Christ— "Sinite parvuulos venire at me" (E5; "Suffer the little ones to come unto me")—to James's own calling the prettiest boys to himself. There may also be a smirk in Robert Tofte's appendix to his love poetry, *Alba* (1598), of a supposed plea to Henri III by the exiled *mignon* Epernon to return to court, whether aimed at James VI or Henri (I3 K1v). See also Robert Sauzet, ed., *Henri III et son temps: Actes du colloque international du Centre de la Renaissance de Tours, octobre 1989* (Paris: Vrin, 1992); Guy Poirier, *Henri III de France en Mascarades Imaginaires* (Quebec: Presses de l'Université Laval, 2010); and, on slander as a creator of community, Luc Racaut, *Hatred in Print: Catholic Propaganda and Protestant Identity during the French Wars of Religion* (Aldershot: Ashgate, 2002).

16. Pierre de Ronsard, *Oeuvres complètes,* ed. Jean Céard, Daniel Ménager, and Michel Simonin (Paris: Gallimard, 1994), 2:1246 («vostre semence chet en terre qui n'est bonne»), in "attributed pieces." Another sonnet (1247) complains of the king's taste for "culs devenus cons."

17. Hillman, *Shakespeare, Marlowe and the Politics of France,* 72.

18. For such images see in particular Jacobson's collections.

19. Lisa Ferraro Parmelee, *Good Newes from Fraunce: French Anti-League Propaganda in Late Elizabethan England* (Rochester, N.Y.: University of Rochester Press, 1996), 47, notes Gabriel Harvey's list of pamphlets he has seen (including misdoings and "practiques" that have "refined divers French wittes, even aboove the Sharpest Italians or Spaniards at this instant)." Parmelee and Voss each have valuable lists of publications.

20. See Voss, chap. 5 ("The News Quarterly and National Identity").

21. *The Pilgrimage to Parnassus with The Two Parts of the Return from Parnassus,* ed. from MSS by W. D. Macray (Oxford: Clarendon Press, 1886), I.iii, 88–89.

22. "Sol in Cancro" ("Sun in Cancer") is on B3. On the same page, the bishop asks the priest, "to prove his Latine," "*Es tu dignus?*" and the priest, "beleeving that *Dignus* had bin to dyne," says "no sir I thanke you, I will dyne with your servauntes." In *C Mary Talys* the dim son is asked about Noah, not Amon.

23. My Columbia colleague James Shapiro, for example, tells me that he had heard the story about the idiot son and the dog's pups from his grandfather, but applied to a would-be rabbi in Eastern Europe. With a shift of aim, much of post-Reformation polemic can be redeployed from the other side: if the Whore of Babylon helped make publics in England, the whore Elizabeth I could do the same in areas dominated by the Guise.

24. London: Nelson, 1590.

25. *Wonderfull Newes of the Death of Paul the III* (London, 1552?), trans. William Baldwin. The former ascription to Matthias Flaccus Illyricus is now in dispute.

26. Sig. A4. The Huguenot Philippe de Mornay, in his misleadingly entitled *Letter, written by a french Catholicke gentleman . . . Conteyning* (London: Wolfe, 1589), scoffs at Catholic claims that the Calvinist Beza had told the assassin of François duc de Guise that the murder would win him Heaven: Calvinism "importeth that no worke whatsoever can merite Paradice" (A3).

27. London: Cadman, 1589. I./J. L. could be James Lea.

CHAPTER FIVE

Making Public the Private

LENA COWEN ORLIN

IN 1982, Richard Helgerson prepared to enter the private sphere. A production of *Arden of Faversham* introduced him to a "level of everyday particularity" and an "extraordinary realism" he had not encountered before in Renaissance drama. Struck by *Arden*'s "richness of social detail," he resolved that his next project would be a "microhistory" of the real-life murder on which this play was based. He had first to finish the landmark book we now know as *Forms of Nationhood,* however. *Forms of Nationhood* includes a reading of a two-part play by Thomas Heywood, *Edward IV,* that eventually contributed to his rethinking of the original attraction to *Arden.* This took him "out from *Arden* to the broader representational field to which it belonged and which it helped open."[1] By the time *Adulterous Alliances* appeared in 1995, Helgerson had become interested in the publics that *Arden* and *Edward IV* (and also *Merry Wives of Windsor* and Dutch genre painting and Spanish peasant drama) made.[2]

The private murder of Thomas Arden was, Helgerson now emphasized, full of "public entanglements" (23). These included "the dissolution of the monasteries, the establishment of a state religion, the growth in royal sovereignty, the networks of national patronage and affiliation, the laws of marriage and divorce" (31). Yet most of the public issues were suppressed, both in the lengthy report of the murder included in Holinshed's chronicle and in the anonymous stage play that inaugurated the genre of domestic tragedy. To the degree that the literary tradition narrowed in on the troubled Arden marriage, the story was an imperfect vessel for Helgerson's widening concerns. *Arden,* he noted, managed "to keep alive . . . a sense of the early modern interpenetration of the public and private," but "only barely" (26), and it was interpenetration in which he had come to be interested. For this theme, the Heywood plays made a more useful case study than did

Arden. "To a far greater extent," he noted, *Edward IV* "puts the intersection of home and state at the very center of attention" (34). Helgerson conceptualized the relationship between public and private as a rivalry, and, as is not the case in *Arden,* in *Edward IV* "the bourgeois domus . . . suffers disruption from without, not from within" (54). There, and in many other works, he found competition between the two spheres to be figured in the person of a sexual predator, a representative of the public arena who enters the private home with aggressive and illicit designs on a private woman. The tragedy of Edward's enforced mistress Jane Shore "comes as close as we are likely to get to providing a paradigmatic, perhaps even a founding case" (34). Helgerson's thesis was that "The sexual predation of a soldier, a courtier, an aristocrat, or the king takes on broader cultural and political meaning because the object of that predation belongs to a different and more vulnerable social order, whether bourgeois or peasant" (189).

Like *Adulterous Alliances,* this chapter engages with the attention newly commanded by the domestic as a symptom of public recognition for an early modern private sphere. My way into the argument is through the idea of the window—as an instrument allowing public access to private life in *Edward IV,* as the object of protectionist legislation in late sixteenth-century London, and as both subject of reproduction and trope for representation in seventeenth-century Dutch genre painting. If I seek to rebalance our understanding of the public and the private through the organizing concept of display rather than invasion, and then to reengage the energies released by the display of "everyday particularity," I nonetheless write in dialogue with and in tribute to the work of Richard Helgerson.

In *Forms of Nationhood,* Helgerson distinguished the type of chronicle history represented in *Edward IV* from Shakespeare's cycle plays. Shakespeare, he said, presents a "royal image of England." He excludes and ignores the "popular, the socially marginal, the subversive, and the folk." Heywood, by contrast, makes room for the ruled as well as the rulers. *Edward IV* features the rebellion of Falconbridge, and Helgerson spent some time on the carnival elements in Falconbridge's representation. He also discussed the encounters of the disguised king with the comic Hobs, the tanner of Tamworth. But the burden of Helgerson's argument about these contrasting visions of England's history was carried by the characters Matthew and Jane Shore. "Inclusion emerges as an inverse function of power," Helgerson wrote; "the more inclusive" a play is, "the greater the place it gives to women and commoners, the less concerned it will be to assert the prerogatives of monarchic rule." In *Edward IV,* Jane Shore "overshadows the kings who seduce and torment her."[3] Helgerson returned to the meanings of Jane Shore in *Adulterous Alliances.*

In the opening scene of *The First Part of Edward IV,* to review briefly, the new king Edward IV insults England, France, and his mother by marrying the widow Elizabeth Woodville. He also receives news of an uprising by those loyal to the monarch he has displaced, Henry VI. In scenes 2–7, Falconbridge and his rebels march on London but are defeated by Lord Mayor Crosby, prosperous goldsmith Matthew Shore, and other citizens and apprentices. In scene 8, Shore explains to his famously beautiful wife Jane why he could not stand self-protectively by as king, city, order, private wealth, and personal safety were threatened by Falconbridge. In scenes 9 and 10 the rebels rise again and are defeated, and Edward IV finally makes a battlefield appearance that, it does not go unnoticed, is belated. Shore scrupulously declines the king's subsequent offer of a knighthood. In scenes 11–14 the royal party goes hunting, and the king, in disguise, dines with a monarchic agnostic, the tanner Hobs. Falconbridge is led to execution in scene 15. In scene 16, the widowed Crosby relies on Jane Shore to help him entertain Edward at a victory feast. Smitten, the king disguises himself again in scene 17 in order to make a surreptitious visit to Shore's London shop. Hobs travels to London and encounters the king's men in scene 18. In scenes 19 and 20, Jane Shore consults her friend and neighbor about the moral dilemma posed by the king's desire for her, but her free choice is abrogated when Edward removes her to court. Learning that his worst suspicions about the king's interests are confirmed, Matthew Shore determines to cash out. He will leave England and everything he has just fought for. In scene 21 Edward's advisers report on taxes they have collected for his foreign wars. These include a remarkably generous contribution from the convert-royalist Hobs. In scene 22, the outward-bound Shore witnesses Jane's new life as a compassionate mediator between king and commons. She receives the petitions of the poor and disenfranchised, occasionally dispenses justice, but more often offers aid, comfort, and mercy. In the final scene of *The First Part of Edward IV* the king reveals his true identity to Hobs and prepares to make war on France. (War will be one of the subjects of *The Second Part of Edward IV,* as are Jane's plight when Edward is succeeded by her antagonist, Richard III, and the wretched deaths of the Shores.)

The Shores appear in nine of the twenty-three scenes of *The First Part,* a play that by its title purports to be occupied with royal history. Theirs are, moreover, episodes full of ethical content and emotional power. Neither Falconbridge, with his gang of rowdies, nor Edward, whose abuse of power Helgerson terms "tyrannical," commands our sympathies as do the goldsmith and his wife. In interlocking patterns of meaning, Falconbridge threatens Shore that when he rules London he will take possession of Jane, and Shore sees Falconbridge defeated, but then the king Shore so loyally defended takes possession of Jane. Under the spell of Jane's beauty, Edward draws the parallels between himself and Falconbridge: "thou, traitor heart, / Wouldst thou shake hands in this conspiracy? / Down, rebel! Back, base treacherous conceit" (16.123–25).[4] The language of Jane's lament, that the king "with a violent siege / Labours to break into my plighted faith" (19.10–11), is a domestic echo of Falconbridge's assault on London. Reencountering her husband, she says, "I must confess I yielded up the fort. . . . But yet, sweet Shore, before I yielded it / I did endure the long'st and greatest siege / That ever battered on poor chastity" (22.86, 88–90).

The king and the city wife share three scenes: Edward's visit to the mayor's house by invitation, Edward's resort to Shore's shop as an ostensible customer, and Edward's incursion into Shore's house to remove Shore's wife. The last, with the king announcing, "I intrude like an unbidden guest" (19.78), best fits Helgerson's paradigm. In full measure of the destruction Helgerson emphasizes, Shore gives up "Lands, goods, and all I have," mourning that "Where kings are meddlers, meaner men must rue" (20.87, 79). Setting aside Helgerson's idea of public and private in rivalry, though, and attempting instead to understand early modern constructs that involved less adversarial notions of the private made public, I would focus not, as he does, on the "rape" of Jane Shore in scene 19 but instead on their shop-centered encounter two scenes earlier.

Despite having bidden his own "idle eye" to "Keep home, keep home" (16.147), the king cannot resist assuming a disguise and searching out Shore's premises. The action begins with a stage direction: *Enter two Apprentices, preparing the goldsmith's shop with plate.* One confirms that the full complement of plate is displayed, and the other reports that "weights and balance" are ready to hand. The first of the two apprentices exits. Jane Shore enters, a stage direction specifying that she has *her work in her hand.* She cross-questions the remaining apprentice about the recent commission of a gold cup and then sends him off to Cheapside, "while I attend the shop myself." According to a fourth stage direction, *The boy departs, and she sits sewing in her shop. Enter the King, disguised* (17.0s.d.–18s.d.).

Edward does not see Jane at first. We are to understand that he is in the process of making his way to the shop known as the "Pelican." Walking, he congratulates himself that in his "secret shape" he has passed unrecognized in the city, even among the watermen at Lion Quay who know him well. But "Soft," he soon interrupts himself: "here I must turn," and next,

"Here's Lombard Street," and finally "here's the Pelican; / And there's the phoenix in the pelican's nest." It has taken eleven lines for Edward to narrativize his movement across the stage as if toward Shore's shop; there follows his pause for nine lines of rhapsodic praise for Jane's beauty. The eyes he had once admonished to "keep home" he now describes as "greedy," and he fully indulges their desire to "gaze." When Jane eventually senses his attention, she calls out, "What would you buy, sir, that you look on here?" Edward uses the pretext of her sapphire ring to draw near. The two then joust verbally until, with the stage direction "*He discovers himself*," Jane "*kneels*" and says, "Whatever we possess is all your highness', / Only mine honour, which I cannot grant." The seduction scene is interrupted by the entrance of Shore, who, in one last stage direction, "*looks earnestly, and perceives it is the King, whereat he seemeth greatly discontented*" (17.19–115s.d.).[5]

The level of visualization here is highly detailed. The scene incorporates thirteen stage directions, calls for a clutter of props, and is elaborated with multiple local referents: Cheapside, Lion Quay, Lombard Street, and the shop called the "Pelican." Heywood re-creates on stage the ocular experiences of his London audiences. On a daily basis they walked through streets past shops that were open for business, the upper shutter of the window raised out as an awning, the lower shutter propped up to display goods, the shopkeeper taking advantage of the window's light as she occupied her time between customers. From the moment Jane sits till the moment she challenges the onlooking king, there are twenty long lines in which we are invited to gaze at the tableau of this actor seated as if in a shop window. The episode has not been recognized as a dumb show because of the king's soliloquy, but I want to emphasize how similar is its effect.

A key element is the implied framing by a shop window. Some years ago I wrote a short speculative piece on the threshold areas between public and private in the built environment—that is, windows and doors.[6] I remarked the frequency with which women deponents in early modern church courts were willing to state that they had been standing on their doorsteps but how infrequently they admitted to having looked out from a chamber window above. Sometimes they professed to be busy on the doorstep, sweeping or shaking out laundry. Sometimes they heard the "great noise" of neighbors quarrelling and rushed to the door; why, then, did a "great noise" not send them more often to a window? I hypothesized that windows and doors had different social codings or moral significations, and that while women might have had irreproachable pretexts to stand in their doorways, it was less respectable for them to admit to having looked out from their windows.

I wrote this without having yet encountered a corroborating discussion in Alberti's *Della Famiglia.* Burckhardt's ideal of the *uomo universale,* Leon Battista Alberti has too often been taken as a guide to spatial practice in the Renaissance.[7] His ideologically motivated abstractions mislead us on the subject of the real. But in the area of cultural superstitions about space, especially patriarchal and gynephobic ones, he is perhaps our most useful witness. Alberti's fictional alter ego, Giannozzo, reports that he has instructed his wife to avoid their window: "To perform your duties well, you cannot spend the whole day sitting idly at the window with your elbows on the sill, as some lazy and foolish women do, who as a pretext keep something to sew in their hands but never finish it." At the same time, he has encouraged her to make public appearances at their door, in a manner "very dignified and serious, so that our neighbors would come to know and appreciate her as a prudent lady, and the family would respect her."[8]

The gendering of windows, usually related today to such red-light districts as that in Amsterdam, has a longer history than we may have realized. In Thomas Middleton's *Women Beware Women,* Bianca, having recently married the modest factor Leantio, calls it "a sweet recreation" "to stand in a bay window, and see gallants" (3.2.49–50).[9] When the Duke of Florence summons her to a banquet, we know that it is because "The Duke himself first spied her at the window" (2.2.8). Leantio, who has tried to hold his wife secret and has charged his mother to chaperone her strictly, is outraged to think of the way in which she may have attracted the Duke's attention; surely, the two women have been "gadding" in the streets. Stung, his mother retorts:

> When last you took your leave, if you remember,
> You left us both at window. . . .
> And not the third part of an hour after,
> The Duke passed by . . . and to my apprehension
> He looked up twice to th'window. (3.2.148–52)

Too late, Leantio bids his wife withdraw: "Thou art a gem no stranger's eye must see" (3.2.94). The window has already made public his private.

Amanda Flather's work on gender and space in the Renaissance is, to my mind, precisely right and importantly corrective on how spatial practices blurred the boundaries between public and private in the period. But she follows a less useful line with prescriptive texts. For Renaissance women, Flather says, "Too much time abroad" was believed to lead to "distraction from domestic duties." It "encouraged idleness, or worse still immorality." Thus, "male moralists repeatedly recommended that solitude and confinement within the home was a necessary protection for women against temptations to their chastity that they might be unable to resist."[10] Familiar as this discourse is to us now, it was not universally accepted then. To the contrary, many writers, Thomas Heywood among them, located agency for immorality in men. They recommended the confinement and surveillance of women less out of fear that women were easily tempted than out of awareness that men's resistance to temptation was low. Flather herself quotes Robert Cleaver from 1615: a woman "abroad in the streets" will "entice men to folly by her looks and behavior."[11] In 1620, the anonymous author of *Hic Mulier* warns husbands to have "every window closed with a strong casement and every loophole furnished with such strong ordinance that no unchaste eye may come near to assail them"; unquestionably, the unchaste eye is that of the man looking in rather than of the woman looking out.[12] More contemporaneously with *Edward IV,* in 1608, John Denison writes that "a woman gorgeously and sumptuously attired . . . is a snare and dangerous provocation to lewdness." He admits that "every one that is thus attired doth not intend to entrap any thereby." Nevertheless, "admit there be no such intent, yet may there easily be such an effect."[13]

This is certainly the window effect of *Edward IV,* where Heywood is at pains to delineate Jane's irreproachable conduct—her shop stewardship, her needlework—and where the king claims that the very sight of her nonetheless causes him to set aside royalty and reason. Masculine onus is also at issue in *Women Beware Women,* where, although Bianca is less innocent, Leantio's mother nonetheless throws the responsibility for Bianca's abduction back on Leantio ("You left us both at window"). "Love," ran an old proverb, "comes in at the window and goes out at the door."[14] Bianca, like Jane Shore before her, will soon be out the door and away to court. For a jealous husband in John Ford's *The Broken Heart,* responsibility for dishonor attaches rather more to the admiring male than to a desiring female, but finally his grief is displaced to the window itself: "I'll have that window next the street dammed up. / It gives too full a prospect to temptation / And courts a gazer's glances."[15]

The moral meaning of windows was in constant tension with the daily imperatives of early modern life. Without question, light was essential for productive work.[16] And women had public duties as contributors to the household economy and as practitioners of the retail trades. Matthew Shore explains that Jane sits in his shop "more to respect / Her servant's duty than for any skill / She doth, or can pretend in what we trade" (20.37–39). This is excessively fastidious on Heywood's part, putting Jane Shore on a par with Katherine Stubbes as a model of the implausible and eschewer of common practice.[17] Even the sternest moralists admitted that women must be allowed to supervise their servants, and Heywood toes this line, not only in Jane's dialogue with the apprentices but also, earlier, when he depicts her assisting the widowed mayor by marshalling his household staff ("My servants are so slack, his majesty / Might have been here before we were prepared," 16.58–59). But it serves Heywood's larger objectives for Jane to be otherwise represented as remote from the real, when the facts were, first, that there were many early modern women who had manufacturing and commercial skills and also, second, that the sight of women in shop windows was a regular one.

While the primary, necessary purpose of the window was to admit light to those within, it also permitted the exchange of glances that adumbrated other exchanges. *Women Beware Women* identifies a further erotic charge that is more peculiar to windows than to doors, which is their greater proximity to the private. When he first spies Bianca, the Duke is said to have "pointed to the wonder warily / As one that feared she would draw in her splendour / Too soon, if too much gazed at" (2.2.11–13). For current purposes, I pass over the titillating effect on the observer of an apprehension that the object of observation may step back into inaccessibility. Instead, I would emphasize simply that this apprehension acknowledges the existence of the inaccessible. In other words, it recognizes—and, in recognizing, creates—a private zone.

This is the subtext of a 1623 case from the London Consistory Court.[18] It was alleged that one Hall, a single man in Acton, had gotten his servant Elizabeth Carter pregnant. Her father, Leonard Carter, was deposed. Carter reported that about a year after Elizabeth went into service, her mother noticed her growing belly. Elizabeth admitted that her master "did diverse times come to her bedchamber" and have "carnal knowledge of her body." Shortly after, Hall alleged to a justice of the peace that Elizabeth had run away. This the Carters seem not to have believed, because they went to Hall's house and demanded to know what had become of their daughter. Hall insisted that she was no longer in Acton. About three months later, a servant in the house that was "a near opposite neighbor" of Hall's said that she had seen Elizabeth "look out of a chamber window" in Hall's house. Carter went to the neighbor's house and, himself "standing in an upper chamber of the said house," glimpsed Elizabeth "in an upper chamber of the said Hall's house at a window." Then she disappeared.

Eventually, two women who "usually on market days resort to London with wares" told Carter that they saw Hall and Elizabeth near Charing Cross. Carter found his daughter and learned that she had been first to

Westminster, where Hall had arranged for her to deliver her child in the house of a shoemaker, and then to the Strand, where Hall had obtained a new position for her with a linen draper. Hall had warned Elizabeth to "keep herself from the knowledge of" her family, because, he said, "if her mother knew where she was she would spoil her and slit her nose." This is not an uncommon story. But it is the liminal moment of Elizabeth's loss that is peculiarly haunting, the idea that Leonard Carter could have seen his daughter in a window without being able to get any nearer to her.[19] In confirming testimony, an Acton man named Peter Thorney said that Hall "did keep the said Elizabeth in some private room in his house for the space of a quarter of a year in the time that she was with child." During those months, Elizabeth vanished into the private, to which only Hall had access and of which Leonard Carter had only the briefest of glimpses, through a window.

For Helgerson, scene 16 of *The First Part of Edward IV* would presumably have seemed of limited use for understanding the "interpenetration" of public and private because shops were not strictly private spaces: they engaged with the public for commercial purposes. And, staffed as mercantile establishments would have been by householder, housewife, male apprentices, or female servants, shop windows might also appear to be insusceptible of contemporary gendering. In *Edward IV,* however, no distinction is made between the Shores' ground-floor shop window and any upper chamber window. Shore attributes to his shop the ocular effect ascribed in *Women Beware Women* to Leantio's house: "Keep we our treasure secret," laments Shore, "yet so fond / As set so rich a beauty as this is / In the wide view of every gazer's eye?" (18.149–51). The character speaks out of a theatrical context in which shops were "discovered" on the early modern stage at least as often as studies, the visual reveal creating for both the voyeuristic effect of viewing sequestered space.[20] In historical archives, there are few other references to a gynephobia surrounding shop windows, perhaps because the working lives of London women were as important as those of men. But one further indication that shop windows nonetheless participated in the discourses of private and public emerges from the scholarship of Lien Luu concerning aliens trading in sixteenth-century London.[21]

Immigrants had certain protections of religious liberty in Tudor England, but politically and economically they suffered disabilities that remind us of gender discrimination in the period. They could not own, inherit, or bequeath property; they could not bring lawsuits relating to real property; they could not vote or hold office (59). As Luu demonstrates, they were also prohibited from keeping "open" shops. In other words, they were barred from publicly displaying their goods and, thus, from selling at retail. The intention was that they should be wholesalers exclusively so that their profit margins were reduced and their labor went uncompensated. Luu explains the regulations for closed shops in language that is strongly reminiscent of that we encounter among the early modern moralists of gender relations: "The aim was to prevent passers-by from being tempted to go [in] and place orders" (64).

Statutes regarding trade restrictions against aliens were passed in 1523, 1539, and 1540, and by the 1580s and 1590s there was a second generation of "foreigners" who were born on London soil but who were still subject to these proscriptions and who were, in addition, precluded from serving apprenticeships in the livery system (59). As with restrictions on women, however, the alien statutes ran afoul of practical concerns. Some members of London's native mercantile community believed that it was dangerous for production to be hidden from public view, because it might encourage dishonest workmanship. Goldsmiths, who employed the most expensive raw materials, were especially worried about fraud (64). Officials of the various livery companies routinely conducted "searches" among manufacturers to make sure that standards of weight, material, and measure were observed, but they found it difficult to monitor those who pursued their crafts in "odd corners" rather than public shops. English craftsmen also complained that, renting out a room or a garret, aliens had lower overhead costs than those who kept shops (64). In 1571 London citizens took their concerns outside the City to petition the queen with a list of grievances against them, among other things claiming that foreigners managed to sell at retail by "keep[ing] shops inward and private chambers" (66). Some aliens established themselves in London's liberties and claimed exemption not only from the wholesaling laws but also from searches, civic responsibility, and taxation (69–70). By the early seventeenth century, many of the restrictions had been found to be unenforceable (70).

This is the context for a language of open and closed, public and private, that dominated the discourse of the alien economy in Elizabethan London. Windows, it turns out, were raced as well as gendered. In 1556 the city aldermen decreed that the shop windows of all foreigners should be "shut" by having lattices placed across them—that is, obscured from public view (64). Lattice, William Harrison was to explain, was made "either of wicker or fine rifts of oak in checkerwise" (fig. 5.1).[22] Ten years later, in 1566, the order for foreigners to block their shop windows was repeated. In 1571 the City aldermen specified that a "stranger" goldsmith was permitted "to open his shop windows and to work therein so long as he sets a lattice be-

FIGURE 5.1. Hans Suess von Kulmbach's *Girl Making a Garland* (ca. 1505–8) is oil on wood, with the reverse of the panel showing a *Portrait of a Young Man*. Thus it may be a courtship painting, perhaps for separated lovers (the scrolled inscription reads "ICH PINT MIT, VERGIS MEIN NIT," "I bind with forget-me-nots"). The young woman who is taking advantage of the light coming through a window is fully absorbed in her project, but the fact that she is displayed to view is emphasized by a raised and disused lattice nearby. The painting considerably predates the works discussed by Helgerson and is German rather than Dutch or Flemish. The visible signature AD, presumably intended to make an attribution to Albrecht Dürer, is a later addition; Kulmbach had worked in Dürer's workshop. (Metropolitan Museum of Art, New York).

fore his shop windows according to the old orders and laws of this city."[23] This was an acknowledgment that natural light was fundamental to productivity, and in 1587 the authorities allowed that foreigners' windows and doors could "leave convenient light for them to work." But the windows should be "made in such sort as people passing by may not see them at work, and so as their wares and merchandizes remaining and being within the same their shops or places give no open show to any people passing by" (64). Importantly at issue here, as also in *Edward IV*'s tableau of Jane Shore, is the concept of display.

The idea of display is an alternate route to another of the subjects of analysis in Helgerson's *Adulterous Alliances*. In contrast to "the monarchic and seignorial state," he wrote, "the home made do . . . by presenting itself as the refuge of the real" (7). For him, this was the signature achievement of *Arden of Faversham,* but it was also key to the work of Jan Vermeer, Pieter de Hooch, Nicolaes Maes, and other northern European artists. "If what interested me was the realistic depiction of everyday domestic life," he wrote, "where better to look than at Dutch genre painting of the mid-seventeenth century?" (2–3). In paintings he observed the near-total absence of husbands in household scenes and the frequent presence of soldiers with apparently libidinous intents.[24] The latter, he said, "threatens to transform an otherwise respectable woman into a whore and to make a brothel of a bourgeois home" (84). Helgerson pointed out that the so-called "Paternal Admonition" by Gerard ter Borch is not a cozy family scene with father, daughter, and grandmother (fig. 5.2). Rather, with a coin in his hand, the soldier is a solicitor of sexual services and the older woman is a procurer. Helgerson read similar stories in ter Borch's "Gallant Officer," his "Lute Player and Officer," Pieter de Hooch's "Interior Scene," and Vermeer's "Soldier and Laughing Girl." His most brilliant readings were of Emmanuel de Witte's "Interior with Woman at the Clavichord," where a man who has doffed his uniform is dimly visible in a nearby bed, and Nicolaes Maes's "The Eavesdropper," where the discarded coat of a visiting officer is a subtle shot of color to one side. All these paintings advanced Helgerson's thesis about "representations of the everyday and its violation" (85). He characterized the visit of the soldier as an intrusion into the private sphere by a sexually predatory agent of the state.

Ter Borch was unusual in creating dark and confined scenes. Few other northern painters located their light in the satin of a skirt. Elsewhere, as Martha Hollander says, the "standard 'Dutch interior'" featured "a visible light source indicated by a window."[25] There were good painterly reasons to have a window; it provided the artist with an opportunity to create visual

FIGURE 5.2. The painting once known as *Paternal Admonition,* by Gerard ter Borch (1654), is now called *Gallant Conversation* for the reasons Helgerson discusses: with the aid of an elderly procurer, the soldier appears to be soliciting sex. (Rijksmuseum, Amsterdam; another version exists in the collection of the Staatliche Museum, Berlin).

interest through the play of light on dark surfaces, as in de Hooch's "Woman Reading a Letter." But to include a window was also to reference the real because of the importance of natural light for the occupations shown in these genre paintings. Sitters were kitchen workers, spinners, lace makers, and child minders. They checked household reserves of linen, scoured pots, peeled apples, swept, kept accounts, played the clavichord, and read books as well as letters.[26] Theirs were windows of practical purpose, not of sexual display. The reader in Pieter Janssens Elinga's painting (fig. 5.3) keeps the lower shutters modestly closed, letting the light from above suffice. And Vermeer made windows as important to his male "Astronomer" and "Geographer" as to his housewives and serving women.

It is important to note that the windows of northern art were not restricted to representations of the real. They were also metonymic metaphors, displaced referents to the painting of the whole. Alberti, the theo-

FIGURE 5.3. Pieter Janssens Elinga's *Woman Reading* (1668–70) keeps the lower shutters decorously closed, using only the light from above. Helgerson discusses Samuel von Hoogstraten's *View of an Interior* (1658), which is unpopulated except for a pair of slippers meant for wearing inside (the painting is also known as "Les Paoufles"). The slippers are taken to imply the housewife's inattention to duty; she has left them, and her house, behind. Elinga's interior makes an interesting counterpoint, his sitter having discarded the shoes she would have worn outside. Though she is not occupied with household chores either, the shuttered windows seem to indicate that her propriety is not at issue. (Alte Pinakothek, Munich).

retician of space, wrote about painting too: "I inscribe a quadrangle of right angles, as large as I wish, which is considered to be an open window through which I see what I want to paint."[27] Rayna Kalas emphasizes that Alberti's window is to be understood not as glass but as frame, a "frame through which to behold a scene."[28] And, following Alberti, Erwin Panofsky describes the method by which an "entire picture" is "transformed . . . into a 'window' . . . we are meant to believe we are looking through this window into a space."[29] Some painters, including Gabriel Metsu, Nicolaes Maes, and especially Gerrit Dou, made the illusion overt by placing a sitter in a *nisstuk* or *vensternis* ("niche piece" or "window niche"), a framed opening, often with a ledge and sometimes with shutters (fig. 5.4). Such window scenes featured characters in isolation rather than in the relationships Helgerson found so potentially compromising. Moreover, it cannot be said

FIGURE 5.4. Gerrit Dou's *Old Woman Watering Flowers* (1660–65) is an example of a "niche" painting that seems more documentary than suggestive or moralizing. (Kunsthistorisches Museum, Vienna).

that the self-portraits of Dou and Samuel Von Hoostraten were erotic. Nor were Dou's painting of an elderly woman watering flowers, his portrait of an aged schoolmaster, Gottfried Shalcken's scene of an old woman scouring a pot, and, perhaps arguably, Francis Mieris's image of a boy blowing bubbles. These works expand on Helgerson's catalogue of home-invasion paintings by offering different and desexualized windows onto what was "real" in seventeenth-century domestic life.

For Helgerson, "domestic drama and domestic painting emerged as a by-product of early modern state formation" (6). The private sphere achieved its public character in "response to a new organization of public power," in "conflicted relation to the competing cult of monarchy," and in "competition with the state and its history" (6, 50, 4). "Competition," "rivalry," and "antagonism" were embodied in the image of a male from the public sphere making predatory incursion on a female from the private sphere. "As a subject for tragical or historical . . . representation," Helgerson said, "the bourgeois house *comes into existence* only in relation to the more usual protagonists of those lofty genres, protagonists who enter its space with destructive effect" (54; emphasis added). He established the domestic dramas as "the refuge of the real" (7), arguing that they achieved meaningful definition exclusively through what I might call the rape of the real. In such a figuration, the private is always already secondary, subsumed, disempowered, reactive, and vulnerable.

The evidence from other windows on the early modern, however, makes it fair to ask whether this was indeed the genesis of the private and whether these were the necessary relationships of parts. Now, display and invasion are not wholly incompatible terms, as Thomas Heywood showed. In *Edward IV,* the first invader of that which is displayed is the eye of the royal observer, the "greedy eye" that "gazes" at the tableau of Jane Shore (17.37). And the Dutch Vasari, Karel van Mander, in his *Painter's Book* of 1604 described the layered spaces of northern painting in the visually invasive terms of *insien,* "view into," and *doorsien,* "view through."[30] Admirably, Helgerson refused to insist upon his reading of the subjects of northern painting. It is not that the presence of a soldier "makes a brothel of a bourgeois home," for example, but that it "*threatens* . . . to make a brothel of a bourgeois home" (84; emphasis added).

Such ambiguity is key to the window effect: the very fact that we cannot be sure of our interpretation reminds us that we make an act of interpretation. Displayed before us is something other than what we can know, because the window opens into another's private zone. We are offered glimpses of things that would otherwise be beyond our reach, as Elizabeth

Carter was out of reach to her father. To take any phenomenon as a subject of display is to make an object of it. At the most basic level, it becomes an object of recognition, in this case the recognition that by the sixteenth century there were entities or spheres that were known to be private and that these had their own prerogatives. There can have been no violation without a prior integrity. My argument, then, is for a different and less victimized "coming into existence" than Helgerson describes.

Many of the contributors to this volume are occupied with asking (in the words of Brendan Dooley) "Are we having a public sphere yet?"[31] One way of making Habermas movable is to posit different kinds of publics from that he so influentially identified. This is a line followed by Peter Lake and Steve Pincus, for example, who speak of "public spheres of [various] sorts" and a "series of public spheres" in the sixteenth and seventeenth centuries.[32] In their view, post-Reformation religious controversy forged pathways for political debates that engaged more diffused and less homogeneous publics. No longer were the participants in dialogue simply "ruler" and "ruled." Now, diverse interest groups were represented, and topics of exchange ranged "from the quotidian to the controversial and even the allegedly seditious" (275). For Lake and Pincus, Parliament was a signal site of public making; there, local matters were transformed into objects of national concern as subjects of public reports and public legislation. They observe that political discourse in its various oral, manuscript, and print media "called into being an adjudicating public or publics" (277). Thus, the public sphere of their narrative is "an arena for the public discussion of political and religious issues," and over the course of the sixteenth and seventeenth centuries it developed from something "opportunistic" (289) and "episodic" (280), occasionally tolerated as a "necessary evil" (292) and "resorted to, in extremity" (277), to something regularized, normative, and, in effect, institutionalized.

If later seventeenth-century parliamentary reports and newsletters contributed to a public sphere of political discourse that could be characterized as coherent rather than chaotic, the domestic drama of the public stage did the same for the private sphere in the later sixteenth century. By the time the private was documented in mid-seventeenth-century northern genre painting, it had become thoroughly recognizable as a space of shelter and sustenance, labor and leisure, sex and generation, property and propriety, accumulation and privation, authority and service, sociability and interiority, men, but especially—and thanks in no small part to the earlier gendering of windows and to *Arden of Faversham* and *Edward IV*—women.[33]

The questions that have impelled my chapter are: "When did we have a private sphere?" and "What was the nature of the relationship between public and private?" Was the relationship as defined, as adversarial, and as hierarchical as Helgerson posits, as early as Helgerson posits? Such fungible social constructions as those for shop windows and chamber windows are among the leading indicators, for me, that even at the end of the sixteenth century, when *Edward IV* was staged, public/private borders remained softer than they were to become. And the public things that went to make a private, such as domestic drama and domestic painting, went also, as an extension of their mutual embeddedness, to make the public. For instance, the feminizing of the private sphere, a phenomenon of the sixteenth and seventeenth centuries, informed a contrasting gendering of the public sphere as Habermas was to define it for the eighteenth century. He would remark that this was an arena for men.

For Habermas, theories that involve a "private sphere" that is described as having been "born as a distinguishable entity in contrast to the public, [glance] over"—that is, ignore—a history in which the economic activity of the private sphere had already become "publicly relevant."[34] The English private sphere had become publicly relevant in the 1530s, when Henry VIII's break with Rome was described as the product of his private conscience. There then followed the series of big public events, economic activities, and state-sponsored formulations that produced the contours of English private life: Protestant emphasis on personal responsibility in spiritual engagement, wider individual opportunity following the redistribution of church lands, the restructuring of poor relief and social responsibility with the dissolution of the monasteries, troubled transitions to a proto-capitalist system, surplus wealth expended on and concentrated in the creature comforts of homes and goods, justifications of an expanding monarchic authority by analogy to normative family structures, the politicization of household organization to mirror state pyramids of power, monitory attention to family and household in public ideology. The private was on the public agenda in homilies, sermons, conduct books, ballads, and also stage plays.

But while the state found it to be in its own interest both to recognize the private as an explanatory model for social organization and also to define the private in ideologically expedient ways, domestic dramas did not simply reproduce publicly authorized constructions. Had they done so, there would have been no more to the *Edward IV* story than the emblematic scene of coercion on which Helgerson focuses. Admittedly, the state sought to co-opt the domestic just as the king kidnapped Jane Shore. In fact, however, the public theater released energies that were to produce a populace that was less compliant than was the enforced mistress. For Lake and Pincus, the public sphere was constituted in the response that controversy solicits. So, too, I would argue, for the stage. As a character Jane Shore is an emblem for the rape of the private; as an idea, for its resistant power.

In *An Apology for Actors* (1612), Thomas Heywood described the theater as a moral medium: "Women likewise that are chaste are by us extolled and encouraged in their virtues, being instanced by Diana, Belphoebe, Matilda, Lucrece, and the Countess of Salisbury." (With the first-person plural he referred first to playwrights and then, in the phrase that follows, also to fellow constituents of English history.) By contrast, "The unchaste are by us showed their errors, in the persons of Phrine, Lais, Thais, Flora, and, amongst us, Rosamond and Mistress Shore." Heywood asked rhetorically, "What can sooner print modesty in the souls of the wanton, than by discovering unto them the monstrousness of their sin?"[35] However disingenuous he may have been about drama's ethical agencies, evidence is that Jane Shore's life was not received simply as a cautionary tale. Two years after Heywood defended the stage against those who were made uneasy by it, and fifteen years after the publication of the *The First and Second Parts of Edward IV,* Jane Shore reappeared in a long ottava-rima poem by Christopher Brooke. *The Ghost of Richard the Third* documented that "her fame by a vild play doth grow." The character Richard, famously Jane's persecutor, almost certainly makes reference here to Heywood's *Edward IV* plays in which, as Helgerson recognizes, Jane "overshadows the kings who seduce and torment her." Audiences in London's public theaters were so far from condemning Mistress Shore that, Brooke's Richard goes on to say, they were known to "commiserate her fate." Even though by his (imagined) lights he did "justice on that sinner," among women playgoers there was not a one to be found who "drinks not her tears"; they made "her fast, their dinner."[36] Sympathy seems to have been a dominant response to the impossible predicament in which Jane was placed by the conflict of allegiance that involved both her husband and her monarch. Opening a window onto the ways in which the real of private life exposed fault lines in public ideology, the Shore scenes in *The First Part of Edward IV* were, like all domestic dramas, radical tragedies.[37]

My quarrel with *Adulterous Alliances,* then, brings me back to *Forms of Nationhood,* to Helgerson's initial recognition of the theatrical muscle of Jane Shore and of the anarchic energy of inclusion. To his list of the "popular, the socially marginal, the subversive, and the folk," I would add the domestic and the female, which were so much more his subjects in

Adulterous Alliances. Jane's abduction may, as he has it, signify the rape of the real, but there is a revenge of the real, too, in the power of the private to make the public—that is, to contribute to a discourse of resistance that was to shape its future.

NOTES

1. Richard Helgerson, *Adulterous Alliances: Home, State, and History in Early Modern European Drama and Painting* (Chicago: University of Chicago Press, 2000), 1–2. Subsequent references to this book are included in the text. Research for this essay was completed in 2009 for a workshop in Helgerson's honor.

2. Helgerson often retold the story of making an initial fact-finding trip to Faversham and learning of my own interest in the Arden murder. My microhistory came out in 1994 in *Private Matters and Public Culture in Post-Reformation England* (Ithaca, N.Y.: Cornell University Press, 1994). Helgerson was always generous about saying that my "scoop" had played a part in redirecting his interests.

3. Richard Helgerson, *Forms of Nationhood: The Elizabethan Writing of England* (Chicago: University of Chicago Press, 1992), 244, 245, 297–98, 235.

4. Thomas Heywood, *The First and Second Parts of King Edward IV,* ed. Richard Rowland, *The Revels Plays* (Manchester: Manchester University Press, 2005).

5. This scene has also been discussed by Leslie Thomson in "'As Proper a Woman as any in Cheap': Women in Shops on the Early Modern Stage," *Medieval and Renaissance Drama in England* 16 (2003): 145–61. Describing a number of plays with a shopkeeper's wife or daughter "put on display like a commodity for sale," Thomson says the "theatrical convention" originated with *Edward IV* (145, 150). She calls it the "Jane Shore paradigm" (151).

6. "Women on the Threshold," in a forum on "Studying Early Modern Women," ed. Leeds Barroll for *Shakespeare Studies* 25 (1997): 16–23.

7. See, for two examples, Orest Ranum, "The Refuges of Intimacy," in *The Passions of the Renaissance,* vol. 3 of *A History of Private Life,* ed. Roger Chartier, trans. Arthur Goldhammer, gen. ed. Philippe Ariès (Cambridge: Harvard University Press, 1989), 207–63; and Mark Wigley, "Untitled: The Housing of Gender," in *Sexuality and Space,* Princeton Papers on Architecture, ed. Beatriz Colomina (Princeton, N.J.: Princeton Architectural Press, 1992), 327–89.

8. For this reference I am grateful to Jane Tylus, "Women at the Windows: 'Commedia dell'arte' and Theatrical Practice in Early Modern Italy," *Theatre Journal* 49.3 (October 1997): 323–42. For the translation from Alberti, see Guido A. Guarino, *The Albertis of Florence: Leon Battista Alberti's "Della Famiglia"* (Lewisburg, Pa.: Bucknell University Press, 1971), 230, 237. Compare also that of Renée Neu Watkins in *The Family in Renaissance Florence* (Columbia: University of South Carolina Press, 1969): "To do this well, however, you must not spend all day sitting idly with your elbows on the window sill, like some lazy wives who always hold their sewing in their hands for an excuse, but their sewing never gets done" (222); and "On a few occasions, in order to teach her a certain air of authority and to have her appear as she should in public, I made her open her own door and go outside practicing self-restraint and grave demeanor. This led our neighbors to observe her air of discretion and to praise her" (229).

9. Thomas Middleton, *Women Beware Women,* ed. J. R. Mulryne, *The Revels Plays* (Manchester: Manchester University Press, 1975).

10. Amanda Flather, *Gender and Space in Early Modern England* (Woodbridge, Suffolk: Boydell Press for the Royal Historical Society, 2007), 94.

11. Ibid., 23.

12. *Hic Mulier,* excerpted in *Half-Humankind: Contexts and Texts of the Controversy about Women in England, 1540–1640,* ed. Katherine Usher Henderson and Barbara F. McManus (Chicago: University of Illinois Press, 1985), 271.

13. John Denison, *A Three-Fold Resolution Very Necessary to Salvation* (London, 1608), sigs. 14^{r-v}. See also Flather, *Gender and Space,* 27–28.

14. Ad De Vries, *Elsevier's Dictionary of Symbols and Imagery,* ed. Arthur de Vries, 2nd ed. (Boston: Elsevier, 2004), for "window." Compare George Chapman in *All Fools:* "Though he come in at the window, he sets the gates of your honor open, I can tell you"; *All Fools,* ed. Frank Manley, Regents Renaissance Drama (Lincoln: University of Nebraska Press, 1968), 3.1.420–21.

15. John Ford, *The Broken Heart,* ed. T. J. B. Spencer, *The Revels Plays* (Manchester: Manchester University Press, 1980), 2.1.1–3. On *Women Beware Women* especially, see Hanna Scolnicov's *Women's Theatrical Space* (Cambridge: Cambridge University Press, 1994) for a chapter on "The Woman in the Window": "The closedness of the house is a symbol of its dweller's chastity, while, conversely, her appearance at the window may be taken for an invitation and a provocation" (54); "Using the convention of the woman in the window presupposes a society based on male authoritarianism and a plot which works out ways of getting round the obstacle posed by the locked door" (63). Cynthia Lewis reconsiders the constructs in "'You were an actor with your handkerchief': Women, Windows, and Moral Agency," *Comparative Drama* 43 (2009): 473–96. For *Edward IV,* see also Leslie Thomson, "Window Scenes in Renaissance Plays: A Survey and Some Conclusions," *Medieval and Renaissance Drama in England* 5 (1991): 225–43.

16. See also on this subject my "Boundary Disputes in Early Modern London," in *Material London, ca. 1600,* ed. Lena Cowen Orlin, New Cultural Studies Series (Philadelphia: University of Pennsylvania Press, 2000), 361.

17. See Philip Stubbes, *A Crystal Glass for Christian Women, Containing a Most Excellent Discourse of the Godly Life and Christian Death of Mistress Katherine Stubbes* (London, 1592).

18. Consistory Court of London Deposition Book (1622–1624), London Metropolitan Archives DL/C/A/003/MS01989/001, fols. 115^{r}–117^{r}.

19. It is not possible to know the full truth of this story. It was an office case, which means that Hall appeared on a charge brought by church officials, not in consequence of a complaint brought by the Carters. Although I emphasize that Carter's daughter was withheld from him in an apparently unbreachable private zone, it could have been the case that Elizabeth's inaccessibility was a protection to her. Hall may not have legitimated her child, but it seems that he saw to her medical care, found her a new position, and may even have sheltered her from abuse by her family.

20. See Alan C. Dessen and Leslie Thomson, *A Dictionary of Stage Directions in English Drama, 1580–1642* (Cambridge: Cambridge University Press, 1999), for both "shop" and "discovery." In "'As proper a woman as any in Cheap,'" Thomson identifies thirty-two plays with shop scenes between 1580 and 1642, ten of these between 1602 and 1613.

21. Lien Luu, "Natural-Born Versus Stranger-Born Subjects: Aliens and their Status in Elizabethan London," in *Immigrants in Tudor and Stuart England,* ed. Nigel Goose and Lien Luu (Brighton: Sussex Academic Press, 2005), 7–75. Subsequent references are included in the text.

22. William Harrison, *The Description of England,* ed. Georges Edelen (Ithaca, N.Y.: Cornell University Press for the Folger Shakespeare Library, 1968), 197.

23. Repertory of the London Court of Aldermen 17 (March 13, 1570–April 14, 1573), London Metropolitan Archives COL/CA/01/01/019, fol. 150.

24. In *Private Matters and Public Culture,* I argued that in the sixteenth and early seventeenth centuries the private home ceased to be seen as the principal site of production; in domestic conduct literature and in stage plays, men were depicted as departing the house in

order to earn the income to support it (244). Thus, as John Dod and Robert Cleaver put it in 1598, "the duty of the husband is to get goods; and of the wife, to gather them together and save them" (*A Godly Form of Household Government,* sigs. M4v–M5r). With this, the house was feminized in common understanding. Helgerson passes over the chronological gap between English plays of the 1590s and northern European paintings of the 1650s and 1660s. To my mind, though, the absence of husbands in the paintings is true to a public perception that was by then increasingly well established, that the private home was "the woman's place."

25. Martha Hollander, *An Entrance for the Eyes: Space and Meaning in Seventeenth-Century Dutch Art* (Berkeley: University of California Press, 2002), 42.

26. See, for example, Jan Vermeer's kitchen-worker "Milkmaid" (1658), Nicolaes Maes's "The Spinster" (1655), Caspar Netscher's "The Lacemaker" (1662), Pieter de Hooch's "A Woman Nursing an Infant" (1660), Pieter de Hooch's "The Linen Closet" (1663), Godfried Shalcken's "Old Woman Scouring a Pot" (1660s), Nicolaes Maes's "Old Woman Peeling Apples" (1655), Pieter Janssens Elinga's "A Woman Reading a Letter and a Woman Sweeping" (n.d.), Nicolaes Maes's "The Account Keeper" (1656), and Gerrit Dou's "Woman at the Clavichord" (1665).

27. Leon Battista Alberti, *On Painting,* trans. John R. Spencer, rev. ed. (New Haven, Conn.: Yale University Press, 1966), 56.

28. Rayna Kalas, *Frame, Glass, Verse: The Technology of Poetic Invention in the English Renaissance* (Ithaca, N.Y.: Cornell University Press, 2007), 152.

29. Panofsky quoted by Kalas, *Frame, Glass, Verse,* 152.

30. Van Mander cited by Hollander, *An Entrance for the Eyes,* 8.

31. Brendan Dooley, "News and Doubt in Early Modern Culture; or, Are We Having a Public Sphere Yet?" in *The Politics of Information in Early Modern Europe,* ed. Brendan Dooley and Sabrina A. Baron (London: Routledge, 2001), 275–90.

32. Peter Lake and Steve Pincus, "Rethinking the Public Sphere in Early Modern England," *Journal of British Studies* 45 (April 2006): 270–92. I quote here from 273–74 and 277; subsequent references are included in the text.

33. See, for some fairly arbitrary examples: for shelter, Cesar van Everdingen's "A Woman Warming Her Hands over a Brazier" (1650); for sustenance, Emmanuel de Witte's "Kitchen Interior" (1660s); for labor, Quiringh Gerritsz van Brekelenkam's "The Tailor's Workshop" (1661); for leisure, Gerard ter Borch's "The Music Lesson" (1668); for sex, Frans Van Mieris's "The Oyster Meal" (1661); for generation, Pieter de Hooch's "Mother Lacing her Bodice beside a Cradle" (1663); for property, Samuel Hoogstraten's "View of an Interior (Les Paoufles)" (1658); for propriety, Gerard ter Borch's "The Suitor's Visit" (1658); for accumulation, Pieter de Hooch's "The Linen Closet" (1663); for privation, Adriaen Jansz van Ostade's "Peasant Family in a Cottage" (1661); for authority, Hendrick Cornelisz van Vliet's "Portrait of Michiel van der Dussen, His Wife Wilhelemina van Setten, and their Children" (1640); for service, Gerrit Dou's "Lady at her Toilet" (1657); for sociability, Jacob van Velssen's "A Musical Party" (1631); for interiority, Pieter Coode's "A Woman Seated at a Virginal with a Letter" (n.d.); for men, Jan Vermeer's "The Geographer" (1668–69); for women, Dirck Hals's "A Woman Tearing a Letter" (1631).

34. Jürgen Habermas, *The Structural Transformation of the Public Sphere: An Inquiry into a Category of Bourgeois Society,* trans. Thomas Burger (Cambridge: MIT Press, 1991), 19.

35. Thomas Heywood, *An Apology for Actors* (1612; STC 13309), sig. G1^v.

36. Christopher Brooke, *The Ghost of Richard the Third* (1614; STC 3830), sig. F1^r. I owe this reference to Arthur Melville Clark, *Thomas Heywood: Playwright and Miscellanist* (Oxford: Basil Blackwell, 1931), 16.

37. This is the main thesis of my *Private Matters,* where I also discussed the meanings of Jane Shore (118–30). There, I used Holinshed's term for the Arden murder, "impertinent," rather than Jonathan Dollimore's, "radical."

CHAPTER SIX

Public and Private Intercourse in Dutch Genre Scenes

*Soldiers and Enigmatic Women / Painters
and Enigmatic Paintings*

ANGELA VANHAELEN

Study of these pictures destroys the belief that anything enters them
by chance.

SIR LAWRENCE GOWING

THERE IS an appealing myth of origins that occurs repeatedly in histories of Dutch genre painting: this art was born together with the Dutch
Republic itself. As Théophile Thoré succinctly put it: "A société nouvelle,
art nouveau"—"A new art for a new society."[1] This claim was no doubt
derived from Hegel's *Lectures on Fine Arts.* In his influential interpretation
of seventeenth-century Dutch painting, Hegel celebrated the liberation of
the Dutch people from the double tyranny of the Roman Catholic Church
and the Habsburg Empire. Throwing off the restraints of Church and
monarchy, the Dutch, he argued, freely turned in their art to the enjoyment of everyday life. Leaving behind a tumultuous past, Dutch realism
engaged with the here and now; the struggle and suffering of Reformation
and Revolt do not reverberate through quiet genre scenes of the mundane
world.[2]

Richard Helgerson's important essay on Dutch genre painting, "Soldiers
and Enigmatic Girls," provides a critical challenge to this axiomatic myth
by reexamining the relationship between Dutch realism and Dutch history.[3] Helgerson focuses on a peculiar kind of genre scene produced by
artists such as Johannes Vermeer, Pieter de Hooch, and Gerard ter Borch:

pictures of soldiers being entertained by Dutch women in domestic interiors (fig. 6.1). These types of paintings were produced mainly in the 1650s and 1660s, just after the conclusion of the long conflict with Spain. Without a war to fight, the soldier enters the home, sits down with the housewife, and turns his attention to a different kind of conquest. Sir Lawrence Gowing wryly notes the implied outcome of such encounters: "The extent of the hospitality that will be exacted of the agreeable hostess is rarely open to doubt."[4] In some paintings, the soldier actually proffers coins, a rather unsubtle device that effectively blurs the boundaries between home and brothel, housewife and prostitute. As we shall see, other variations are much more reticent about their own moral force, staging the consummation of the narrative as an open-ended question.

The imagery is both humorous and disquieting. It presents a limit case to Hegel's assertion that the new art conveys "the superabundant sense of the joys of ordinary existence."[5] As Helgerson astutely points out, genre scenes of domestic interiors almost never depict the male householder. The man who actually buys and hangs such paintings in his house is thus situated as a voyeur outside of the picture, who watches soldiers invade his home to seduce his wife or daughters. What types of pleasures could this strange twist on voyeurism possibly offer? These paintings seem to have sold well; there are hundreds of extant variations on the theme, indicating a market for such imagery and attesting to its widespread appeal.

Helgerson's argument takes up the question of the broader cultural functions of these pictures. By situating this uneasy imagery within its political context, he effectively demonstrates its resonance with specific political anxieties. The events of 1650 are especially relevant. At this time, the unity of the new republic was disrupted by internal conflicts, which culminated in Stadholder William II's attempt to invade Amsterdam. The Dutch stadholderate was a hereditary position, filled by the heirs of the nobleman William of Orange, military leader of the Dutch Revolt. The States General, a representative body, was the sovereign ruler of the United Provinces, and the stadholder was in theory its servant who had charge over the military. There was a delicate balance of power between these two bodies of authority, however, for the stadholder had widespread popular support, which allowed him to step out of his mandated place and at times take on a quasi-monarchical role.[6] William II's failed invasion of Amsterdam was followed only months later by his sudden death from smallpox. The States General seized this unanticipated opportunity to reassert its sovereignty and established what was later called the First Stadholderless Period (1650–72). Supporters of this new form of government called it the

FIGURE 6.1. Johannes Vermeer, *Officer and Laughing Girl,* ca. 1657. Oil on canvas, 50.5 x 46 cm. (Copyright The Frick Collection, New York).

"True Freedom," and it was during this time that images of military men intruding on Dutch domesticity proliferated.

By being attentive to these political conflicts, Helgerson argues that the True Freedom itself—the nature and survival of the Republican government—is what is at stake in scenarios that intimate the potential violation of Dutch home life. The pleasure of these paintings therefore extends beyond sexual innuendo by affording an odd enjoyment of the moral and constitutional uncertainties of the polity that male householders collectively possessed. The fear of invasion is brought under control by being deflected into the aesthetic realm of paintings that evoke an omnipresent danger.[7] The soldier, in this interpretation, represents the incursion of state military power, while the absent householder is the defender of the Republic's True Freedom. The woman gets to choose between them. The viewer (or voyeur) teases out the enigma: Will she opt for the True Freedom or subject herself to the Stadholderate?

In this chapter, I work outward from this suggestive argument in order to consider its implications for rethinking the connections among painting, history, politics, and the interconnectedness of public and private life in the Dutch Republic. Dutch genre painting traditionally has been defined in opposition to history painting, and I start with Helgerson's significant claim that genre, which is often dismissed as an apolitical and ahistorical form of art, is in fact actively political in its engagement with history. Helgerson deftly negotiates historiographic and methodological disputes about the interpretation of Dutch realism, and his interventions have important connotations. For, when we consider the distinctive ways that genre painting does history—from below, from a seated position, from a conversational domestic setting—we gain new insights into what made it such an efficacious medium for fostering the participation of private individuals in the Republic's extremely divisive political life.

The insights of Czech writer Karel Čapek provide an evocative starting point for a consideration of these issues. Čapek visited the Netherlands in the early 1930s and published a pithy commentary in a small book called "Letters from Holland." Here is what he says about Dutch painting:

> And so, partly through lack of space, partly as the result of the Reformation, there arose a Dutch art which is secular, small-scale and bourgeois. But I haven't yet come to the point I wanted to make, and that is, that the Dutch painter did not work standing like Titian, or prone on a scaffolding, like Michael Angelo, but sitting down. . . . Dutch art is the work of seated painters for sedentary townsfolk; an urban art. . . . These pictures were not painted for galleries where people walk about, but for rooms where they sit down. Dutch art revealed a new reality by betaking itself home and sitting down there. . . . Make an excited man sit down; immediately he drops his heroics and all his grandiose posturings. Nobody can preach sitting down; all he can do is talk. By sitting down permanently on its wicker footstool, Dutch art banished all high-flown heroics from itself and the world which it portrays.[8]

I cite Čapek at length here because I think that Richard Helgerson would have appreciated how these witty observations corresponded to his own. Čapek points out that the grandiose posturing and didactic heroics of Italianate history paintings are at odds with Dutch genre scenes. History painting, the preferred genre of state power, takes the viewer into an exalted realm of ideals and allegory, religion and myth; whereas genre painting stays closer to the homely realities.

History painting also gives up its didactic and ideological meanings more readily than does genre painting, because it is devised in relation to corresponding texts. Helgerson makes this point through an analysis of Jan Steen's picture of two women in an interior. At first glance this painting looks to be a genre scene until we decipher the note that the younger woman is holding up: "alderschonte Barsabe—omdat" (most beautiful Bathsheba—because . . .). The ambiguities of genre painting dissipate as we turn to the biblical passage that describes King David's summoning of Uriah the Hittite's wife to his own bed. Once we have found the text, we can interpret the painting. Now we see, in Helgerson's words: "A royal intrusion into a domestic interior and into the body of the woman identified with that interior."[9] History painting, the idiom of politics, often expresses political power through imagery of the control, possession, abduction, or violation of women's bodies, signifying the control that sovereign power had over its subjects and territories. Indeed, as Helgerson demonstrates, the seventeenth-century language of politics commonly elided with the language of sexual rivalry and adultery.[10]

Dutch genre painting, by contrast, usually is defined in opposition to history painting by virtue of the fact that it is not text based. Clearly influenced by Hegel, the nineteenth-century painter and art critic Eugène Fromentin claimed that "The revolution which had just rendered the Dutch people free, rich, and prompt for all undertakings, had despoiled them of what elsewhere formed the vital element of the great schools [of painting]. It . . . abolished the representation of antique fables as well as the gospel."[11] Freed from the text, Dutch artists turned to the world they saw around them and painted, in Fromentin's influential words, "the portrait of Holland, its exterior image, faithful, exact, complete."[12] They painted clouds and trees, the polders and the seas, cows, windmills, milkmaids, taverns, fairs, and, of course, home life.[13]

This new art of the mundane generated a new kind of art criticism, which had to come to terms with the loss of explanatory texts. Sir Joshua Reynolds, on a journey through Flanders and Holland, prefaced his description of the Dutch art collections by asserting that "history has never flourished in this country"[14] and concluded by stating that "The account which has now been given of the Dutch pictures is, I confess, more barren of entertainment, than I expected . . . however uninteresting their subjects, there is some pleasure in the contemplation of the truth of the imitation."[15] The content of Dutch art, as Hegel too argued, does not captivate us; it is too familiar, too close to nature and everyday life. What, then, is its appeal? Hegel writes: "so what is most important here is the individual recreation

of the external world. . . . And consequently the interest in the objects delineated tends to revert to the fact that it is the unique powers of the artist
himself which are thus consciously displayed."[16] These paintings accord-
ingly shift attention from mundane prototypes to the powers of inventive
creators and discerning beholders. Uninteresting content serves as pretext
for the individual ability of artists in the exercise of formal innovation.

This compelling characterization of Dutch realism has had a significant
impact on the field. Dutch art, as Svetlana Alpers famously argued, is an
art of describing. She concludes: "The fact that Dutch art was so often independent of the texts that were the basis of history paintings made them
also independent of commentary . . . you cannot tell the story of a Dutch
painting, you can only look at it."[17] A curious stasis characterizes the in-
stantaneity of these pictures. The actors are on stage; they gesture, open-
mouthed, and then nothing happens. By arresting a moment in time, the
paintings frustrate narrative and history. In this way, as Helgerson notes,
questions of history and politics often are evacuated from the interpretation of these works. The influential writings of Dutch art historian I. Q.
van Regteren Altena, for instance, frame the Dutch Golden Age as an era
of peaceful leisure: "The whole of the seventeenth century reminds us of
one long Sunday, during which the Dutch gradually awoke after the evil
dream . . . of which the shaken minds of the older generation had but
slowly recovered. It resembled a day of rest when people . . . had leisure
to explore with new eyes, and to find inexhaustible joy in studying every
aspect of God's creation, and work done by the hand of man."[18]

Dutch art, according to this formulation, served as a means of forgetting the politics of the past. Having thrown off repressive ecclesiastical and
aristocratic patronage, it did not look back at the traumas of history. As
Fromentin asked: "Do the people remember it? Where do you find living echoes of these extraordinary emotions?"[19] Helgerson's response to this
kind of question would be that history and political conflict lurk close to
the edges of genre paintings, just waiting to be read into them. Like the
soldier who disrupts the quiet, orderly Dutch home, that which has been
repressed of Dutch art—history, the text, the military, the stadholder—
stages a return in these paintings.

Helgerson's argument is persuasive, yet it also raises methodological dif-
ficulties, which he critically addresses in the essay. Confronting the problem head-on, he concedes that in seeing soldiers as representatives of the
stadholder and threats to the True Freedom, he is "reading for the text"
even though genre scenes lend themselves to often diametrically opposed

readings. Helgerson's review of the critical literature reveals that many of the repeated motifs in these paintings—fruit, wine, beds, musical instruments, and maps, for instance—could function as symbols of sexual promiscuity and worldliness *or* as emblems of everyday homeliness and national virtue. Iconographic interpretations have found text-based evidence for both kinds of reading. Indeed, both are equally convincing precisely because of the ways in which genre paintings evade being tied to a single authoritative text. Helgerson is forthright about acknowledging that his reading in support of the True Freedom could be an over-avid reading of these intractable works. It is but one among the multiple interpretative possibilities the paintings offer.[20]

In short, Helgerson comes up against a methodological impasse familiar to all historians of Dutch art. Ann Adams has summarized it succinctly: "Either [art historians] describe these works as created exclusively for visual delight, or they argue that such paintings hide their symbolic content, usually a moralizing message. Some scholars split the difference and celebrate these works for making instruction palatable through delight."[21] The strength of Helgerson's essay is that it points to a way out of this dilemma. Although he reads symbolic content in terms of the True Freedom and republican autonomy, in an important passage he underlines the fact that the choice of subjects for the paintings "was richly overdetermined, and the ways in which those paintings were received were no doubt equally varied."[22] A case in point is the impossibility of choosing between opposed readings of Vermeer's *Soldier and Laughing Girl* (see fig. 6.1). Is the woman a virtuous Hollandia, true to her husband, or is she Vrouw Wereld, a personification of worldly vice? Will she accept or reject this soldier's advances? Helgerson concludes: "the very force of Vermeer's painting derives from its undecidability."[23]

So, there he sits, the soldier, waiting indefinitely for the woman to decide. "The eye is never satisfied, desire is never sated, as long as one courts art and love."[24] Vermeer's painting seems to illustrate this seventeenth-century maxim. In fact, early modern treatises on Dutch art repeatedly returned to the trope that painting's seductive surfaces were designed to titillate the art lover, whose desiring eyes sought to penetrate the picture.[25] Realist painting, according to these contemporary accounts, is a "seductress of sight." As it tempts and teases the viewer, its sensual charms conflate with the pleasures offered and withheld by the painted women.[26] The beauty depicted can never be had, however; she stirs but does not satisfy longing. Painting remains impenetrable. It teases with evocative symbols, yet a final interpretation or single, true meaning is ever-elusive. The plight of the viewer/voyeur is thus analogous to that of the soldier in these pictures: he is held in suspense, seeking but not receiving a definitive answer.

Indeed, the erotic language used to describe painting often elided with military rhetoric in these treatises. By captivating the art lover's eye, the painter overcomes, subdues, and conquers it.[27] Like the art of love, the powers of art are forces in peaceful battles, skillfully and persuasively won. Making art, making love, making war. The art handbooks describe the painter as a peaceful soldier, who mobilizes his skills of seduction. Gowing, himself a painter, came to a similar conclusion about Vermeer's works: "The attention of man to woman is finally identified with the attention of a painter to his subject. . . . However an artist love the world, however seize on it, in truth he can never make it his own."[28]

Following from Gowing's and Helgerson's insights, I want to suggest that the very undecidability of these unresolved and richly overdetermined seduction scenes functions on one level as a meta-discourse about genre painting itself—a means for painters to self-critically comment on their own practice. Realism attempts to capture the everyday world in paint, but it can never completely possess it. The subject of genre painting, in many cases a woman, retains her separateness, her decisive power to spurn or welcome the soldier's and the painter's forays into her realm. If painters are peaceful soldiers, then their paintings are as enigmatic and evasive as the girls in them.

This interpretation seems to move us away from the important questions Helgerson raised about the relation of painting, politics, and history toward a formalist analysis of painting in its autonomous realm. In order to counter this, I shall turn to some seventeenth-century Dutch commentary that brings together soldiers, painters, and different genres of painting. Following Helgerson's example, I've chosen three exhibits: a text and two paintings that help to sharpen our sense of the historical and political potential of the genre paintings created in the 1650s and 1660s.[29]

Exhibit A is Dirck van Bleyswijck's civic history of Delft, published in 1667. Van Bleyswijck discusses both soldiers and painters in his history of the city and its illustrious men. A series of biographies of military and naval heroes is followed by a section on the lives of Delft artists. In conclusion, he bestows on them the same status, stating: "The war-heroes and artists are similarly renowned because of their deeds and works . . . on account of these, everyone shares in and enjoys the honour of the Fatherly City."[30] Like the soldier celebrated for his defense of the population, the artist is described as a citizen-hero. According to van Bleyswijck, the works and deeds of both soldiers and artists served the greater good.

Genre painting developed in interesting ways in Delft, where artists like Vermeer and de Hooch repeatedly took up the soldier and enigmatic girl motif. But how could this make them good citizens? *Exhibits B and C* offer some clues. They are a pair of paintings done by de Hooch after he had moved from Delft to Amsterdam in the early 1660s. Both works present unusual variations on the soldier and enigmatic girl theme. In *Leaving for the Walk* (fig. 6.2), we see a soldier and a woman strolling in an interior. Behind them are two stone archways, and one of these offers a glimpse into a familiar setting: a domestic interior. Inside it, a chair is pushed back from a table under the window as if moments before the couple had been sitting there conversing. Close to the arched doorway stands another woman, possibly a maid, with a young child in her arms; it looks as if they too have just stepped out of the home. This painting seems to respond to questions raised by the seduction scenes examined by Helgerson: What happens next? How might the story of the soldier and the enigmatic girl continue once she makes her decision? What if she does indeed walk out with him?

Where would they go? The answer posited here is somewhat surprising, for this is not the usual tavern, inn, or brothel of so many Dutch genre scenes. This architectural setting, with its colonnade, pilasters, archways embellished with relief carving, and elaborate inlaid floor is distinctive and recognizable. This is in fact the Citizen's Hall of Amsterdam's new Town Hall. Arguably a monument to the True Freedom, every part of the Town Hall celebrated the history, glory, and honor of the fatherly city. De Hooch takes liberties with the interior here, for this archway does not actually open into a private apartment. The painting thus presses its viewers to consider the interpenetration of intimate and public spaces. While Helgerson did not include this painting in his analysis, I think it resonates with one of his main assertions, which is that the everyday lives of ordinary people took on a new immediacy in this period as the home became less of an adjunct to state power and more of an alternative to it.[31] It is as if every home had a door that opened directly into the Citizen's Hall, and the many doors of the Town Hall led right back into the home, so that the stock figures of genre painting could move easily between private and civic life.

This painting thus gives us a different view of the relationship of the soldier to the home and its denizens. His role here is to accompany the woman into the Citizen's Hall, making it seem as if he invaded the home with the aim of bringing private people into public space. The soldier of genre painting does not abduct the Republic's women after all. He does

FIGURE 6.2. Pieter de Hooch, *Leaving for the Walk*, ca. 1663–65. Oil on canvas, 72 x 85 cm. (Musées des Beaux-Arts de Strasbourg. Photo Musées de la Ville de Strasbourg, M. Bertola).

not force himself on them, or carry them off and violate them in the way that the soldier of history painting does. Instead of ravaging women, the off-duty soldier of Dutch genre sits down and talks with them (see fig. 6.1). If, as Helgerson argues, he represents public state power and she the interests of private people, then all of these paintings emphatically depict the two joined together in the intercourse of conversation rather than violation. They are not antagonists locked in an unequal physical battle. In de Hooch's painting, they walk arm-in-arm from the home to the Town Hall. If marriage is implied, then it is "companionate marriage," amicable and mutually beneficial. Unlike other paintings of this genre, this one does not blur the boundaries of home/brothel and wife/prostitute; rather it reveals similarities between home/citizen's hall and husband/soldier.

In this way, de Hooch plays with the well-established trope that the boundaries of the home correspond to the boundaries of the housewife's body.[32] As Lena Cowen Orlin argues in her chapter in this volume, architectural openings such as windows have multivalent gendered associations. In de Hooch's painting, the open archway and pushed-back chair under the window suggest the prior entry of the soldier into the domestic sphere. In the moment depicted, however, we see this open doorway more as exit than entryway. Here it is as though the opening created by the male intruder provides an egress for the housewife. While the breaching of domestic boundaries usually is depicted in terms of the desecration of virginal purity, in this scene we see that the crossing of boundaries can disrupt domestic constraints in ways that are potentially liberating rather than damaging. Here, the home is not a separate and sealed sanctum closed to a potentially polluting world. Home and state, or private and public, are not pictured as two opposite and antagonistic spheres. Rather, they are joined together—architecturally by the arched opening, and metaphorically by the alliance between housewife and soldier, private subject and public power.

Indeed, as Helgerson argues in *Adulterous Alliances,* the new domestic genres that proliferated at this time treated the domestic sphere with "unaccustomed seriousness and sympathy," putting the home into a significant and signifying narrative relation with the state—an adulterous alliance that indicates the growing importance of private life in the definition of the polity.[33] Dutch genre paintings, he argues, do this kind of work. Hung almost exclusively in the domestic interior, genre scenes had the potential to transform this space by explicitly interrogating the home and its boundaries, opening the space itself up to debate. In this way, they publicize the home in innovative ways that draw attention to the very interconnectedness of the private and public spheres. Framed genre paintings often play on their likeness to framed doorways or windows. They occupy the same symbolic space at the threshold of the domestic realm, a point of interface that both separates and joins it to the world outside of the home. If, following from the art treatises, we see the peaceful soldier as painter, then it follows that the medium of painting itself also acts as intermediary between the public and private spheres. In this way, paintings that seem intractable to history actually operate as historical agents.

Helgerson shows us how genre paintings of seemingly mundane subjects could bring public concerns—political, military, and civic matters—into the home. This process, I argue, is not pictured as a violent invasion. History painting, the preferred genre of state power, produced multiple images of the forceful subjection of female bodies to violent male soldiers. Genre paintings—pictures made of and for the domestic interior—consciously alter this well-established pictorial tradition by wittily replacing violation with conversation. The brutal soldier and the victim-ized woman become the peaceful soldier and the enigmatic woman. With this strikingly new motif of intercourse between a soldier and a woman, these self-aware paintings signal their own capacity to bring about a new kind of reciprocity between public and private life. Above all, these images of intercourse indicate the potential of genre painting to enter and thus transform the private realm into a new type of public space where matters of concern—like the merits of the True Freedom—could be subjected to explicit analysis by private people in their own homes.

Exhibit C. Council Chamber of the Burgomasters in the Amsterdam Town Hall. De Hooch explores another aspect of this process in a related paint-ing of the interior of the Town Hall (fig. 6.3). This painting depicts the Burgomaster's Chamber, a room that was open to private people when meetings were not in session. The chamber is hung with two very large history paintings, one at either end. The work that is partly visible be-hind the large draped curtain in De Hooch's rendering is Ferdinand Bol's painting of the incorruptible Roman consul Fabritius, who would not be threatened or frightened by a monstrous elephant into accepting bribes from the corrupt King Pyrrhus. The soldier and man and woman in the foreground of De Hooch's painting look up at a complementary work that hangs on the facing wall. The viewer cannot see this painting but would likely know that it is Govert Flinck's depiction of the incorruptibility of the consul Marcus Curius Dentatus, who turned down a rich inducement in favor of a simple and honest meal of root vegetables. Both are text-based paintings, derived from historical accounts extolling the virtues that every good burgomaster and citizen should possess. They are not terribly enig-matic, but even so, the Dutch poet and playwright Joost van den Vondel was commissioned to compose an explanatory poem. His interpretation of the Flinck painting runs as follows:

> During the watch of the burgomasters, Rome sleeps in safety
> As Marcus Curius refuses the proffered gold
> And is satisfied with a meal of turnips.
> Thus is the city built through moderation and faithfulness.[34]

These instructive verses clearly enforce the intended meaning of the work, concurrently closing off the possibilities of divergent interpretations.

In de Hooch's painting, small groups stand together as households and as citizens to discuss these edifying history paintings. Notable is the cen-tral male figure dressed in black, who gestures toward Flinck's work. The

FIGURE 6.3. Pieter de Hooch, *The Interior of the Burgomaster's Council Chamber*, ca. 1665. Oil on canvas, 112.5 x 99 cm. (Copyright Museo Thyssen-Bornemisza, Madrid).

absent householder of genre scenes seems quite at home in this civic space explaining history painting to his female companion. Her body is placed in front of the doubled openings of a background doorway and window; her covered head, silhouetted against the window, is precisely at a point of overlap between the door and window frames. Intriguingly, these architectural elements do not conform to the actual space, for this door does not actually open into the bright corridor depicted here, but into a small windowless alcove.[35] The fictional window balances the large windows at the right of the composition, where another woman stands between the open shutters and looks out toward the town square. The juxtaposition of these female figures with conspicuous openings seems to call attention to the entry of women into civic life. The new Town Hall created something that was quite unusual in the Dutch Republic, and this is what De Hooch highlights: the interior doubled as an exhibition space, where a broad segment of the general public could come together to view and talk about the political meanings of publicly commissioned works of art.[36]

In light of this, what do we make of the soldier who stands prominently in the foreground and gazes up at Flinck's painting? Is he a threat to the True Freedom or an ideal citizen and supporter of the Amsterdam government? Is he the peaceful soldier/viewer of the art treatises, who attempts to penetrate the painting he views in order to capture its meaning? If so, does he internalize or contest the republican values it imposes? It is, of course, impossible to know. This enigmatic soldier indicates how genre paintings function: their characteristic ambiguity suggests multiple possible meanings for their viewers to decipher.

Indeed, as a genre painting of people viewing history paintings, de Hooch's image of the burgomaster's chamber calls attention to the very different viewing practices that different types of paintings solicit. The didactic gesture of the central male householder who explicates Flinck's history painting resonates with Čapek's assertion that Dutch realism differed from history painting because it "was not painted for galleries where people walk about, but for rooms where they sit down. . . . Nobody can preach sitting down; all he can do is talk" (see fig. 6.1). The difference Čapek highlights—the contrast between standing and lecturing about a history painting or sitting and talking about a genre painting—is central to my argument. Genre images of soldiers and enigmatic girls do not preach a single political or moral doctrine; they are conversation pieces. In this way, they transform the home into a discursive realm and thus a new kind of public realm.

Notably, such works were not specially commissioned to serve public authorities who traditionally interpreted matters of common concern, like civic virtues, for the people in public representations like the history paintings displayed in the Town Hall.[37] Genre paintings did not directly serve the interests of politics in this way. Sold on the market, these were not custom-made works, like the Town Hall paintings, in service to the ideologies of Republican government. Breaking from traditional patronage patterns, genre painting, as Fromentin asserted, "released itself from the *obligations* of history."[38] The genre painter's successful participation in public life depended on the skill and ambition required to attract, or even seduce, an audience in an open-market situation. In this way, the painter was no longer an adjunct of public authorities but became a public figure in his own right.[39] It is this new social role that self-aware paintings of painter/soldiers highlight. Paradoxically, the act of painting history from below served to elevate the public status of the genre painter.

By creating works of art that functioned independently of prior structures of authority, the painter engaged in new forms of publicity that generated what Habermas famously identified as a new phase of the public sphere constituted by discussion and debate among private householders and their families. Self-awareness was a crucial part of this process. Habermas writes of the formation of a public sphere "within which the subjectivity originating in the interiority of the conjugal family, by communicating with itself, attained clarity about itself."[40] For Habermas, this new self-criticality takes the form of rational-critical debate. Helgerson, by contrast, importantly highlights the pleasures offered by the aesthetic realm of painting, wherein the forces of ambiguity and anxiety are equally at play, and where the conjugal family may never attain complete clarity while pondering its own enigma.

As relatively inexpensive market commodities, genre paintings entered homes, thus allowing private people to enter into public debates through discussion of their open-ended and anxiously pleasurable connotations. It is in this manner, as Helgerson recognized, that the conflicts of history and politics lurked close to the edges of genre paintings, just waiting to be read into them by viewers with potentially divergent interpretations. Indeed, it is the viewer who completes such paintings, for the multiple meanings of these enigmatic works are created by the interpretive strategies of their beholders.

This creative process of interpretation is especially powerful when considered in light of the intense divisiveness caused by the Dutch Republic's internal political conflicts, which at times brought it to the brink of civil war, as in 1650. The seventeenth century was anything but a long peaceful Sunday afternoon. Though some householders were defenders of the States' True Freedom, many were staunch supporters of the House of Orange. Others may have held conflicting loyalties. The paintings do not overtly uphold one type of political formation over another. In practical terms, genre painters did not tend to limit their potential market in this way. Instead, they created alluringly ambiguous works that appealed to a wide range of buyers with varying political, social, and religious affiliations.

Not only did this make painters astute businessmen, it also made them good citizens who, as van Bleyswijk pointed out, made significant contributions to public life. Cultural historians recently have argued that during the political crisis that followed the events of 1650, the Dutch Republic was held together by a vibrant *discussiecultuur,* which served as a fundamental means to manage the many tensions that threatened to divide this diverse society. A culture of discussion was generated by the widespread circulation of various media, which allowed people to deliberate crucial political issues, including what form of new structure sovereignty should take. In other words, sovereign authority was no longer tacitly accepted by the subjects of the state but was scrutinized and debated by them. As we have seen, the imagery of soldiers and enigmatic girls that proliferated at this time had the potential to generate this kind of interrogation. Thus we should consider the functions of genre paintings within the broader cultural context of *discussiecultuur,* a new forum of public life in which such debates among private people became a predominant means to negotiate political conflicts and thereby to avoid violence and war.[41]

In this context, the making, viewing, and discussion of enigmatic paintings had the potential to transform both painters and beholders into peaceful soldiers engaged in conversation instead of physical violence. Richard Helgerson's important work on genre painting points us in this direction, shifting the interpretation from elusive meanings to broader social functions by indicating how this medium could foster new ways for private people, including women, to engage with national affairs and thus enter the public sphere. History and politics are not evacuated from Dutch genre scenes, and Helgerson's questioning of this assumption makes us see how such paintings allowed people to sit down in their homes and work through the dangers and pleasures of divisive historical conflicts, in the process developing new ways to do politics.

NOTES

Thank you to Paul Yachnin for inviting me to write this paper, and to the members of the Making Publics research team, especially Shankar Raman and our wonderfully generous summer seminarians, for all of their astute insights and suggestions. Thanks also to Rebecca Zorach for her response paper, which critically addressed an earlier version of this paper presented at the 2011 American Historical Association annual meeting. The epigraph is from Lawrence Gowing, *Vermeer* (1952; repr., London: Gilles de la Mare, 1997), 24.

1. For Théophile Thoré, see W. Bürger [pseud.], *Musées de la Hollande* (Paris: Renouard, 1858–60), 2:xv.

2. G. W. F. Hegel, *Aesthetics: Lectures on Fine Art,* trans. T. M. Knox (Oxford: Clarendon Press, 1975), 2:885–87.

3. Richard Helgerson, "Soldiers and Enigmatic Girls," in *Adulterous Alliances: Home, State and History in Early Modern European Drama and Painting* (Chicago: University of Chicago Press, 2000), 79–119.

4. Gowing, *Vermeer,* 48.

5. G. W. F. Hegel, *The Philosophy of Fine Art,* trans. with notes by F. P. B. Osmaston (London: G. Bell, 1916–1920), 2:383.

6. Herbert H. Rowen, *The Princes of Orange: The Stadholders in the Dutch Republic* (Cambridge: Cambridge University Press, 1988), 41–42.

7. Helgerson, *Adulterous Alliances,* 85, 95.

8. Karel Čapek, *Letters from Holland,* trans. Paul Selver (London: Faber & Faber, 1933), 77–79.

9. Helgerson, *Adulterous Alliances,* 110.

10. Ibid., 105. He draws evidence from Dutch political pamphlets, theater plays and history paintings to substantiate this claim. An important article that explores the sexual politics of history painting is Margaret D. Carroll, "The Erotics of Absolutism: Rubens and the Mystification of Sexual Violence," *Representations* 25 (Winter 1989): 3–30.

11. Eugène Fromentin, *The Old Masters of Belgium and Holland,* trans. Mary C. Robbins (1876; repr., New York: Schocken Books, 1963), 130.

12. Ibid., 131.

13. Ibid., 134.

14. Joshua Reynolds, *A Journey to Flanders and Holland,* ed. Harry Mount (Cambridge: Cambridge University Press, 1996), 83.

15. Ibid., 107.

16. Hegel, *Philosophy of Fine Art,* 2:385.

17. Svetlana Alpers, *The Art of Describing: Dutch Art in the Seventeenth Century* (Chicago: University of Chicago Press, 1983), 1.

18. I. Q. van Regteren Altena, "The Drawings by Pieter Saenredam," in *Catalogue Raisonné of the Works of Pieter Jansz Saenredam* (exh. cat., Centraal Museum, Utrecht, 1961), 18.

19. Eugène Fromentin, *The Masters of Past Time: Dutch and Flemish Painting from van Eyck to Rembrandt* (1876; repr., London: Phaidon Press, 1948), 107. This passage is discussed in Svetlana Alpers, *The Vexations of Art: Velázquez and Others* (New Haven, Conn.: Yale University Press, 2005), 86, 95.

20. Helgerson, *Adulterous Alliances,* 112, 114.

21. Ann Jensen Adams, "Money and the Regulation of Desire: The Prostitute and the Marketplace in Seventeenth-Century Holland," in *Renaissance Culture and the Everyday,* ed. Patricia Fumerton and Simon Hunt (Philadelphia: University of Pennsylvania Press, 1999), 232.

22. Helgerson, *Adulterous Alliances,* 84.

23. Ibid., 103.

24. Eric Jan Sluijter, "Introduction: 'With the Power of the Seemingly Real We Must Conquer and Capture the Eyes of Art Lovers,'" in *Seductress of Sight. Studies in Dutch Art of the Golden Age,* trans. Jennifer Kilian and Katy Kist (Zwolle: Waanders, 2000), 13.

25. Samuel van Hoogstraten, *Inleyding tot de Hooge Schoole der Schilderkonst* (1678; repr., Doornspijk: Davaco, 1969). Karel van Mander often used sexual terms to describe the optical penetration of a picture by desiring eyes in *The Lives of the Illustrious Netherlandish and German Painters, from the First Edition of the Schilderboek (1603–1604),* ed. and trans. Hessel Miedema (Doornspijk: Davaco, 1994). Philips Angel argued that pleasing the art lover's eye was the primary function of painting. Philips Angel, "Praise of Painting," intro. and ed. Hessel Miedema, trans. Michael Hoyle, *Simiolus* 24.2–3 (1996): 227–58. On these commentators, see Walter Melion, *Shaping the Netherlandish Canon: Karel van Mander's Schilder-boeck* (Chicago: University of Chicago Press, 1991), 8; Eric Jan Sluijter, *De Lof der Schilderkunst. Over schilderijen van Gerrit Dou (1613–1675) en een Traktaat van Philips Angel uit 1642* (Hilversum: Verloren, 1993); and Celeste Brusati, *Artifice and Illusion: The Art and Writing of Samuel van Hoogstraten* (Chicago: University of Chicago Press, 1995), 232.

26. See Eric Jan Sluijter, "On *Fijnschilders* and 'Meaning,'" in *Seductress of Sight,* 265–95.

27. On the trope of the artist as soldier in art handbooks, see Brusati, *Artifice and Illusion,* 230; also Svetlana Alpers, *The Vexations of Art,* 104.

28. Gowing, *Vermeer,* 54, 66.

29. Helgerson, *Adulterous Alliances,* 105.

30. "De Krijgs-helden en Constenaren sijn ingelijcr door hare daden en wercken befaemt / maer d'eere die haer Vaderlijke Stadt wegens dese alle mede-deelt en geniet / . . . Nu sal den lof van d'een en d'ander des te bestendiger in wesen blijven en voor de kancker der vergetenheyt des te seeckereder bewaert zijn." Dirck van Bleyswijck, *Vervolg van de Beschryvinge der Stadt Delft . . .* (Delft: Arnold Bon, 1667), 860.

31. Helgerson, *Adulterous Alliances,* 4.

32. There is much written about this. Two key art historical studies are: Elizabeth Honig, "The Space of Gender in Seventeenth-Century Dutch Painting," in *Looking at Seventeenth-Century Dutch Art,* ed. Wayne Franits (Cambridge: Cambridge University Press, 1997), 187–201, 240–44; and Martha Hollander, *An Entrance for the Eyes: Space and Meaning in Seventeenth-century Dutch Art* (Berkeley: University of California Press, 2002).

33. Helgerson, *Adulterous Alliances,* 3, 6.

34. Op de wacht van de burgemeesters mag Rome veilig slapen
Als Marcus Curius het aangeboden goud afslaat,
En zich tevreden stelt met een gerecht van rapen.
Zo wordt door Matigheid en Trouw de stad gebouwd.

35. Hollander, *An Entrance for the Eyes,* 194.

36. The increased participation of middle-class women in political opinion and discussion culture was notable in this period. See Willem Frijhoff and Marijke Spies, *1650: Hard-Won Unity. Dutch Culture in a European Perspective* (Assen: Royal Van Gorcum; New York: Palgrave Macmillan, 2004), 1:223. On the Town Hall, see Katharine Fremantle, *The Baroque Town Hall of Amsterdam,* Orbis ertium; Utrechtse kunsthistorische studien, 4 (Utrecht: Haentjens Dekker & Gumbert, 1959).

37. Jürgen Habermas, *The Structural Transformation of the Public Sphere. An Inquiry into a Category of Bourgeois Society,* trans. Thomas Burger (Cambridge: MIT Press, 1994), 37.

38. Fromentin, *The Old Masters,* 125 (emphasis added).

39. Leo Braudy, *The Frenzy of Renown: Fame and Its History* (Oxford: Oxford University Press, 1986), 330.

40. Habermas, *The Structural Transformation,* 51. See also 7–19.

41. See Frijhoff and Spies, *1650: Hard-Won Unity,* esp. 49–50, 220–25; and the essays in *Public Opinion and Changing Identities in the Early Modern Netherlands. Essays in Honour of Alistair Duke,* ed. Judith Pollman and Andrew Spicer (Leiden: Brill, 2007).

CHAPTER SEVEN

Sonnets from Carthage, Ballads from Prison

Entertainment and Public Making in Early Modern Spain

JAVIER CASTRO-IBASETA

SPANISH poetry of the Golden Age underwent two momentous transformations in a short period of time. Each was quite different in nature
but both were equally decisive in the evolution of modern Spanish and
European literatures. The first shook the literary field between around 1530
and 1550; the second began a few decades later, around 1580. In his last
two books, *Adulterous Alliances* (2000) and *A Sonnet from Carthage* (2007),
Richard Helgerson situated these two transformations in their wider European contexts. *Adulterous Alliances* studied the novel representations
of nonaristocratic households in the late Renaissance. In its fifth chapter
("The Liberty of Spanish Towns"), he analyzed the representation of peasant households in the *comedia nueva,* a new formula of commercial theater
that, from the 1580s on, rose to dominate the Spanish stage. Lope de Vega's
Fuente Ovejuna (ca. 1615) thus found its context among English plays such
as *Arden of Faversham* (ca. 1590), as well as among Dutch domestic paintings of the mid-seventeenth century. Helgerson's second systematic approach to Spanish literature, and his last book, *A Sonnet from Carthage,*
was originally conceived as one chapter of an ambitious monograph that
would have been dedicated to the spread in Renaissance Europe of the
new (Italianate) poetry. He dedicated the entire book to Garcilaso de la
Vega's Sonnet no. 33—"To Boscán, from La Goleta" (1535)—as exemplary
of "the deepest ambitions, longings, reservations, affections, jealousies,
disillusionments, and interdependencies that had shaped the new poetry
wherever it appeared."[1]

In this chapter I wish to add a layer to Helgerson's analyses, considering those two poetic transformations from the perspective of "public

making"—that is, "the active creation of new forms of association that allowed people to connect with others in ways not rooted in family, rank, or
vocation, but rather founded in voluntary groupings built on the shared
interests, tastes, commitments, and desires of individuals."[2] How did these
two literary revolutions affect traditional collective identities and shape
forms of association in early modern Spain? It is in discussing this question that this chapter is a contribution to the theory of the Making Publics
project. Helgerson became deeply involved in that project during its early
phase (2005–7). He collaborated decisively in the creation of transhistorically usable ideas about "publics" and "public making." Unfortunately, he
did not have the chance to incorporate all this insightful thought into his
own published work. Thus, in a sense this chapter is also a tribute to Helgerson's scholarship, exploring the directions in which the idea of making
publics might have taken his work.

Around the year 1530, two relatively young Spanish noblemen, the Catalan
Joan Boscà (usually Castilianized as Juan Boscán, ca. 1490–1542) and his
friend, the Castilian Garcilaso de la Vega (ca. 1498–1536), began to experiment with a new poetic style based on Italian Renaissance poetry. One of
their novelties was the appropriation into Spanish of the hendecasyllabic
meter and the displacement of the Spanish traditional octosyllable. After
the initial surprise, and not before having to overcome some resistance,
the new metric began to be adopted by many Spanish poets. Soon, almost
everyone who counted was writing in the new Petrarchan fashion. By the
1550s, the new poetry's success among learned poets was so overwhelming that it had almost reduced traditional metric to the margins of folk,
popular, or burlesque literature. The sonnet—until just a few years before
a foreign and exotic form—soon became the measure of all poetry.[3]

    Helgerson chose a 1535 sonnet as representative of the form. In that
year, the soldier and poet Garcilaso de la Vega had followed his lord, the
Emperor Charles V, to a campaign against the city of Tunis. Wounded
in battle, he composed the sonnet while recovering. According to Helgerson, the convalescent poet intuitively resorted to his knowledge of the
classics in order to make sense of his experience in Africa. Tunis did not
manifest itself to the poet as either a den of Moorish pirates or a site
of crusading warfare. Instead, in his eyes the city recovered its ancient
identity: it was Carthage. The sonnet was a remembrance of Virgil and
the Roman Empire and an evocation of Dido. In the Italianate manner,
Garcilaso invoked the classical past in order to celebrate the rebirth of the
Roman Empire while at the same time casting doubts on its legitimacy—

an ambiguity that, in Helgerson's interpretation, was the constitutive dialectic of the new poetry, which he saw as being stretched between the erotic and the political poles.[4]

The second literary revolution began a few decades later, in the early 1580s, when a new group of young and anonymous but accomplished poets began to experiment with what—especially after Garcilaso—were considered minor forms of the traditional octosyllabic poetry, and to alternate the writing of Italianate poetry with that of *romances,* the Spanish equivalent of the English folk ballad. Although these young poets—artists like Lope de Vega (1562–1635) and Luis de Góngora (1561–1627)—were equally skilled in both registers, it was their *romances* that first made them famous. Traditionally transmitted orally, the old medieval *romances* found their way to the printing press during the sixteenth century, first as broadsheets and, from the 1550s on, collected in books called *romanceros.* These *romances,* commonly sold and sung in public by blind singers, were an extremely popular form of poetry, especially among the urban lower classes, low-ranking soldiers, and so forth. Their structure was quite simple, consisting of long series of octosyllabic verses with all the even lines rhyming. It was this vulgar but charming kind of poetry that the new generation of authors began to exploit and adapt.[5]

Helgerson thought that Garcilaso's Sonnet no. 33 could be used to represent the entire movement of the new poetry. It seems much more difficult to find a single *romance* that exemplifies the second literary transformation, but to illustrate the extent to which the new forms could depart from the standards of the earlier poetry we may compare Garcilaso's sonnet from Carthage with a famous *jácara*: Escarramán's love ballad from prison. *Jácaras* were comic *romances* featuring outlaws or *jaques* (hence the name of the genre), typically represented in love with their partners—usually prostitutes—in a parody and inversion of the Petrarchan conventions.

Escarramán's love letter—written in 1605 by Francisco de Quevedo (1580–1645), a poet who followed in the footsteps of Lope and Góngora—and his lover's reply to it are considered the first in the genre.[6] Escarramán is a thief awaiting the carrying out of his sentence in the prison of Seville. The ballad is a love letter he writes to his syphilitic lover, a prostitute called "la Méndez," after he has been publicly flogged and just before he is sent as a slave rower to the king's galleys. The rogue describes his hardships and asks his lover for money. In a second letter, la Méndez replies from a hospital in Toledo with discouraging news about the gang and herself and refuses to send him money. Both poems are written in a burlesque manner, exploiting pun after pun, sparking laughter from the reader as he hears of the grotesque couple's misfortunes while deciphering the obscure *germanía*—the slang of the Spanish underworld—in which the poems were written. Escarramán's letter began its circulation in manuscript and oral form around 1603–5. It probably became popular in the public playhouses when it was performed by theatrical companies as a comic interlude during the intermissions of the main play. By 1613 it was already so famous that someone decided to print it in a broadsheet for the cheap-print market. Its popularity soon led to a series of imitations, thus initiating the new poetic subgenre of the *jácaras*.[7]

Despite their apparently striking differences, Garcilaso's lyric poetry and Quevedo's *jácaras* had important similarities, as the latter were not intended to be truthful descriptions of the underworld but encrypted representations of real courtly love affairs. Quevedo's friend and editor, José González de Salas, commented how at least some of the *jácaras* "concealed the courting of great lords and celebrated the beauty of excellent ladies," which explained their use of "some polished terms and idioms" otherwise inappropriate to the voices of these rogues.[8] The *jácaras* are thus best understood in their origin as ironic inversions of the classic tropes of courtly love and as grotesque exaggerations of the logic of the pastoral genre. If noble lovers could be represented in the guise of shepherds, why couldn't they also take the shape of crooks and prostitutes? It was no satire: it was celebratory playfulness.

But this grotesque celebration of aristocratic gallantry implied a profound change of paradigm from the one established by Garcilaso and Boscán. The elements of the new poetry as exemplified by Garcilaso's sonnet (the mixture of epic, melancholy, love lyricism and courtly but unaffected rhetoric) appear in the *jácara* inverted and deformed. Escarramán and Garcilaso's poetic personae coincided in seeing war and empire as obstacles to love, but the ways in which they experienced both love and empire were quite different. They lived imperial warfare from asymmetric positions: Garcilaso had reached Tunis in a galley rowed by dozens of "Escarramanes," and while the soldier-poet could at least dream of eternal glory, the most common fate of a galley slave was infamous death. As for the lyricism, nothing could be as far from the piercing allusions to love in Garcilaso's sonnet as the selfish and grotesque relationship between Escarramán and his harlot. The *jácaras* were an extreme form of the *romance*—extreme in their recourse to the low and plebeian, for example—and therefore not an entirely typical expression of the genre. Other *romances*, although folksy, were not necessarily vulgar. Nevertheless, the contrast between Garcilaso's sonnet from Carthage and Quevedo's ballad from prison—both expressions of courtly love—illustrates the transformation of paradigms from one poetic revolution to the other.

Boscán and Garcilaso explicitly presented their innovation as "grave and artful" in contrast to traditional octosyllabic verses (*coplas,* as they called them), which were seen as childish and unworthy.[9] The couple's attack on traditional Castilian poetry was part of a wider (and hysterical) rejection of Spanish letters in general that made Garcilaso famously exclaim: "I do not know what plagues us that hardly anyone has written anything in our tongue except what we could easily have done without."[10] In their battle to transform Spanish letters, Garcilaso and Boscán adopted Baldassare Castiglione's ideal of *sprezzatura*—that "certain nonchalance so as to conceal all art and make whatever is done or said appear to be without effort and almost without any thought about it."[11] Boscán's own translation of Castiglione's *Book of the Courtier* was, according to Garcilaso, the first example of *sprezzatura* in Spanish prose, "avoiding affectation without lapsing into dryness."[12] The long periods of hendecasyllabic poetry achieved a parallel effect of *sprezzatura* by hiding poetic artificiality under the appearance of gracious but prosaic, conversational language—at least that is how the new poetry sounded to the ears of those accustomed to the faster and more obvious rhythms of traditional octosyllabic poetry: many complained that in the Italianate poetry "the rhymes are not as apparent, nor resound as much, as in the Castilian."[13]

The shift from the *coplas* to the new poetry was thus seen as a progression from childish unpolished jesting to the prestigious gravity of unaffected courtliness. To Boscán and Garcilaso, the need for this evolution appeared all the more urgent in the context of 1527–30, when they first conceived of the possibility of imitating Italian poetic forms. Those were the years when many Spaniards thought that the emperor would move his court to Italy, maybe permanently. People like Boscán, Garcilaso, and their patron, the duke of Alba, were willing to follow Charles but feared the prospect of having to compete with Italian courtiers in their own country for the emperor's favor. To this vanguard group of Spanish courtiers prepared to abandon Spain for Italy in the trail of their emperor, Boscán and Garcilaso proposed imitating Italian cultural idioms in order to compete with the prestige of Italian courtiers.[14]

The nature and context of Boscán and Garcilaso's project is thus relatively easy to ascertain; explaining the revival of the *romancero* and the wide success of Quevedo's *jácara* is much more complicated. In order to provide an adequate account, we first need to situate this revival in the context of a larger and revolutionary literary transformation. In the short period between 1580 and 1610 a whole host of new genres appeared or reached maturity, of which the new *romance* was just one among many. If around 1580 Lope de Vega and Góngora began to experiment with the *romancero* (creating the "romancero nuevo"), just a decade later the same Lope "invented" a successful formula to create commercial theater: the "comedia nueva." In the sphere of prose, Mateo Alemán revolutionized the novel with the reinvention of the picaresque in the first part of his *Guzmán de Alfarache* (1599), an influential book that—among many other responses—prompted Cervantes to write what is arguably the culmination of this momentous literary transformation: *Don Quixote* (1605–15). All these "new" genres and forms—from poetry to theater, from verse to prose—seem so diverse that each one requires a separate analysis. However, the common elements of the emergence of the new genres—their proximity in time (they all appeared within roughly thirty years) or the coincidence of some key names (Lope)—point to the need for a unified approach. One of the things these new genres had in common was their systematic problematization of the strict barrier that Garcilaso and Boscán had erected between courtly and popular literature. Another was their connection with an effervescent literary market.

The market is a crucial element if we are to understand the 1580s poetic revolution, and I will come back to it. But before that, and in order to see the issue in its broadest scope, we need to address these two poetic paradigms from a "making publics" perspective, beginning with an obvious question: Who was the literary audience in each case?

Helgerson masterfully described the social environment in which the "new Spanish poetry" of the 1530s took root. Garcilaso's was poetry created by and for a restricted group of noblemen who could address one another personally in terms of friendship and service.[15] Boscán and Garcilaso aspired to refashion the small and elitist milieu of the Spanish court nobility, not to create it anew or to alter its social constitution. On the contrary, they were rather conservative: in order to fashion the new courtiers, they stressed even more the cultural barrier that separated them from the plebs. Octosyllabic poetry was to be avoided by the nobles because it was dangerously close to folk verse.[16] Garcilaso and Boscán did not want to create a new social group but to transform an old one. Their project presumed the preexistence of a community of peers, and their poetry simply addressed that community. If by public making we understand the creation of new forms of association and identity, we must conclude that Garcilaso and Boscán were not involved in any kind of public-making activity.

The exact reader of the new forms produced from 1580 onward is, by contrast, much more difficult to establish. Who formed the audience of the new *romances,* the new *comedia,* or the new novelistic prose? Nothing as discernible as the Garcilasian courtier stands out. Nobles read it, but so did merchants, craftsmen, peasants, priests, and so forth. Lope's and Góngora's *romances* can be found in manuscript volumes in the libraries of private collectors (often noblemen) but also in affordable printed books that the urban middle classes could buy and in cheap printed broadsheets sold by blind men at the city corners. They circulated orally in the court and literary circles but were also sung in the public playhouses and the streets. The same can be said about Quevedo's *jácaras.* Escarramán's letter was very probably, in the beginning, a private joke among courtiers, a burlesque description of a secret gallant adventure. But it soon found its way to a wider audience in the public theaters and in printed broadsheets sold in the streets. Clearly, we cannot take for granted the audiences of the second literary revolution the same way we can for the first one. In order to understand the literary earthquake of the late sixteenth century, an inquiry into terms of "public making" is not only fitting but crucial.

This may have been Helgerson's intuition, too, when in the introduction to *Adulterous Alliances* he drafted an audience-based explanation of the book's central problem (the dignifying of nonaristocratic households in many early modern cultural productions):

> Why were stories of the nonaristocratic home and its sexual disruption, stories that regard the home with an unaccustomed seriousness and sympathy, so frequently told at just this time and in just these places? An obvious answer would be the increasing influence among consumers of drama and painting of people like those portrayed: town-dwellers of middling status and significant means. But this sociological explanation, appealing as it is, cannot be made to fit a good part of the evidence. Certainly all these works were the product of newly established or newly invigorated commercial sites [among these Helgerson included the Dutch market for paintings and the public theaters of England, Spain, and France]. . . . Without these new sites neither the plays nor the paintings would exist. But the fit I was expecting is not to be found—at least not consistently.[17]

According to Helgerson, "the new commercial patrons and the stories they paid to see only sporadically mirror[ed] one another." For example, the audience of Heywood's *Edward IV* "shared roughly the status of those whose home is disrupted in the play." But one cannot account in the same manner for the interest of the Spanish audiences of Lope's *Fuente Ovejuna:* "Whatever audience demand helped produce Spanish peasant drama, it did not come from peasants themselves."[18]

Helgerson thus rejected a narrow *sociological,* audience-based thesis and elaborated an *ideological* one instead. He interpreted the mysterious dignifying of nonaristocratic households as an expression of anti-absolutist ideals, with the nonaristocratic households (bourgeois and peasant alike) as the symbol and "site" of premodern corporate constitutionalism.[19] Helgerson saw the political ideology, not the audience's social identity, as the explanatory key.

But, as the above quotation shows, when Helgerson wrote *Adulterous Alliances* he was thinking of early modern theatrical audiences in terms of class—that is, as a physical coalescence of a preexisting group distinguished by its socioeconomic identity. He saw playhouse audiences as instances of the rising bourgeoisie: "town-dwellers of middling status and significant means," "consumers of drama and painting."[20] Helgerson assumed that, while in the theater, the bourgeois spectator kept his preexisting social identity intact: he attended the playhouse and enjoyed the play *as a bourgeois;* and therefore with a peasant character all he could establish was an ideological tie, never a true social identity (association).

In order to tackle the problem from a making-publics perspective, we first need to acknowledge that classes, audiences, and publics, although interconnected, are very different kinds of entities.[21] A *class* is a group of people bound together by a strong social identity. (Other similarly robust social identities are nations, confessions, etc.; sociologists sometimes call these kinds of associations *communities.*) An *audience* is a group of people who, aside from sharing the circumstance of consuming the same cultural product (a book, a show, etc.), are otherwise unconnected. In contrast, one can *simultaneously* be a member of a community and a member of an audience, for those two commitments do not interfere with one another; in fact, "commitment" is too strong a concept to be applied to the idea of an audience. An audience lacks social identity; it is basically passive and accidental and does not demand anything from its members.

A *public* stands somewhere between a community and an audience. Like an audience, it is centered around a cultural good. But a public is not as weak or accidental as an audience is. A public comes into being precisely when partaking in a cultural interest creates a certain bond among the members of an audience—a bond that is then not all that easily broken. Therefore, unlike an audience and more like a community, a public has some kind of identity as a social group. It implies some active (rather than passive) engagement both with the cultural activity and with other members of the public. On the one hand, being a member of a public implies some commitments; but on the other hand, the commitments and demands that a public imposes upon its members are limited. Unlike the members of a nation, a religion, or a class, who are often willing to sacrifice their lives for the good of the community, the idea of someone dying for the sake of a public is ridiculous. In any case, should it happen, a group that can demand such a strong sacrifice from its members is no longer a public: it has evolved into a community.

The existence of publics and audiences as different social creatures prevents us from making a priori judgments about collective aesthetic experiences. A close, empirical study of the process of reception and its effects on an audience's social identity is required before determining whether we are in front of an audience or of a public. Helgerson's imagined bourgeois spectator may well simply be a circumstantial playgoer, a member of an audience whose basic class identity is not challenged in the process (at least not fundamentally). But he also may have been absorbed into a *public-making* process, in which case his identity as a bourgeois is at stake and cannot be taken for granted (at least not entirely). In the first case, the bourgeois spectator stands among the audience *as a bourgeois.* In the second, he does so primarily *as a member of the play-going public* and only secondarily as a bourgeois.

Preexisting social identities of course affect the ways in which people interact with cultural objects, but we should never underestimate the degree to which art creates its own publics—publics whose members are *relatively* unencumbered by those preexisting social identities. Public making is the process through which people gathering around an artifact, a text, or a shared interest acquire, even if just momentarily, new social identities. According to Michael Warner, "a public is a space of discourse organized by nothing other than discourse itself. It is autotelic. . . . It exists *by virtue of being addressed.*" That is, as long as they are engaged in the public-making process, the members of a public are not primarily bourgeois, aristocrats, or Christians but members of *that* public.[22] "A public is poetic world making"[23]: by virtue of their aesthetic interest the bourgeois member of a public is, at least temporarily, liberated from his bourgeois identity and freed to explore new *social* (and not just *ideological*) bonds between him, the other members of the public, and even a peasant (or the representation of one).

We can now begin to understand some differences between Garcilaso's sonnet from Carthage and Quevedo's ballad from prison. Garcilaso wrote for his own social class, assuming its preexistence and knowing its exact boundaries. The poet was perfectly aware of who his audience was. He wrote for his peers about epic and lyric experiences proper to the court nobility. These readers, in turn, could easily identify themselves with the heroes of the poems (the abandoned lover, the valiant knight, the melancholic shepherd). There were strong bonds of identity between author, reader, and character. Such identity "in literature" mirrored the strong social identity of the class to which they all belonged.

All that transparent equivalence suddenly disappears, however, when we consider the new literary genres and forms that appeared between 1580 and 1610. On the one hand, the new audiences were extremely heterogeneous. People of different social groups (nobles, priests, artisans, commoners, etc.) consumed and enjoyed the same novels, plays, *jácaras,* and *romances.* On the other hand, the distance between readers' preferences and literary characters was usually considerable: the courtiers, for example, were fascinated by picaresque stories about rogues and outlaws; urban populations enjoyed plays about peasants; and peasants enjoyed stories about knights and kings. It is impossible to reduce the audiences of these genres to a preexisting group such as a rank, class, or confession. This fact often serves as circumstantial evidence of a public-making process and, as I shall argue, there was indeed one such process involved in the emergence of these new genres. At the center of that process was the literary market.

By the late sixteenth century, Spain had one of the most developed literary markets in Europe. In response to the entertainment needs of a rapidly growing urban population, literature became a commodity. The rise of a market for literary products revolutionized the entire literary system. Like their English counterparts, many accomplished Spanish authors, unlucky in securing aristocratic or ecclesiastical patronage, decided to write for the market instead, which proved to be both challenging and liberating. Commercial writers were looked down on by other poets, but they were also freed from traditional constraints and conventions, and they rapidly learned to exploit this newly gained liberty in creative ways. Mixing high and low traditions, they invented new literary genres and formulas with which to satisfy a new and avid popular demand for entertainment. Among them were many excellent writers, and the average production for the market was of a remarkably high aesthetic quality: for example, many of the classics of early seventeenth-century European literature (Shakespeare's plays, Cervantes' novels) were texts produced for the popular market. All in all, it was a quite revolutionary process.[24]

But what mostly interests me here is not how the market altered the genre system or how it provoked the appearance of the professional writer but rather the ways in which the commodification of literature changed audiences' relationships to the poetic voice and fostered the emergence of new practices of reading (and listening to) poetry. As opposed to court-ly circles, whose exposure to literature was theoretically unmediated by money, urban audiences seeking entertainment had to pay for it—and although it often goes unsaid, the mediation of money affects an audience's approach to a text. The commodification of literature is a crucial episode in the history (and theory) of early modern publics.

In his analysis of Renaissance drama, Paul Yachnin has shown that "the early modern theater was where nobodies went to pretend that they were somebodies."[25] This is a wonderful description of the process through which theatrical public making created new identities. But it also suggests that the creation of those new social identities required the absence or suspension of preexisting ones: for truly, as Yachnin hints, only "nobod-ies" can become "somebodies." What this explanation lacks is an analysis of how the preexisting social identities were suspended in the first place, or of how the members of an early modern theatrical audience were trans-formed into "nobodies" in the first place—for in early modern Europe hardly anyone was a private person, a "nobody." On the contrary, most people had a public identity in which their being "somebody" consisted. Society was conceived as a "body politic" in which everyone had a political role, however small. Almost no one was a purely private person, for every-one was considered a distinct and necessary organ of the political body, each with its distinct public and political functions. In this regard there was no distinction between kings, nobles, or commoners: everyone was a necessary member of a hierarchically structured social body.

This social metaphor was given legal and practical existence through the idea of the community (*universitas*). Virtually everyone was a mem-ber of at least one community, and usually they belonged to more than one (the guild, the town, the third state, the realm, Christendom). Public identities in early modern Europe were solid and widespread. The vari-ous overlapping communities provided their members with strong "social selves" that they proudly represented in public. Even the dependents in a household were seen as members of a domestic body and given public visibility through the patriarchal head. Only outcasts and vagrants were truly "nobodies"—"private" people in the sense of being "deprived" of the protection of any community.[26]

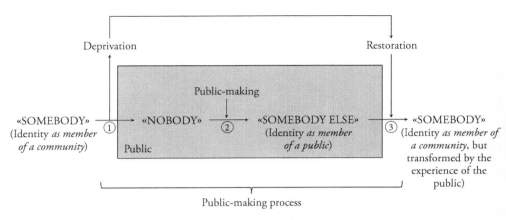

Figure 7.1. Diagram: public-making process. Graphics by author.

Most of the members of any early modern audience belonged to one or more communities and were thus social "somebodies," even if only of very local importance. In order for a process of theatrical public making to take place (that is, in order for audience members to form a public), the early modern spectator, were he an artisan or the king, had to be temporarily *deprived* of his social self. We can think of the whole process as being divided into three steps (fig. 7.1). A "somebody"—someone invested with a strong social identity, like a member of a guild or the king—entered a playhouse. If a process of theatrical public making was to take place, that person needed to undergo a *deprivation:* he had to dispense with his social self in order to become a "nobody" (step one). Only then could public making take place, temporarily transforming the person into a member of a public, a "somebody *else,*" by virtue of his association with other members of the theatrical public (step two). This association led to interactions among members of the public that had little to do with the ways in which they would have interacted outside of the theater (the king and the artisan could laugh *together*). The "somebody else" persona would of course be *affected* by the previous occurrences of his outside-the-theater social identity, but the overall experience of being part of a public would not be *determined* by those occurrences. Once back outside the theater, the spectator's original social identity would be restored (step three), only in some way it had now been affected by the experience of having been a member of a public. The old "somebody" had learned something from his having been "somebody else"; even though he still was the "old" somebody, there was something "new" about him.

Scholarship about publics tends to focus on steps two and three but does not say much about step one.[27] How did a "somebody" become a "nobody"?

"Poets wish either to profit or delight, or to say at the same time what is agreeable and convenient to life. . . . He who blends usefulness and sweetness, instructing and pleasing the reader in equal parts, wins every applause."[28] Thus Horace described the double function of poetry: to instruct and to please. Although he preferred them in combination—whence sprang the idea of poetry as sweet moral medicine—those two *moments* seemed to him separate enough that they could exist in isolation, implying that they operated at different levels. Horace's authority in Renaissance poetic theory was matched only by that of Aristotle, and his ideas are a good guide to the sixteenth and seventeenth centuries' notions about the workings of literature. But still today it is assumed that pleasure and doctrine are different aspects, perhaps coexisting but in fact demanding separate analysis. New historicism, for instance, focuses on the doctrinal, political moment of literature and neglects the pleasing aspects of poetry as more proper to the ahistorical, aestheticistic, formalistic approach—as if pleasure and entertainment did not require contextualization, or as if they were the nonsocial, inconsequential part of literature. But as I shall argue here, it is only by taking seriously and analyzing—both socially and historically—the pleasing moment of poetry that we shall be able to make sense of Renaissance public making.

The doctrinal and pleasing moments of literature are not essential qualities of the literary text itself but the effects of reading practices. They are basically different ways in which texts interact with their readers' identities. Pleasurable readings are instances of what Kant called *aesthetic judgment,* which requires that readers temporarily disregard their social interests.[29] Assuming that those interests are basically dictates of an individual's "social self," what Kant was asking from the aesthetic reader was that, while engaged with the text, he temporarily dispense with his social self. Conversely, a nonaesthetic approach to a text takes place when the reader approaches it invested in his social self, relating to the text in a manner mediated by his social interests. This approach generates a doctrinal, as opposed to pleasurable, reading of a text. (The classic example is that of a nobleman reading the *Iliad* in order to learn the aristocratic ethos; such a reading requires that he approach the poem invested in his "noble" persona.) Doctrinal instances of reading—either conservative or subversive—operate on the reader's social self, either to reinforce it (encouraging knights to be brave), to reflect upon its condition (problematizing bourgeois culture), or to metamorphose a given social self into a new one (transforming an artisan into a radical proletarian). Texts with a doctrinal vocation will openly or covertly invoke the reader's social self, addressing the knight *as* knight, the king *as* king, the peasant *as* peasant.

Garcilaso and Boscán conceived of their poetry as doctrinal, addressing their peers' courtly selves with the intention of securing their reproduction as a class in the midst of a political crisis. They expected a doctrinal reading on the part of their noble readers, who would approach the poems as aristocrats and not as aesthetes. On the contrary, Renaissance commercial theater aimed primarily to please the audience. Although every play included doctrinal moments designed to address the social selves of particular groups of spectators, the play as a whole—and commercial theater as a genre—invited its general audience to enjoy themselves, to make aesthetic judgments, to free themselves from the constraints of their social selves.[30] That is why Helgerson's attempt to identify a Renaissance theatrical audience with a class (the bourgeoisie) was ill-fated and had to be abandoned.

Thus, aesthetic pleasure and entertainment are the veritable foundations of public making. Pleasure and entertainment have the capacity to transform social selves into "nobodies," who then can associate freely in the form of publics. The *potential* political effect of a play like *Fuente Ovejuna* gets actualized not only directly, through doctrine and ideology, but also indirectly, by pleasing and through public making.

Commercial theater—and commercial literature of the late Renaissance in general—fostered public making by emphasizing the entertaining and aesthetic moment of literature over the doctrinal one. Theater and literature did so both directly and indirectly. Directly, because there was a conscious strategy to sell more, and commercial writers knew that their urban audiences demanded entertainment rather than education. Lope de Vega understood his own successful theatrical formula (the "new comedy") as a market strategy that disregarded the classical principles of poetics in order to please the *vulgo* (plebs, crowd). When his enemies attacked Lope because of the peculiar mixture of tragedy and comedy in his plays—thus opposing the Aristotelian rigid doctrinal barriers between the two genres and between the socially high and the socially low—he replied:

> I write according to the art invented
> By those who the vulgar applause pretended,
> For as it is the plebs (*vulgo*) who pay the content,
> We must speak foolishly to make them content (*gusto*).[31]

Gusto (content, delight, pleasure) was what justified the infringement of the Aristotelian principles, in a move to—very explicitly—sell more.[32]

Commercial literature also fostered entertaining public making indirectly because the writers did not know beforehand who would read their work. This moved them to evoke the figures of the *vulgo* and the "curious reader." Unlike courtly poets like Garcilaso, who knew exactly for whom he was writing, commercial playwrights like Lope could count on having a mixture of commoners, members of the Church, nobles, and even the royal family as potential spectators of his plays. He therefore could not address his audience by appealing to their social selves. Instead, he referred to all those who enjoyed his plays as *vulgo* regardless of their rank—and regardless, too, of the fact that among them he could count kings and nobles: in regard to theatrical spectatorship, all were part of the same crowd.

Commercial writers thus addressed their audiences as members of a public they called the *vulgo*. In the mind of the commercial authors, what characterized this public were the *vulgo*'s rejection of moral doctrine and the seeking of pure pleasure—*gusto* and entertainment. In the words of one of these new authors, Francisco López de Úbeda, "such is the inundation of weird plays and vain books, that it has suffocated any trace of holy mindfulness in the crowd." Entertainment and pleasure seem to have completely displaced doctrine, for which reason López de Úbeda decided to openly advertise his book as a "book of entertainment."[33]

If *vulgo* was the name for their audience as a collective, commercial authors used another term for the individual members. Ignoring the identity, status, and rank of the person who would be reading the book, they often addressed him by calling him "curious reader" (*curioso lector*), like the *pícaro* Guzmán did in the opening lines of his fictional autobiography.[34] But if *vulgo* meant the rejection of doctrine and the search for pleasure and entertainment, what did the expression "curious reader" imply?

The early modern period witnessed an explosion of curiosity, an attitude that extended from activities like traveling and collecting to scientific experimentation.[35] It also affected reading. (Curiosity in the realm of readership has still not received as much attention as it has in other fields, like science; other expressions of it, such as political curiosity, and the relationship between all these forms of the curious attitude, also await exploration.) In response to this proliferation of curiosity and curious people, the meaning and connotations of the words "curious" and "curiosity" changed over the course of the first half of the seventeenth century, at least in Spain.

In his *Tesoro de la lengua castellana* (1611), Sebastián de Covarrubias offered the following definition: "Curious. The person who deals with something with especial care and solicitude." According to Covarrubias, "curious" derived from the Latin *curiosus* and this from *cura,* or care. The term therefore had a positive connotation: that of studiousness. In its second edition (1673), the *Tesoro* juxtaposed an alternative etymology (without even erasing the original one): "The words curious and curiosity come from the Latin adverb "why" (*cur*) . . . and from the word otiosity (*ociosidad*), because curious people are usually otiose and nosy, like their master [Satan]." *Cur* and *ocio* had combined to form *cur-ocio,* whence the modern term *curioso.*[36] Curious inquisitiveness had thus drastically shifted its connotation from studiousness to snoopiness.

The slick association of the curious and the otiose is extremely revealing. The curious man was literally one who inquired too far into things that did not belong to his professional sphere (*otium*). Disregarding the proper boundaries of his rank, office, and occupation, the curious man's studiousness was propelled neither by a desire to perform his public duties well nor by practical social or professional interests. Curious people engaged in all kinds of activities out of which neither they nor the body politic obtained any form of obvious material, social, or practical benefit. They showed interest in politics without engaging in political activities; they collected heterodox and prohibited religious books without being heterodox; they read novels and plays from which they could not obtain any useful moral lesson.[37]

Curious reading can thus be described as pleasure-seeking and aesthetically driven. The curious reader did not engage with a text motivated by the interests dictated by his social self. On the contrary, a curious reader was defined by the extent to which his readings fell *outside of* the realm of his professional or social interests. Echoing the *pícaro* Guzmán's call to his anonymous "curious reader," Cervantes addressed the prologue of *Don Quixote* (1605) to a hypothetical "idle reader."[38] Idle, curious reading belonged to the opposite extreme of doctrinally driven reading (the kind favored by moral authorities). Curiosity was what propelled a shoemaker to read chivalric novels: the moralists rightfully questioned what doctrine he could learn from them (absolutely none!). "Curious readers" endangered a social order (the body politic) that was basically organized around doctrinal reading: each person had to restrict his field of interest to the limits dictated by his public persona (that is, by the status and professional community to which he belonged). The aberrant etymological addition of 1673 to the definition of curiosity in Covarrubias's *Tesoro* should be seen as a reflection of the moral authorities' concerns about the expansion of this new, corroding attitude.

By their emphasis on pleasure and entertainment, and through their recurrent calls on the curious reader and the *vulgo* (which was nothing but a physical gathering of curious people), writers for the market fostered this novel form of reading: a curious approach to literature, a fundamentally aesthetic engagement with the poetic product that encouraged the members of the audience to dispense temporarily with their social identities and their professional interests in order to genuinely enjoy the literary experience. In order to entertain themselves, the readers and spectators were being invited to become nobodies. The noble lady who read a novel thus turned into a curious, idle reader. The prince who enjoyed a play became, if only momentarily, part of the *vulgo*—at one with the rest of a public formed by all those who enjoyed *vulgar,* non-Aristotelian drama. Princes, shoemakers, knights, and bourgeois, by responding to the call of entertainment, were all being aesthetically deprived of their social selves—they were becoming "nobodies." Opening the first page of a novel, filled by curious expectation, or crossing the threshold of the public playhouse to watch the latest play were thus liminal moments, ritual acts of aesthetic deprivation through which people of different social conditions came together and associated in groups of idle, anonymous nobodies, regardless of who they were outside the public.

This helps to explain a remarkable aspect of early modern Spanish entertainment literature. As the case of the *jácaras* perfectly illustrates, the readers or spectators of commercial works very often shared neither social background nor rank with the literary characters. Picaresque literature is a clear example, but far from unique. Commoners were fascinated by plots involving kings, ministers, knights, and courtiers. Nobles were equally beguiled by stories of peasants. And both groups loved tales about *jaques,* rogues and criminals. The *vulgo,* the curious readers, did not approach literature in order to become good subjects, good rulers, good citizens, good fathers, or good Christians. They were not looking for the doctrinal examples, positive or negative, that the authors might (or might not) have included in their novels or plays. As temporary nobodies, they did not seek social identification with the characters and were free to associate in the form of publics with the other "nobodies" with whom they shared an aesthetic experience, regardless of their social rank. And that is how in Spain the late Renaissance literary market, by multiplying the instances of entertainment, acted as a vigorous public-making catalyst.

In conclusion, it is true that literature has social and political effects but, contrary to conventional thought, those effects are not always (and not even primarily) a direct consequence of political doctrine traceable in the texts—the social or political "message." The doctrines and ideologies contained in a literary work are important and do clearly have political effects, but the historical reconstruction of the political effects of literature cannot be reduced to an analysis of its ideological content. A literary work may also have *indirect* social and political consequences as a result of its "making publics" role. Those indirect effects are often unexpected and may on occasion be much more consequential than the direct effects of doctrine and ideology. As I have tried to demonstrate, those indirect effects may actually have very little—sometimes nothing at all—to do with the manifest political content of the work as such. It is precisely my argument that public making (one of the most consequential social effects that literature may have) depends little on the manifest political content of a text and much more on its entertaining and aesthetic elements.

However, the fact that public making depends primarily on the apparently unimportant, nonideological component of literature should not lead us to think that public making is politically inconsequential. My intention in this chapter has been simply to show how the commodification of literature in late sixteenth-century Spain was a crucial factor in the proliferation of literary publics in the decades around 1600. No space remains here to describe the significant political effects brought about by such proliferation. As an example, let me just say that the public formed in the Spanish playhouses during the first two decades of the seventeenth century (the theatrical *vulgo*) would immediately become an important factor in Castilian politics. This public was not a political actor but formed an influential audience for politics. Composed of spectators who consumed political news as if it were part of an ongoing national drama, the *vulgo* did not mobilize itself as a political actor would have done (the *vulgo* was not "the people"), but nonetheless it profoundly affected the ways in which Spanish rulers conducted politics once they understood that they were being scrutinized.[39] Through the process of public making, even nonpolitical texts may have consequential political effects!

NOTES

1. Richard Helgerson, *Adulterous Alliances: Home, State, and History in Early Modern European Drama and Painting* (Chicago: University of Chicago Press, 2000), 123–49; Richard Helgerson, *A Sonnet from Carthage: Garcilaso de la Vega and the New Poetry of Sixteenth-Century Europe* (Philadelphia: University of Pennsylvania Press, 2007), x. I am most thankful to my colleagues Michael Armstrong-Roche, Lucy Guenova, Laurie Nussdorfer, and

Khachig Tölölyan, and to the patient editors of this volume for their invaluable comments on the earlier drafts of this essay.

2. Bronwen Wilson and Paul Yachnin, "Introduction," in *Making Publics in Early Modern Europe: People, Things, Forms of Knowledge,* ed. Bronwen Wilson and Paul Yachnin (New York: Routledge, 2010), 1.

3. There are two good recent books on the reception of Italianate poetry in Spain: Begoña López Bueno, *La renovación poética del Renacimiento al Barroco* (Madrid: Síntesis, 2006); and Leah Middlebrook, *Imperial Lyric: New Poetry and New Subjects in Early Modern Spain* (University Park: Pennsylvania State University Press, 2009).

4. Helgerson, *Sonnet from Carthage.* See also Anne J. Cruz, "Self-Fashioning in Spain: Garcilaso de la Vega," *Romanic Review* 83.4 (1992): 517–38, on whose interpretation Helgerson partly based his own.

5. A good overview of the new romancero is Antonio Carreño, "Introduction to Luis de Góngora," in *Romances* (Madrid: Cátedra, 2000), 15–40. See also Pedro M. Cátedra, *Invención, difusión y recepción de la literatura popular impresa (siglo XVI)* (Mérida: Junta de Extremadura, 2002); and López Bueno, *Renovación poética,* 128–37.

6. Francisco de Quevedo, *Poesía original completa,* ed. José Manuel Blecua (Barcelona: Planeta, 1999), nos. 849–50.

7. On the dates, see Pablo Jauralde, *Francisco de Quevedo, 1580–1645* (Madrid: Castalia, 1999), 265. On the genre, Rafael Salillas, "Poesía rufianesca (jácaras y bailes)," *Revue Hispanique* 13 (1905): 18–75; and Emilio Cotarelo y Mori, "Introduction," in *Colección de entremeses, loas, bailes, jácaras y mojigangas desde fines del siglo XVI a mediados del XVIII* (Madrid: Bailly/Bailliére, 1911), 1: cclxxiv–ccxc.

8. Joseph Antonio González de Salas, "Introduction to the Muse 'Terpsichore,'" in Francisco de Quevedo, *El Parnaso español* (Madrid: Diego Díaz de la Carrera, 1648), 311.

9. Juan Boscán, "Preface," in *Las obras de Boscán y algunas de Garcilaso de la Vega* (Barcelona: Carles Amorós, 1543), 2:19r. On the poetic theories of Pietro Bembo upon which these ideas relied, see Javier Lorenzo, "Poética e ideología: La aristocratización del endecasílabo en la 'Carta a la Duquesa de Soma,'" *Hispanic Review* 73.1 (2005): 25–40.

10. Garcilaso de la Vega, "Preface," in *Los quatro libros del cortesano,* trans. Juan Boscán (Barcelona: Pedro Monpezat, 1534). Helgerson's translation of this fragment is in *Sonnet from Carthage,* 32.

11. Baldassare Castiglione, *The Book of the Courtier,* Norton Critical Edition, ed. Daniel Javitch, trans. Charles S. Singleton (New York: Norton, 2002), 32.

12. Garcilaso de la Vega, "Preface," in *Los quatro libros del cortesano.*

13. Boscán, "Preface," in *Las obras,* 2:19v. Lorenzo, "Poética e ideología," 29–30. On hendecasyllabic poetry and the ideal of *sprezzatura,* see also Ignacio Navarrete, *Orphans of Petrarch: Poetry and Theory in the Spanish Renaissance* (Berkeley: University of California Press, 1994), esp. 58–71.

14. On the cojuncture of 1527–30, see Manuel Rivero Rodríguez, *Gattinara: Carlos V y el sueño del Imperio* (Madrid: Sílex, 2005), 103–48.

15. Helgerson, *Sonnet from Carthage,* xv, 56–65.

16. Navarrete, *Orphans of Petrarch,* 38–72. See also Peter Burke, *Popular Culture in Early Modern Europe,* 3rd ed. (Farnham, UK: Ashgate, 2009), 369, 374, 375–76.

17. Helgerson, *Adulterous Alliances,* 5–6.

18. Ibid.

19. Ibid., 6–7.

20. Ibid., 5.

21. Wilson and Yachnin, "Introduction," in *Making Publics in Early Modern Europe,* 1–5; Michael Warner, *Publics and Counterpublics* (New York: Zone Books, 2005), 65–124.

22. Warner, *Publics and Counterpublics,* 67.

23. Ibid., 114–24.

24. On the rise of the Spanish literary market, see D. W. Cruickshank, " 'Literature' and the Book Trade in Golden-Age Spain," *Modern Language Review* 73.4 (1978): 799–824; B. W. Ife, *Reading and Fiction in Golden-Age Spain: A Platonist Critique and Some Picaresque Replies* (Cambridge: Cambridge University Press, 1985), 1–24; Juan Carlos Rodríguez, *El escritor que compró su propio libro. Para leer el Quijote* (Barcelona: Debate, 2003); Carlos M. Gutiérrez, *La espada, el rayo y la pluma: Quevedo y los campos literario y de poder* (West Lafayette, Ind.: Purdue University Press, 2005), 8–59; Donald Gilbert-Santamaría, *Writers on the Market: Consuming Literature in Early Seventeenth-Century Spain* (Lewisburg, Pa.: Bucknell University Press, 2005); and Alejandro García-Reidy, *Las musas rameras. Oficio dramático y conciencia profesional en Lope de Vega* (Madrid: Iberoamericana, 2013).

25. Paul Yachnin, "Shakespeare and the Spaces of Publicity," in *Opinión pública y espacio urbano en la edad moderna,* dir. Antonio Castillo Gómez and James S. Amelang, ed. Carmen Serrano Sánchez (Gijón: Trea, 2010), 15–24 (the quotation is on page 18). See also his "The Populuxe Theatre," in Anthony B. Dawson and Paul Yachnin, *The Culture of Playgoing in Shakespeare's England: A Collaborative Debate* (Cambridge: Cambridge University Press, 2001), 38–65.

26. A good introduction to the legal structure of medieval and early modern societies is Paolo Grossi, *A History of European Law* (Chichester: Wiley-Blackwell, 2010), 1–80. I borrow the term "social self" from David Gary Shaw, *Necessary Conjunctions: The Social Self in Medieval England* (New York: Palgrave MacMillan, 2005).

27. See, e.g., Warner, *Publics and Counterpublics,* 65–124; and Yachnin, "Populuxe Theatre."

28. Horace, *Ars poetica,* lines 333–44. My translation.

29. Kant, *Critique of Judgment,* 1.1.1.1–2.

30. A similar argument in Jürgen Habermas, *The Structural Transformation of the Public Sphere: An Inquiry into a Category of Bourgeois Society* (Cambridge: The MIT Press, 1989), 36–41. Habermas seems here to be following Kantian aesthetics as well.

31. Lope de Vega, *Arte nuevo de hacer comedias,* lines 45–48. My translation.

32. On the importance of "gusto" and entertainment in Renaissance Spanish literature, see Michael Armstrong-Roche, *Cervantes' Epic Novel: Empire, Religion, and the Dream Life of Heroes in Persiles* (Toronto: University of Toronto Press, 2009), 6–7, 14–19.

33. Francisco López de Úbeda, *Libro de entretenimiento de la pícara Justina* (Medina del Campo: Christóbal Lasso Vaca, 1605), prologue.

34. Mateo Alemán, *Primera parte de Guzmán de Alfarache* (Madrid: Várez de Castro, 1599), 1.

35. Barbara M. Benedict, *Curiosity: A Cultural History of Early Modern Inquiry* (Chicago: University of Chicago Press, 2001); *Curiosity and Wonder from the Renaissance to the Enlightenment,* ed. R. J. W. Evans and Alexander Marr (Aldershot: Ashgate, 2006); Neil Kenny, *The Uses of Curiosity in Early Modern France and Germany* (Oxford: Oxford University Press, 2004).

36. Sebastián de Covarrubias, *Tesoro de la lengua castellana o española,* ed. Felipe Maldonado and Manuel Camarero (Madrid: Castalia, 1995), 384.

37. I have dealt with this form of curiosity in "Mentidero de Madrid: La corte como comedia," in *Opinión pública y espacio urbano,* 43–58.

38. Cervantes, *Quixote* 1, prologue.

39. Castro-Ibaseta, "Mentidero de Madrid." I will deal with this in the book I am currently writing, *Beware the Poetry: Political Satire and the Emergence of the Public Sphere in Spain, 1600–1645.* In my PhD dissertation ("Monarquía satírica. Poética de la caída del conde duque de Olivares," Universidad Autónoma de Madrid, 2008, available at www.tdx.cat/handle/10803/50097) the curious reader may find some more material on all these questions.

PART THREE

Networks and Publics

CHAPTER EIGHT

Forms of Nationhood and Forms of Publics
Geography and Its Publics in Early Modern England

LESLEY B. CORMACK

RICHARD HELGERSON's book, *Forms of Nationhood,* included a ground-breaking examination of the ways in which geographical thought helped a nation imagine itself. Although not situated specifically within the theoretical framework of publics and public making, Helgerson was nevertheless developing an important understanding of the ways in which publics were created, interacted, and changed over time. Helgerson's work on geography and chorography provides an ideal starting point from which to investigate the development of publics in early modern England. In order to place his work within a new interpretation of publics and public making, we must begin with a close reading of his seminal essay "The Land Speaks," published first as an article in 1986 and then as chapter 3 of *Forms of Nationhood.* The present chapter provides an ideal foundation, arguing as it does for the importance of geographical thought to the development of local identities and radical political thought. If this new geographical thought was involved and invoked in the creation of a public, an examination of this geographical public might explain how publics in general changed the political, economic, and cultural landscape of early modern England. It is in an examination of chorography, the study of local places and local history, that we can most clearly test the argument that publics were created in the study of the local and ascertain whether the creation and nurturing of such a public could take on the political weight suggested by Helgerson. In particular, a chorographic public was formed around the creation and rearticulation of William Camden's often expanded *Britannia.* This public was a loose band of strangers, held together by a political vision of the antiquity of Britain and an intense loyalty to the land.

The Land Speaks

"In 1579, while Edmund Spenser, Philip Sidney, and their Areopagitican friends were struggling to have, as Spenser put it, 'the kingdome of our own language,' Englishmen made another, more immediately successful conquest. For the first time they took effective visual and conceptual possession of the physical kingdom in which they lived."[1]

So Richard Helgerson begins his 1986 article, "The Land Speaks." Influenced by the new deconstructivist stance of geographers such as J. B. Harley,[2] Helgerson took up the question of the interaction between mapping and geographical description on the one hand and socioeconomic and political change in early modern England on the other. Helgerson argued that maps and chorographies (that is, the descriptions of local places) both created and demonstrated the changing attitudes toward the land as constitutive of England and the English people. By mapping the island and describing its localities, English people began to define themselves as belonging to the land and to express a loyalty toward the land first and the monarch second. This was the beginning of a move from a kingdom to a nation state; and so, for Helgerson, mapping and chorography played a vital role in the political revolution in England in the seventeenth century.

The first step in this transformation of the land, according to Helgerson, can be seen in the publication of Christopher Saxton's groundbreaking *Atlas of the Counties of England* (1580).[3] As Helgerson points out, it is not really accurate to call this massive work Saxton's alone, as several other people played important roles in its creation. Elizabeth commissioned the work; Sir Thomas Seckford, Master of Requests, paid for and organized it; and Saxton surveyed the countryside and produced the maps and the atlas itself. Helgerson sees this as an elision "from royal authority, through gentry patronage, to commoner craftsmanship."[4] In the process, the message of the *Atlas* changed as well.

This *Atlas* was a huge undertaking. Many of the counties had never been surveyed before, so much had to be done from scratch. Saxton tried to do it all himself, but both time and funding were insufficient. In the end, it took significantly longer to accomplish than Saxton had anticipated, and even so he cut corners and did not survey all the counties properly.[5] Nevertheless, the results were impressive. This atlas of maps, depicting all the counties of England, was the first such collection ever conceived or produced. It provided the first clear image of the entire space of England, county by county. The royal coat of arms was displayed prominently, for the message of this work, according to Helgerson, was that England and Elizabeth were to be identified with the land.

This is well illustrated by the frontispiece (fig. 8.1). In this magnificent engraving, Elizabeth is enthroned at the center, as patron and ruler to the book, the land, and the nation. To her right we see Geography, personified with compass and globe. To her left sits Astronomy with an armillary sphere. Above Elizabeth's head, Righteousness and Peace—both female—embrace under Elizabeth's rule, while below two aspects of mapmaking, geometric and panoramic, set their sights on England and Elizabeth's patronage. Helgerson suggests that the Ditchley portrait (fig. 8.2), part of the cult of Elizabeth, is based on this frontispiece.[6]

The maps themselves (fig. 8.3) contain overt representations of the monarch in the guise of royal coats of arms (under the canopy at the bottom right). Of equal significance, the maps show musters, lords lieutenant, and places of fortification. The presence of these details of governance indicates that William Cecil, Lord Burghley, must have had some role in this atlas, as he was the person in Elizabeth's government who had an interest in maps, and particularly in this sort of administrative detail.[7] And yet, according to Helgerson, although the frontispiece and the coats of arms show the power of Elizabeth, the *Atlas* itself undermines this power, because the land has become more important than the monarch in this book. In other words, the message of the work was one of loyalty to the land and identity based on the land. As Helgerson puts it, this cartographic representation of England "strengthened the sense of both local and national identity at the expense of an identity based on dynastic loyalty."[8]

We therefore see that, even with a work such as Saxton's *Atlas,* commissioned by Elizabeth, the focus of loyalty and interest has begun to shift from the monarch to the lived-in place. The following decades see this development continuing. Chorography, both as cartography and description, became even more focused on the land, but, according to Helgerson, with an important twist. The monarch was disappearing from the scene, so chorography was now either in opposition to the monarch or indifferent to the monarch as the holder of national loyalty.

The first work in this new generation of descriptive geographies was John Norden's *Speculum Britanniae* (conceived in 1583, published from 1594 to 1597; with one more map in 1604) (fig. 8.4). Saxton's *Atlas* was incomplete, and so Norden hoped to secure similar support to survey and map the remaining counties more accurately. He approached Elizabeth and William Cecil, seeking royal patronage, but they were not interested. The political concerns and costs of the war with Spain took up most of

FIGURE 8.1. Title page, Christopher Saxton, *Atlas of the Counties of England and Wales* (1580). (Stock photo. By permission of the Folger Shakespeare Library).

FIGURE 8.2. Attrib. Marcus Gheeraerts the Younger, *Queen Elizabeth I* ("The Ditchley Portrait"), 1592? (National Portrait Gallery, London).

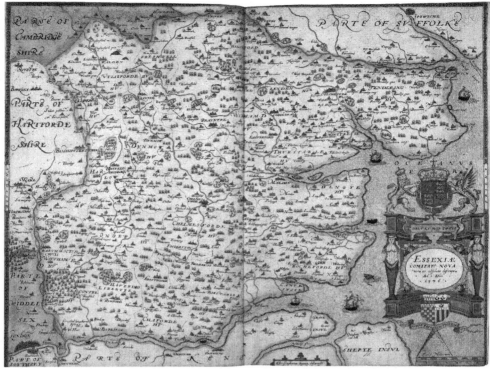

FIGURE 8.3. Map of the county of Essex, from Christopher Saxton's *Atlas of the Counties of England and Wales* (1580). (Stock photo. By permission of the Folger Shakespeare Library).

their time and attention, so Norden was forced to survey with some insufficient private patronage, hoping that he could make enough on the sales to warrant the expense. He also published religious works as he surveyed, as those sold well and helped finance his mapmaking venture.[9] Given this patronage story, it is not surprising that the royal crests did not appear in this atlas, but rather local coats of arms took their place. As Norden hoped to attract local gentry and aristocracy to buy his book or provide support, the presence of coats of arms of those local notables made perfect sense. The resulting message, according to Helgerson, was one of loyalty to the local—to the place—rather than to the monarch; the land was stressed and the monarch marginalized.[10]

Michael Drayton, in *Poly-Olbion* (1613), goes even further down this path (fig. 8.5).[11] The land itself becomes the symbol of authority; the history of Britain is the history not of a single people but of a single land.

Poly-Olbion is a romance of the rivers, an odd chronology as it has no people. Elizabeth (now dead) becomes the personification of the land, as can be seen from the frontispiece. As Helgerson says, "Drayton's Britain is 'peopled' by its natural and man-made landmarks. Its streams are nymphs; its hills, shepherds; its differing regions, rival choirs. Its only crowns are worn by towns and natural sites. And its scepter, as shown on Drayton's frontispiece, is held by the land as a whole."[12] Drayton dedicated his long poem to Prince Henry, demonstrating a certain antagonism toward James and therefore toward the monarch both as the land and as the focus of loyalty for her people.[13]

Helgerson argues that in Drayton's work we can see the growing separation of court and countryside in this chorographical move. Elizabeth becomes the land and the land becomes the focus for local loyalties. The

FIGURE 8.4. Map of the county of Hartfordshire, from John Norden's *Speculum Britanniae,* Part 2 (1594–97). (Stock photo. By permission of the Folger Shakespeare Library).

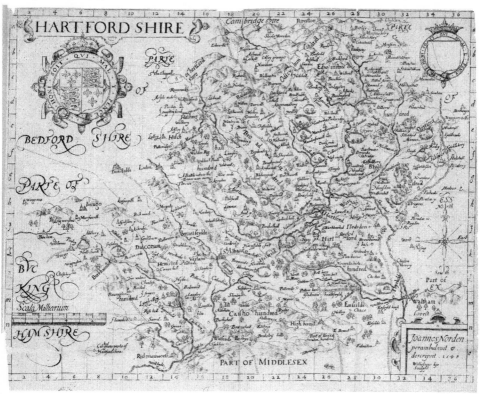

FIGURE 8.5. Title page, Michael Drayton, *Poly-Olbion. Part 1* (1613) (Stock photo. By permission of the Folger Shakespeare Library).

corruptions of court seem ever more distant from the wondrous gifts of God, nature, and industry, seen in the local marvels, the natural beauty, and the fruits of human enterprise. According to Helgerson, this alienation became even more pronounced in the seventeenth century, and this split between court and country was one of the triggers for the civil war.[14] By the 1620s, Helgerson claimed, chorography was being produced as an overt call against the monarch.[15]

Problems with This Interpretation

Helgerson has more to say in this rich article, including his discussion of the relationship between chorography and chronology. But this brief synopsis gives us sufficient material to examine the interaction of Helgerson's work and theories of publics and public making. There are several problems with the argument delineated thus far, even though it contains some fascinating insights into the growing identity of the map readers with the lived space of the land.

First, early modern viewers would not necessarily have understood maps in the way a twenty-first-century viewer sees them, even assuming they would have had access to these maps in the first place. Modern observers have learned to internalize the semiotics of the map, but these strange objects were much less clear to a sixteenth-century audience.[16] Until the sixteenth century, no one except cartographers and navigators would have been able to read the information encoded on a map, especially one involving geometry and mathematical measurements.[17] During the sixteenth century, a larger group of observers developed what Peter Barber calls "map-consciousness," that is, an understanding of what maps were and what they depicted.

In England, gentry and yeoman farmers first used maps in a sustained manner as documents in legal disputes over land. Until the 1580s, people used descriptions rather than "plats," but after 1580 maps appeared more often either as subsidiary evidence or eventually as primary evidence.[18] In the final years of the sixteenth century, prosperous merchants and gentry began to purchase maps that represented their own regions and parts of the world in which they might have some interest, from the Holy Land to new world trading locales.[19] Saxton and Norden began producing maps and atlases just at the time when the gentry would have been beginning to understand and value maps, but Norden's money woes and his inability to finish his project due to lack of funds indicates that gentry were not lining up to buy his wares.

Further, Elizabeth herself does not seem to have particularly valued maps, nor is there evidence that she could read them.[20] Although it was ostensibly Elizabeth who sponsored Saxton's *Atlas,* in reality it was Burghley, who did appreciate and understand maps, collecting them throughout his career. Indeed, much of the rich source of maps remaining in the State Papers owes its existence to Burghley's careful collecting. Therefore, royal interest in Saxton and the lack of interest in Norden must be seen as originating with Burghley and probably represents changing political needs rather than a shift in ideological understanding on the part of the monarch.

Finally, historians of the civil war no longer believe that a court and country split was responsible for the war, something that Helgerson was able to take for granted when he wrote this article.[21] Therefore, finding evidence of a growing court and country divide does not carry the explanatory weight that it once did.

What If We Added Publics?

More interesting than finding fault with individual bits of interpretation, however, is to see how Helgerson's work would combine with an analysis of the creation of publics. By "publics" I mean a loose collection of people, not all of whom have personal knowledge of one another, connected by a common interest in a particular subject and with some social or political goal in mind. There would be many publics in a society, and publics are always coming into being, evolving, and decaying.[22] Because Helgerson himself saw his work as implicitly dealing with publics and as he was part of the interdisciplinary Making Publics research team that developed this interpretation of publics, it would seem likely that he would see elements of these publics in his earlier work. Did these works of local mapping and local description create publics? Were they produced by publics? Did they, as Helgerson seems to suggest with his court/country thesis, produce counterpublics? What is the relationship between public making and nation building in this instance? Can they be connected? Does Helgerson's argument change with the addition of publics? Or are publics really there without being named?

These chorographic works did participate in the making of publics: first, through the representation of shared space and a shared understanding of its importance; and second, through the creation of a public of chorographers and consumers of chorography. The difference between the definitions of publics and their making as defined above and Helgerson's original argument in *Forms of Nationhood* lies in the scale of connections proposed. In Helgerson's earlier work, the connections created by geographical study were overwhelmingly personal. Our definition of publics must allow them to be open to strangers. These are not, of course, in complete opposition; early modern England had a small population, especially of those interested in chorography, and at some level all connections had an element of personal interaction, even among people who never met.

Chorography and Its Publics

When Sir Julius Caesar recorded "The Singularities of England" in his commonplace book, he was participating in chorography. He described London Bridge, one of the great wonders of the world, and the four naturally occurring hot baths of England, and he discussed the abundance of jewels and minerals to be found on the island.[23] Chorography owed its early definition, as well as its subsequent reintroduction in the fifteenth century, to Ptolemy's *Geographia*. Ptolemy had separated chorography from the more elevated study of geography proper, defining its purview as the description of ports, villages, peoples, rivers, and so forth.[24] Thus, the term "chorography"—or "local history," as it might be called—came to be applied in the sixteenth century to any study of local places or people. This study often, although not always, focused on one town or country and through its detailed enumeration of local sights, marvels, and commodities, helped engender local pride and loyalty. The division between chorography and history was often quite blurred, as describing local phenomena often included the famous battles fought there or histories of prominent families of the region.

Chorographies were written by those who lived in and knew the local places of which they wrote. Individual scholars, working in their own parishes, collected information, some of which they shared, some of which they did not. They wrote diaries or commonplace books, like Sir Julius Caesar's, in which they recorded the presence of dripping wells, Roman inscriptions, natural phenomena, and family histories. Some men like Richard Carew and William Lambarde published their accounts.[25] Others read papers at meetings of the Society of Antiquaries (founded 1586).[26] Some just corresponded, both inside England and internationally as part of the Republic of Letters. Some lived their whole lives in their local region, others traveled widely in England and abroad. At one level, these men were a sort of public involved in parallel play. They each wrote their own accounts, describing their own locality. They participated in the large chorographic public to the extent that they corresponded, read published chorographies, and recognized the larger ideological import of such study.

Richard Carew (1555–1620) provides a good example of a chorographer who knew the larger community of scholars and yet stayed in his locality for most of his life.[27] Carew was a member of the landed gentry, with family holdings in Cornwall. He went to university at Christ Church, Oxford, where he met William Camden and Philip Sidney, both of whom influenced his choice of avocation. After university, he completed his education at the "third university of England," reading law at Middle Temple, London.[28] He settled on the family estate in Cornwall in 1577, married into the Arundell family, had ten children, and settled into the life of the landed gentry. He became a justice of the peace and a Member of Parliament.

Carew was a typical landed gentleman, albeit a well-educated one, except that he was an active scholar his whole life. He taught himself Greek, Italian, German, Spanish, and French, translated histories, poetry, and geographies. He wrote a panegyric on "The excellencie of the English tongue," first published in the second edition of William Camden's *Remaines* (1614). This was part of a major debate with, among others, Richard Verstegan, Thomas Nashe, and Edmund Spenser over whether English should use foreign words and on the importance of maintaining the purity of Saxon roots.[29] Turning from language to chorography, Carew spent most of his life exploring the geography and antiquities of his home county. He published *The Survey of Cornwall* in 1602 and continued to work on additions to the work throughout his life. The *Survey* consisted of two books, the first a general description of Cornwall and the second a perambulation of the county from east to west. Given the isolation of Cornwall, both geographically and as one of the few places with a surviving Celtic minority, few Englishmen had had access to this rich chorographic description before the publication of Carew's work. Through his work he claimed the significance of this backward region to the nation as a whole and argued that Cornwall was integral to the English nation.

Carew was part of a loose network of scholars, many of whom knew each other from university days. He corresponded with several other local historians regarding the history and description of England and its peoples, particularly with William Camden, whom he supplied with substantial information for Camden's own national chorography. This network of scholars was not a public, but their loose group of correspondents, emphasizing the importance of the local to the nation and the land to subject loyalty, provided the foundation on which a chorographic public could be built.

William Camden and *Britannia* (1586)

In many ways, the life and work of William Camden provides a better model for the creation of a chorographic public than the mapping enterprise discussed by Helgerson, a public that created a new message of loyalty to and identification with the land and its history rather than loyalty to / identification with the monarch, the court, or the government. In other words, here is a public that has the potential to perform the ideological and political work posited by Helgerson.

William Camden (1551–1623) was born at the Old Bailey in London.[30] His father had been a painter-stainer; while this was a respectable London guild, the Camden family was not rich, and so William never had the resources of someone like Richard Carew. Camden attended Oxford from 1566, first at Magdalen College and eventually moving to Christ Church, where he met Carew and Sidney. In *Britannia,* Camden speaks with affection and gratitude for Sidney's encouragement of him and his work.[31] Camden left Oxford in 1571 with no degree, perhaps because his religious politics were too conservative for the time. He was eventually awarded a BA, which was clearly very important to him. He also petitioned later for an MA but never received it. Camden needed to earn a living and so turned to education. He became Master and later Head Master at Westminster School in London, where he remained for much of his life.

With a secure income, Camden turned to his interest in chorography and began work on what would become his lifelong project, a description of the historical remains of all parts of the ancient Roman province of Britain, to be published as *Britannia: sive Florentissimorum Regnorum Angliae, Scotiae, Hiberniae et Insularum adiacentium ex intima antiquitate Chorographie description* (London, 1586) (fig. 8.6). On his visit to England in 1577, Abraham Ortelius had suggested to Camden that he write a complete description of the island and its Roman antiquities, a project Camden had already begun and happily moved forward.[32] He compiled previous accounts, especially that of John Leland, and supplemented this by personal travel and extensive correspondence with scholars such as Alexander Nowell, William Lambarde, schoolmate Richard Carew, and others. As he describes his methods: "I have travailed over all England for the most part; I have studiously read over our owne countrie writers, old and new; all Greeke and Latine authors which have once made mentione of Britaine. I have had conference with learned men in other parts of Christendome: I have beene diligent in the Records of this Realme."[33] In other words, his research was multifaceted; he used firsthand observation; he consulted all possible manuscripts and other sources; and he conferred with experts. Camden also used work written by others, although he was not making a compilation such as that of Richard Hakluyt.[34] His work for the *Britannia*, then, was conducted in the field, through study and collaboration, and through research into original sources, both printed and manuscript.

We can get some indication of Camden's research network by examining the scholars named in *Britannia*.[35] Camden is quite scrupulous in assigning credit and so lists the vast majority of his sources. As would be expected, the largest number of references are to classical and medieval sources. But there are many contemporary correspondents, including men from all parts of the British Isles and the Continent. The more than fifty correspondents identified included fellow antiquarians such as Daniel Rogers, an expert in ancient coins; Edward Palmer, another numismatist who had attended Oxford and Middle Temple with Camden; and Francis Tate, a judge and legal scholar who composed the first list of members of the Society of Antiquaries.[36] Robert Cotton, William Lambarde, and Richard Carew also contributed. Camden exchanged information with scholars from Wales (David Powel), Scotland (David Chambers, George Buchanan, and John Jonston), and Ireland (John Bale traveled there). Michael Maschert, a Church of England clergyman, contributed a Latin verse describing Clarendon Park near Salisbury: "A famous parke for Stag and hind, neere Salisburie doth lie."[37] Camden praised the diligence and helpfulness of several of his contributors. For example, he said of Thomas Talbot, a collector of medieval manuscripts, "Not to conceal my obligations to any, I must acknowledge myself under very great ones to Thomas Talbot, a diligent examiner of records and a perfect master of our antiquities."[38]

The network of contributors included Roman Catholic priests and continental Protestant reformers. Geographers such as Ortelius, local historians such as John Stowe, and physicians such as John Caius were all part of this diffuse network of scholars. This was not a coterie of men who knew each other from university or London, although some did. Rather, this was a loosely connected group of people, all interested in antiquities and local history. Several also connected through the new society for those sharing this interest in London, the Society of Antiquaries.

The Society of Antiquaries was an organization whose creation corresponded with the publication of *Britannia*, and whose membership consisted of a subset of the network of contributors and correspondents in contact with Camden himself.[39] The society first met in about 1586; they held thirty-eight documented meetings at Derby House in London, where the members debated questions concerning British antiquities.[40]

FIGURE 8.6. Title page, William Camden, *Britannia: sive Florentissimorum Regnorum Angliae, Scotiae, Hiberniae et Insularum adiacentium ex intima antiquitate Chorographie description* (London, 1586; **1607 ed.). (Stock photo. By permission of the Folger Shakespeare Library).

The aim of the society was "to establish a 'cultural longevity' for their country,"[41] to demonstrate the antiquity and nobility of their native land. These men had a new vision of Britain, both as an island with ancient rights, traditions, and history and as a focus for the encouragement of local loyalties. Camden attended meetings of the society, at which chorographically minded men read papers of direct importance to the composition of *Britannia*.[42] Camden himself delivered several papers there, including one on Roman epitaphs in 1600.[43] The society, then, was part of the creation and embodiment of the network of scholars connected with the development of British chronology.

As his reputation spread (even before publication of *Britannia* in 1586), scholars from across Europe, both Protestant and Roman Catholic, included a meeting with Camden on their itinerary when they came to England. Geographers such as Abraham Ortelius and Gerardus Mercator consulted with Camden. Equally, lawyers such as Alberico Gentili, statesmen such as Barnabé Brisson, president of the *parlement* of Paris, and scholars and poets such as the Hungarian Parmenius visited and exchanged information and opinions.[44] Camden corresponded with Justis Lipsius, Janus Gruter, and Jacques-Auguste de Thou, among other continental scholars with historical and antiquarian interests.[45] He was part of a European scholarly community at the same time that he helped create and nurture a domestic chorographic public.

Network or Public?

In the seventeenth century Camden's groundbreaking work was altered substantially. The Society of Antiquaries ceased to meet by about 1608.[46] An interest in history seemed to be overtaking a history of antiquities. By mid-century, methods for conducting a national survey of the local had been utterly transformed. When organizations such as the Royal Society of London and the Académie des Sciences began to conduct national surveys, a committee would decide which questions to ask and questionnaires would be sent out.[47] Camden, on the other hand, had employed a very personal methodology based on his own knowledge and erudition and combined with networks of like-minded humanist scholars. These were networks based on mutual interests and trust, with common visions of the end project and its importance. Sebastian Münster had employed a similar methodology in composing his *Cosmographia*, in which he had corresponded with leading geographers in each country and region of Europe.[48]

Given these personal connections, we would be mistaken to call Camden's web of correspondents a public. However, his network was to provide the frame on which this public would develop.

Britannia itself constituted and nurtured a public, particularly through its rewriting and republishing. For *Britannia* took on a life of its own. The first edition, in Latin (1586), was a relatively modest octavo. During Camden's lifetime, the work was continually expanded and was published in five separate editions: 1587, 1590, 1594, 1600, and 1607. At each iteration, more material was added. By 1607, Camden had reworked the organization, modeling it on Jacques-Auguste de Thou's history of France.[49] This final Latin version was in folio and included an index, maps by Saxton and Norden, and various engraved illustrations. An English translation of the 1586 edition was made by Philemon Holland in 1610. Furthermore, there were two Latin editions published in Frankfurt in 1590 and 1610. It was translated anew into English in 1695 by Edmund Gibson, a very influential edition that was reprinted with additions in a 1722 edition. Finally, there was an edition by Richard Gough in 1786, reissued in 1806. During Camden's lifetime, various people, some of them strangers, sent him more and more information about Roman coins, inscriptions, and ruins, as well as local histories and places of interest. After his death, this group of correspondents and contributors continue to grow; Richard Gough's 1786 version was thousands of pages long. In this way, the earlier humanistic network had now been superseded by a public—a group that strangers could enter as long as they had the expertise.

How did *Britannia* form a public? First, an ever-expanding group of people contributed to the various editions. These people did not know each other; what they had in common was an interest and expertise in local phenomena. Second, this group of strangers shared a political belief in the antiquity of Britain and a loyalty to the land and its history that superseded any contemporary loyalty to monarch or government. This is not to say that all antiquarians were political radicals, but the view of the antiquity of common law, of tradition, and of the transitory nature of particular rulers was part of the message to be read between the ever-widening covers of Camden's *Britannia*. Finally, the readership of *Britannia* and other such chorographies produced in the following years can also be seen as a public. It was a numerous public, evidenced by the many editions of *Britannia* published over the years. It, too, partook of the radical messages of such chorographic writings, although perhaps in a more attenuated way than the contributors themselves.

The Land Speaks

What difference does it make that *Britannia* formed a public? Did there thereby exist a different view of England or Britain in any way akin to Helgerson's changing identity and affiliation with the land? Do we see a different political attitude? Has the land indeed spoken? I would argue that it has, and that this is a public with political import.

A large and multifaceted public developed around the research, publishing, and reading of *Britannia,* a public that survived for many years and in all parts of England. By thinking about the chorographically interested community (as opposed to just chorographical thought itself), we discover the subtle ways in which people in England were able to manage their destiny. They could develop new ways of living in the land, new loyalties to the land and its history, and new expectations of what a monarch or a government should do for its people. The chorographic public gained a strong identification with the land and its history, an identification that encouraged criticism of perceived domestic political abuse and enthusiasm for imperial adventures. They were no longer simply subjects of the monarch; they were members of a nation.

Richard Helgerson, in his 1986 article, pointed the way toward such an interpretation. While "The Land Speaks" dealt first with the mapping of England and the semiotics of such mapping, the addition of the contributors and readers of these chorographic works—the makers and partakers of this organic and ever-changing public—adds a layer of complexity to his analysis and makes the argument for a politics of chorography much more compelling.

NOTES

1. Richard Helgerson, "The Land Speaks: Cartography, Chorography, and Subversion in Renaissance England," *Representations* 16 (1986): 51.

2. J. B. Harley, "Deconstructing the Map," *Cartographica* 26.2 (1989): 1–19; reprinted in J. B. Harley, *The New Nature of Maps: Essays in the History of Cartography,* ed. Paul Laxton, intro. J. H. Andrews (Baltimore: Johns Hopkins University Press, 2002).

3. Christopher Saxton, *Atlas of the Counties of England* (1580), reprinted in *Christopher Saxton's Sixteenth-Century Maps* (Shrewsbury, UK: Chatsworth Library, 1992).

4. Helgerson, "The Land Speaks," 53.

5. Sarah Tyacke and John Huddy, *Christopher Saxton and Tudor Map-making* (London: British Library, 1980), 40. I. M. Evans and H. Lawrence, *Christopher Saxton: Elizabethan Map-maker* (Wakefield, UK: Wakefield Historical Publications, 1979), 9, 66 ff.

6. Helgerson, "The Land Speaks," 54. William Ravenhill, introduction to *Christopher Saxton's Sixteenth-Century Maps,* 15. For discussion of the cult of Elizabeth, see especial-

ly Roy C. Strong, *The Cult of Elizabeth: Elizabethan Portraiture and Pageantry* (London: Thames & Hudson, 1977), and Frances A. Yates, *Astraea: the Imperial Theme in the Sixteenth Century* (London: Routledge & Kegan Paul, 1975).

7. Peter Barber, "Was Elizabeth I Interested in Maps—and Did It Matter?" *Transactions of the Royal Historical Society,* 6th ser. 14 (2004): 185–98. Helgerson does not mention this.

8. Helgerson, "The Land Speaks," 56.

9. Most popular, judging by the number of times they were reprinted, were *A Pensive Mans Practice* (1584), with at least sixteen editions by 1640, and *A Poore Mans Rest,* with its twentieth edition in 1684 (Edward Lyman, "English Maps and Map-Makers of the Sixteenth-Century," *Geographical Journal* 116 [1950]: 16). Frank Kitchen, "Cosmo-choro-poly-grapher: An Analytical Account of the Life and Work of John Norden, 1547?–1625" (PhD diss., University of Sussex, 1993), discusses the reasons for Norden's lack of success in obtaining crown or government patronage. Helgerson, "The Land Speaks," 66.

10. Helgerson, "The Land Speaks," 58.

11. For a recent discussion of Drayton, see David Galbraith, *Architectonics of Imitation in Spenser, Daniel, and Drayton* (Toronto: University of Toronto Press, 2000).

12. Helgerson, "The Land Speaks," 59–60.

13. Roy C. Strong, *Henry, Prince of Wales and England's Lost Renaissance* (London: Thames & Hudson, 1986); Timothy Wilks, ed., *Prince Henry Revived: Image and Exemplarity in Early Modern England* (London: Southampton Solent University, in association with Paul Holberton, 2007).

14. Much of the early work on the English Civil War emphasized the growing tensions between the court and the puritan country, e.g., Christopher Hill, *The English Revolution, 1640* (London: Lawrence & Wishart, 1940) and *The Intellectual Origins of the English Revolution* (Oxford: Clarendon Press, 1965); Hugh Trevor-Roper, *Religion, the Reformation and Social Change; and Other Essays* (London: Macmillan, 1967); Richard Henry Tawney, *The Rise of the Gentry, 1558–1640* ([Utrecht?]; repr., *The Economic History Review* 11 (1941): 1–38; and Lawrence Stone, *The Causes of the English Revolution, 1529–1642* (London: Routledge & Kegan Paul, 1972).

15. Helgerson, "The Land Speaks," 82.

16. See J. B. Harley and David Woodward, eds., *The History of Cartography,* vols. 1–3 (Chicago: University of Chicago Press, 1987–2007), for a full description of the changing nature of maps in different cultures through time. See especially vol. 3, *Cartography in the European Renaissance,* for the development of cartography during the sixteenth century.

17. Peter Barber, "England II: Monarchs, Ministers, and Maps 1550–1625," in *Monarchs, Ministers and Maps: The Emergence of Cartography as a Tool of Government in Early Modern Europe,* ed. David Buisseret (Chicago: University of Chicago Press, 1992), 58, argues that by 1580 "map-consciousness—the ability to think cartographically and to prepare sketch maps as a means of illuminating problems—was becoming ever more widespread." See also P. D. A. Harvey, *Maps in Tudor England* (Chicago: University of Chicago Press, 1993).

18. Harvey, *Maps in Tudor England,* 83–93. A number of popular books on surveying, written in the period, indicate the growing interest in this area: e.g., Valentine Leigh, *The Most Profitable and Commendable Science of Surveying* (London: [J. Kingston] for A. Maunsell, 1577); Leonard Digges, *A Geometrical Practise, named Pantometria* (London: H. Bynneman, 1571); Edward Worsop, *A Discoverie of Sundrie Errours and faults . . . by Land-meaters* (London: H. Middleton, 1582).

19. Svetlana Alpers, *The Art of Describing: Dutch Art in the Seventeenth Century* (Chicago: University of Chicago Press, 1983).

20. Barber, "Was Elizabeth I Interested in Maps?"

21. Revisionist interpretations include Conrad Russell, *The Causes of the English Civil War* (Oxford: Oxford University Press, 1990); Nicholas Tyacke, *The English Revolution c.1590–1720: Politics, Religion and Communities* (Manchester: Manchester University Press,

2007); Kevin Sharpe, *The Personal Rule of Charles I* (New Haven, Conn.: Yale University Press, 1992).

22. For a much more extended discussion of publics by the Making Publics research group, see Paul Yachnin and Bronwen Wilson, eds., *Making Publics in Early Modern Europe: People, Things, Forms of Knowledge* (New York: Routledge, 2010). I have been most influenced by Peter Lake and Steven Pincus, "Rethinking the Public Sphere in Early Modern England," *Journal of British Studies* 45 (2006): 270–92; Brian Cowan, *The Social Life of Coffee: The Emergence of the British Coffeehouse* (New Haven, Conn.: Yale University Press, 2005); Benedict Anderson, *Imagined Communities: Reflections on the Origin and Spread of Nationalism* (London: Verso Editions, 1983); Michael E. Gardiner, "Wild Publics and Grotesque Symposiums: Habermas and Bakhtin on Dialogue, Everyday Life and the Public Sphere," *Sociological Review* 52 (2004): 28–48; and Michael Warner, *Publics and Counterpublics* (New York: Zone Books, 2003).

23. BL Add. MS 6038, fol. 250a. For a full discussion of the teaching of chorography at the English universities, see Lesley B. Cormack, *Charting an Empire: Geography at the English Universities 1580–1620* (Chicago: University of Chicago Press, 1997), especially chapter 5.

24. Ptolemy, *Geographia*, sig. a1a.

25. Richard Carew, *The Survey of Cornwall* (London: S. S[tafford] for J. Jaggard, 1602); William Lambarde, *A Perambulation of Kent* (London: n.p., 1576).

26. Little has been written about this society. Still useful is Joan Evans, *A History of the Society of Antiquaries* (Oxford: Oxford University Press, 1956).

27. S. Mendyk, "Carew, Richard (1555–1620)," in *Oxford Dictionary of National Biography*, online ed., ed. Lawrence Goldman; www.oxforddnb.com/view/article/4635.

28. Sir George Buck, *The Third Universitie of England* (London, 1615). For a discussion of the Inns of Court, see Wilfred R. Prest, *Rise of the Barrister: A Social History of the English Bar, 1590–1640* (Oxford: Clarendon Press, 1986,) and R. Julian Martin, *Francis Bacon, the State, and the Reform of Natural Philosophy* (Cambridge: Cambridge University Press, 1992).

29. See Helgerson, "The Land Speaks," 51. This shows one of the connections between the "kingdom of his own language" and the geographical nation.

30. See Wyman H. Herendeen, *William Camden: A Life in Context* (Woodbridge, UK: Boydell Press, 2007), for a comprehensive and authoritative biography. This supersedes his earlier important article, "William Camden. Historian, Herald, and Antiquary," *Studies in Philology* 85 (1988): 192–210.

31. William Camden, *Britain, or A chorographicall description of the most flourishing kingdomes, England, Scotland, and Ireland, and the ilands adioyning, out of the depth of antiquitie*, trans. Philémon Holland (London: G. Bishop and J. Norton, 1610), 6.

32. Daniel R. Woolf, *The Idea of History in Early Stuart England* (Toronto: University of Toronto Press, 1990), 116.

33. Camden, *Britain*, preface.

34. Richard Hakluyt, *Principal Navigations, Voyages, Traffiques, and Discoveries of the English Nation* (London: Vol. 1, 1598; Vol. 2, 1599; Vol. 3, 1600).

35. This analysis is based on the 1610 English version of *Britannia*.

36. Unless otherwise noted, all biographical information in these two paragraphs comes from the *Dictionary of National Biography*.

37. Camden, *Britain*, 250.

38. Ibid., 148.

39. Linda Van Norden, "Henry Spelman on the Chronology of the Elizabethan Society of Antiquaries," *Huntingdon Library Quarterly* 13 (1949–50): 158. Cormack, *Charting*, 201–2.

40. Evans, *History of the Society of Antiquaries*, 10.

41. Ibid., 11.

42. Many of these papers were published by Thomas Hearne as *A Collection of Curious Discourses* (London: W. and J. Richardson, 1720; expanded ed. 1771).

43. Woolf, *Idea of History,* 116.

44. Wyman H. Herendeen, "Camden, William (1551–1623)," in *Oxford Dictionary of National Biography,* ed. H. C. G. Matthew and Brian Harrison (Oxford: Oxford University Press, 2004); online ed., ed. Lawrence Goldman, January 2008, www.oxforddnb.com/view/article/4431.

45. Woolf, *Idea of History,* 34, 116, 118.

46. Van Norden, "Henry Spelman," 159.

47. Kathleen H. Ochs, "The Royal Society of London's History of Trades Programme: An Early Episode in Applied Science," *Notes and Records of the Royal Society of London,* 39.2 (April 1985): 129–58. For the Royal Society more generally, see Michael Hunter, *Establishing the New Science* (Woodbridge, UK: Boydell Press, 1989); Lisa Jardine, *Ingenious Pursuits: Building the Scientific Revolution* (New York: Nan A. Talese, 1999). This method can be seen with the mapping of Scotland in the early eighteenth century (Charles W. J. Withers, *Geography, Science, and National Identity: Scotland since 1520* [Cambridge: Cambridge University Press, 2001]) and with Oglivy's maps (Meredith Donaldson Clark's article in this volume).

48. Matthew McLean, *The* Cosmographia *of Sebastian Münster: Describing the World in the Reformation* (Aldershot, UK: Ashgate, 2007).

49. Woolf, *Idea of History,* 118.

CHAPTER NINE

"The Land Speaks"

John Shrimpton's Antiquities of Verulam and St. Albans *and the Making of* Verulamium

MEREDITH DONALDSON CLARK

IN *Forms of Nationhood,* Richard Helgerson documents the "generative energy" that flowed through a generation of Elizabethans: those poets, playwrights, antiquarians, cartographers, lawyers, explorers, and theologians who, in their efforts to describe what they saw as the preexisting nation of England, themselves contributed to the creation and definition of early modern England's conception of itself and its history. As Helgerson himself acknowledged, such an argument is made possible only with "the bright light of retrospection"; it took centuries of history, self-reflection, and interpretation before the nascent elements of the modern English nation, present in a collection of texts written approximately between 1590 and 1620, became evident. Early moderns themselves "did not know where either they or their history were going."[1] Yet in order for those texts to have had such a transformative influence, they needed to have been read, referenced, discussed, and tested. In effect, they needed to become public documents capable of assembling a public readership through "uptake, citation, and recharacterization," that is, through the attention, discussion, and collaboration of interested individuals.[2] The significance of those texts was felt almost immediately, as the subsequent generation who came of age reading the works of William Camden, Edmund Spenser, Michael Drayton, and others turned to them with their own questions of national, civic, and individual identity and were thereby largely responsible for establishing which texts would participate in the early stages of the long process of English nation building.

This chapter will present the work of John Shrimpton (ca. 1591), a largely unknown amateur antiquarian from St. Albans, as an illustrative example of how the "concerted generational project" of writing English nationhood described by Helgerson was taken up by the next generation.[3] Around the year 1630, fuelled by curiosity about his own backyard and a distaste for the "envious times" in which he found himself, Shrimpton compiled *The Antiquities of Verulam and St. Albans,* a local history of his hometown and the adjacent ruins of the ancient Roman settlement of Verulamium.[4] Shrimpton's study exhibits all the hallmarks of early modern chorography and antiquarianism. The manuscript, which was never published, combines paraphrases of medieval authors, facts about Verulamium, observations on the physical condition of the Roman remains, accounts of significant local historical events and personages, transcriptions of monuments, anecdotes from his own life in St. Albans, and information about local topography. The *Antiquities* also details Shrimpton's specific reading practices. As one of the earliest readers of works by Camden, Spenser, Drayton, and John Weever, Shrimpton relied on those recent texts, alongside established authorities including Tacitus, Gildas, and Bede, for his account of the history of Verulamium. By granting the recent texts equal, if not more, weight than the classical and medieval texts, Shrimpton showed that those texts Helgerson would later identify as foundational to English nationhood were quickly recognized to possess authority and legitimacy.

Such authority depends largely on uptake, and Shrimpton's little-known town history offers clear evidence for how regional information was shared both directly and indirectly through chorographical writing during the early seventeenth century. For his historical account of Verulamium, Shrimpton relied heavily on commonplaces, that is, on passages excerpted and reduced from larger works that, in their repackaged form, entered into textual circulation independent of their original source. Shrimpton not only copied out commonplaces found elsewhere but also transcribed excerpted passages from Camden, Spenser, Weever, and others, thereby creating new commonplaces. The practice of commonplacing, as "a quintessentially humanist method of reading and storing information," was one way in which texts became public documents, capable of enabling collaborative thought among strangers.[5] "Public," in this sense, refers to what the Making Publics Project defined as "forms of association that allowed people to connect with others in ways not rooted in family, rank, or vocation, but rather founded in voluntary groupings built on the shared interests, tastes, commitments, and desires of individuals."[6] Commonplaces are "common" because they are available to anyone who also has access to texts, thus creating a textual public "by the reflexive circulation of discourse" that "takes place not in closely argued essays but in an informal, intertextual, and multigeneric field."[7] The texts Shrimpton chose to include as commonplaces allowed his *Antiquities* to belong, a generation later, to a specific textual public, or what Helgerson identifies as the "various intermediary social figurations" that "formed around Camden's *Britannia*."[8] Helgerson describes how Camden and his *Britannia* served as a hub connecting the antiquarian interests shared by poetry, history, cartography, and many other fields during the sixteenth and seventeenth centuries. Spenser's *Ruines of Time,* Drayton's *Polyolbion,* and Weever's *Ancient Funeral Monuments* each owes aspects of its form and content to Camden's *Britannia,* and Shrimpton drew heavily on commonplaces from all four in his *Antiquities.* Camden's *Britannia* became such a pivotal text across genres and generations precisely through the mechanisms of public making, as will be clear from the example of Shrimpton's *Antiquities.*

The incidences of uptake and citation in Shrimpton's *Antiquities* reveal an intertextual public that coalesced around the idea of Verulamium during the turn of the seventeenth century. Camden, Spenser, Drayton, and others created a poetic idea and cartographic image of Verulamium that Shrimpton superimposed on his own quotidian experience. Verulamium became a symbol of the antiquarian enterprise, demonstrating how a site with few remaining monuments could nevertheless be restored for posterity through textual monuments and the circulation of information. The contemporary reality of Verulamium was one of loss and ruin. However, through historical prose, narrative, and poetry, Shrimpton's antiquarian endeavor allowed him to reimagine and revitalize what Michel de Certeau calls "the invisible identities of the visible": a sense of place in which the narrative layers of the past, together with the archaeological layers of earth, produce "the presences of diverse absences." De Certeau's meditation on the physical reality of the past and its impact on the present mirrors Shrimpton's everyday experience of St. Albans:

> Objects and words also have hollow places in which a past sleeps, as in the everyday acts of walking, eating, going to bed, in which ancient revolutions slumber. . . . It is striking here that the places people live in are like the presences of diverse absences. What can be seen designates what is no longer there: "you *see,* here there used to be . . . ," but it can no longer be seen. Demonstratives indicate the invisible identities of the visible: it is the very definition of a place, in fact, that it is composed by these series of displacements and effects among the fragmented strata that form it and that it plays on these moving layers.[9]

In a literal sense, St. Albans was constructed using layers of stone from Verulamium, and much more of the ancient city lay hidden underground only to be discovered several centuries later. And in a figurative sense, the layers of meaning introduced by poets and antiquarians helped to reshape Shrimpton's "very definition of place." Like the chorographers of a generation earlier, Shrimpton's engagement with the public image of Verulamium created through texts allowed him to discover "Rome lying just under the surface of his own England."[10]

Shrimpton's *Antiquities* gives us a rare glimpse not only of participation in a public but of participation at a temporal remove. Publics allow for vicarious association, connecting individuals who may have no knowledge of each other, but evidence for this is difficult, if not impossible, to reconstruct. Shrimpton's manuscript contains little evidence of direct correspondence with other like-minded antiquarians. Rather, his participation in a public of regional antiquarianism was mediated locally by texts: he bought, borrowed, and read books, measuring them against his own observations. His reading practices, well documented in his *Antiquities,* show both how quickly excerpted passages from those texts identified by Helgerson as foundational to English nationhood began circulating as commonplaces, and how, despite their national scope, those texts had a regional impact and could influence an individual's everyday experience and perception of his own hometown.

Reading Shrimpton's Sources

By all contemporary accounts, there was little to see of the ancient, ruined Roman city of Verulamium by the late sixteenth century. The majority of the ancient structures and artifacts a twenty-first-century visitor encounters at Verulamium are the result of major excavations carried out during the mid-twentieth century, but they were still deeply buried during John Shrimpton's lifetime.[11] Camden reports in his *Britannia* that "there remaineth nothing of it to be seene, beside the few remaines of ruined walles, the checkered pavements, and peeces of Roman coine other whiles digged up there."[12] John Norden's description of the sparse ruins of Verulamium in his *Speculum Britanniae* includes the earthy detail that "[i]n the ruinous walles of this Citie groweth licoras."[13] Much of what had been left after the Roman occupation had been salvaged and reused in constructing the monastery and abbey of St. Albans.[14] By the time Camden and Norden composed their descriptions, little remained of the once-thriving Roman city.

Yet this tantalizing lack of physical evidence fuelled curiosity and imagination. From the 1580s to 1630s, chorographers, antiquarians, and poets built on what little archaeological evidence remained, supplementing it with archival research, rumor, and personal experience to create a powerful image of Verulamium as an emblem of the destructive force of time. The power of this chorographical image of Verulamium grew to affect even St. Albans's own citizens. The idea of Verulamium was a public thing, made and remade from one chorographical text to the next through the accretion, citation, repetition, and occasionally rejection of historical facts. Shrimpton participated in this textual public by reading and writing, and his *Antiquities* demonstrates how such a public—wherein a group of strangers forms a network through their interactions with various print media, objects, shared interests, and scholarly practices—has the potential to affect an individual's lived experience.

Shrimpton's reading practices—particularly his reliance on the work of Camden, Drayton, and Weever—are clear from the opening page of *The Antiquities*. He begins with a list of "the principall Authors names from whence this History is Extracted," including ancient and medieval historians and chroniclers (Tacitus, Gildas, Bede, Jacobus de Voragine), authors local to St. Albans (Alexander Neckham, Alfric of St. Albans, Abbot John Whethamstede, the author of the *Flores Historiarum,* the author of "The golden Leager booke" of St. Albans), and recent authors (Camden, Drayton, and Weever).[15] Nearly four hundred years later, Helgerson would begin *Forms of Nationhood* with a list of the eight most substantial contributions to the writing of English nationhood under Elizabeth, and the two lists overlap on the names Camden and Drayton, two of only three contemporary authors Shrimpton includes. In addition, although Spenser, who appears on Helgerson's list, is not included in Shrimpton's, the influence of Spenser's poetry, particularly his *Ruines of Time,* is felt throughout Shrimpton's *Antiquities.* One generation after the publication of Camden's *Britannia,* Spenser's *Ruines of Time,* and Drayton's *Poly-Olbion,* Shrimpton recognized the significance of these works and turned to them not only as sources of historical knowledge but also as models for organizing information. It was the image of Verulamium developed by Camden, Spenser, and Drayton (who themselves drew on the works of John Leland, William Harrison, John Norden, and William Vallans) that supplied the textual material for the commonplaces Shrimpton used both to distinguish and to transmit these nascent forms of nationhood.

Prior to the publication of Camden's *Britannia* (1586), Verulamium received limited attention in chorographical works, but the attention it did receive would shape the image of Verulamium prevalent by the end of the sixteenth century. John Leland visited Verulamium in the 1530s and made notes on the ruins, including observations on the reuse of bricks in the construction of the abbey. He also transcribed lengthy passages from the *Gesta Abbatum Monasterii Sancti Albani,* which was compiled over several centuries by monks working in the St. Albans *scriptorium,* including the medieval chronicler Matthew Paris.[16] A few decades later, William Harrison relied on Leland's notes for his *Description of England* (1577; enlarged 1587), which was appended to Holinshed's *Chronicles* and thereby reached a wide readership. In the thematic chapter on Britain's cities, Harrison included the major events of Verulamium's history and referenced the writings of Matthew Paris, Tacitus, Gildas, and others.[17] However, Harrison was a critical reader of his sources, at one point including the marginal gloss "this soundeth like a lie."[18] Many of the details Harrison included, such as Abbot Alfric's purchase and draining of the royal fishpond and the erroneous claim that the Thames once flowed through Verulamium, became commonplace and were repeated in subsequent chorographies, including Camden's. Harrison recognized the importance of transcribing passages from older authors in order to save them from loss:

> Good notice hereof also is to be taken by *Matthew Paris,* and others before him, out of whose writings I haue thought good to note a few things, whereby the maiestie of this ancient citie may appeare vnto posteritie, and the former estate of Uerlamcester not lie altogither (as it hath doone hitherto) raked vp in forgetfulnes, through the negligence of such as might haue deserued better of their successours, by leauing the description thereof in a booke by it selfe, sith manie particulars thereof were written to their hands, that now are lost and perished.[19]

Harrison's meditation on Verulamium's rescue from oblivion was a precursor to the image of Verulamium as a symbol of mutability, which developed several decades later. The evocative image of resurrecting the past "maiestie" of a place and thus saving it from being "raked vp in forgetfulnes" became a common antiquarian trope, and one frequently used with reference to Verulamium. The verb "to rake" means to assemble or collect together, but it has a more specific sense of raking coals to put out a fire, and the phrase "rake up" means to "bring to wider notice" or "revive the memory."[20] "Raked vp in forgetfulnes," then, articulates the antiquarian fear of "historical loss," which Andrew Escobedo defines as the "sense that the past was incommensurate with and possibly lost to the present."[21] For Harrison, Verulamium is an example of a historical artifact in danger of becoming so badly deteriorated by the passage of time that future generations would know only that *something* had once existed there, but not what it was; what would be "raked vp" is not the memory of the site's "former estate" but, paradoxically, only "forgetfulnes." Sites with few physical remains, such as Verulamium, fostered in antiquarians like Harrison a reverence and respect for textual monuments as bulwarks against the destructive power of time that Camden would echo a decade later in his *Britannia.*

The form and content of Camden's *Britannia* owes much to the work of Leland and Harrison before him.[22] However, Camden managed to avoid the hindrance—which had plagued Leland—of lacking a suitable structure to accommodate the sheer quantity of collected material by adopting the county-by-county form popularized by Christopher Saxton's landmark *Atlas* (1579).[23] Although he incorporated information and sources from Leland and Harrison, Camden's discussion of Verulamium and St. Albans far surpassed those of his antecedents, as he took a site, which in his day was "being turned into fields," and reinvigorated it with a vivid account of its history.[24] Camden's account of Verulamium is typical of his overall method, where, in Bernard Klein's words, "history sets the stage for geography."[25] In *Britannia,* he describes each county's notable places (including etymology of place-names), monuments, and historical events with the aim "to restore antiquity to Britaine, and Britain to his antiquity."[26] When faced with a location like Verulamium, which possessed few artifacts and monuments of its own, Camden, like Harrison before him, turned to the textual monuments of the archive to supplement his field research. As Jennifer Summit observes, in Camden's approach to antiquarian writing "books become a form of archeological artifact, the physical remains of the past that speak in a language that is no longer that of the researcher."[27]

Camden describes the scant physical evidence at Verulamium as fully as he can, including descriptions of the Roman-era remains and a sketch of the ancient coins found in farmers' fields, but for details he bases his account largely on other texts, including those by Tacitus, Gildas, Suetonius, Alexander Neckham, and the *Flores Historiarum.* When he repeats information obtained through networks of antiquarians, he credits his correspondents, including Hubert Goltzius and David Powel.[28] He also quotes lengthy sections from primary sources, including the passages from the *Gesta Abbatum Monasterii Sancti Albani* that describe the discovery of artifacts in underground vaults under the site of Verulamium.[29] Thus, Camden's account of Verulamium weaves together the various strands of English history that took place there and in the surrounding Hertfordshire countryside: Britain's Roman past, the martyrdom of Saint Alban, the building of the abbey, and several key battles of the Wars of the Roses. By uniting historical narratives, etymology, topographical descriptions, and reproductions of artifacts, Camden's account of Verulamium served as both the standard for subsequent chorographers and their main source.

Through Camden, Verulamium became a site of keen contemporary interest. When the mapmaker and chorographer John Norden compiled the *Hartfordshire* volume of his *Speculum Britanniae,* he was one of the first mapmakers to feature Verulamium on his county map, and he included a substantive prose description of the ancient Roman city.[30] Norden included many of the historical details found in Camden and elsewhere, but his attention was drawn to cataloguing the ruins and artifacts found on the site, as he enthusiastically noted the "sundry pottes of gould, brasse earth, glasse and other metal, some frawght with the ashes of the dead, some with the coyne of the auncient *Britons* and Romane Emperours. And in a stone were found certayne Brytish books, whereof one imported the historie of *Albans* martyrdome."[31] For Norden, the material traces, scant as they were, confirmed the existence and the former glory of Verulamium above and beyond the textual accounts: "the sundry Roman coyns tumbled out of their obscure denns, by the painefull plough, doe, as it were, proclaim vnto vs, so many hundred years after Verulamium's fall, that it is no fable that is written of her antiquitie."[32] As F. J. Levy notes, Norden had a "strong visual sense" that responded to "the vicissitudes of time as shown in ruins" and "[u]nlike almost everyone else in the sixteenth century, he went beyond describing a ruined castle merely because it was there: Norden almost automatically saw it peopled and thriving, as it must once have been."[33]

Norden's account of Verulamium demonstrates an awareness of how history permeates everyday life or, in de Certeau's words, how "objects and words also have hollow places in which a past sleeps."[34] Norden's map image of Verulamium in turn influenced Camden, as he incorporated it in all editions of *Britannia* after 1607, including the 1611 English translation, which Shrimpton would have likely seen.[35] As the expanding editions of Camden's *Britannia* and Norden's chorography make clear, the ruined Roman city of Verulamium became a public image. Although its actual site offered only the faintest hint of what had once existed, this absence was elaborated and enlivened not only by mapmakers and chorographers but also, increasingly, by poets.

For example, after Camden's *Britannia,* references to the Roman city became more frequent in poetry. William Vallans's *A Tale of Two Swannes* (1590) features swans who, on their journey along the river Lea through Hertfordshire to London, pass "not farre from ancient Verolame."[36]

Although this reference is limited to a half-line of poetry, more than one-third of the accompanying prose commentary on the poem focuses on Verulamium, with information largely adapted from Camden. The most extensive poem taking Verulamium as its subject, however, is Spenser's *The Ruines of Time* (1591), which, by contrasting the ruined state of Verulamium with the power of the written word to preserve the past, engages with many of the themes present in Leland, Harrison, Camden, and Norden. Contained in Spenser's larger *Complaints* volume, *The Ruines of Time* features a speaker, a late sixteenth-century man like Spenser himself, who comes face-to-face with a figure from England's Roman past.

The poem opens with the speaker positioning himself beside the "silver streaming" Thames, near to where the ancient Roman city of Verulamium once stood. There he sees a weeping woman (Verlame, or the genius of Verulamium) who tells him that she once was "that Citie which the garland wore / Of *Britaines* pride" but has now become "but weedes and wastfull gras."[37] With this declaration, Verlame fully embodies the land that speaks. She then recites a long complaint, locating the fate of Verulamium in the context of other fallen classical civilizations, as well as the more recent deaths of Robert Dudley, earl of Leicester, and Sir Philip Sidney. The thrust of the genius's complaint is a longing for earthly glory that recognizes the vanity and futility of human endeavor, "For how can mortall immortalitie give?"[38] *The Ruines of Time* is a meditation on loss at the individual, the local, the national, and the civilizational levels. In it, Verulamium becomes a trope that allows Spenser to mourn and monumentalize the recent losses of Sidney and Dudley alongside the fall of ancient civilizations, thus placing their deaths in the broader dignity of time's assault on all that would seem great and permanent.

The Ruines of Time reveals much about Spenser's reading practices: most of his factual information about Verulamium comes from Camden's *Britannia,* but his poetic account adapts and responds to Camden's antiquarian portrayal of Verulamium. At times, Verlame's complaint echoes Harrison's meditation on the antiquarian enterprise:

> Nor anie liues that mentioneth my name
> To be remembred of posteritie,
> Saue One that maugre fortunes iniurie,
> And times decay, and enuies cruell tort,
> Hath writ my record in true-seeming sort.[39]

Just as Harrison wished to prevent Verulamium from being "raked vp in forgetfulnes," so too is this "One," whom Verlame identifies as "*Cambden* the nourice of antiquitie," able to rescue Verulamium from her state of near-oblivion.[40] As she laments, "all but ruines now I bee, / And lye in mine owne ashes, as ye see," yet Camden is a "lanterne unto late succeeding age" who can "see the light of simple veritie, / Buried in ruins."[41]

Spenser often made use of antiquarian sources for his poetry, yet several elements in *The Ruines of Time* suggest some ambivalence, or at least a degree of uncertainty, toward these sources. Verlame's assertion that Camden "writ my record in true-seeming sort" has led some scholars, including Bart van Es, to suggest that the discrepancy between "true-seeming" and "veritie" reveals a subtle criticism: "the city's 'genius' remains uncertain whether Camden has created or discovered her past."[42] Moreover, in his poetic representation of Verulamium, Spenser is not tied to "veritie" but can rather adopt legends and false information for his own purposes. Although previous accounts of Verulamium emphasized the falsity of the claim that the Thames once flowed through the city, attributing it to "a corrupt place in *Gildas*," Spenser makes the Thames the meeting place for the speaker and the Genius of Verlame, "Nigh where the goodly *Verlame* stood of yore."[43] He places Verulamium "on the featureless banks of the Thames (the river of time)" in order to connect that particular site to the universal experience of change, where "all that in this world is great or gaie, / Doth as a vapour vanish, and decaie."[44] For Spenser, the image of Verulamium as a symbol of mutability supersedes the factual information about it. He blurs the distinction between poetry and history, presenting an image of Verulamium where fact and legend, excised and rearranged from their original contexts, combine to transform the sparse allegory of the antiquarian enterprise as a whole.

Spenser used the antiquarian creation of Verulamium to articulate a response to the ubiquitous claim in his sources that texts can create a monument able to withstand the destructive force of time. *The Ruines of Time,* as Spenser asserts in its final lines, is a "moniment of praise," and with this word "moniment" he ends where he began. In the opening of the poem, the speaker declares he stands "Nigh where the goodly *Verlame* stood of yore, / Of which there now remaines no memorie, / Nor anie little moniment to see."[45] Thus the poem moves from the tragic absence of a monument to finally becoming itself a monument. Yet, as van Es has observed, for the early moderns, "monument" was "an evocative but also a troubling term."[46]

The figure of the monument moves in two directions at once: it holds the promise of permanence, memory, and eternity while ultimately being a fallible subject to the devouring course of time. As "a monument-less monument," Verlame fears the dreaded state of nothingness, which is to be

"[w]asted . . . as if it never were" or, in Harrison's phrase, "raked vp in forgetfulnes."[47] Only the written word, Verlame declares, can protect against
such dissolution, as "wise words taught in numbers for to runne, / Recorded by the Muses, live for ay."[48] Again, her exemplar of the permanence
of text is Camden, and she declares that, "though time all moniments
obscure, / Yet [his] just labours ever shall endure."[49] These paired traits of
the monumental impulse ("ever shall endure") and the fear of historical
loss ("all moniments obscure") are continuously in tension in *The Ruines
of Time,* and they underpinned and motivated a broad range of poetic and
cartographic enterprises of the late sixteenth and early seventeenth centuries, including the shaping of the powerful image of Verulamium.

Drayton's account of Verulamium in *Poly-Olbion* (1612; expanded in
1622), which Shrimpton drew from directly for his *Antiquities,* was strongly
influenced by Spenser's creation of the Genius of Verlame and the emphasis on the twin themes of mutability and monumentality. Echoing Harrison's reflections on Verulamium's past glories and Spenser's meditations on
the fallibility of human monuments, Drayton describes "*Verlam* once her
head aloft did beare / (Which in her cinders now lies sadly buried heere)."[50]
Drayton's chorographical poem has a tripartite form: songs (written in
hexameter and prefaced with a verse argument), maps (based on Saxton's
county maps, but populated with figures allegorizing topographical features), and prose commentary (written by the antiquarian John Selden
to complement and elucidate Drayton's references). In Song 16, Drayton
creates a poetic response to his antiquarian sources by taking historical anecdotes and facts about Verulamium and translating them into a conversation in hexameters between an anthropomorphized river Ver and Watling
Street. Vine argues that Drayton's prosopopoeia, which is a common feature of *Poly-Olbion,* "brings a continuity between past and present that
even the most compendious antiquarian catalogues and descriptions cannot achieve."[51] Providing a balance to Drayton's poetic account, Selden's
prose commentary to *Poly-Olbion* more closely resembles the antiquarian
works by Leland and Camden that he frequently references. Also, alongside the familiar citations to Tacitus and Gildas, Selden transcribes three
lengthy passages from *The Ruines of Time,* thereby ascribing to Spenser the
same degree of authority as his ancient sources. Drayton's and Selden's engagement with Spenser's poem demonstrates that soon after its publication
excerpted passages from *The Ruines of Time* circulated as commonplaces
and could be used for the purpose of substantiating historical claims.

During the sixteenth century, the idea of Verulamium developed
through the collection, reiteration, and arbitration of details about its lo-

cation and history. These details circulated within an antiquarian public keen to share information and methodologies; yet as the progression from Leland to Drayton shows, this circulation of commonplaces also had the power to shape and reshape the very public that had created this idea of Verulamium in the first place. By the time Shrimpton began compiling his *Antiquities,* Verulamium had become a symbol both of mutability and of the antiquarian desire to discover and create monuments for the preservation of history. By depending so heavily on the depictions of Verulamium present in the works of Camden, Spenser, and Drayton, Shrimpton's *Antiquities* is situated in what Helgerson calls a "dense net of intertextual relations" existing between texts that "refer so often and so conspicuously to one another."[52] While I have been arguing that we should interpret this "net of intertextual relations" as a public, the public Shrimpton participates in differs markedly from Warner's model, where publics, even though they are "created by the reflexive circulation of discourse," can nevertheless only "act historically according to the temporality of their circulation," and their participants "understand themselves as directly and actively belonging to a social entity that exists historically in secular time and has consciousness of itself."[53] In contrast to the relative immediacy of Warner's model, the public that created the idea of Verulamium in the early modern period is diachronic: it was little concerned with the present, instead being oriented to the past (the source of the people, texts, and artifacts it takes as its interest) and the future (in its desire to restore and preserve the past for posterity). It is fitting that this public participated in establishing what Helgerson would later identify as "forms of nationhood," as this designation also implies the dual focus of transmitting the nation's past to future generations.

Shrimpton's Verulamium

Shrimpton's *Antiquities of Verulam and St. Albans* provides ample evidence that the chorographical and poetic texts identified by Helgerson as "forms of nationhood" were immediately recognized as having the weight and authority commonly granted to ancient texts. By listing his sources and repeating many of the details about Verulamium found in them, Shrimpton's *Antiquities* provides documentary evidence of late English Renaissance reading practices as well as examples of the uptake inherent in the formation of the public that engaged with these sources and turned to them to define the nation. The *Antiquities* allows us to "look over the shoulder of a local historian of the 1630s as he bends to the task," and, in doing so, we can plausibly detect Shrimpton's uptake of contemporary commonplaces circulating about Verulamium and gauge their effect on his local experience.[54] *The Antiquities* proceeds in roughly chronological order from its settlement by the Romans to the dissolution of its monastery, and many of details Shrimpton includes come directly from his sources. His use of these sources ranges from attributing a certain fact to an author by name, to borrowing phrasing and quotations, to transcribing long passages outright.[55]

Shrimpton likely did not consult all his sources directly, however, as his citations to the ancient sources nearly always appear in excerpts from Camden and Weever; for instance, he transcribed some quotations, such as the poetry of Neckham, directly from Camden's *Britannia*.[56] Massive texts such as *Britannia* or Drayton's *Poly-Olbion* became repositories of antiquarian learning, and they provided access to a wide array of primary sources. Only a generation after their publication, they were actively consulted by readers who used them "in the manner that they might have used any other historical or antiquarian book."[57] Shrimpton's most heavily used source for both content and form was Weever's *Ancient Funeral Monuments* (1631), a comprehensive account of both existing and defaced funeral monuments in Britain.[58] Weever, who seems to have been a personal friend of Shrimpton, traveled and collected notes over two or three decades before assembling them into his expansive text a year before his death. Four features of Weever's book appear to have influenced Shrimpton's presentation of Verulamium: his frequent "use of illustrative extracts from the poets," his use of other manuscripts "from which he again took whatever he found interesting," his "adopting [of] an emphatically personal point of view," and his conviction that books could serve as a monument more lasting than brass.[59] Weever opens his lengthy catalogue of monuments with the assertion that "all religious Foundations, all sumptuous and magnificent Structures, Cities, Townes . . . as well as Tombes and Sepulchres, are called Monuments," but they are all subject to decay and so, "for worthinesse and continuance, bookes, or writings, haue euer had the preheminence" as monuments.[60] As corroborative evidence, he cites numerous commonplaces taken from ancient authors, as well as Joachim Du Bellay, Drayton, and Spenser. He cites two passages from *The Ruines of Time* to demonstrate, first, that cities are subject to decay ("all but ruines now I bee, / And lye in mine owne ashes, as ye see"), and second, that only books can provide true permanence ("But wise wordes taught in numbers for to runne, / Recorded by the Muses, live for ay").[61] For Weever, Spenser's representation of Verulamium as a symbol of the desire for permanence, which was the culmination of the preceding antiquarian descriptions of the Roman site, informed his approach to the ruins and monuments of the entire nation.

Shrimpton adopts Weever's scholarly practices but narrows his focus to a town rather than a county or the nation. It is Spenser's portrayal of Verulamium and its significance that sets the tone of Shrimpton's *Antiquities*. Shrimpton inserts the same stanza Weever quotes, which begins "I was that Citie, which the garland wore," into his list of abbots in order to illustrate the historical moment when "Verulamium was for ever layd in her grave."[62] The significance of this commonplace for Shrimpton is clear from the opening page. After the initial list of authors, Shrimpton begins with a meditation and verse on the fragility of material monuments and the destructive force of time:

> Verulamium was one, whose name although it survives her ancient glory, or if you please her miserable desolation, yet of the same nothing nowe remaines but a few fragments of the old ruinous walls with the trenches which went about it, to be seen, all the rest of it *being buryed in its own ashes as if it had never been.*

> > Thus still devouring time to ruines brings
> > & changeth oft the greatest States that are
> > it doth not spare the Monuments of Kings
> > but makes them lye as if they never were
> > it layes the mountaines level with the plaine
> > makes sea dry land, and dry land sea againe[63]

These verses imitate the genius of Verlame's declaration that "ruines now I bee, / And lye in mine owne ashes, as ye see," and that the city is "Wasted . . . as if it never were, / And all the rest that me so honord made, / And of the world admired ev'rie where, / Is turnd to smoake," an image Drayton also echoed in *Poly-Olbion.*[64] Yet Shrimpton goes a step further and links Spenser's image to the image of a phoenix in a passage describing the rebuilding of Verulamium after Boadicea's rebellion. Here Shrimpton quotes another commonplace, Symphosius's riddle on the phoenix, and provides both a prose and verse translation:

> > Vita mihi mors est; morior si coepero nasci;
> > sed prius est fatum leti quam lucis origo;
> > sic solus Manes ipsos mihi dico parentes.

Death is like to me, I dye if I begin to be borne, first comes death, then follows life, so that only my dead ghosts are my parents, of thus if yow please.

> > My death is life to mee my boddye dyes
> > e're I can be new borne, for first comes death

> by which dissolved to dust from thence I rise
> Unto the light & reassume my breath
> Thus my dead Ashes my parents bee
> & thus I dye to live as yow may see.[65]

Shrimpton's transcription of material from both direct and indirect sources demonstrates that commonplaces were available to anyone who also had access to texts, and that attention to them included their readers and users in an impersonal and anonymous public form of association.

Yet little about Verulamium and St. Albans was impersonal or anonymous to Shrimpton, and the *Antiquities* is remarkable for his poetic and personal approach to his subject. In addition to quoting medieval and contemporary verse, he included a fifteen-stanza poem on the mythological marriage of the small river Cott to the town of Verulamium. Written in the mode of Camden's *De Connubio Tamae,* Spenser's river marriage canto in *The Faerie Queene,* book 4, and Drayton's *Poly-Olbion,* the poem seems to be an original composition. Also, the few glimpses into his own daily life in Hertfordshire indicate that the constructed image of Verulamium as a monument to mutability affected Shrimpton deeply. At several points he refers to the "envious times" in which he lives and stops himself from making overtly political statements, lest he give offense.[66] He openly and vehemently disparages the dissolution of the monasteries, however, which he calls "that terrible Thunderclap": "such sacraledg, cruelty & disorder was committed, that under pretence of pulling down the Abbeyes with other religious structures, they defaced the monuments of ye dead, breaking up their graves, & burning their bones."[67] Such a desecration is immediate and personal for Shrimpton: the graves broken open could very well have housed his own family. In fact, when he catalogues the monuments still existing in the cathedral, he includes his own parents' graves alongside that of nobility. Shrimpton endorses tolerance toward the Roman Catholicism of his ancestors: "Howsoever these things were applyed & used by the Papists, yet were they the guifts & religious offerings of devout men, & therefore ought to have been bestowed to the mentainance of Leirning & relieife of the poore; & not to mentaine the pride & prodigality of those in whom both religion, leirning, & charity was wanting."[68]

Although writing as a chorographer, Shrimpton conveys a sense of place in the *Antiquities* shaped distinctly by his role as inhabitant. His everyday life in St. Albans was shaped by what de Certeau describes as the "series of displacements," "fragmented strata," and "moving layers" that define those places in which "the presences of diverse absences" are palpable. For Shrimpton, the absences were at once familial, religious, archaeological, and historical, and he turned to texts as compensation for what was lacking. At once intimate and detached, specific and general, quotidian and timeless, Shrimpton's study of Verulamium articulates an awareness of loss that is deeply personal alongside a desire to fill gaps in the historical record and monumentalize what remained.

Conclusion

Many of the chorographical and antiquarian projects during the early modern period shared a desire to serve as monuments, preserving through words what was otherwise lost through decay and ruin. These texts, including those identified by Helgerson as "forms of nationhood," frequently identified themselves either explicitly or implicitly as monuments, and there is an overlap between the early modern usage of the term "monument" and Helgerson's definition of "forms": "forms . . . are as much agents as they are structures. They make things happen."[69] Texts by Camden, Spenser, Drayton, and others became "forms of nationhood" because they could provide the monumentality that nationhood entails. However, this required uptake; it required individuals to pick up, read, and engage with these texts. The example of John Shrimpton is a reminder of the necessity of such involvement and the potential it has to transform an individual's experience of place. In writing a local chorography, then, Shrimpton incorporated the rhetoric of monumentality that drove the considerable literary production of the sixteenth and seventeenth centuries. The *Antiquities* shows that the tensions and debates inherent in elite English antiquarian circles could be no less palpable to the son of a brewer who participated in the writing of his nation's history in the context of his own hometown.

NOTES

1. Richard Helgerson, *Forms of Nationhood: The Elizabethan Writing of England* (Chicago: University of Chicago Press, 1992), 13, 11.

2. Michael Warner, *Publics and Counterpublics* (New York: Zone Books, 2005), 145.

3. Helgerson, *Forms of Nationhood*, 1.

4. John Shrimpton, *The Antiquities of Verulam and St. Albans,* ed. Carson I. A. Ritchie (St. Albans, UK: St. Albans and Hertfordshire Architectural and Archaeological Society, 1966), 77. Shrimpton's work has received scant attention in early modern scholarship. See Carson I. A. Ritchie, "A Forgotten Antiquary," *Hertfordshire Countryside* 11.42 (Fall 1956): 54–56; Carson I. A. Ritchie, "An Elizabethan Looks at Verulamium," *Notes and Queries* 202 (June 1957): 233–34; and Angus Vine, *In Defiance of Time* (Oxford: Oxford University Press, 2010), 197–98.

5. Ann Blair, "Humanist Methods in Natural Philosophy: The Commonplace Book," *Journal of the History of Ideas* 53.4 (1992): 541–52, 541.

6. Bronwen Wilson and Paul Yachnin, "Introduction," *Making Publics in Early Modern Europe: People, Things, and Forms of Knowledge* (London: Routledge, 2010), 1.

7. Warner, *Publics and Counterpublics,* 90, 145.

8. Helgerson, *Forms of Nationhood,* 131.

9. Michel de Certeau, *The Practice of Everyday Life,* trans. Steven Rendall (Berkeley: University of California Press, 1988), 108.

10. Frank Kitchen, "Cosmo-Choro-Poly-Grapher: An Analytical Account of the Life and Work of John Norden, 1547–1625" (DPhil diss., Sussex University, 1992), 29.

11. On these excavations, see Rosalind Niblett and Isobel Thompson, *Alban's Buried Towns: An Assessment of St Alban's Archaeology up to AD 1600* (Oxford: Oxbow Books, 2005).

12. William Camden, *Britannia,* trans. Philemon Holland (London, 1610), 408.

13. John Norden, *Speculi Britanniae Pars: The Description of Hartfordshire* (London, 1598), 25.

14. Rosalind Niblett, *Verulamium: The Roman City of St Albans* (Gloucestershire: Tempus Publishing, 2001), 7–8, 143–46.

15. Shrimpton, *Antiquities,* 1.

16. John Leland, "Commentarii," *Cygnea Cantio* (London, 1545), O3v; for Leland's notes on Verulamium, see John Leland, *De Rebus Britannicis Collectanea,* ed. Thomas Hearne (London, 1774), 4: 164–68.

17. William Harrison, "The Description and History of Britaine," in Raphael Holinshed, *The First and Second Volumes of the Chronicles* (London, 1587), 191–92.

18. Ibid., 192.

19. Ibid., 191. This passage also appears in the 1577 edition.

20. *Oxford English Dictionary,* 3.a., 3.c.

21. Andrew Escobedo, *Nationalism and Historical Loss in Renaissance England: Foxe, Dee, Spenser, Milton* (Ithaca, N.Y.: Cornell University Press, 2004), 3.

22. On Camden's *Britannia,* see Lesley Cormack, *Charting an Empire: Geography at the English Universities, 1580–1620* (Chicago: University of Chicago Press, 1997), 177–80; Bernard Klein, *Maps and the Writing of Space in Early Modern England and Ireland* (New York: Palgrave, 2001), 143–45; and Stan Mendyk, *'Speculum Britanniae': Regional Study, Antiquarianism, and Science in Britain to 1700* (Toronto: University of Toronto Press, 1989), 49–56.

23. Klein, *Maps,* 140–44.

24. Camden, *Britannia,* 412.

25. Klein, *Maps,* 143.

26. Camden, *Britannia,* fol. 4r.

27. Jennifer Summit, *Memory's Library: Medieval Books in Early Modern England* (Chicago: University of Chicago Press, 2008), 175.

28. Camden, *Britannia,* 408–13.

29. For facing Latin/English translations of the pertinent ancient and medieval sources on St. Albans, see Niblett and Thompson, *Alban's Buried Towns,* 349–88.

30. On Norden's *Speculum Britanniae* project, see Edward Lynam, "English Maps and Map-Makers of the Sixteenth Century," *The Geographical Journal* 116.1/3 (July–September 1950): 15–23; Mendyk, *'Speculum Britanniae',* 57–74; and Klein, *Maps,* 145–48.

31. Norden, *Speculi Britanniae Pars,* 24.

32. Ibid.

33. F. J. Levy, *Tudor Historical Thought* (San Marino, Calif.: Huntington Library, 1967), 162.

34. De Certeau, *Practice,* 108.

35. Ritchie argues that Shrimpton was familiar with Norden's *Speculum Britanniae* as well

as John Speed's *The Theatre of the Empire of Great Britain* (1611); See Ritchie, "Introduction," in Shrimpton, *Antiquities,* xii–xiii.

36. William Vallans, *A Tale of Two Swannes* (London, 1590), A4r.

37. Edmund Spenser, *The Ruines of Time,* in *The Yale Edition of the Shorter Poems of Edmund Spenser,* ed. William A. Oram et al. (New Haven, Conn.: Yale University Press, 1989), lines 36–37, 42.

38. Ibid., line 413.

39. Ibid., lines 164–68.

40. Ibid., line 169.

41. Ibid., lines 39–40, 170–72.

42. Bart Van Es, *Spenser's Forms of History* (Oxford: Oxford University Press, 2002), 32.

43. Camden, *Britannia,* 411; Spenser, *Ruines,* line 3.

44. Van Es, *Spenser's Forms,* 36; Spenser, *Ruines,* lines 54–55.

45. Spenser, *Ruines* lines 4–5.

46. Van Es, *Spenser's Forms,* 23.

47. Ibid., 34; Spenser, *Ruines,* line 120.

48. Spenser, *Ruines,* lines 402–3.

49. Ibid., lines 168–75.

50. Michael Drayton, *Poly-Olbion* (London, 1622), 16.43–44.

51. Vine, *In Defiance of Time,* 183.

52. Helgerson, *Forms of Association,* 131.

53. Warner, *Publics,* 90, 68, 75.

54. Ritchie, "Introduction," iii.

55. Shrimpton's borrowings are usually unattributed. E.g., the biographical sketches of the Abbots (32–38) are taken nearly verbatim from John Weever, *Ancient Funerall Monuments* (London: Thomas Harper, 1631), 557–62.

56. Shrimpton, *Antiquities,* 21. Ritchie catalogues numerous other examples, see "Introduction," ix–xiii.

57. Vine, *In Defiance of Time,* 196.

58. See E. A. J. Honigmann, *John Weever* (Manchester: Manchester University Press, 1987), 68–79.

59. Honigmann, *Weever,* 71, 72–73, 77.

60. Weever, *Ancient Funerall Monuments,* 1.

61. Ibid., 4–5.

62. Shrimpton, *Antiquities,* 27.

63. Ibid., 1; emphasis added.

64. Spenser, *Ruines,* lines 39–40, 120–23.

65. Shrimpton, *Antiquities,* 7. Symphosius, *Symphosii uteris poetae elegantissimi erudita iuxta ac arguta et festiua Aenigmata* (Paris, 1533), A4r.

66. Shrimpton, *Antiquities,* 32, 77.

67. Ibid., 76.

68. Ibid., 77. For the description of Shrimpton's parents' graves, see 51.

69. Helgerson, *Forms of Association,* 6.

CHAPTER TEN

Collectors, Consumers, and the Making of a Seventeenth-Century English Ballad Public

From Networks to Spheres

PATRICIA FUMERTON

IN 2005, when I joined Richard Helgerson as part of the UCSB branch of the Making Publics Project centered at McGill University and under the direction of Paul Yachnin, I had a sneaking suspicion that the combined scope and necessary granularity of this project could drive one mad. In writing this chapter, I have felt that foreboding madness more closely creep upon me as I have tried to make sense of some five years of my own work on making publics while at the same time paying tribute to the lifetime making of Richard Helgerson, a guiding genius for the MaPs project before his too early demise in 2008.

Both are impossible tasks. Making Publics became a great success, but the sign of its success—as we have moved in our discussions from defining a public to defining publics in the making—is that we are always making ourselves making and unmaking publics being made and unmade. That is, just as one's finger is placed on the pulse of a public in the making, it is in the process of being—*by virtue of its definition of being a public and not* the *public*—unmade. I recall George Wither's emblem, which tellingly riddles, "As soone, as wee to bee, begunne; / We did beginne to be Vndone" (fig. 10.1). I am here beginning or—I guess in the grander scheme of things—*continuing* my being undone. Writing in this chapter of the processes specifically of making a ballad public with an eye to the makings of the great Richard Helgerson, I by definition must embrace simultaneously their and my own unmaking, especially as I could never attain Richard's uncanny breadth and depth of vision that can sweepingly take in all of history while remaining acutely attuned to the historical moments of both the then and the now.

If Richard in this emblem is the all-encompassing Ouroborus that consumes its own tail in a representation of his eternity, I am the enclosed babe lying within, propped on the skull of my mortal limits. Like that babe, I begin undone. I shall nevertheless strive to capture some of Richard's devotion to the larger historical picture and to the way he thought complexly about history—including the marginal together with great affairs of state—about generations of people talking together within historical moments of time, and also about how individuals involved in those discussions took unique positions, not necessarily sharing the same viewpoint even though they might be excitedly gathered around, and looking at, the same thing.

Richard's generational thinking, as well as his inclusive vision of what "counts" as historically important, especially sets the stage for my own strategy in this discussion. I deal with a popular printed form that was often dismissed as inconsequential in its own time by those with aesthetic and/or political authority but that was the most popular form of contemporary print and spoke volumes about generations, private individuals, and histories of early modern England, written with both a big and a little *h*. I speak

FIGURE 10.1. George Wither, *A collection of Emblemes*, 3 vols. (London 1656), illustration and caption to vol. 1, emblem 45.

As *foone*, as *wee* to bee, *begunne*;
We did *beginne*, to be Vndone.

of the English broadside ballad. Thinking about the collecting and circulation of the broadside ballad in early modern England allows us to tease out further Lesley Cormack's distinction between networks and publics and to provide a conceptual and working model for a ballad public.

Some background: I have been directing the English Broadside Ballad Archive, or EBBA, for only a little longer than the Making Publics project came into being (since 2003). Like MaPs, EBBA is a protean creature always in the making. Funded mostly by large NEH grants, the project is devoted to mounting online all surviving seventeenth-century broadside ballads printed in English (some ten to eleven thousand works). We prioritize black-letter ornamental ballads published in the ballad's heyday of the first half of the seventeenth century, although—and this is what makes the project so unstable—the continually evolving format of the broadside ballad necessitates inclusion of both earlier and later printed ballads in order to grasp meaningfully the genre's shifting format at any one time. The ballads are further digitally mounted in EBBA in various facsimile representations reflective of their multiple cultural roles—as art, as history (multiply defined), as song, and as literature. EBBA is thus an ambitious project that, babe-like, aspires to the kind of grand ambitions of Making Publics and the laureate career of Richard Helgerson.

Most recently, I have been researching the networks of collectors of primarily black-letter broadside ballads in seventeenth-century England. These networks include prominent and recognizable figures such as Samuel Pepys and Robert Harley, but also more historically obscure persons such as Humphrey Wanley, Anthony Wood, and John Bagford. Focusing on any one collector and his assemblages reveals an individual but also a maze of connections with other collectors. To the extent that this collecting network drew in strangers and had a scholarly and social agenda (as we shall more fully see), it could be argued to form a public. It certainly fits Leslie Cormack's thumbnail definition of publics in her essay in this volume as "a loose collection of people, not all of whom have personal knowledge of one another, connected by a common interest in a particular subject and with some social or political goal in mind."

As was the case with Cormack's chorographers, the black-letter ballad collectors I shall trace formed a relatively small network. But, as Cormack herself notes, the population of early modern England was itself relatively small. More important than size, it would seem to me, is the level of engagement between participants of a network with their subject and with each other. By this gauge, if we might feel unsure about the "publicness" of a ballad-collecting network, we can with confidence identify a ballad public actively at play in watching Pepys as he expands upon his collecting network. By focusing, as in Google Maps, specifically on Pepys's ballad collecting, and then further zooming in to look at his wider social interactions in circulating ballads, as told in his *Diary,* we can extend our vision beyond the relatively small but important assemblages of collectors to include a much larger and more engaged ballad public. As we shall see, this public may not share the same scholarly values as the serious ballad collectors of black-letter scriptural and printed ballads, and it may not be as "invested" in ballads per se, but its members reflexively used ballads to private, social, and political ends, relying on shared public expectations about what ballads are and can be. I conclude by proposing that such a ballad public, which includes collecting and consuming as well as ballad-producing relationships, strangely resembles Clifford Geertz's landmark model of the social spheres of the Balinese cockfight.

As in Richard's focus throughout his career on generational formations, it is important to contextualize black-letter ballad collectors, such as Pepys, within changing generations of ballad collectors as well as changes in ballad production, which to some extent influenced what was "out there" to be collected. Sixteenth-century collectors, such as Captain Cox and William Fitch (whose collection was later split up to become the Huth ballads at the British Library and the Britwell ballads at the Huntington Library)[1] were necessarily limited in their collecting practices to the kinds of broadside ballads being printed at the time: simple artifacts typically printed on one side of a relatively small folio sheet of paper in black-letter (what we know today as "gothic") type with few, if any, ornaments, only the occasionally named tune title, and a modest range of topics that favored religion, elegies/epitaphs, and wonders. The generation that lived through, or close to, the seventeenth-century heyday of the broadside ballad (1600–50) had the opportunity to collect a very different kind of ballad. During this period, the ballad's multidimensional and multi-media potentials blossomed: we find decorative, if sometimes crude, artifacts consisting of much larger folio sheets—on which the ballad was usually expanded and divided into two "parts"—still printed in black letter but with multiple woodcuts as well as other ornaments, a named tune title, and a dizzying variety of topics ranging from religion, elegies/epitaphs, and wonders to familiar "historical" stories, such as Chevy Chase, to romantic love or marriage or sex, to murders or other timely news, to alehouse good fellowship, to politics, and so on (see, for example, fig. 10.2). There was no topic or stance that such broadside ballads could not adopt. Ballads issued by the same author or printer/publisher often presented in the very same ballad

Anne VVallens Lamentation,

For the Murthering of her husband *Iohn Wallen* a Turner in Cow-lane neere Smithfield; done by his owne wife, on satterday the 22 of Iune. 1616.
who was burnt in Smithfield the first of Iuly following.
To the tune of Fortune my foe.

G Reat God that sees al things that here are don
 & seeing thy Court with thy celestiall Son;
Heare her complaint that hath so sore offended,
Forgiue my fact before my life is ended.

Ah me the shame vnto all women kinde,
To harbour such a thought within my minde:
That now hath made me to the world a scorne,
And makes me curse the time that I was borne.

O would to God my mothers haples wombe,
Before my birth had beene my happy tombe:
Or would to God when first I did take breath,
That I had suffered any painefull death.

If euer dyed a true repentant soule,
Then I am she, whose deedes are blacke and foule:
Then take heed wiues be to your husbands kinde,
And beare this lesson truely in your minde,

Let not your tongue oresway true reasons bounds,
Which in your rage your vtmost rancour sounds:
A woman that is wise should seldome speake,
Vnlesse discreetly she her words repeat.

Oh would that I had thought of this before,
Which now to thinke on makes my heart full sore:
Then should I not haue done this deed so foule,
The which hath stained my immortall soule.

Tis not to dye that thus doth cause me grieue,
I am more willing far to die then liue;
But tis for blood which mounteth to the skies,
And to the Lord reuenge, reuenge, it cries.

My dearest husband did I wound to death,
And was the cause he lost his sweetest breath,
But yet I trust his soule in heauen doth dwell,
And mine without Gods mercy sinkes to hell.

In London neere to smithfield did I dwell,
And mongst my neighbours was beloued well:
Till that the Deuill wrought me this same spight,
That all their loues are turnd to hatred quight.

Iohn Wallen was my louing husbands name,
Which long hath liu'd in London in good fame.
His trade a Turner, as was knowne full well,
My name An Wallen, dolefull tale to tell.

FIGURE 10.2. "Anne Wallens Lamentation" (1616), Pepys 1.124–125. (Reproduced by permission of the Pepys Library, Magdalene College, Cambridge. English Broadside Ballad
Archive, EBBA 20053: http://ebba.english.ucsb.edu/ballad/20053/image.)

Anne wallens Lamentation,

Or the second part of the murthor of one *Iohn Wallen* a Turner in Cow-lane neere
Smithfield; done by his owne wife, on saterday the 22 of Iune 1616.
who was burnt in Smithfield the first of Iuly following.
To the tune of Fortune my foe.

MY husband hauing béene about the towne,
And comming home, he on his bed lay downe:
To rest himselfe, which when I did espie,
I fell to rayling most outragiously.

I cald him Rogue, and slaue, and all to naught,
Repeating the worst language might be thought
Thou drunken knaue I said, and arrant sot,
Thy minde is set on nothing but the pot.

Swéet heart he said I pray thée hold thy tongue,
And if thou dost not, I shall shall doe thée wrong,
At which, straight way I grew in worser rage,
That he by no meanes could my tongue asswage.

He then arose and strooke me on the eare,
I did at him begin to curse and sweare:
Then presently one of his tooles I got,
And on his body gaue a wicked stroake

Amongst his intrailes I this Chissell threw,
Where as his Caule came out, for which I rue,
What hast thou don, I prethée looke quoth he,
Thou hast thy will, for thou hast killed me.

When this was done the neighbours they ran in,
And to his bed they streight conueyed him:
Where he was drest and liu'd till morne next day,
Yet he forgaue me and for me did pray.

No sooner was his breath from body fled,
But vnto Newgate straight way they me led:
Where I did lie vntill the Sizes came,
Which was before I there thrée daies had laine.

Mother in lawe, forgiue me I you pray,
For I haue made your onely childe away,
Euen all you had; my selfe made husbandlesse,
My life and all, cause did so transgresse.

He nere did wrong to any in his life,
But he too much was wronged by his wife,
Then wiues be warn'd, example take by me,
Heauens graunt no more that such a one may be.

My iudgement then it was pronounced plaine,
Because my dearest husband I had slaine:
In burning flames of fire I should fry,
Receiue my soule swéet Iesus now I die.

T: Platte.

FINIS.

Printed for *Henry Gosson*, and are to be solde
at his shop on London bridge.

a dialogue debating two sides of an issue and/or produced whole ballads that promoted opposing stances. The idea was to market something for everyone, aiming at the widest groups of consumers, especially the large market base of the middling and the low—at least, those who could afford to pay a penny or halfpenny for a ballad and could appreciate its tunes and illustrations, if not always, or fully, its printed words.

While most other types of printed literature in England transitioned from black-letter to white-letter or roman font by the early seventeenth century, the broadside ballad held onto its black-letter roots well into the late seventeenth century, though the size of the sheets on which ballads were printed was typically reduced by half. There was also a revival of the ballad heyday's two-part format in some remakings in the 1670s–1680s of the earlier-century productions. Collectors who lived through or close to the ballad heyday had the most access to ornamental black-letter ballads. They included John Selden (1584–1654), George Thomason (1602–66), Elias Ashmole (1617–92), Anthony Wood (1632–95), Samuel Pepys (1633–1703), John Bagford (1650–1716), Narcissus Luttrell (1657–1732), and Robert Harley (1661–1724), among others. Of these, Selden, Wood, Pepys, Bagford, and Harley favored collecting black-letter ornamental ballads. Thomason, Ashmole, and Luttrell, however, favored the newly emerging white-letter or roman-type ballad, which came to dominate the ballad scene.

In the seventeenth century, white-letter ballads, like later black-letter ballads, were usually printed on smaller sheets. But, unlike their black-letter cousins, they sported less ornamentation—sometimes little more than a plain line dividing columns of stanzas—and, though they could embrace various topics, politics ruled. Political white-letter broadside ballads exploded at heightened political times (in the 1640s, 1660s, and—among extant ballads—especially the 1680s), and it is telling that collectors of these ballads typically collected political pamphlets as well.[2] Along with the typographical shift to white letter and its accompanying aesthetic and topical changes, fewer and fewer tune titles appear printed on the ballad sheet. Interestingly, we also see some later ballads printed with musical notation, but the music is often declared by musicologists to be "meaningless."[3] By the eighteenth century—with some notable exceptions, as in the productions of William and Cluer Dicey (who printed a range of white-letter ballad formats, often reintroducing illustrations)—ballads were typically distributed on mere slips of paper called "slip songs." Some collectors of a later generation than Pepys's sought out the much earlier heyday black-letter ornamental format and their half-folio black-letter cousins. But white letter continued to dominate what was being produced by printers and thus what was available for collection, as evidenced in the mammoth assemblage of twenty-four white-letter volumes by Sir Frederick Madden (1801–73).

To capture the wide arch of collecting and production history and so place seventeenth-century black-letter broadside ballad collectors in full perspective, we must further note that among the generations of ballad collectors and producers of the eighteenth century there emerged a significant counter-collecting/producing group. They tellingly appeared on the scene soon after the ballad lost the prominence of its eye-catching ornament, including its swirling, decorative black-letter type, and also its printed tune titles. As if in response to these losses, they became intent on redefining the ballad not as occasional print but as "traditional" oral history and—somewhat ironically—folded together the practice of ballad publication and collecting. These include the anonymous but influential author/editor of *A Collection of Old Ballads* (3 vols., 1723–25) and his older contemporary, Thomas Percy (1729–1811), who published *Reliques of Ancient English Poetry* (3 vols., 1765). Their most influential generational successor was Francis James Child (1825–96), author of *The English and Scottish Ballads* (8 vols., 1857–59, with two subsequent editions, 1860, 1866), reissued and retitled *The English and Scottish Popular Ballads* (5 vols., 1882–98).

Both in alliance with and in counter to the broadside ballad's loss of ornament and tune titles as well as its newly elevated roman type in its later formats of the seventeenth century, these collectors/scholars/editors extended their gaze far back to classical times to find authentication for their theory of the traditional oral ballad in Homer, who had newly been identified as a ballad singer. At the same time, they asserted that oral ballads before the coming of print expressed the "true," "pure," and "ancient" history of England—history here being characterized as "popular" or "folk."[4] Child, who referred to the Pepys and Roxburghe collections of mostly black-letter ballads as "on the whole . . . *veritable dung-hills*," printed instead scholarly editions of ballads that he declared to be derived from uncorrupted country singers and ancient manuscripts (such as the Percy Folio).[5] But what about the seventeenth-century collectors of the "veritable dung-hills" of printed broadside ballads?

If we focus on those collectors of roughly the same generation who not only collected seventeenth-century broadside ballads but privileged, rather than scorned, black-letter heyday ballads—Wood, Pepys, and Bagford— we find a network of exchange that touches even the next generation, Harley. This collecting network promotes its own distinctive ideas of what a ballad is/should be as well as its place in history. What the collectors share,

unlike the later antiquarian collector-scholar-editors, is an acute appreciation for print, especially for black-letter print and ornamental woodcuts.
This appreciation extends to admiration for the interconnectedness of the
hand-printed *together with* the machine-printed as marking a crucial, if
passing, historical moment in print history, as well as an appreciation for
actual history writ or printed small.

Pepys makes it clear on the title page to his collection of ballads, notably handwritten in black letter, that the broadside ballad format of the
time is changing and that his collection is intended as a personal record
of that change. Under "My Collection of Ballads" and a prominent picture of himself, Pepys writes: "Begun by Mr. Selden [referring to John
Selden]; Improved by the additions of many Pieces elder thereto in Time;
and the whole continued to the year 1700. *When the Form, till then peculiar
thereto, vizt. of the Black Letter with Picturs seems (for cheapness sake) wholly
laid aside, for that of the White Letter without Pictures*" (emphasis added).[6]
Pepys's table of contents to his collection then divides the collection into
ten "Heads of Assortment" or topics, such as "Devotion and Morality"
and "Marriage, Cuckoldry Etc." He also divides up his five-volume collection by volume and format according to a rough chronology, beginning in
volume 1 with manuscript copies of four sixteenth-century printed ballads
(all copied out in black-letter script, with the exception of one consisting
mostly of musical score), which he groups together with "Long Ballads an-
tient"—by which he does not mean long narrative tales like Chevy Chase,
but big folio sheets of two-part ornamental black-letter broadside ballads,
most of which he acquired in purchasing Selden's collection. These are the
ballads from the broadside ballad's ornamental heyday, as described above
and exemplified in figure 10.2. Pepys names his next, large section (vols.
2–4) "Common Ballads in the Black Letter"—which were still ornamental
with printed tune titles but of half-folio, not folio, size—and finally calls
his last section, the fifth volume, "Verse Ballads in the White Letter."

The fact that Pepys grouped together manuscript and long ancient ballads in black letter is telling and links him to other collectors of black-letter
ballads and their intermediaries. At about the same time Pepys seriously
began work on his ballad collection (likely in the 1680s) he, as seriously
started his collection of calligraphy to chronicle the history of handwriting
before and after the introduction of printing "*& the Competition for Mastery, between the Librarians* [meaning masters of penmanship] *& Printers,
upon the first breaking-out of the Latter*" (emphasis added).[7] For Pepys, that
is, expert penmanship and printing are actively engaged with each other
at this point in history. The foundation of that engagement lies in black

letter. Indeed, as Gerald Egan explains, drawing on the landmark work of Daniel Berkeley Updike and Stanley Morison, the first English printing presses imitated the scribal style of *textura* lettering (angular, close-together, thick strokes—giving the impression of "blackness" of the page) that was widely used for formal ecclesiastical documents and for less formal, commercial postings.[8] As other styles of print type became available in England, black letter continued to dominate elite scholarly texts, but also popular broadside ballads and other forms intended for mass dissemination, such as proclamations. Charles Mish and Keith Thomas attribute this "hanging on" of black letter in popular print to its being used in elementary texts, such as hornbooks (by which children first learned to read), catechisms, psalters, and primers. "Black letter was the type for the common people," Thomas argues, requiring "a more basic skill than roman-type literacy." But Mark Bland, Zachary Lesser, and others see the holdover of black letter as a culturally constructed "*nostalgia* for a traditional, communal English past."[9]

Such a constructed print community anticipates the imagined oral community advanced by later antiquarians, but when combined with the ongoing actual practice of learning to read in black letter, the savoring of black-letter type appears to occupy a charged convergence of historical past and present. Pepys thus concludes his collection on calligraphy with examples of black-letter printing imitating black-letter handwriting imitating black-letter printing. His "Conclusion" begins, "Being a Moderne Proof, from the following Ballad, of the Imitableness of Printing by Hand-Writing [a ballad is shown] Equall to those of Hand-writing by Printing, exhibited at the Beginning of this Collection, Page[s 11–15, vol. 1]" (fig. 10.3).[10] One experiences a moment of confusion here. Isn't the ballad pictured in this "Conclusion" part of a *printed* ballad, specifically one typical of the "common" black-letter format of the later half of the seventeenth century (with title printed in mixed roman/black-letter type, including a verse in roman type, and then, below the picture, black-letter text)? Where, then, lies the imitating handwriting within? For the solution to this perplexing question, one must turn the page. There, on the page's verso, one discovers a handwritten and hand-drawn imitation of the machine-printed ballad previously shown (fig. 10.4). This handmade version is placed on the page slightly askew with two colored playing cards superimposed on top of it in trompe l'oeil fashion. The page is titled "The Performance of Mr. Samuel Moore, One of the Surveyors of the Customs, [the ballad is shown] *Being no Professor of Penmanship*" (implying that most anyone can do this; emphasis added).

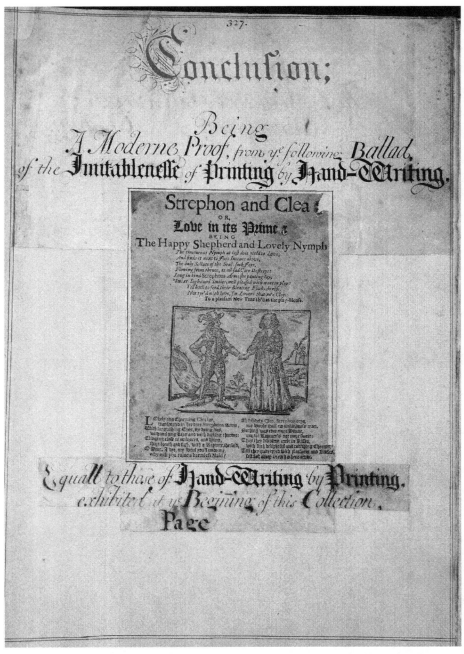

FIGURE 10.3. "Conclusion" to Pepys's three-volume collection of calligraphy, PL 2983 (vol. 3), 327. (Reproduced by permission of the Pepys Library, Magdalene College, Cambridge. English Broadside Ballad Archive, EBBA 2983: http://ebba.english.ucsb.edu /ballad/32073/image.)

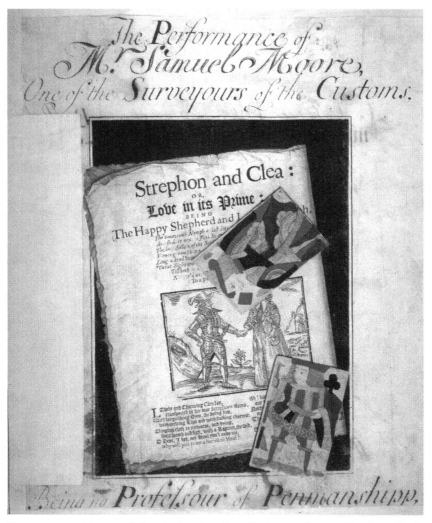

FIGURE 10.4. Verso to "Conclusion," to Pepys's three-volume collection of calligraphy, PL 2983 (vol. 3), 328. (Reproduced by permission of the Pepys Library, Magdalene College, Cambridge. English Broadside Ballad Archive, EBBA 2983: http://ebba.english.ucsb.edu/ballad/32074/image.)

Pepys is not alone in his evident perception that he is at a crossroads in the history of both handwriting and printing—a competition per se— and that ballads, with their black-letter print derived from scribal printing practices, exemplify that historical moment. It is a moment wherein the trace of the personal "hand" can be seen in printing even when machine-made. Other collectors of primarily black-letter broadside ballads were thinking along the same lines, forming a kind of collecting network that promoted the appreciation of ballad-printing-handwriting.

Indeed, the first nineteen manuscript fragments in Pepys's calligraphy collection were supplied to him by the same bookseller who frequently provided him with ballads, John Bagford. Humphrey Wanley was also drawn into this network as early as 1695 via Pepys's friend Dr. Arthur Charlett (Master of University College, Oxford). Only twenty-three at the time, Wanley was already renowned as an expert paleographer and, with Charlett acting as intermediary, later helped Pepys identify the early fragments Bagford supplied.[11] Wanley had himself planned a calligraphy collection, which was never realized.[12] A good friend of Bagford, Wanley also supported Bagford's long-in-the-works plan to write a history of print (the two of them promoted that scheme in letters addressed to Sir Hans Sloane and published in the 1706–7 issue of the Royal Society's *Philosophical Transactions*). Pepys's nephew, John Jackson (helper in assembling Pepys's library and bringing to conclusion his collections of calligraphy and ballads), subscribed to Bagford's project, as did Charlett, but it never got off the ground. Still, Bagford was assembling huge volumes of fragments of manuscripts and print—including many title pages and, not incidentally, a still uncut broadsheet printed with sixteen black-letter hornbooks—all in preparation for his history.[13] At the same time, he supplied not only Pepys but also Robert Harley with ballads for Harley's personal collection.[14] Bagford's own three-volume collection of ballads begins with twenty-seven pages of snippets of manuscript and print fragments before becoming solely focused on printed broadside ballads, moving from black letter to white letter, like Pepys's. Wanley, furthermore, provided Pepys with ballads that were handwritten. In 1701 he secured one from his friend Michael Bull at Bennet (Corpus Christi) College, Cambridge, who was another subscriber to Bagford's projected history of printing. Bull's transcription was of a sixteenth-century black-letter broadside ballad in celebration of Mary Tudor's ill-fated pregnancy, which, Bull promises, he transcribed "with all the Exactness I could." The ballad is in Pepys's collection, along with an excerpt from Bull's handwritten letter to Wanley.[15] For Pepys, a handwritten ballad was as good as a printed ballad, if it was written exactly.

Pepys often had ballads copied out—by Bull, by William Hewer (who ended up housing both Pepys and his library at Clapham late in 1701), by a Captain Allen, and by others.[16] He was discriminating, though, as instanced when a servant, Will Swan, offered him a ballad to the tune of Mardike (a tune by John Playford, whose music store Pepys often visited). Pepys praises the ballad as "incomparably writ in a printed hand" and so borrows it, but on returning it, he declares, "the song proved but silly and so I did not write it out" (1.41). Meanwhile, by 1701 Wanley was also work-ing part-time for Robert Harley, another acquaintance of Pepys. He had become Harley's full-time librarian by 1708 and was a major spur to Har-ley's interest in manuscripts, early printed books, *and* black-letter ballads. Wanley acted as Harley's intermediary in purchasing Bagford's collections on his death, including his collection of ballads (though these were kept separate from Harley's own growing ballad collection).[17]

Anthony Wood, living in Oxford and devoted to recording its history, might appear here to be the odd man out. But in addition to compiling information about Oxford's ancient past, Wood also gathered "heaps" (his own word) of fresh-off-the presses pamphlets, advertisements, and any-thing else he could snatch up in town, including many black-letter broad-side ballads. And here again we see the interconnection between writing and print, for Woods freely annotated the printed ballads he collected, handwriting on them information first and foremost about the printer and the date and the place of printing, and then about persons or incidents referenced therein.[18] Wood's ballad collection, in sum, embodies the hand as much as the printed word. Dr. Charlett, who advised Pepys on his cal-ligraphy collection, was also a good friend of Wood and acted as interme-diary between Pepys, Wood, and Wanley when in 1701 Wanley wrote to Charlett on behalf of Pepys asking Charlett if he could obtain the titles of Scotch ballads from Wood's collection, which Pepys wanted to see.[19] There is a network of ballad collecting at play here that ties together in a relatively small but expandable company Pepys, Wanley, Charlett, Wood, and Har-ley (and extending to include figures like Bull, Hewer, Jackson, and even lesser persons such as Mr. Moore, a workman who retrieved and returned "Ballads, old" for Pepys).[20]

So does this rhizomatic network of collectors, many of whom are work-ing together on the historical documentation of the timely intersection between scriptural and black-letter print, especially as exemplified in bal-lads, form *just* "a loose network of scholars," to quote Lesley Cormack? Or could it also rise to the status of what Cormack and other members of the Making Publics project would call a public? Certainly, as with publics, this network was organic: it was open to strangers (Wanley, for example, was at first a stranger to Pepys), and it had a scholarly agenda that it tried to disseminate to a larger public, as in the projected and advertised history of print promoted by Bagford and his supporters. If not everyone in the black-letter ballad-collecting network signed on to Bagford's project, most shared his mission not only of collecting black-letter ballads but, via such ballads, of capturing the momentous intersection between the handwritten and the printed page.

Nor should we underestimate the extent to which their networked scholarly cause was socially relevant and thus further available to others. Like Wood, all of those interconnected through black-letter ballad collecting, however antiquarian their interests, also valued ballads as products and records of lived history—of history in the making. At the beginning of his collection, Pepys foregrounds a passage attributed to John Selden that praises ballads precisely as occasional records, which Selden calls "libels"— meaning short pieces of paper, not necessarily written slanders: "Though some make slight of Libels; yet you may see by them, how the Wind sits. As take a Straw, and throw it up into the Air; you shall see by that, which way the Wind is; which you shall not do, by casting up a Stone. More Solid things do not show the Complexion of the Times so well as Ballads and Libels."

All of these collectors clearly relished ballads as records of a nostalgic old-style English print and of age-old English stories—tales of Chevy Chase or Guy of Warwick or Robin Hood or of long-ago romantic love— later to become the focus, reimagined as oral, of the promoters/collectors of the "traditional" ballad. But they also relished the ballad's printed words as words in the making (whether by hand or by press) recording the passing here and now—historical straws blowing in the wind. They thus amassed popular ballads that addressed topical domestic debates and gender disputes, recent wonders, in-the-talk news, current politics, the latest fashion, and so on. Debates and answer ballads are common in their collections because such ballads circulate multiple views for mass consumption.

So, once again, is this socially aware, sometimes publication-seeking, always preservation-seeking, network of collectors in fact more than "just" a network? I would think it could be considered to be such at times and, perhaps most interestingly, was sometimes considered so by its members, whatever we might think about its size or agenda. This would seem especially likely at times of excited collectivity, exchange, and potential growth, as in the instance when many of them came together on paper, if not in person, to publish and solicit support for Bagford's proposed history of print. Their attempt to solicit enough subscribers to publish Bagford's project ultimately failed, but its very effort suggests that the participants (and others connected to them) might well have imagined themselves as forming a significant public. By my own gauge—admittedly flawed by the distance of time and limitations of available evidence—what gives me some pause in definitively calling them a public is not so much their relatively small size or failure to grow substantially but rather what appears to be, for the most part, their relatively weak interactions with each other. That is, I have not found much evidence of sustained affective reciprocity within their network. And though interested in collecting socially relevant ballads, as a group they, for the most part—again, so far as I have found—appear to have been relatively uninterested in participating socially or politically in the larger forum of mass-market ballad consumerism of which they willy-nilly were a part.

Pepys, as we shall see, is the noticeable exception. It is precisely in this larger forum of mass-market ballads, in the interactive dissemination and consumption of ballads in which he eagerly participated, I would argue, that we can more definitively find a ballad public in the making. For ballads were not only, or even primarily, for cutting and pasting into collector's books or piling into "heaps" or transcribing. They were for gathering around, exchanging, singing or reading out loud, and pasting up for all (or for just a select few) to see. They were cultural artifacts that circulated in complex reflexive and nuanced ways formative of an expansive, multivalenced, and organic ballad public. The interests of this more expansive and more interactive ballad public cannot be as specifically pinned down as those of our ballad-collecting network. A big and dynamic ballad public is protean. In this sense, one might more accurately speak of ballad publics than *a* ballad public. But I hold to the singular because, at any point in their varied employment of ballads, most participants shared a common familiarity with and interest in popular ballad forms and their potential personal, social, and political uses.

If we zoom further in on Pepys and the way he wove ballads into his day-to-day social relations, based on his *Diary* of 1660–69, we can gain a better sense of how such a vibrant ballad public could work. The potential for ballads to serve individuals and groups depended on the way they were made by authors, printers, and others, but also on a common understanding of how the manufactured product could be variously used. I recall, in its simplest interpretation of such interplay, Michael Warner's discussion in *Publics and Counterpublics* of the "talk value" built up around multifarious vocalizations of the widely popular catchphrase "Whassup?" first marketed in 1999 by Budweiser. "Talk value allows a structured but mobile interplay between the reflexivity of publics (the talk) and the reflexivity of capital (the value)," Warner notes. He adds, "In contemporary mass culture, the play between these different ways of rendering the field of circulation reflexive has created countless nuances for the performance of subjectivity."[21] Mass-produced ballads created their own market reflexivity and complex interarticulation with public reflexivity that made for myriad nuances of what was—by virtue of the social circulation of ballads—a collective performativity.

On April 11 and April 17, 1661, as an instance, Pepys sang a bawdy ballad in a local tavern with Captain John Allen (Clerk of the Ropeyard in Chatham). The song took the form of a medley—one of the forms mass-marketed by ballad makers in the seventeenth century—consisting of proverbs and catchphrases often taken from other ballads. Significantly, the first time Pepys refers to the ballad it is by the last line of the fourth stanza: "*Goe and bee hanged; that's twice god b'w'y*" (2.72). The second time, however, he calls the ballad by the third line of the third stanza: "*Shitten come Shits the beginning of love*" (2.78). That the title to this ballad keeps changing in Pepys's mind is not a sign of early dementia but rather of the fact that the ballad itself is a composite of "Whassup?"-like catchphrases, each of which, at any moment, depending on the context of the singing or recollecting, might be the one Pepys most recollects. In each case, Pepys and Allen "took great pleasure" (2.72) in turning the ballad market in popular consumer phrases into a reflexive moment performative of male middle-class bonding, in which clearly a larger male public familiar with such catchphrases could also take part.

On another, very different social occasion, at a large dinner party hosted by Lord William Brouncker on January 2, 1665, Pepys turns popular knowledge of ballad content into an in-joke among those present that could also be interpreted as a nuanced personal and political jab. Pepys brings a broadside ballad along to the party and is most pleased with its reception, saying, "I occasioned much mirth with a ballet I brought with me, made from the seamen at sea to their ladies in town—saying Sir W. Penn, Sir G. Ascue, and Sir J. Lawson made them" (6.2). It is unclear whether the "much mirth" at the party ensued from the ballad itself or from Pepys's tongue-in-cheek naming of its authors as Sir William Penn, Sir George Ascue, and Sir John Lawson—all naval commanders. The actual author of the ballad, as most at the dinner party would have likely known, was Charles Sackville, later earl of Dorset, a familiar court and satiric wit. The ballad had been entered in the Stationers' Register just three days earlier, entitled "The Noble seamans complaint to the Ladies at Land," and is extant in a later printing (6.2n1).[22] It gently parodies the many ballads about common seamen departing from, returning to, or writing to their ladyloves. Sackville has raised their status to "noble" but also makes them a tad dim-witted, as they complain about how difficult it is to write not only because of "our empty brain" (l. 9) but the rough seas, which make writing literally hard (ll. 10–13)! The joking could be interpreted as all in good fun, and in no way pointed. But stanza 5, especially line 4, is unsettling at this moment in time:

> Should foggy Opdam chance to know
> Our sad and dismal story,
> The Dutch would scorn so weak a foe,
> *And quit their fort at Goree;*
> For what resistance can they find
> From men who've left their hearts behind?—
> With a fa, la, la, la la! (emphasis added)

Opdam was a Dutch admiral, and references to the Dutch are scattered throughout the song. But the mention of Fort Gorée was most current for January 1665.[23] On October 24, 1664, the Dutch had captured Gorée and proceeded to seize back all their other holdings on the West Coast of Africa that had been lost to the English a year earlier. On December 22, 1664, news of the disaster had reached London, and Pepys writes in disgust of the "cowardice" of the British fleet, which despite having a major presence in the area, surrendered the fort with little resistance.[24] So Pepys's clearly invented attribution of the ballad's authorship and bringing this particular Sackville ballad to a dinner party filled with naval officers in January 1665, just eleven days after the news arrived of such shameful naval loses, could be a veiled insult: "What are you naval commanders doing writing about love at sea when you are being humiliated by the Dutch?" However, the song is so light in tone that any intended insult, though likely perceived by some with a wink and a nod, could also be most assuredly ignored or denied.

Like his contemporaries, Pepys not only knew how to use popular ballad topics but also typical ballad modes for his own purposes, such as "answers" and role-playing, sometimes to create a private public, so to speak, between knowing ballad aficionados. At another dinner party at Lord Brouncker's on January 2, 1666, he meets the actress Elizabeth Knepp, who sings the ballad "Barbara Allen" for the group. Pepys experiences "perfect pleasure . . . to hear her sing, and especially her little Scotch song" (7.1).

And so begins an infatuation that becomes a flirtation and sexual dalliance facilitated through performing ballad characters. When three days later Pepys traveled to Greenwich to another dinner party, he went hoping to "get" Mrs. Knepp, but she was busy. Her substitute? She sent Pepys "a pleasant letter, writing her [i.e., signed by her] *Barbary Allen*" (7.4). The next day, at a "great dinner" at Greenwich with "much company," Pepys again missed getting Knepp and was especially frustrated because he had "wrote a letter to her in the morning, calling myself *Dapper Dicky* in answer to hers of *Barb. Allen*" (7.5). "Dapper Dicky" is the title of another Scottish ballad in which a girl laments her lover's absence. What are Pepys and Knepp doing? They are self-consciously inhabiting a ballad public that allows one to voice roles and play with them to one's own personal but still public ends, as anyone seeing these letters or hearing Knepp and Pepys adopt these ballad personae would know exactly what the two were about. They made a private ballad public of lamentable love turned to sexual courting.

Pepys participates with self-reflective resistance in the making of an even broader ballad public, this time with serious political stakes. On March 5, 1667, he travels alone by water, "reading a ridiculous ballad made in praise of the Duke of Albemarle, to the tune of *St. George*." He adds, "the tune being printed too" (8.99). A close if not exact version of the ballad, in white letter with musical notation, is titled "A heroical song on . . . George Duke of Albemarle . . . made in August 1666." It shamelessly remakes the much cherished ballad of an already established national hero by the same first name: Saint George, patron saint of England. The refrain runs: "Lord George was born in England, restored his Country's Joy, / Come let us sing 'Vive le Roy'" (8.99n2). The title date of August 1666, during the Second Anglo-Dutch War, is most telling. George Monck, 1st Duke of Albemarle, was at that time commander of England's fleet. The famously drawn-out Four Days naval battle of the war, June 1–4, 1666, at times resembling a confusing "melée," ended with both sides claiming victory, though in fact the English lost many more ships than the Dutch and accusations spread widely of "great bad management" on the part of both Albemarle and Prince Rupert.[25] The subsequent two-day engagement known as St. James's Day Battle, July 25–26, 1666 (August 4–5 on the Dutch Gregorian calendar) was also commanded by Monck. It ended more clearly in English victory; however, the English failed decisively to cripple the Dutch fleet. Certainly Pepys does not buy into the ballad's great praise of Albemarle's feats. Not only does he call the ballad "ridiculous," but he suspects political machinations in its making: "I observe that people have some great encouragement to make ballads of him [Albemarle] of this kind; there are so many, that hereafter will sound like *Guy of Warwicke*" (8.99)—referring to another beloved English ballad hero. Who exactly are "the people" making and encouraging these ballads remains unclear, but likely the Crown and/or Albemarle himself were behind them. Pepys is fully aware that the broadside ballad—as a single "libel" sheet easily printed off for mass distribution—could be turned to political purposes with ease. He is also more than aware that the public could be persuaded to think about Albemarle as a hero by exploiting the form and content of previous popular ballad texts, such as "St. George of England." Indeed, though Pepys repeatedly calls Albemarle a "blockhead," he expresses admiration that he "hath strange luck to be beloved" (8.499). Ballads likely played a significant part in such "luck."

With this instance of large-scale marketing intended to make a ballad public that will "buy into" Albemarle's heroism—as into the "Whassup?" marketing by Budweiser—I propose that we consider what might at first seem an unlikely model for conceptualizing the making of ballad publics or, more broadly speaking, a ballad public. I propose we think of a ballad public (indeed potentially all publics) in terms of Clifford Geertz's groundbreaking vision of the Balinese cockfight.[26] Geertz essentially envisions the cockfight of Bali in terms of encircling spheres of a culture-making public that affirms social status. At the center of the cockfight ring are the leaders of Bali, who lovingly nurture their cocks as if they were an extension of themselves, as well as their allies, who together form coalitions of bettors. Occupying the ring just outside these central fighters are individuals who occasionally enter their own cocks in small matches, might make bets on the big ones, and are still very much invested in the outcome of the "battle." Beyond these are the petty bettors, who do not fight cocks themselves but still publicly take sides at the fight. Farther out, on the fringe of the cockfight, are the socially marginal and the poor, who are far less invested in the specific fights but take part in assorted sheer-chance gambling at encircling concession booths, as in a small fair.[27]

So too with the making of a broadside ballad public, we can image a kind of Balinesian nesting of public spheres, from the more intense or strong at the center to the less invested or weak at the margins. Center stage are the important "makers"—not so much the mostly anonymous "authors" or occasional sponsors like Albemarle as the major printers and publishers or booksellers of ballads and their allies in the trade; next invested are the hawkers and purchasers of ballads; and on the outskirts of the ballad public are the occasional listeners/viewers/readers/singers (many of them too poor to be able to afford to buy a ballad). On these margins might also stand those who passingly cite ballads in historical or fictional texts (such as Shakespeare in *The Winter's Tale* or Jonson in *Bartholomew Fair*).

Where, in this Balinese sphere model of a ballad public, would we place our network of black-letter ballad collectors? In working on this chapter, I originally drew a sketch of concentric circles and placed the collectors just outside the makers of ballads because, with the exception of later antiquarian scholar-editors and creators of the "literary ballad," most collectors valued and promoted the printed ballads, even if they didn't literally "make" them. But the more I talked with long-term UCSB Making Publics member Eric Nebeker (a MaPs Graduate Student Associate who joined the project with Richard Helgerson and has since earned his PhD), and the more I extended my discussions to include graduate students in my recent class on ballad culture, which I co-taught with Eric, the more I recognized that ballad collectors should best be positioned slightly askew in my neat Balinesian public-sphere model, as in figure 10.5. In this rendering, the ballad collectors can be seen as having participated in and helped generate a larger ballad public; but they can also be seen to have had an "eccentric" agenda (documentation and preservation of black-letter script/ print) that was relatively small-scale and situated outside the mass-market consumerism of a ballad public. To the extent that they constituted a small network with little dissemination, however "open" they might have been to interested strangers, the collectors did not participate in a larger ballad public. Of course, by this logic, any "group" within a ballad public might go "askew" of that public if its interests became too specialized.

In this conception of the making of a ballad public, we also see that any public has a core of strength and an outside that is weaker. Furthermore, as we have seen in Pepys's *Diary,* hot spots can flare up at any moment at any place in this spheric model. Certain printers or publishers can become very influential, a coalition of sorts may form between collectors of ballads (as happened when ballad printing and print history became the double-pronged focus of Pepys, Bagford, Harley, and Wanley—to the extent that their interests might not be shared by the larger public of which they were otherwise a part, thus pushing them to the outside of the larger public), and occasional makers might suddenly produce lots of ballads on a single subject, as in the mobilizing of ballads in praise of Albemarle. We see similar dramatic hot spots form in *The Winter's Tale* around Autolycus at the sheep-shearing feast, and even more intensely in *Bartholomew Fair,* where,

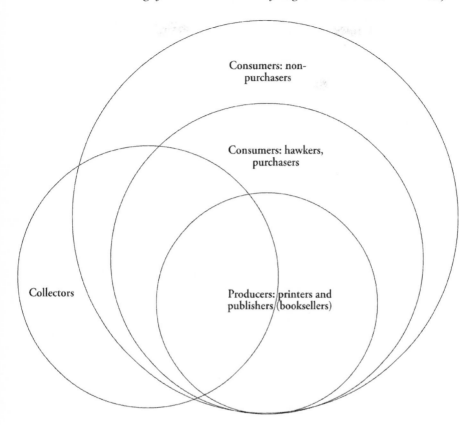

FIGURE 10.5. A Ballad Public Sphere Model. Graphics by Eric Nebeker.

again, layers of an onion of intensity of investment circle around the ballad singer, Nightingale, and his cutpurse partner, Edgworth.[28] Jonson always scathingly put down ballads, as did most of the aspiring laureates of his time, but he also knew precisely how the ballad market functioned and how it could be performatively worked upon by individuals with a collective goal—just as he and his players improvised on the reflexive "Whassup?" of ballad marketing to their own commercial ends.

And on that idea of ends, I here end where I began, with my own undoing—"As soone, as wee to bee, begunne; / We did beginne, to be Vndone" (see fig. 10.1). I end with yet one more hot spot out on the fringe of the Balinese sphere of an early modern English ballad public, where the naval pride in Pepys's *Diary* have turned out en masse on May 15, 1668, for the funeral of Sir Thomas Teddemen (another naval officer criticized in the Four Days Battle; 9.200n4). Pepys is impressed by the turnout: "But Lord, to see among the young commanders and Thomas Killigrew and others that came" (9.200). This comment could have led to a critique by Pepys of those very young commanders, as there was a general opinion, shared by him, that the navy was being stocked by Charles and York with inexperienced courtiers rather than seaworthy officers. Instead, Pepys's attention is diverted: "*how unlike a burial this was, Obrian taking out some ballets out of his pocket, which I read and the rest came about me to hear; and there very merry we were all, they being new ballets.*" [new paragraph] "*By and by the Corpse went*" (9.200; emphasis added). The new youthful commanders, in violation of the decorum of somberness at funerals, bring ballads in their pockets, but instead of criticizing them, Pepys cannot help but be drawn into their circle, reading the ballads out loud for the rest to gather round and hear, and "very merry we were all, they being new ballets." As if in afterthought, he notes Teddeman's corpse passing by.

One might judge this moment severely as a violation of ceremony; but one might also appreciate the power of the ballad to make a public, and a merry one at that, out of a group of divergently interested persons. Here, they come together in the moment of merrymaking that is a moment of forgetting—forgetting the death that punctuates so many of the diaries of the seventeenth century, as of all time. And ironically they remind us of the life in the making of a public. I remember at Richard Helgerson's memorial service how a young graduate student spontaneously offered as commemoration a hand-drawn portrait he had made of Richard, and how an emeritus faculty member composed two sonnets in Richard's honor—one a translation of Garcilaso de la Vega's "Sonnet from Carthage," the focus of Richard's last book, and the other a sonnet on Richard Helgerson himself, spoken in echoing form across the centuries. People gathered round and admired both in a momentary making of a Helgersonian public. And ballads do just that by drawing both on the passing historical moment and on the power of the little paper in print to circulate and attract.

I conclude now by pulling a handmade ballad out of my virtual pocket in solemn remembrance and honor of Richard Helgerson. I call upon you to gather round to view and read it along with this chapter. If you agree to join in, we shall have momentarily created a ballad public out of strangers, even if only in passing. Indeed, it is in the very moment of flashing into existence and undoing that is one way a ballad public is made—in lasting memory (fig. 10.6).

A Ballad upon the Death of our Great Garcilaso, RICHARD HELGERSON,

on this past Saturday the 27th of April 2008 in his home with his beloved wife by his side. Pictured as he was in life by M. Oliver.

To the Tune, *The King's last good-night.*

Sonnet to Boscán from Goleta

Boscán, the arms and turbulence of *Mars*,
  now sprinkling blood upon our *African*
earth, bringing back to life the former *Roman*
Imperium to flourish in these parts,
have led back into memory the arts
  and ancient valor of the Italians,
  by dint of whose great power and valiant hands
vast *Africa* was laid low in every part.
Here where the *Roman* bonfires blazed their fill,
  where fire and flames promiscuously left
  only the name of *Carthage*, and a void,
love turns and turns my thoughts again, until
  they wound and scorch my timorous soul, bereft,
  and I in tears and ashes lie destroyed.

Garcilaso de la Vega
1535.

Sonnet to Richard from Goleta

A Dying man sips water through a straw
  and holds it down as best he can. He sees
  the friends who come to see him in their needs,
obeying an inexorable law:
see as you would be seen; say what you saw.
  His feet grow cold. The chill reaches his knees.
  His hands are hot. There is no way to please
this body any more--it's stuffed with straw.
Which makes the play and work he made of mind
  more apt than ever, and immune to pity:
  scholar and teacher, parent, husband, leader,
he leaves a huge and ragged hole behind
  in this part of the universe and city.
  Think kindly of him. Think well, gentle reader.

John Ridland
April 2008.

Printed by K. McAbee for P. F. at the sign of the *Ermine*, UCSB.

FIGURE 10.6. A Ballad in Memory of Richard Helgerson. Illustration: M(ac) Oliver. Sonnets by Garcilaso de la Vega, trans. John Ridland (*left*) and John Ridland (*right*). Printer: K(ris) McAbee. Publisher: P(atricia) Fumerton. The ermine is the "sign" of the Early Modern Center, UCSB.

NOTES

I want to thank the members of the McGill Making Publics project, especially Paul Yachnin, as well as those of the UCSB division of MaPs, for helping me germinate this essay over the years of the project. I am especially grateful to Eric Nebeker for many conversations in which he has shared with me his deep expertise on ballad culture; on making publics, in particular, see his "Textual Publics and Broadside Ballads," *Studies in English Literature* 51.1 (Winter 2011): 1–19.

1. On Cox, see Margaret Spufford, *Small Books and Pleasant Histories: Popular Fiction and Its Readership in Seventeenth-Century England* (Cambridge: Cambridge University Press, 1981), 143; the provenance of the Huth and Britwell (also referred to as the Heber) ballads is nicely hand-diagrammed on a page accompanying the Huntington collection, HEH 18262–18348 (reproduced on the EBBA Web site, ebba.english.ucsb.edu/page/provenance2).

2. See Angela McShane-Jones, " 'Rime and Reason': The Political World of the Broadside Ballad, 1640–1689" (PhD diss., University of Warwick, 2005), as well as her *The Political Broadside Ballads of Seventeenth-Century England: A Critical Bibliography* (London: Pickering & Chatto, 2010).

3. Claude M. Simpson, *The British Broadside and Its Music* (New Brunswick, N.J.: Rutgers University Press, 1966), xii.

4. *A Collection of Old Ballads,* vol. 1 (London: n.p., 1623), iii.

5. Quote from Mary Ellen Brown, "Child's Ballads and the Broadside Conundrum," in *Ballads and Broadsides, 1500–1800,* ed. Patricia Fumerton and Anita Guerrini, with the assistance of Kris McAbee (Burlington, Vt.: Ashgate, 2010), 67.

6. See EBBA 32621, ebba.english.ucsb.edu/ballad/32621/image.

7. Handwritten title page to Pepys's "My Calligraphical Collection," vol. 1 (of three volumes), dated 1700, in *Catalogue of the Pepys Library at Magdalene College Cambridge, Vol. IV: Music, Maps, and Calligraphy* (Wolfeboro, N.H.: D. S. Brewer, 1989), p. l of Calligraphy catalogue (each catalogue section of the volume is independently paginated); hereafter cited as *Calligraphy.*

8. Gerald Egan, "Black Letter and the Broadside Ballad," in *Broadside Ballads from the Pepys Collection: A Selection of Texts, Approaches, and Recordings,* ed. Patricia Fumerton (Tempe, Ariz.: Arizona Center for Medieval and Renaissance Texts and Studies, 2013), 29–30; much of my section on black letter is indebted to Egan's essay as well as to personal conversations with him on the subject.

9. Ibid., 30–32.

10. *Calligraphy,* 327.

11. Richard Luckett, "Introduction" to *Calligraphy,* vi, v. On Pepys's befriending of Wanley via Charlett and Bagford's providing Pepys with ballads as well MSS and printed fragments, see Luckett, "The Collection: Origins and History," in *Catalogue of the Pepys Library at Magdalene College Cambridge, Vol. II: Ballads, Part ii: Indexes,* comp. Helen Weinstein (Wolfeboro, N.H.: D. S. Brewer, 1994), xvi–xv. See also Milton McC. Gatch, "John Bagford as a Collector and Disseminator of Manuscript Fragments," *The Library,* 6th ser., 7.2 (June 1985): 96–97.

12. Luckett, "Introduction," *Calligraphy,* v; Wanley mentions his plan to Pepys's nephew, John Jackson, in 1701 (n1).

13. Gatch, "John Bagford, Bookseller and Antiquary," *The British Library Journal* 12 (1986): 153, and for a full description of Bagford's proposal, 158–64. Gatch lists the subscribers in "John Bagford as a Collector," 99–100. For Bagford's folio sheet of printed hornbooks, see Andrew White Tuer, *History of the Horn-Book* (New York: Charles Scribner's Sons, 1896), 2:133–34.

14. J. W. Ebsworth, ed., *The Bagford Ballads*, 3 vols. collected into 2 (1878; repr., New York: AMS Press, 1968), 1:v, viii–ix.

15. Gatch, "John Bagford as a Collector," 100. For a facsimile of Bull's transcription and of his letter to Pepys, see EBBA 31607 and 31608 (Pepys 1.23 and 1.24–25, respectively), with Bull's letter in the latter, ebba.english.ucsb.edu/ballad/31608/image.

16. Luckett, "The Collection," xvi. For Hewer and Allen, see *The Diary of Samuel Pepys*, ed. Robert Latham and William Matthews, 11 vols. (Berkeley: University of California Press, 1995), 9.242 (June 16, 1668) and 2:77–78 (April 11, 1661); citations to Pepys's *Diary* will hereafter appear in the body of my chapter by volume and page, separated by a period.

17. C. E. Wright and Ruth C. Wright, eds., *Humphrey Wanley and the History of the Harleian Library: A Reprint of the Introduction to "The Diary of Humphrey Wanley, 1715–1726,"* 2 vols. (London: Bibliographical Society, 1966), 1:xv. The editors attribute Wanley's interest in printing largely to his early friendship with Bagford, xvii, xxv. See also Luckett, "Collection," xvii–xviii.

18. Nicholas K. Kiessling, *The Library of Anthony Wood* (Oxford: Oxford Bibliographical Society, 2002), xxv, xxviii–xxxviii.

19. Luckett, "Collection," xvi.

20. Ibid.; *Private Correspondence and Miscellaneous Papers of Samuel Pepys, 1679–1803,* ed. J. R. Tanner, 2 vols. (New York: Harcourt Brace & Company, n.d.), 1:167.

21. Michael Warner, *Publics and Counterpublics* (New York: Zone Books, 2002), 101, 102.

22. The editors of the *Diary* mistyped "London" for "Land" in the title of the ballad; 6.2n1; for the correct entry, see Hyder E. Rollins, *An Analytical Index to the Ballad-entries (1557–1709) in the Registers of the Company of Stationers of London* (Hatboro, Pa.: Tradition Press, 1967), 170. I cite from the earliest extant printed version, in *Wit and Mirth* (1714), as provided online with lines numbered, in *Representative Poetry Online,* rpo.library.utoronto.ca/poems/song-written-sea. Norman Ault gives the earliest found manuscript version, which is missing the "fa, la, la, la, la" refrain; *Seventeenth Century Lyrics from the Original Texts* (London: Longmans, Green, 1928), 334–35.

23. Apparently due to the "foggy Opdam" reference (Obdam commanded the Dutch fleet at the Battle of Lowestoft, June 13, 1665, in which action he died), Matthew Prior says that Sackville composed the song the night before the engagement; dedication to Prior's *Poems on Several Occasions* (1718), A3v. But, as Ault points out, "it is now generally supposed that Dorset wrote it while serving under the Duke of York in his first cruise in November 1664, when the Dutch avoided an action by retiring into port; note for p. 335 on p. 438.

24. *Further Correspondence of Samuel Pepys, 1662–1679,* ed. J. R. Tanner, 3 vols. (London: G. Bell and Sons, 1929), 1:34. See also *Diary,* 5:352–53.

25. *Diary,* 7.143; see also 7.147.

26. Clifford Geertz, "Deep Play: Notes on the Balinese Cockfight," in *The Interpretation of Cultures: Selected Essays by Clifford Geertz* (New York: Basic Books, 1973), 412–53.

27. Ibid., 435; see also 432n18.

28. William Shakespeare, *The Winter's Tale,* ed. Frank Kermode, 2nd ed. (New York: Signet, 1998), 4.4.220–327; Ben Jonson, *Bartholomew Fair,* ed. E. A. Horsman (London: Methuen, 1960), 3.5.11–194.

CHAPTER ELEVEN

Forms of Internationality

The Album Amicorum *and the Popularity of John Owen*
(1564–1622)

VERA KELLER

THE PUBLIC studied by scholars since Habermas is a scientific object. That is, it does not exist in concrete reality as the mundane objects of everyday life do, nor does it even equal the sum total of human bodies gathered in any one place. Rather, the public is an abstracted category of thought. Scientific objects become more or less real as they come to be and pass away as the targets of inquiry.[1] This has been true for publics just as it was for other new concepts, such as energy or temperature.

In the seventeenth century, forms of association became new objects of study. The rise of empirical politics in the sixteenth century motivated the survey of territory, demographics, trade, taxation, popular opinion, customs, forms of association, national character, and mass movements. As res publica (public affairs) grew in scope as an object of inquiry, the public came more and more into view as an entity. As such categories of thought came from political writings, studying the early modern study of forms of association would point to the role of the state in public making.

Authorities on publics often argue that publics must organize themselves "independently of state institutions."[2] For Habermas, the public sphere served to connect state and society.[3] Yet such a conceptual division between state and society does not fit early modern practice. For instance, the emergence of "methodical travel," and the many genres developed alongside it to map land, peoples, and knowledge, offers an example of how state and society intersected in the early modern period. Historians of modern Europe have pointed to the ways bureaucratic surveys of populations, such as official paperwork, forms, and censuses, created categories

220

for the conceptualization of individual identity such as race, profession, and nationality.[4] Likewise, Justin Stagl has traced a central modern genre of social enquiry—the survey questionnaire—to the early modern practice of politically motivated methodical travel, the *ars apodemica,* as it was known to academics of the time. The ancestor of the eighteenth-century Grand Tour, sixteenth- and seventeenth-century academic travel differed in its adherence to predetermined goals, categories, and clearly codified practices—thus earning it its moniker of "methodical travel." Methodizers of travel intentionally structured experience. The Swiss Theodor Zwinger, for instance, prescribed influential query lists and categories in his *Methodus Apodemica* of 1577 written for the learned traveler.[5] Methodical travel helped forms of association to come into view as objects of study and offered ways for individuals to insert themselves into such categories of thought.

Methodizers of travel defined travel as both political and personal. The peregrinator traveled "To get knowledge for the bettering of himselfe and his Countrie."[6] It was the methodical traveler's task to map out knowledge for the benefit of his or her (usually his) homeland, using the previously supplied query lists and itineraries designated by experts in the *ars apodemica.* Methodizers of travel such as Zwinger urged voyagers to observe certain forms and places of association, especially the markets, universities, gardens, libraries, and art collections found in urban spaces. In the act of observing, the traveler also participated in such associations. Experiencing them firsthand was the point of travel, but it was an experience structured by presupplied categories. The personal experience of methodical travel reinforced the existence and importance of these generalized categories, especially when travelers compared one place to the next.

Writers on methodical travel conceptualized the ideal traveler as a faithful gatherer of knowledge abroad for the benefit of his own country—that is, as a loyal, if unpaid, observer on behalf of the state. However, the analogue today for such methodical travelers would not be the Foreign Service (a cadre of trained and paid government employees) but the junior year abroad. This was especially so before Jean-Baptiste Colbert's development of an internal state information-collection system in Louis XIV's France.[7] Early modern states often lacked extensive government-paid internal bureaucracies, and public services were perforce often mixed with personal profit. Methodical travel is a case in point. While ostensibly providing a service for his country, the traveler was also an individual member of society with his own interests, concerns, and political entanglements. From the state's perspective, the mixture of the public and the personal in methodical travel had the disadvantage of having to train individuals as politically acute observers. Methodical travel (increasingly considered integral to higher education) made categories of political observation and analysis available to the individual traveler. Guides to travel were intended to inculcate habits of observation in travelers, and these were habits which might also be directed toward one's own land. Due to the interpenetration of state and society, the observer (the state) might become the observed.

The genres for categorizing international knowledge associated with methodical travel might be compared to the genres of nationhood analyzed by Richard Helgerson in his *Forms of Nationhood*. Helgerson, although not speaking explicitly in terms of public formation, described a process of separation and communication between feudal monarchies and an emerging modern nationhood through new genres consolidating a national identity. In "The Land Speaks," for example, he described an emerging sense of belonging associated with the land of a country itself, crystallized in cartography rather than identified with a feudal (and international) monarchy.

In Helgerson's account, the identity of the ordinary individual thus became entangled with an emerging political entity—the nation—which did not brook invasion by an international Other: "The rhetoric of nationhood is a rhetoric of uniformity and wholeness. The unified self of the Englishman or Frenchman, the Italian or German, is founded on the political and cultural unity of the nation to which each belongs. The denial of nationhood is experienced as a denial of integrated selfhood."[8] The integrated self sprang from a sense of unsevered belonging to the very ground upon which the individual stood, thus placing and concretizing national and individual identities.

In the new genres studied by Helgerson, national and individual identity became more and more materialized—in thick law books, lengthy epics, and bulky atlases. In the land itself, identity gained the material status of an almost mundane object as feudal fealty faded from view. However, as Lesley Cormack has pointed out in her contribution to this volume, cartography did not have the status of an everyday object in the lived experience of ordinary individuals in this period. In the era studied by Helgerson, cartography was a specialized skill, patronized by state ministers famed for their expertise in the collection and management of information, such as William Cecil. Rather than materializing a concrete bond, cartography was a tool for a critical survey at the highest level of the state. The designations affixed to maps by cartographers were not natural entities but categories of thought. The proliferation of cartographic bodies on maps was not so much the personification of an immediately felt link between individuals and the land, but part of an effort to categorize and classify peoples from the perspective of international politics through the creation of new scientific objects.

This does not mean, however, that local individuals or landholders might not also reinterpret such categories and grant them an existence as lived realities in ways that differed from their original purpose. For instance, despite the proliferation of maps in Dutch domestic interiors described by Svetlana Alpers (as Richard Helgerson pointed out in "The Folly of Maps and Modernity"), early modern representations of mapping, from Holbein's *The Ambassadors* to Dutch Golden Age painting, were often used to depict what Helgerson called "the vanity of national identity." Rather than new tools for the study and control of the world, maps were often deployed in popular representations to display timeworn *vanitas* themes of the uncontrollable mutability of the world.[9]

Methodical Travel and the Form

Methodical travel, whose undoubted home was Ramist central Europe, was a highly textually mediated form of travel. A coterie of writers in Paris, including George Villiers, 2nd Duke of Buckingham, ridiculed a pedantic German traveler in their play *Sir Politick Would Be* for the huge number of books he carried with him. He required an itinerary to show him the routes, a small book telling him what was curious in each country, and a beautifully bound blank book, called an *album amicorum,* in which savants were asked to inscribe pregnant messages in all sorts of languages. Finally, he carried a journal in which he recorded his observations each day.[10] Before the traveler actually came to experience the world, his experience was already mediated by well-traveled itineraries and guides to observation. Through his own journal notes and his own inscriptions in the albums of others, the traveler inserted himself into the categories of thought laid out by the methodizers of travel.

The *album amicorum,* or book of friends, emerged in the 1540s in Wittenberg. In these pre-bound books, travelers collected inscriptions and images from a wide range of figures they encountered in travel. Comparable to today's Facebook, the book of friends, despite its name, was (circa 1600) generally not an intimate genre but a widely seen, often multivolume collection of diverse individuals from varying walks of life and even religions. It offered a means to survey, collect, and arrange society in the form of a book.[11]

The practice of methodical travel encouraged the personal collection and reuse of diverse prefabricated materials. While abroad, a traveler might visit a workshop specializing in frequently repeated views of city sights, like early modern postcards, in order to further ornament his book with local scenes. For instance, the lavishly illustrated album of the Nuremberg patrician Jakob Fetzer, who traveled for two decades and as far afield as Ireland and Jerusalem, was filled out with a series of London tourist scenes. The same scene of London Bridge found in his album can also be found in the album of the Dutch traveler Michael van Meer.[12]

Alba amicorum of methodical travelers were often replete with stock images of town sights, costumes, and character types (such as Venetian courtesans), either cut out and pasted in, executed by professional *alba amicorum* illustrators, or preprinted in ready-made albums or interleaved printed books (often emblem books or costume books).[13] The images included in *alba amicorum* frequently came from other new or newly popular genres offering categories for social knowledge, such as the costume book, the cartographic body, and the survey of professions.[14]

The costume book, which emerged in the 1560s, provided fixed images of the habits of diverse cultures and was another popular source for album illustration.[15] It was one of many pictorial genres categorizing social knowledge in the period. Comparable to the emergence of the costume book was the proliferation, in the late sixteenth and early seventeenth centuries, of bodies personifying geographical areas upon maps.[16] Surveys of professions also became popular in the late sixteenth century. In 1582, Ambrogio Brambilla published what would prove an influential print including over two hundred thumbnail images of different street vendors. "As in a collection of scientific specimens," writes Evelyn Welch, "the emphasis was on the type or genus that unified these creatures, not on their differences.[17] Tomaso Garzoni's one-thousand-page description of all professions first appeared in 1585. Garzoni both cited and was cited by authors of political studies, for instance in *On a Sufficiency of Things in a Republic,* a 1625 work by the political writer and proponent of the *ars apodemica,* Jakob Bornitz.[18]

In short, by the turn of the seventeenth century, an array of interrelated new genres offered categories for social observation and for the association of individuals into groups. Although, as Valerie Traub argues, categories of race and gender only consolidated in the Enlightenment, this late sixteenth- and early seventeenth-century mapping of peoples contributed to a shift in such taxonomies.[19] Categories of race, gender, professions, social hierarchies, and nationalities were of interest to the students of the res publica, who sought in travel the answers to queries preordained by the methodizers of travel.

John Owen's Popularity

Through their own inscriptions in the albums where so many of these new pictorial genres appeared, individuals fitted themselves into this mosaic of recognizable materials. Such individual inscriptions were not, however, expressions of a subjective selfhood or of an intimate friendship, as the name "book of friends" might suggest. They were also usually commonplace expressions, often classical, biblical, or patristic in origin but also including vernacular adages and Neo-Latin epigrams. Album inscriptions, including the epigram, provide another example of how the methodical traveler associated him- or herself with a formulaic and recognizable cultural reservoir.

The epigram, a genre notoriously difficult to define, was based on classical epigraphy but also intersected with vernacular proverbs and was frequently macaronic. Its chief attributes were brevity and wit.[20] As Debora Shuger has argued, epigrams did not provide access to an inner self but exhibited a public persona active in the realm of politics.[21] The characteristic displayed by the epigram was magnanimity or greatness of spirit. This was precisely the quality the methodical traveler attempted to demonstrate. When seeking a position at the court on his return home, methodical travelers ought to display "Spirit; which shall free them from reproche, quarrels, and putting up of dishonourable injuries," while seeking a friend "that is magnanimous."[22]

Although urged to be "sociable," the traveler was also warned that, "though it be requisite, to be thus generally knowen of all; yet let such take heede to intrude into the friendship of any, but with great respect, and for good cause: using modestie and sparingness evermore in revealing of any thing observed in travaile, unless upon demands, and in urgent causes."[23] The politic traveler moved with his true beliefs and ideas held close to his chest. Travelers' knowledge was a precious political resource to be doled out sparingly. The Welsh poet John Owen put such advice into epigrammatic form: "Esto multorum, soli tibi notus, amicus, / Et quod vis alios ipse silere, sile" (Be a friend to many, but known only to yourself, and stay silent about those things you wish others would not talk about).[24]

The epigram did not open a window to the soul but slammed it shut smartly. Astute verbal fencing and epigrammatic repartee were tools of the prudent navigator of politics, who defended injuries to honor through the point of a verse rather than a sword. The paragon of the cunning and learned political put-down was Queen Elizabeth's extemporaneous Latin exchange with a Polish ambassador, an incident admiringly recounted by those seeking to mold political communication into an astute, learned exchange vital to the prudent practice of policy.[25]

The Neo-Latin epigrams of the Scot George Buchanan (1506–82), tutor to the future King James I of England, and the Welshman John Owen proved immensely popular internationally, not because they were expressive of a subjective individuality or of a national literature, but because they were formulaic. They could serve as shared currency by offering prefabricated repartees, which, by drawing upon widely spread categories of thought, could easily be fit into diverse contexts. In addition to some epigrams addressed to individuals, Owen's epigrams included a cast of types: professions (alchemist, courtier, politician, divine, poet, historian); objects (mirror, magnet, water clock); polities (Britannia, "To the noble Venetians," "To the French,"); parts of the state (king, populace, senate, "the eyes of the *res publica*," "on the crowd, the king, and the law," "*ragion di stato*"); vices and virtues; various characters drawn from Martial (Zoilus, Cotta); and biblical subjects (God, man, the devil, the fall of Adam).

In the manner of occasional poetry or "casualcarmina," Owen often identified an addresser, an addressee, and an occasion for his epigrams, such as "Albion, to the King," "The King, to Britain," "To England, on the British Union," "Union, to the British," or "The State of the British Union to the King." In other words, when reading the epigrams, the reader does not feel that she is engaging directly with an authorial self but rather witnessing an exchange, often concerning a widely recognizable event, between two other parties. In the examples above, the epigram served as a medium of communication between the land (whether England alone or all of Britain), the ruler, and a political event, the Union of the Crowns.

Given the prominence of epigrams addressing the Union of the Crowns, Owen's work might well have served to help imagine an international identity for James's subjects and their foreign observers, just as the forms of nationhood studied by Helgerson concretized an English identity. It is significant that the most popular British epigrammatists on the Continent were Scottish and Welsh—Buchanan and Owen—rather than English. Owen frequently drew attention to the newly hyphenated identities of the British in his epigrams "Cambro-Britannus," "Anglo-Scoti," and "A Paire Royall of Friends, Ad Anglo-Scoto, Scoto-Cambro, Cambro-Anglo Britannos," among others.

Owen himself reached out to an international audience. When the young duke of Braunschweig-Lüneburg, Friedrich Ulrich, nephew of Queen Anne, was prominently received at the court of King James in 1610, his cousin Prince Henry gave him a suit of armor; Owen seized the chance to present him with an autograph volume of 124 epigrams, many of them newly composed.[26] They are still in the ducal library in Wolfenbüttel.[27]

Owen's gift of a holograph bound volume of his original poems directly to Friedrich Ulrich suggests the self-presentation of a single author working to collect and protect his own distinct corpus. Indeed, James Doelman has argued that epigram authors strove to protect their corpus as recognizable in a world of epigram citation and imitation. "John Owen, for example, put the stamp of ownership on his texts and his craft in his volumes of Neo-Latin epigrams," said Doelman.[28] Yet Owen's encounter with Friedrich Ulrich was but one example, and an extreme one, of his meetings with a large number of foreign visitors. That volume remained in manuscript in the ducal library of Braunschweig-Lüneburg and was not published until the nineteenth century.[29] His meetings with other international visitors, and his inscriptions in their albums, produced a vibrant back-and-forth between Owen's printed corpus of epigrams and an international public via a culture of citation.

Poetry fitted to generalized categories and matters of common debate was made for a culture of common-placing and citation. As a result, Owen's epigrams, like other epigram collections of the period, shared a very fertile relationship with the *album amicorum*. Epigrams both came from album inscriptions and were repeated as album inscriptions. For example, his epigrams "To Jakob Fetzer," "Rose," and "In someone's album" can be traced to the album of the young Nuremberg patrician traveler and future politician Jakob Fetzer. Owen's inscription in Fetzer's album appeared in Owen's collection of printed epigrams, and from there "In someone's album" was reused as inscriptions in the *alba amicorum* of others.[30] In fact, Owen's epigrams were widely cited in *alba amicorum* across Europe. They appear in thirty-seven inscriptions in surviving albums of Hungarian provenance—on a par with citations from Ovid—and in over forty surviving albums of German provenance.[31]

Such interaction was partly responsible for Owen's international popularity. Seventeenth-century editions of his poetry appeared in England (London) in 1606, 1607, 1612, 1618, 1619, 1622, 1628, 1633, 1634, 1653, 1659, 1668, 1671, 1676, 1677, 1678, and 1686 (five of these are English translations, one composed in the New World).[32] Almost as many editions appeared that century in Holland (Leiden and Amsterdam) in 1628, 1633, 1634, 1640, 1642, 1644, 1646, 1647, 1650, 1657, 1662, 1669, 1679, and 1682—all in Latin.[33]

These editions all derive from the 1628 edition, produced after Owen's death by a young German-speaking Silesian traveler, Gottfried Hegenitius, who included the inscriptions from the album of Jakob Fetzer. Owen's works appeared even more often in German-speaking lands in the seventeenth century in 1608, 1609, 1610, 1612, 1614, 1615, 1617, 1620, 1622, 1641, 1649, 1651, 1653, 1658, 1661, 1668, 1678, 1683, 1684, and 1694 (three of these are German translations).[34] Owen remained in print in German-speaking lands through the first decades of the nineteenth century.[35]

In contrast to Owen's past European celebrity, his position in the canon of British literature today reflects Ben Jonson's opinion of the poet. Jonson told William Drummond of Hawthornden in 1619 that "Owen is a pure pedantique Schoolmaster sweeping his living from the Posteriors of litle children, and hath no thinge good in him, his Epigrames being bare narrations."[36] Perhaps it was precisely to the "pedantique" nature of his poetry that Owen owed his long-lived and widespread continental reception.[37] Although he often addressed contemporary issues, stylistically he based his epigrams very closely on Martial, earning himself the title of the "British Martial." Owen's success lay not in his radical departure from Martial and his development of an authorial voice but in his ability to take Martial up and re-characterize him in such a way that his poetry, rather than Martial's, became a new model for imitation.

Owen's epigrams proved popular precisely because their Latinity, brevity, wit, and allusiveness suited them well for travel through and conversation with international audiences moving between state and society. The epigrams spread rapidly, not because they were distinctive, but because they were made from and for imitation. This citation-ready aesthetic did not appeal to those seeking national voices within the field of literature, and this is one reason why Owen is so little studied today. In an era when the value of literature was judged by the authenticity of its national voice, Erich Urban, the author of the central study of Owen's influence on German literature (1900), made his "dislike" for his own subject manifest, as Ruth Angress pointed out.[38] Suitability for international uptake was the reason for the popularity of Owen's epigrams in the seventeenth century as well as for their current marginal status.

Formulaic Neo-Latin epigrams, to modern ears, might appear to have little to do with the practice of political observation and discussion. Such citation-ready verse, however, did not entail an avoidance of contemporary engagement; fitting one's self into shared forms directly addressed a reformulation of public and private and the conceptualization of the self within new civic identities. As David Allan had written concerning Buchanan's poetry, the "literary sensibility which resulted was in fact the means by which the fraught relations between public and private life, between states-manlike and scholarly endeavour . . . were first directly confronted by perplexed Scottish intellectuals."[39] Though Allan hoped to show what was distinctively Scottish about Buchanan's Neo-Latin poetry, the agency of an international public is apparent in both shaping and receiving Owen's work.

Global Travel and the Epigram

The *Forms of Nationhood* studied by Helgerson can be seen, not as a mod-ern nationalism opposed to medieval feudalism, but as a reaction to a dis-turbingly new internationalism. The methodical international observation integral to continental travel triggered a backlash from some English ob-servers such as Ben Jonson. Jonson was opposed not only to the aesthetic qualities of Owen's epigrams but to the entire culture of learned and (from Jonson's perspective) pedantic travel in which they were employed. Several English writers, among them Francis Bacon, Thomas Palmer, and Thom-as Coryate, tried to bring German-style methodical travel to England. Thomas Coryate was ridiculed as "Brittaine's Perspicill" for his attempt to become one of the new instruments of observation.[40] Jonson satirized international methodical travel in his poem, "On the Famous Voyage" (published in his own *Epigrammes*), which detailed a lengthy trip through the London sewers. He often poked fun at Englishmen who attempted to gain a political reputation through the forms of internationality, as in his character Sir Politick Would-be, who claimed, "All tooke me for a citizen of Venice: / I knew the formes, so well."

This new internationalism has sometimes appeared in historiography not as a highly mediated and artificial tool of observation but as inte-gral to the organic emergence of new national selves. Garrett Mattingly's classic work on the emergence of modern diplomacy and intelligence gathering, *Renaissance Diplomacy* (1955), traced the origins of the stand-ing embassy to the competitive Italian Renaissance city-states. Rather than the previous temporary orators sent to negotiate alliances for a Europe presumed to exist in Christian communion and a state of peace, the new diplomats assumed a state of warring interests that required information gathering about presumed competitors. For Mattingly, diplomacy was of a piece with the entire age and but one "adaptation of the new type of self-conscious, uninhibited, power-seeking competitive organism." In his link-age of worldly empiricism and modern selfhood, Mattingly was arguably influenced by Jakob Burckhardt's view of the Italian Renaissance as the "discovery of man and the world."[41]

More recently, however, global perspectives have challenged Mattingly's account. Daniel Goffman has argued that it was the increasing interaction between Italy and the encroaching Ottoman Empire that gave rise to a newly empirical study of peoples and the assumption of competition and antagonisms between states. This assumption of a difference of interests was only augmented by the Protestant Reformation and the breakup of Latin Christendom. Emerging European diplomatic professions, such as those of standing ambassadors and familial dynasties of interpreters, grew from an international, alien observation of cultures rather than a new Renaissance self-consciousness growing organically from within.[42]

This was the world in which diplomatic investigations gave rise to new bodies of international knowledge based on empirical collection, and therefore on fragments, periodical dispatches, clever aphorisms, and tentative essays, rather than on polished humanist oratory.[43] In contrast to the national rhetoric of wholeness and immediate belonging to which Helgerson alluded, new political writings were celebrated for a "pointed" aesthetic of clever and fragmented *sententiae* developed in an atmosphere of intersubjective social doubt.

In its very name, the book of friends appears to delineate a zone of intimacy and trust, but it belonged to the prudent and political culture of methodical travel. The book of friends, which could encompass hundreds of inscriptions of strangers met in the course of travel, was far from intimate.[44] As the books were ordinarily inscribed in hierarchical order, which could range from kings in the front of the book to artisans at the end, the *album* required both its owner and its inscribers to conceptualize how international society might be integrated, and where each individual would stand in an international order. The seemingly private interaction between owner and inscriber was in fact a negotiation for rank within an international and competitive society. Furthermore, this rank would be viewed by many. Inscribers were not restricted to members of a particular confession, or indeed to Christians[45]; this was especially so for travelers who brought their albums on journeys outside lands ruled by Christians.[46] Within the album, Latin and Greek epigrams interacted with many macaronic and polyglottal inscriptions, as inscribers competed in a display of their mastery of foreign languages. For instance, the future English ambassador to the Ottoman Empire, Thomas Glover, signed the album of the Scot Georg Craig in Ottoman Turkish in 1605. Tellingly, two pages later, a (crossedout) comment noted, "This Book is not English nor Scotch."[47]

In their brevity and international aesthetic, Owen's epigrams are the very opposite of the consolidating English national genres studied by Helgerson.[48] This contrast is mirrored by the fact that, although many signed *alba amicorum,* strikingly few Englishmen kept them, especially in comparison to their Northern European Protestant peers (including the Scots). The few who did were cosmopolitan in the extreme. These included William Bedwell, the English Arabist at Leiden whose album was signed by the Moroccan ambassador, and Francis Segar, gentleman of the bedchamber for Maurice of Hesse-Kassell, whose album was signed among others by Shah Abbas of Persia.[49]

Conclusion

The book of friends, despite its name, does not reveal the subjective interiority of individuals or affective intimacy. The epigrammatic inscriptions often contained in it protectively cordoned the interior self off from the world of politically oriented international travel. It was not because they were so individual but because they were so formulaic that Owen's epigrams provided a convenient currency for cosmopolitan sociability.

The emerging nationalism of England and the increasing cosmopolitanism of methodical travel appear to have been contradictory trends. However, like the public and the private, one might expect nationalism and internationalism to emerge together as complementary opposites. Rather than contradictions, perhaps we can see both as taking up the same tools of categorization in different ways.

Such an international perspective can shed light on the development of new genres for the study of territories and peoples, and the ways in which such genres, like the red tape of a later era, provided categories of thought for the formation of publics, even though such categories were often deployed at cross-purposes to the original intent of the form. The agency of generic literature for public formation within a zone shared among states, peoples, and individuals makes it ripe for historical analysis. Such analysis might even uncover the aesthetic attractions of Owen's "bare narrations."

NOTES

1. Lorraine Daston, ed., *Biographies of Scientific Objects* (Chicago: University of Chicago Press, 2000).

2. Michael Warner, "Publics and Counterpublics," *Public Culture* 14.1 (2002): 49–90.

3. Jürgen Habermas, *The Structural Transformation of the Public Sphere: An Inquiry into a Category of Bourgeois Society,* trans. Thomas Burger (Cambridge: MIT Press, 1991), 231.

4. Ian F. McNeely, *The Emancipation of Writing: German Civil Society in the Making, 1790s–1820s* (Berkeley: University of California Press, 2003). Peter Stallybrass is currently studying "blanks," or printed forms providing spaces for manuscript, which allow for individual inscription within shared categories.

5. Justin Stagl, *A History of Curiosity: The Theory of Travel, 1500–1800* (Chur, Switzerland: Harwood Academic Publishers, 1995), and Joan-Pau Rubiés, "Instructions for Travellers: Teaching the Eye to See," *History and Anthropology* 9 (1996): 139–90.

6. Thomas Palmer, *An Essay of the Meanes how to make our Travailes, into forraine Countries, the more profitable and honourable* (London: Lownes, 1606), 53.

7. Jacob Soll, *The Information Master: Jean-Baptiste Colbert's Secret State Intelligence System* (Ann Arbor: University of Michigan Press, 2009).

8. Richard Helgerson, *Forms of Nationhood: The Elizabethan Writing of England* (Chicago: University of Chicago Press, 1992), 22.

9. Richard Helgerson, "The Folly of Maps and Modernity," in *Literature, Mapping and the Politics of Space in Early Modern Britain,* ed. Andrew Gordon and Bernhard Klein (Cambridge: Cambridge University Press, 2001), 241–62.

10. George Villiers, *Plays, Poems, and Miscellaneous Writings associated with George Villiers, Second Duke of Buckingham,* ed. Robert D. Hume and Harold Love (Oxford: Oxford University Press, 2007), 230–31; Charles de St. Évremond, *Oeuvres* (London: Tonson, 1705), 293.

11. Max Rosenheim, "The Album Amicorum," *Archaeologia* 62 (1910): 251–308; Alfred Fiedler, *Vom Stammbuch zum Poesiealbum: Eine volkskundliche Studie* (Weimar: Böhlau, 1960); Margaret Annie Eugénie Nickson, *Early Autograph Albums in the British Museum* (London: The Trustees of The British Museum, 1970); Gertrude Angermann, *Stammbücher und Poesiealben als Spiegel ihrer Zeit: Nach Quellen des 18.–20. Jahrhunderts aus Minden-Ravensberg* (Münster: Aschendorff Verlag, 1971); Kees Thomassen, *Alba Amicorum: Vijf Eeuwen Vriendschap op Papier gezet: Het Album Amicorum en het Poeziealbum in de Nederlanden* (The Hague: Maarssen, 1990); Christiane Schwarz, *Studien zur Stammbuchpraxis der Frühen Neuzeit: Gestaltung und Nutzung des Album amicorum am Beispiel eines Hofbeamten und Dichters, eines Politikers und eines Goldschmieds, etwa 1550 bis 1650* (Berlin: Peter Lang, 1999); Werner Wilhelm Schnabel, *Das Stammbuch: Konstitution und Geschichte einer textsortenbezogenen Sammelform bis ins erste Drittel des 18. Jahrhunderts* (Tübingen: Max Niemeyer, 2003); Johan Oosterman, "Women's Albums: Mirrors of International Lyrical Poetry," in *I Have Heard About You: Foreign Women's Writing Crossing the Dutch Border: From Sappho to Selma Lagerlöf,* ed. S. van Dijk et al. (Hilversum: Verloren, 2004), 94–99; Walther Ludwig, *Das Stammbuch als Bestandteil humanistischer Kultur: Das Album des Heinrich Carlhack Hermeling, 1587–1592* (Göttingen: Vanedenhoeck & Ruprecht, 2006); and Marie Ryantová, *Památníky aneb štambuchy, to jest alba amicorum: Kulturně historický fenomén raného* (Ceske Budejovice: Historický Ústav Filozofické Fakulty Jihočeské Univerzity, 2007).

12. The *album amicorum* of Michael van Meer, Edinburgh, MS.La.III.283, 408. See June Schlueter, "Michael van Meer's *Album Amicorum,* with Illustrations of London, 1614–15," *Huntington Library Quarterly* 69.2 (2006): 301–13. The cassowary can be found in Fetzer's *album amicorum,* Herzog August Bibliothek, Ms. Blankenburg 235, 83r. On Fetzer and his *album amicorum,* see James Cameron, "Some Continental Visitors to Scotland in the Late Sixteenth and Early Seventeenth Centuries," in *Scotland and Europe, 1200–1850,* ed. T. C. Smout (Edinburgh: John Donald Publishers, 1986), 50–51. An impressive portrait of Fetzer survives in the Herzog Anton Ulrich Museum in Braunschweig. Joachim Jacoby, *Die Deutsche Gemälde des 17. und 18. Jahrhunderts* (Braunschweig: Herzog-Anton-Ulrich-Museum, 1989), 179.

13. The prints of Jost Amman were often copied in *alba amicorum,* and Amman even issues prefabricated *alba* including his popular images and ready to be filled in with inscriptions and heraldry. Ilse O'Dell, "Jost Amman and the Album Amicorum. Drawings after

Prints in Autograph Albums," *Print Quarterly* 9 (1992): 31–36.

14. Bronwen Wilson, *The World in Venice: Print, the City, and Early Modern Identity* (Toronto: University of Toronto Press, 2005), and "Venice, Print and the Early Modern Icon, Chorographic Impressions: Early Modern Venice through Print," *Urban History* 33.1 (2006): 39–64.

15. Ann Rosalind Jones, "Habits, Holdings, Heterologies: Populations in Print in a 1562 Costume Book," *Yale French Studies* 110 (2006): 92–121.

16. Valerie Traub, "Mapping the Global Body," in *Early Modern Visual Culture: Representation, Race, and Empire in Renaissance England,* ed. Peter Erickson and Clark Hulse (Philadelphia: University of Pennsylvania Press, 2000), 44–97.

17. Evelyn Welch, *Shopping in the Renaissance: Consumer Cultures in Italy, 1400–1600* (New Haven, Conn.: Yale University Press, 2005), 55.

18. George W. McClure, *The Culture of Profession in Late Renaissance Italy* (Toronto: University of Toronto Press, 2004), 12–13; Jakob Bornitz, *Tractatus politicus de rerum sufficientia* (Frankfurt: Tampachius, 1625), 58.

19. Traub, "Mapping the Global Body," 44.

20. R. K. Angress, *The Early German Epigram: A Study in Baroque Poetry* (Lexington: University of Kentucky Press, 1971).

21. Debora Shuger, "Life-writing in Seventeenth-century England," in *Representations of the Self from the Renaissance to Romanticism,* ed. Patrick Coleman, Jayne Lewis, and Jill Kowalik (Cambridge: Cambridge University Press, [2000], 2008), 68–72.

22. Palmer, *An Essay of the Meanes how to make our Travailes,* 129–30.

23. Ibid., 130–31.

24. John Owen, *Epigrammatum Ioannis Owen Cambro-Brittani, Oxoniensis editio postrema* (Leiden: Elzevier, 1628), 271.

25. Bornitz, *Tractatus Politicus,* second letter to the reader. Janet M. Green, "Queen Elizabeth I's Latin Reply to the Polish Ambassador," *The Sixteenth Century Journal* 31.4 (2000): 987–1008.

26. Jill Bepler, "Practical Perspectives on the Court and Role of Princes: Georg Engelhard von Loehneyss' Aulico Politica 1622–24 and Christian IV of Denmark's Königlicher Wecker 1620," in *Pomp, Power and Politics: Essays on German and Scandinavian Court Culture and Their Contexts,* ed. Mara Wade (Amsterdam: Rodopi, 2003), 144.

27. Ms. 1185 Helmstedt, *Johannes Audoëni Cambro-Britanni manuscriptorum epigrammatum liber ad illustrissimum principem Fridericum Huldericum Ducem Brunsvicensem et Luneburgensem* (1610).

28. James Doelman, "Epigrams and Political Satire in Early Stuart England," *Huntington Library Quarterly* 69.1 (2006): 31–46l; here 33.

29. John Owen, *Johannes Audoëni Cambro-Britanni manuscriptorum epigrammatum liber ad illustrissimum principem Fridericum Huldericum Ducem Brunsvicensem et Luneburgensem,* ed. Friedrich Adolf Ebert (Leipzig: Wagner, 1824).

30. Owen, *Epigrammatum* (1628), 271. The album of Jakob Fetzer, Herzog August Bibliothek, Ms. Blankenburg 235, 81r and 84r, and Ms. Blankenburg 231, 161r. K. Schöppe, "Aus einem Studenten-Stammbuche," *Zeitschrift des Veriens für Thüringische Geschichte* 19 (1899): 509–25, 524.

31. *Inscriptiones Alborum Amicorum,* http://iaa.jgypk.hu/index2.php?mutato=1&lang=en. *Repertorium Alborum Amicorum,* www.raa.phil.uni-erlangen.de.

32. According to *Early English Books Online,* http://eebo.chadwyck.com. See also J. J. Enck, "John Owen's Epigrammata," *Harvard Library Bulletin* 3 (1949): 431–34; Leicester Bradner, *Musae anglicanae; A History of Anglo-Latin Poetry, 1500–1925* (New York: Modern Language Association of America, 1940), and Bradner, "*Musae Anglicanae:* A Supplemental List," *The Library,* 5th ser., 22.2 (June 1967): 93–103; here 100–101.

33. According to the *Short-title Catalogue of the Netherlands,* http://picarta.pica.nl.

34. According to the database of seventeenth-century German printing, *Das Verzeichnis der im deutschen Sprachraum erschienenen Drucke des 17. Jahrhunderts,* www.vd17.de/.

35. E.g., John Owen, *Epigrammata, ad usum juventutis studiosae selecta* (Amberg: Uhlmann, 1811), and John Owen, *Epigrammata selecta* (Leipzig: Gleditsch, 1813).

36. Ben Jonson, *Conversations with William Drummond of Hawthornden, 1619* (New York: Barnes & Noble, 1966), 10.

37. Johannes Janssen, "The Microcosm of the Baroque Epigram: John Owen and Julien Wandré," in *The Neo-Latin Epigram: A Learned and Witty Genre,* ed. Susanna de Beer, K. A. E. Enenkel, and David Rijser (Leuven: Leuven University Press, 2009), 275–300; here 280.

38. Angress, 14. Erich Urban, *Owenus und die Deutschen Epigrammatiker des 17. Jahrhunderts* (Berlin: E. Felber, 1900); and Gilbert Waterhouse, *The Literary Relations of England and Germany in the Seventeenth Century* (Cambridge: Cambridge University Press, 1914), 59–68.

39. David Allan, *Philosophy and Politics in Later Stuart Scotland: Neo-Stoicism, Culture and Ideology in an Age of Crisis, 1540–1690* (East Lothian, Scotland: Tuckwell Press, 2000), 46. See also Grahame Castor and Terence Cave, eds., *Neo-Latin and the Vernacular in Renaissance France* (Oxford: Clarendon Press, 1984), and David Halsted, *Poetry and Politics in the Silesian Baroque: Neo-Stoicism in the Work of Christophorus Colerus and His Circle* (Wiesbaden: Harrassowitz, 1996).

40. David J. Baker, "'Idiote': Politics and Friendship in Thomas Coryate," in *Borders and Travellers in Early Modern Europe,* ed. Thomas Betteridge (Aldershot, UK: Ashgate, 2007), 129–46.

41. Garret Mattingly, *Renaissance Diplomacy* (Boston: Houghton Mifflin, 1955), 61; and Evert Janssen, *Jacob Burckhardt und die Renaissance* (Assen: Van Gorcum, 1970), 99.

42. Daniel Goffman, "Negotiating with the Renaissance State: The Ottoman Empire and the New Diplomacy," in *The Early Modern Ottomans: Remapping the Empire,* ed. Virginia H. Aksan and Daniel Goffman (Cambridge: Cambridge University Press, 2007), 61–74.

43. Merio Scattola, *Dalla virtù alla scienza: La fondazione e la trasformazione della disciplina politica nell'età moderna* (Milan: Angeli, 2003).

44. Vera Keller, "Painted Friends: Political Interest and the Transformation of International Learned Sociability," in *Friendship in the Middle Ages and Early Modern Times,* ed. Marilyn Sandidge and Albrecht Classen (Berlin: Walter de Gruyter Press, 2010).

45. The album of Pieter Nuyts, 18–19, for Ahmad ibn Qasim al Andalusi, who signed in Leiden in 1613; John Fletcher, *Pieter Nuyts and His "Album Amicorum"* (Melbourne: The Bibliographical Society of Australia and New Zealand, 1974).

46. See, for instance, Gotha Library Chart B 1039, *Stammbuch* of Johann Reichart von Steinbach, with 27 entries in Istanbul, 2 in Scutari, and 1 in Edirne.

47. *Album amicorum* of George Craig, Edinburgh University Library, Laing III 525, 10v and 13r.

48. For Pietro della Valle's use of the genre in Persia, see Nathalie Hester, *Literature and Identity in Italian Baroque Travel Writing* (Burlington: Ashgate, 2008), 74.

49. The album of Francis Segar is Huntington Library Ms. 743. William Bedwell's album is discussed in Alastair Hamilton, *William Bedwell, the Arabist, 1563–1632* (Leiden: E. J. Brill for the Thomas Brown Institute, 1985).

Theatrical Publicity

CHAPTER TWELVE

The Voice of Caesar's Wounds

The Politics of Martyrdom in Shakespeare's Julius Caesar

DAVID LEE MILLER

FROM *Forms of Nationhood* through *A Sonnet from Carthage,* Richard Helgerson's major work describes literary figurations of public space through a dialectic of the local and the universal. In this dialectic, the immediacies of village and domicile are gathered into imaginary unities of nation and empire, but at a high cost: to be appropriated by the vision of empire, self and community must be alienated from their provincial origins, emptied of specific content. In *Adulterous Alliances* Helgerson traces a countermovement to this ascendancy of the state, visible in genres that foreground domestic spaces threatened by incursions of power figured as sexual predation. The dialectic is still at work in this countermovement: "Domestic drama and domestic painting," he observes, "emerged as a by-product of early modern state formation and defined themselves by their difference from the newly invented or newly revived genres of state."[1] This resistance of the domestic to the imperial finds a sympathetic echo within the genres of state, which not only celebrate the fantasy of a universal space but also mourn the loss of the concrete and particular. Garcilaso's *Aqui* in the Carthage sonnet, for example, points not to Rome—nor to Goleta, in spite of the title assigned to the poem by editorial tradition—but rather to a place "of which Rome's violence has left only the name," the location, as the poem goes on to declare, of the poet's own undoing, the *me deshago* into which the speaking voice dissolves.[2]

Like most things, this dialectic of the local and the universal comes from Hegel. In the *Encyclopedia of the Philosophical Sciences,* Hegel identifies a similar contradiction as the paradox of deictic language: pointers like "I," "here," and "now" evoke an immediate moment of self-presence even as they establish the generality of an abstract category. In Paul de Man's translation, Hegel argues that "When I say 'I,' I *mean* myself as *this* at the exclusion of all others; but what I say, I, is precisely anyone; any I, as that which excludes all others from itself."[3] Michael Warner observes that the shiftiness of such pointers is crucial to the ability of discourse to generate publics, since a certain indeterminacy of address—"this discourse is intended for whoever chooses to join its audience"—precedes our identification with the addressee position when we take public speech into ourselves.[4] Hegel's version of this paradox indicates that the universal placelessness of empire arises from within language; it implies that the imperial art Helgerson has studied draws on the categorical emptiness of language as such to project fantasies of universality invested with power and authority. Such art offers up its own emptiness in displaced form as an object of political desire. At the same time, as the example of Garcilaso reminds us, it registers and regrets the cost of this fantasy, its dissolution of the local and immediate.

In this chapter I want to consider further the ways in which texts and performances can both project and unravel fantasies of shared public space. The imaginary locale we shall visit is the Rome of Shakespeare's *Julius Caesar,* but the topography we encounter there will be less geographical or archaeological than textual and theatrical—not so much a historical place as one of metaphor and layered make-believe. Theater is not itself a fantasy of shared space so much as a shared space of fantasy, a commercial arena dedicated to pretense and illusion as leisure practices. Both the artistic and the commercial success of such a venue depends on its ability to turn the members of a crowd into members of an audience, eliciting endlessly variable moments of engagement—frissons of guilt, stabs of empathy, ripples of sexual desire, passionate idealizations, and pleasures of anticipation—that are neither purely collective nor utterly idiosyncratic but instead are always in flux, literally *at play,* between private and public, or collective and individual, experience. Theater can manage such a transformation because its simulations of human action allow representations of all sorts—words, props, clothing, gestures, social spaces—to float free of the contexts in which they are normally anchored. These simulations do not, of course, abandon their extra-theatrical contexts altogether. An account book, a country dance, a crown and scepter, or a biblical allusion all bear their associations with them onto the stage; but once there, they enter into a welter of more immediate associations, of figuration and projected fantasy, that opens them up to many different meanings and desires.

We see this volatility of representations in *Julius Caesar*'s treatment of social space, for Shakespeare's play summons radically divergent social and textual spaces into a fictional domain where they can then overlap. Richard Halpern, in an astute mapping of the play's symbolic venues, has described the opposition between the Roman Forum and the Senate as anticipating Jürgen Habermas's contrast between the public sphere and mass culture: "The political struggle of *Julius Caesar*," he observes, "is largely a contest between the material, rhetorical, theatrical, and even interpretive practices of its two public spaces," that of an idealized politics and that of economics and the body.[5] Revealing as this account proves to be—and it is a strong reading—I want to suggest that its definitions both of politics and of public space are needlessly constrained by an unstated secularism. The exclusion of religion as a subject of serious thought has been so common among materialist critical approaches that it has given rise to a countermovement, a "religious turn" in early modern literary studies.[6] Even a work like Dawson and Yachnin's *Culture of Playgoing,* which seeks to put these competing approaches into "collaborative debate," tends to sustain their polarization of church and marketplace: "Yachnin is inclined to contest Dawson's account of the religious affiliations of theatre, especially by insisting that theatrical pleasure in Shakespeare's time was founded in the commerce in elite cultural goods and social capital *rather than* in religious habits of thought."[7] Instead of zoning off religion and commerce as discontinuous compartments within the public sphere, I shall argue that in *Julius Caesar* performance turns the stage into a figurative space where other symbolically charged venues, including the church and the marketplace, overlap. They do so in unpredictable ways, with unexpected consequences.

In what follows I will ask you to bear in mind that although the first definition given in the *Oxford English Dictionary* entry on *place* is "public square," there is also a cluster of related textual-rhetorical senses.[8] These are important because Caesar's pagan Rome is not only compounded of different social venues but is also haunted by distinctly biblical "places" in the textual sense. I will invite you as well, because the play itself repeatedly does so, to ponder the ways in which theatrical performance complicates the already contradictory dynamics of deictic utterance.[9] This complication arises because the ambiguity of place extends to voice and persona: if "here" is an imaginary compound of pagan Rome and Elizabethan London, rostrum and pulpit, Plutarch and the Gospels, then "I" and "now" must prove likewise variable.[10] Yet their instability is not quite Hegelian. In *Julius Caesar* we encounter not a dream of imperial space emptied of particularity but an imaginary register in which different localities meet and contaminate each other; a place not where the speaking voice is undone but where we uncover the peculiar mobility of utterance that lends political rhetoric its devastating force.

Tongues in Wounds

Before his death, Shakespeare's Caesar compares himself to the dwelling-place of the gods: "Hence!" he cries, dismissing a swarm of suitors, "wilt thou lift up Olympus?" (3.1.74).[11] Such presumption can hardly go unpunished. And so abruptly the scene is transformed: the suitors turn into assassins and the man who, as Cassius said, "is now become a god" (1.2.116) just as quickly turns into a "bleeding piece of earth" (3.1.254). That is what Antony calls him as he stands over the body, taking in the shock of a god's mortality. And yet in the lines that follow, Antony's words bring Caesar back to life even while prophesying vengeance for his death: "Caesar's spirit," he proclaims, "Shall in these confines with a monarch's voice / Cry 'Havoc!' and let slip the dogs of war" (270–73).

Why "with a monarch's voice"? To cry havoc, to give the signal for slaughter and pillage without quarter, was a royal prerogative. Caesar came to the Senate house to take on that voice, tempted by news that "the Senate have concluded / To give this day a crown to mighty Caesar" (2.2.93–94). The conspirators come to prevent him. As it happens, both parties are taken by surprise: Caesar is not crowned but killed, yet he returns in death to claim "a monarch's voice" and run his shaken assassins to ground. Where does this voice come from? How does it gain such power? In one sense it comes from Antony: "Over thy wounds," he says, "now do I prophesy / (Which like dumb mouths do ope their ruby lips / To beg the voice and utterance of my tongue)" (3.1.259–61). Antony here sees the bloody gashes as mouths desperate to speak, like a dreamer whose voice is paralyzed in sleep. Opening their lips, these mouths bring the corpse not to life but to a kind of life-in-death, unnaturally mobilizing a piece of earth with the will to speak. This will and its urgency are strangely out of place. Where do they come from?

Such a moment intensifies our feeling for the play as theater. Antony projects his voice into Caesar's wounds like a playwright reviving dead Romans to put his words in their mouths: "To beg the voice and utterance of my tongue" might be any actor's motto. Moments earlier we saw Brutus and Cassius exulting to think of "this our lofty scene . . . acted over, / In [states] unborn, and accents yet unknown!" (112–13). Their fantasy is less gruesome than Antony's image but no less dislocated: actors in a state unborn when Caesar lived, speaking accents then unknown, pretend to be Romans anticipating their own performance. Routing themselves through a legendary past, the actors play at imagining what they are, doubling back on their ordinary selves in a way that stretches the illusion very thin. And this is not the only time. Watching a performance, we do not usually worry that as Romans the characters should speak Latin. But Shakespeare insists on this difference when he has Caesar deliver the celebrated line "*Et tu, Brute?*" (77), flaunting the ventriloquism of his art. Through such means he prepares us to catch an unnerving glimpse of this art in the dumb mouths of a corpse animated by someone else's will to speak.

Julius Caesar is a play about political oratory, about a will to speak so deeply embedded in the will to power that they are almost the same thing. On some level every character both seeks and fears "a monarch's voice." At times Rome seems to consist entirely of alpha-male orators. When they stand around the marketplace, flexing their rhetoric and eyeing each other as rivals, no lofty declarations about the sanctity of the republic can disguise the fierce egotism that has them in its grip. Yet for all their egotism, the will to power swirls among them without really belonging to any one Roman. Rather it comes to each one from all the others, like the forged notes that Cassius has thrown into Brutus's window at night, "all tending to the great opinion / That Rome holds of his name" (1.2.318–19).[12]

Marc Antony's vision of speaking wounds points to an irreducible mobility in the voice and its desires. If this mobility is essential to the experience of theater, where all voices and desires are projected and simulated, it is also essential to the politics of emulation, where every competitor sees his own reflection enlarged or diminished in his rivals. But Antony's vision also suggests something beyond the theatrical and the political. In his metaphor the urgency of speech is displaced in a more deeply shocking way, scattered across the surface of Caesar's body in wounds that open "ruby lips" to beg. These gashes are somehow almost lovely, their bleeding edges as precious as the lips of a Petrarchan mistress.[13]

In the strangeness of this image there is a sense of what Freud calls the uncanny, the return of a dreaded and long-repressed fantasy. One such fantasy unearthed by Freud holds that the other lips on a woman's body are also a wound, the mark of a violent castration. Shakespeare makes a knowing joke on this commonplace in *Twelfth Night,* as Malvolio studies an anonymous letter, trying to decide whether the handwriting is Olivia's: "These be her very c's, her u's, and her t's," he concludes, "and thus makes she her great P's" (2.5.86–88). In *Julius Caesar,* Portia slashes her thigh to prove her worth to Brutus, and while I don't want to minimize the complexity of her self-wounding, which is meant to deny female weakness, it does also signify castration, and in this it both mirrors and contrasts with Caesar's bloody wounds.[14]

Shakespeare closely followed the account in Sir Thomas North's translation of Plutarch, and there we read that as Caesar fell, "Brutus him selfe gave him one wounde about his privities."[15] *Et tu, Brute?* Has Caesar been given the unkindest cut of all, the original Caesarean section?[16] So Antony's soliloquy seems to hint. But I don't mean this quite literally. Shakespeare repeats a great deal from Plutarch, but he doesn't say that Brutus stabbed Caesar in the privates. He leaves this thought unstated, perhaps sensing that it will be more powerful as unexpressed fantasy than as fact. So in place of a literally castrated Caesar we get Portia's wounded thigh and a strangely transformed corpse, a punctured and bleeding body that is, somehow, castrated all over.

In this transformation the corpse is weirdly sexualized. Appallingly, its "ruby lips" evoke desire as well as horror. There are many ways in which Caesar's body becomes an object of desire: first to the conspirators washing their hands in its blood; then to Marc Antony asking "that I may / Produce his body to the market-place" (3.1.227–28); and then again to the plebs, told that if they knew the contents of his will they would "go and kiss dead Caesar's wounds, / And dip their napkins in his sacred blood" (3.2.132–33). Sexual, political, and economic desires mingle freely with religious reverence in this body, an emotionally charged image whose meaning fluctuates from scene to scene, speaker to speaker, moment to moment.

Among the desires that swirl around Caesar's body the sexual imagery is most disturbing. Tongues and wounds, tongues in wounds, wounds with lips, lips kissing wounds—Decius Brutus, in his interpretation of Calpurnia's dream, even imagines that Rome will "suck / Reviving blood" from Caesar (2.2.87–88). Antony's first image is more decorous; it keeps his tongue and Caesar's wounds separated by the abstraction of his "voice and utterance." But when he addresses the crowds in the marketplace he collapses this distance. First he calls up the image in its more decorous version: unlike that silver-tongued Brutus, he says, "I only speak right on / . . . Show you sweet Caesar's wounds, poor, poor dumb mouths, / And bid them speak for me" (3.2.223–26). Already something subtle has happened: before, in private, the dumb mouths begged him to speak for them; now, before the crowd, he bids them to speak for him. But then he displaces his own voice even more deviously—"were I Brutus," he continues, "And Brutus Antony, there were an Antony / Would ruffle up your spirits"—and having thrown his voice into this imaginary "Brutus Antony," he condenses the image into its most shocking form: "Would ruffle up your spirits, and put a tongue / In every wound of Caesar that should move / The stones of Rome to rise and mutiny" (3.2.226–30).

What kind of rhetoric is this? The tongue is a conventional metonymy for the power of speech and hence a symbol of rhetoric itself. But to put this tongue into wounds that have already been fashioned as mouths with lips is more than just unconventional, it's repulsive. Shakespeare will come back to this image in *Coriolanus* when he has a Roman citizen explain that "if he [Coriolanus] show us his wounds and tell us his deeds, we are to put our tongues into those wounds and speak for them" (2.3.5–7). But the wounds Coriolanus displays have healed into scars, and besides, the impropriety of the citizen's "tongues" is comically inept, a piece of verbal buffoonery expressing his lack of status and education. There is nothing comical about Antony's speech. There, lips and tongues evoke erotic, parasitic, and cannibalistic fantasies. The conventional metonymy is wrenched into the kind of abusive metaphor to which rhetorical treatises give the name catachresis.

Jesus Christ

Dante's *Inferno* exemplifies a medieval tradition in which Caesar is a type of Christ: Brutus and Cassius appear with Judas Iscariot quite literally in the jaws of Hell, eternally chewed by a three-headed Satan.[17] Shakespeare's Caesar, by contrast, is hardly sympathetic—surely we aren't supposed to see him as Christlike. And yet the play courts this analogy, multiplying references that link the assassination of Caesar to the crucifixion.

There is, for example, Calpurnia's dream the night before the assassination. Caesar tells Decius Brutus:

> She dreamt to-night she saw my statuë,
> Which like a fountain with an hundred spouts
> Did run pure blood; and many lusty Romans
> Came smiling and did bathe their hands in it. (2.2.76–79)

Decius challenges Calpurnia's interpretation of the dream as a warning, but in doing so he makes it sound even more like a gruesome parody of the Last Supper and the Catholic Mass:

> Your statue spouting blood in many pipes,
> In which so many smiling Romans bath'd,
> Signifies that from you great Rome shall suck
> Reviving blood, and that great men shall press
> For tinctures, stains, relics, and cognizance. (2.2.85–89)

For good measure, the last line throws in a reference to the cult of saint-hood. But as these passages invoke the analogy between Caesar and Christ, they also make it strange. What is Shakespeare doing?

The connection is intensified when Antony "produces" Caesar's body to the marketplace. Given the pattern already established, the public display of Caesar's wounds will recall the "doubting Thomas" episode from the Gospel of John: "Except I see in his hands the print of the nails, and put my finger into the print of the nails, and put mine hand into his side, I will not believe it" (20:25).[18] For Shakespeare's audience, the display of Caesar's body would also recall the elevation of the Host during the celebration of the Mass, a practice that reformers in the sixteenth century deplored because of its emphasis on spectacle.[19] The *Catholic Encyclopedia* describes the superstitions that surrounded this practice: "The elevation of the Host at Mass seems to have brought in its train a great idea of the special merit and virtue of looking upon the Body of Christ. Promises of an extravagant kind circulated freely among the people describing the privileges of him who had seen his Maker at Mass."[20] In just this way Antony flourishes the promises contained in Caesar's will.

This connection between the Mass and the body in the marketplace is complicated by a second, equally striking connection to the theater itself. When Antony descends from the "pulpit" (3.1.236) to display Caesar's body, Shakespeare is effectively superimposing on his Roman marketplace two other settings familiar to an Elizabethan audience. The first would be the area at the front of the church called the chancel or sanctuary, where services are performed and the altar is placed. The second is the stage itself, evoked again here as it was earlier, when Brutus and Cassius imagined the assassination performed by players. Once again the theatrical illusion carries Shakespeare's audience from London to ancient Rome only to circle back for a moment to the London stage. Here, as Antony shows Caesar's bloody mantle to the crowd, we see the conspirators' "lofty scene" acted over much sooner, much closer to home, than they anticipated: "Look, in this place ran Cassius' dagger through; / See what a rent the envious Casca made" (3.2.174–75).

The theatricality of this moment is brought to the surface not only because it turns the conspirators' fantasy back upon them but also, in a more immediate way, because Antony's descent from the pulpit is so full of stagecraft. He asks permission of the crowd before coming down and then instructs them to "stand far off," clearing a space for his performance (167).[21] This attention to blocking and staging is followed by Antony's conspicuous and rhetorically brilliant use of both the mantle and the body itself as theatrical props.

The moment when Antony reveals the body—"Look you here. / Here is himself, marr'd as you see with traitors" (196–97)—is at once the pinnacle of the scene's conscious theatricality and the moment that most explicitly recalls the elevation of the Host, which the priest performed immediately after pronouncing the words *Hoc est enim corpus meum* ("For this is my body"). This telescoping of references seems odd, although the association between theatricality and the Catholic Mass was familiar enough. Protestant polemic had long ridiculed the Mass as nothing but costume and theater, while Puritan theater-bashing had likened plays in turn to the vain and worldly spectacles of the Catholic service. But if Shakespeare is evoking another conventional association, he is again giving it a powerful twist. The revelation of Caesar's bloody corpse becomes more shocking, not more sacred, when that corpse is identified with the body of the crucified Christ and its presentation during the Mass.

I have argued elsewhere that Shakespeare at such moments is tapping into submerged, largely inarticulate fears, sorrows, and longings in his contemporary audience.[22] One way he does this is by alluding to the public execution of religious martyrs. England in the sixteenth century witnessed many forms of atrocity, but among the most traumatic was the burning of more than 280 heretics by Mary Tudor. Powerful men like Cranmer and Ridley went to the stake, but so did scores of commoners, sometimes even women and children. The grim stories of these public immolations were gathered in what came to be known as the *Book of Martyrs,* compiled by John Foxe. This volume, expanding through edition after edition, circulated more widely than any other book in England except for the Bible; by order of law in 1570 it was chained next to a copy of the Bible in every parish church.

What did these public executions mean to the English people? There were many points of dispute in the Reformation, but the heart of the matter concerned the sacrament of the Eucharist, and especially the words through which the sacrament of the "Lord's Supper" was instituted: "This is my body . . . this is my blood of the New Testament" (Matt. 26:26–28; cf. Mark 14:22–24, Luke 22:19–20). As historian Lee Palmer Wandel says with stark simplicity, during the Reformation "these words tore apart Western Christendom. Fathers disowned sons, wives left husbands, neighbors massacred neighbors over the relationship between 'this' and 'my body.'"[23] Did the communion simply commemorate Christ's sacrifice, as the reformers argued, or did it in some mystical sense actually repeat that sacrifice, here and now, through the "real presence" of Christ's body and blood in the communion?

Deep within the ideological character of these executions as historical events lurks a terrible irony. Protestants who went to the fire repudiating the doctrine of transubstantiation saw *themselves* as reenacting Christ's sacrifice. As a result, Catholic authorities who burned heretics for repudiating the doctrine were, in the eyes of Protestants, shifting the scene of the Eucharist from the chancel, or sanctuary, to the marketplace—from the bread and wine of the Mass to the body and blood of a real human victim.[24] When Shakespeare telescopes these same two locations on the stage, he is surely playing with fire.

Foxe's *Book of Martyrs* shows us how in the aftermath of the Marian martyrdoms Catholic and Protestant polemicists competed with each other to control the volatile meaning of historical events, much as Brutus and Marc Antony struggle in *Julius Caesar* to control the meaning of the assassination. When Antony finds Brutus and the other conspirators standing over the body of Caesar, red to the elbows with his blood, he says that he will be their ally *if* they can justify what they have done. Brutus quickly agrees that an explanation is necessary, "Or else were this a savage spectacle" (3.1.223). That is to say, the crucial difference Brutus has insisted on all along—"Let's be sacrificers, but not butchers" (2.1.166)—cannot be read on the face of the deed itself. It must be determined by what gets said afterward. So when Antony stands alone over the body, he asks pardon "that I am meek and gentle with these butchers." When he mounts the pulpit in the marketplace, he will turn the sight of Caesar's body into precisely the "savage spectacle" Brutus wanted to avoid.

Foxe's *Book of Martyrs* offers a pointed example of the same dynamic that is at work in these scenes from the play. In this dynamic, the substance of what we see depends on the words that define it, just as the transformation of the Host into the body of Jesus depended on the words *Hoc est corpus meum.* What kind of event *was* burning at the stake? An atrocity, to be sure, unforgettable and deeply disturbing, as the woodcuts are there to remind us. But was it the awful destruction of a heretic, someone whose open break with the holy Church was tantamount to dismembering Christ's body all over again? Or was it the pitiful suffering of a Christian martyr, someone who, just like the martyrs of the early Church, was bearing supreme witness to her faith? If the victim was a heretic, he was cast in the role of a crucifier, tearing apart the holy body of the Church—a sense that lingers even in the modern historian's assertion (quoted earlier) that the words of the Eucharist "tore apart Western Christendom"; but as a martyr, the victim was instead identified as the one crucified, reenacting Christ's sacrifice there in an English town square—one event, terrible enough to send shock waves through the body politic for decades to come, grasped in two diametrically opposed and irreconcilable ways.

This is the politics of martyrdom, and Foxe's book shows it in action. Catholic writers debunked his stories, so in later editions he quotes from their pamphlets to answer their charges. But the more forcefully he argues for a Protestant reading of the burnings as martyrdoms, the more clearly he reveals that *before* they are executions or martyrdoms, they are provocations to debate. The horror of the event may be self-evident, but its meaning is not. Every sermon, every pamphlet and diatribe, demands that its audience take sides, seeing the spectacle as either one thing or the other, as lawful execution or as martyrdom.

The longer this debate goes on, the more it calls attention to the gap between event and meaning, and the more obvious this gap is, the harder it becomes to forestall a third response, a perception that whatever else the atrocities may be, they are a wedge driven into the body politic. This perception is not possible within the polarizing terms of the debate. To see the event as either execution or martyrdom is still to see it from *within* the confines of the struggle that gave rise to it; in order to see the event as what enables the struggle to grow and spread, you have to step back, finding a position outside the push and pull of the ongoing debate. Only then does it begin to be possible to see the whole process at work.

Finding this more detached point of view is easier said than done. The wrenching violence of the atrocity makes detachment almost impossible— this is part of its power. Distance, as opposed to indifference, takes time and must be achieved.[25] I want to suggest that the Elizabethan theater, in plays like *Julius Caesar,* may have contributed to this achievement, and in this way may have played a part in the slow historical process by which English culture began to gain some distance on its deadly religious politics.

Theater did this by helping to foster the third point of view. One of the ways in which *Julius Caesar* creates this possibility is by setting the action in classical Rome. If you take feelings and images that are too threatening, too close for comfort, and project them into the imaginary distance of a pagan empire, you can filter them through this other place, this other story, and let them come back in a less overwhelming form. When this happens in *Julius Caesar,* the action goes forward in a kind of double register. In the story, Calpurnia's dream prophesies Caesar's death. But it also evokes the ritual of communion, a meaning that cannot be intended or understood by characters in the play because it doesn't belong to the world of classical Rome. Such meanings come alive for an Elizabethan audience; they belong to the world of the Reformation.[26]

When they do come alive, I see Shakespeare working to give himself and his audience a different perspective on them, neither Catholic nor Protestant.[27] He does this by staging the politics of martyrdom at a certain distance, not so far as to make them unrecognizable or diminish their power but not so near as to scorch us with their flames. The violence is still there, but we are able to see more clearly how the politics works. Look at the broad structure of the play and you will see, side by side at its center in act 3, two scenes: the assassination and the speeches in the marketplace; the event in its raw violence and the debate that seeks to capture and direct this violence. Critics have wondered about this structure, for one normally expects the title character of a tragedy to die at the end of act 5, not at the start of act 3. What this pattern throws into relief is the relationship between the event and the competition over its meaning. Throughout the last half of the play, the course of events will be governed more by the force of Antony's rhetoric than by the death that occasioned it—more by his tongue than by Caesar's wounds.

Antony declares that the uprooted tongues placed in Caesar's wounds "should move / The stones of Rome to rise and mutiny," and so they do: the plebs riot, the city burns, and in a famous absurdity, Cinna the poet is torn to pieces because he has the same name as one of the conspirators. All this is found in Plutarch, but because of the double register in which the play develops, Antony is declaring more than Plutarch knows. His words also echo the Gospel of Luke: "I tell you, that if these should hold their peace, the stones would cry" (19:40). Here again we see Reformation England superimposed on pagan Rome, for the allusion identifies the voice of Caesar's wounds with Christ's entry into Jerusalem. But how are we to understand this compounding of places? Are the Roman plebs, calling for fire and shredding poets, really comparable to "the whole multitude of the disciples" who "began to rejoice, and to praise God with a loud voice" because the Messiah had come (19:37)?

Indeed, Shakespeare does seem to be courting such an analogy. Antony's words echo a moment in the gospel story when the Pharisees feel intimidated by the crowds: "Then the high Priests, and the Scribes the same hour went about to lay hands on him: (but they feared the people)" (20:19). Yet the analogy extends beyond this single echo, especially for an audience that would not only recognize biblical language but also remember the surrounding passages. The imagery of stones is prominent in both texts.

In the play's opening scene the tribune Marullus derides the plebs: "You blocks, you stones, you worse than senseless things!" (1.1.35). The first time Antony mentions Caesar's will he replies to this charge as if he had been there to hear it: "You are not wood, you are not stones, but men" (3.2.142). Meanwhile back in Luke chapter 20, the priests and scribes worry that if they give a wrong answer to the question Jesus has put to them, "all the people will stone us" (20:6), and a few verses later Jesus prophesies their destruction with the parable of the vineyard, concluding:

> "What meaneth this then that is written, The stone that the builders refused, that is made the head of the corner?
>
> "Whosoever shall fall upon that stone, shall be broken: and on whomsoever it shall fall, it will grind him to powder." (20:17–18)

In the following chapter Jesus hears the temple of Jerusalem praised for its "goodly stones," and replies that "the days will come wherein a stone shall not be left upon a stone, that shall not be thrown down" (21:5–6).

When he prophesies the destruction of the temple, Christ goes on to say that the days to come will be announced by "fearful things, and great signs . . . from heaven" (21:11), much like the "prodigies" and "portentous things" (1.3.28, 31) that terrorize Rome on the eve of Caesar's death. And of course it is also in chapter 20 of Luke that the spies of the priests ask Jesus if it is lawful to give tribute to Caesar, prompting the famous injunction to "Give then unto Caesar the things which are Caesar's" (20:25). This clustering of associations has a cumulative effect, generating a peculiar resonance between the play and the Gospel.

These echoes are amplified by others that link the play to Thomas Nashe's 1593 pamphlet *Christ's Tears over Jerusalem*.[28] Nashe is explicit about the association between contemporary London and what he calls "her great Grand-mother, Jerusalem," and he elaborately recycles many of the same biblical passages that reverberate in Shakespeare's play: "O Jerusalem, Jerusalem, that stonest and astoniest thy prophets with thy perverseness, that lendest stony ears to thy teachers."[29] He extends Christ's prophecy of the destruction of the temple into a relentless diatribe, in the process reimagining Christ himself as an orator much like Antony—who in fact echoes the rhetoric and imagery of Nashe's messiah both in his funeral speech and in his soliloquy over the dead body of Caesar. Nashe also, notoriously, creates in the matron Miriam and the son she devours an appalling travesty of the Eucharist.

Shakespeare's handling of similar materials is reticent by contrast, although a touch of Nashe's rhetorical violence lingers on—perhaps is even meta-rhetorically *commented* on—in Antony's catachrestic tongues. I think this reticence participates in a historical process of distancing: where Nashe seeks out horrors from biblical times to threaten London with destruction, Shakespeare seeks perspective on recent traumas by filtering them through an image of pagan Rome. What I have said about this displacement so far, however, does not entirely capture its effect. When the play takes its distance from the politics of martyrdom, doesn't it necessarily suggest the possibility that this distance might extend to the great martyrdom itself, the one that founded the Christian religion? In other words, if the allusions to Luke in the text of the play *don't* lend an aura of sacredness to the killing of Caesar, then couldn't they have the reverse effect, highlighting the political subtext of intrigue and demagoguery surrounding the crucifixion?

Shakespeare's use of Rome in *Julius Caesar* is like a thought experiment: a what-if scenario created to explore a particular hypothesis. Of course, a dramatist working by intuition and imagination need not be conscious of his hypotheses in the same way a philosopher must. On the contrary, one advantage of a pagan setting is that it provides *enough* distance for a playwright to grapple with just those questions he might not be able to ask in any other way. It enables him to try out thoughts he cannot acknowledge, thoughts that might not quite be thinkable for his time and place if stated explicitly.

Such a thought inhabits the tragedy of *Julius Caesar,* particularly in the way the play aligns the middle part of its own action with chapters 19–21 of the Gospel of Luke. Popular unrest, a sense of looming disaster, politically motivated fear of a man who claims to be god, all leading to betrayal and sacrifice—these are the elements the texts have in common. But the effect is *not* to make religious allegory out of the Roman political struggle, as in Dante. Rather, it is to heighten our sense of political struggle in the gospel story. The unspoken implication is utterly profane: Was Christ's ministry comparable to Antony's speech in the marketplace? Do these charismatic figures channel the same kind of power? Is it simply political rhetoric—the ventriloquist's trick of throwing his voice into a martyr's wounds—that leads the stones of Jerusalem to cry out and the stones of Rome to rise and mutiny?

Shakespeare may or may not have entertained such thoughts. But when he acts over the lofty scene of Christ's ministry in the peculiar guise of Caesar's tragedy, his play does participate in that slow and subtle process of estrangement that, over the next two centuries, would clear a space for the emergence of secular culture. Perhaps it does so only as a side effect of the essentially conservative politics Helgerson described in *Forms of Nationhood* as a theater of exclusion. There Shakespeare and the "author's theater" he helped to create are in full flight from popular culture and the politics of the vox populi, and *Julius Caesar* offers plenty of evidence to support this view. The reading I am suggesting moves in a different direction, not so much opposing Helgerson's account as adding an unexpected twist, one in which the theater's reactionary distrust of the popular casts a skeptical shadow over the gospel narrative, yielding a perspective that in another register—the politics of martyrdom rather than those of carnival and popular revolt—seems arguably progressive.

Such a claim may sound too teleological. Is the "not-yet secular" just another name for the "destined-to-become secular"? I want to resist that implication. Falling back into an older critical language, it would be possible to sum up my argument with the claim that, in Shakespeare and the Elizabethan theater, we witness an effort by the human imagination to free itself from the politics of martyrdom. I still find this familiar, progressive, humanist narrative deeply attractive, even as I know that it doesn't quite let me say what I mean. This is my own moment of estrangement, analogous to that of Shakespeare and his audience, rooted in ambivalence toward an ideology felt to be inadequate but not entirely drained of its former charisma.

In this I join a long line of readers and theater professionals who have invested *Julius Caesar* with the politics of their own times and places.[30] Enlightenment audiences saw the conspirators as noble but doomed Republicans. John Wilkes Booth, an actor who committed his crime in a theater, saw himself as Brutus. Orson Welles used visual cues in his staging of Antony's great speech to evoke the memory of Hitler's mass rallies at Nuremberg. In these ways readers, audiences, and directors have continued to do what Shakespeare was doing: they have projected their own political struggles into a distant time and place in order to gain a new perspective on them.[31] But Shakespeare does this with more subtlety and complexity—more ambivalence, I would say—than his successors, who for much of the play's history on the stage have cut such inconvenient moments as the proscription scene in act 3, or who have underplayed the vanity and self-delusion feeding Brutus's moral idealism.

The lesson I take from this history is precisely *not* to grasp the play as a fable of our own political moment, tempting as that may be. The play's power of estrangement—what Halpern calls its "complexly non-synchronous relation with its historical moment"—is not a fully measured turning-away from the Christ story, nor can it be plotted on a vector leading straight to that conclusion.[32] Along with other deeply disturbing moments in Shakespeare—Antonio's flamboyant self-martyrdom in *The Merchant of Venice,* for example, or Cordelia's unresurrected death at the close of *King Lear*—Shakespeare's handling of the analogy between Christ and Caesar seeks out a deep indeterminacy.

Among literary history's more idiosyncratic responses to the assassination of Julius Caesar we might include the following anecdote about Shakespeare, relayed by John Aubrey in his *Brief Lives:* "His father was a Butcher, and I have been told heretofore by some of the neighbours, that when he was a boy he exercised his father's trade, but when he killed a calf he would doe it in a high style, and make a speech."[33] Since the late seventeenth century was not likely to have seen any neighbors still alive with firsthand knowledge of Shakespeare's boyhood, the documentary value of this evidence is thin. As a retroactive fabrication derived from Shakespeare's texts, however, it has some interest. The killing of Caesar is twice referred to as butchery in act 3 of the play, first in the mode of denial by Brutus and then in the mode of accusation by Antony. The metaphor is recollected in *Hamlet* when Polonius—played by Heminges, the same actor who created the role of Caesar[34]—confirms that he played once at the university: "I did enact Julius Caesar. I was kill'd i'th' Capitol; Brutus kill'd me," to which Hamlet replies, "It was a brute part of him to kill so capital a calf there" (3.2.103–6).

Aubrey's anecdote reads *Hamlet* back into *Julius Caesar* even as it reads both plays back into their author's school days. It does so to conjure an image of young Shakespeare acting over the lofty events of sacrificial history (whether that of Foxe, Eusebius, or Plutarch) in a butcher's stall, rehearsing at once the high style of Roman oratory and a lusty sense of the absurd like the one that quickens Hamlet's mockery. In its compressed way, with an anachronistic but thoroughly pleasurable compounding of butchery, sacrifice, history, fantasy, and their nominally distinct venues—the barnyard, the altar, the book, the London stage—Aubrey's anecdote imitates Shakespeare's spectacularly allusive and heterotopical style. In spite of his gift for anecdote I would not call Aubrey a new historicist, but he does momentarily capture something that historicism has occasionally missed: the destabilizing effects of figuration and performance, which cannot be contained by the essentially narrative form we call history.

NOTES

1. Richard Helgerson, *Adulterous Alliances: Home, State, and History in Early Modern European Drama and Painting* (Chicago: University of Chicago Press, 2000), 6.

2. Richard Helgerson, *A Sonnet from Carthage* (Philadelphia: University of Pennsylvania Press, 2007), 41.

3. Paul de Man, "Sign and Symbol in Hegel's Aesthetics," *Critical Inquiry* 8 (1982): 768–69. Cf. Isobel Armstrong, *The Radical Aesthetic* (Oxford: Blackwell, 2000), 51. De Man translates from G. W. F. Hegel, *Werke in zwanzig Bänden, Enzyklopadie der philosophischen Wissenschaften I* (Frankfurt am Main, 1979), 8:74, par. 20.

4. Michael Warner, *Publics and Counterpublics* (New York: Zone Books, 2002): "The most private, inward, intimate act of reading can be converted by the category of the public into a form of stranger relationality" (84).

5. Richard Halpern, *Shakespeare among the Moderns* (Ithaca, N.Y.: Cornell University Press, 1999), 79. Halpern's reading of the play is extended by Daniel Juan Gil in "'Bare Life': Political Order and the Spectacle of Antisocial Being in Shakespeare's Julius Caesar," *Common Knowledge* 13 (2007): 1–14.

6. See Ken Jackson and Arthur F. Marotti, "The Turn to Religion in Early Modern English Studies," *Criticism* 46 (2004): 167–90.

7. Anthony B. Dawson and Paul Yachnin, *The Culture of Playgoing in Shakespeare's England: A Collaborative Debate* (Cambridge: Cambridge University Press, 2001), 3 (emphasis added). The quoted sentence typifies the dominant tendency in the dynamic of productive disagreement that drives the book's argument; at other moments the authors do speak of the theater as "a place where different cultural avenues cross" (5).

8. *Oxford English Dictionary,* 7.a–c.

9. Dawson and Yachnin explore the phenomenology of metatheatrical awareness as a component of theatrical pleasure, and develop a correspondingly complex notion of the dramatic "person," in *The Culture of Playgoing.*

10. For a parallel analysis of the "Lo" with which Spenser both closes *The Shepheardes Calendar* and opens *The Faerie Queene,* see my essay "Spenser and the Gaze of Glory," in *Edmund Spenser's Poetry,* Norton Critical Edition, ed. Hugh Maclean and Anne Lake Prescott, 3rd ed. (New York: Norton, 1993), 756–64.

11. Passages from Shakespeare's plays are quoted from *The Riverside Shakespeare,* ed. G. Blakemore Evans and J. J. M. Tobin, 2nd ed. (Boston: Houghton Mifflin, 1996).

12. Wayne Rebhorn, "The Crisis of the Aristocracy in Julius Caesar," in *New Casebooks: Julius Caesar,* ed. Richard Wilson (New York: Palgrave, 2002): "although the motives of the conspirators, and especially those of Brutus, must be distinguished from Caesar's as well as Antony's and Octavius's in many respects, all are nevertheless animated by the same fundamental drive, the drive to excel all others, to 'out-imitate' their fellows" (29). Coppélia Kahn, in *Roman Shakespeare: Warriors, Wounds, and Women,* situates this drive within "a discourse instating [the conspirators] and Caesar as well with identity, agency, and masculinity. In this play more than any other," she writes, "Shakespeare grounds virtus in a specific political ideology, one that both constitutes and fractures its male subjects" (New York: Routledge, 1997), 77; see also 88–96, "The Teeth of Emulation."

13. In commenting on an earlier version of this essay, the late Marshall Grossman pointed out that Caesar's wounds and blood also evoke those of Lucrece. The Roman Republic that was brought into being by the affective and symbolic power of her violated corpse receives its coup de grace through the power of Caesar's.

14. On the complex gender symbolism of Portia's wound and its contrast to the wounds in Caesar's body, see especially Kahn, "A Voluntary Wound," in *Roman Shakespeare,* 96–105. Kahn comments perceptively on the way Portia's wound both masculinizes her and signifies emasculation, and on the way Caesar's wounds feminize him. I disagree only with the

assertion that Portia's later death by "swallowed fire" (4.2.206) re-feminizes her (103). For the motif of "swallowed fire" as confirmation of one's place within the charmed circle of Roman masculinity, see David Lee Miller, *Dreams of the Burning Child: Sacrificial Sons and the Father's Witness* (Ithaca, N.Y.: Cornell University Press, 2003), 43–51.

15. Geoffrey Bullough, *Narrative and Dramatic Sources of Shakespeare* (New York: Columbia University Press, 1964), 5:86.

16. For the rumor that Caesar was Brutus's father, alluded to by Seutonius and echoed in both *The Mirrour for Magistrates* and Shakespeare's *2 Henry VI,* see Arthur Humphreys, ed., *Julius Caesar* (Oxford: Clarendon, 1984), "Introduction," 24.

17. Bullough mentions Dante's *Inferno* in the course of his wide-ranging survey of conflicting takes on Julius Caesar in classical, medieval, and early modern sources. See *Narrative and Dramatic Sources of Shakespeare,* 5:3–57 (esp. 19–20).

18. Biblical passages are cited from the *The Geneva Bible: A Facsimile of the 1560 Edition,* intro. Lloyd E. Berry (Madison: University of Wisconsin Press, 1969). I have modernized spelling in the passages quoted.

19. The elevation of the Host was eliminated from the English Church under Cranmer's revision of the *Book of Common Prayer* in 1549. It was reinstituted under the Catholic Mary Tudor, but eliminated again under Elizabeth with the adoption of the Thirty-Nine Articles, which state that "the Sacrament of the Lord's Supper was not by Christ's ordinance reserved, carried about, lifted up, or worshipped" (Article 28). Early in her reign, Elizabeth made a public show of exiting a Christmas Mass "so as not to be present at the elevation of the host"; Philip Benedict, *Christ's Churches Purely Reformed: A Social History of Calvinism* (New Haven, Conn.: Yale University Press, 2002), 243.

20. www.newadvent.org/cathen/05380b.htm.

21. For "far" in the second phrase, the First Folio actually reads "farre," a two-syllable form meaning "farther."

22. Miller, "The Father's Witness: Patriarchal Images of Boys," *Representations* 70 (2000): 115–41. The argument introduced in this essay later appears in *Dreams of the Burning Child,* chap. 3, "Witnessing as Theater in Shakespeare." Anthony B. Dawson sees Elizabethan theater in an analogous way as rehearsing the trauma of "iconophobia," a "period of prolonged iconoclasm in which [the Elizabethans] witnessed massive changes in the iconic landscape that they inhabited." ("The arithmetic of memory," in Dawson and Yachnin, *The Culture of Playgoing,* 161–81; the quoted sentence appears on p. 170.) Developed independently and at about the same time, my historical argument and Dawson's overlap in interesting and complementary ways. We diverge partly because my interest in the dynamics of patriarchy and sacrificial witnessing leads to a specific emphasis on the Eucharist, whereas Dawson is developing a line of criticism focused more broadly on the debate surrounding iconoclasm. Major contributions to this critical conversation include James Siemon, *Shakespearean Iconoclasm* (Berkeley: University of California Press, 1985); Huston Diehl, *Staging Reform, Reforming the Stage: Protestantism and Popular Theater in Early Modern England* (Ithaca, N.Y.: Cornell University Press, 1997); and Michael O'Connell, *The Idolatrous Eye: Iconoclasm and Theater in Early Modern England* (New York: Oxford University Press, 2000).

23. Lee Palmer Wandel. *The Eucharist in the Reformation: Incarnation and Liturgy* (Cambridge: Cambridge University Press, 2006), 1. Since the initial publication of the argument I am here resuming, the scholarly literature on Tudor martyrdoms has expanded considerably. One especially pertinent contribution is the perceptive analysis given to competing martyrologies by Susannah Brietz Monta in *Martyrdom and Literature in Early Modern England* (Cambridge: Cambridge University Press, 2005). Monta describes in fine detail the rhetorical and textual strategies the martyrologists employ in seeking to consolidate a community of belief, ward off factionalism, and manage the epistemological crisis noted by a Catholic recusant whose words Monta quotes at the start of her study: "In the tyme of

Queen Marie were many put to death, and now also in [Elizabeth's] tyme, of two severall opinions; both these cannot bee martyrs" (1).

24. As Monta observes, the title page of *Actes and Monuments* in 1583 "opposes the centerpiece of the Catholic liturgy, the elevation of the host just at the miracle of transubstantiation, to the central witness of Foxe's text: the burning of martyrs, sacrifices for truth. . . . The title page argues that the sacrifice of the martyrs' flesh replaces the Mass's central miracle" (57).

25. Indifference was always possible. In *Christ's Churches Purely Reformed: A Social History of Calvinism,* Benedict concludes that "Those deeply committed to either Catholic orthodoxy or some brand of Protestantism both formed a minority of the population. In between stood a broad middle group willing to adjust its practice in whatever direction the ruling powers deemed appropriate" (243).

26. In the *Actes and Monuments* woodcut illustrating the death of Anne Askew, "the soldiers executing her and her fellow martyrs wear Roman dress" (Monta, *Martyrdom and Literature,* 62).

27. In this sense, Shakespearean drama does appear to be constituting a "public" in the complex way elaborated by Michael Warner: a "virtual entity" involving a relation among strangers that depends on "active uptake" by its participants along with a "temporality of circulation" (*Publics and Counterpublics,* 88, 94). Shakespeare presents a complicated instance, because his plays began as theatrical events but then quickly started to circulate as printed texts, and because their afterlives as canonical texts regularly revived in performance meant that the range and temporality of their circulation were both discontinuous and unusually long-term. To these complications must be added the indirectness of address proper to drama, which only intermittently or obliquely acknowledges the audience whose attention it nonetheless solicits.

28. For a thorough (if possibly overzealous) tracing of these echoes, see J. J. M. Tobin, "Antony, Brutus, and Christ's Tears over Jerusalem," *Notes and Queries* 45 (1998): 324–31.

29. "Christs Teares over Ierusalem," in *The Works of Thomas Nashe,* ed. Ronald B. McKerrow; reprint with corrections, ed. F. P. Wilson (New York: Barnes & Noble, 1966), 2:15, 23 (spelling and font modernized by me).

30. For a detailed stage history, see John Ripley, *Julius Caesar on Stage in England and America, 1599–1973* (Cambridge: Cambridge University Press, 1980).

31. And often, of course, to gain a new perspective on the play as well, as Halpern suggests in developing the "modernist allegory" referred to earlier (n. 3 above).

32. Halpern, *Shakespeare among the Moderns,* 78.

33. *Brief Lives, A Modern English Version,* ed. Richard Barber (Totowa: Barnes & Noble, 1983), 285.

34. T. W. Baldwin, *The Organization and Personnel of the Shakespearean Company* (New York: Russell, 1961), 404; thanks to Stephen Orgel for this reference.

CHAPTER THIRTEEN

Shakespeare's Pains to Please

JEFFREY KNAPP

> If we offend, it is with our good will.
> *A Midsummer Night's Dream*, 5.1.108

WHENEVER Shakespeare plots to kill an English king, he always procrastinates, putting off the murder till late in the play; but in *Macbeth* (ca. 1606) the Scottish king Duncan is murdered early in the second act, having suffered repeated attacks, first from rebels, then from invaders, and finally from one of the generals who had just defended him against both rebels and invaders. What makes Duncan so irresistible a target for his enemies, and for Shakespeare? It is characteristic of the play that not even Duncan's eventual killer can explain. Shortly before stabbing his king, Macbeth rehearses the many reasons why he should continue to shield Duncan instead: not only is Duncan Macbeth's ruler, kinsman, and guest, but he

> Hath borne his faculties so meek, hath been
> So clear in his great office, that his virtues
> Will plead like angels, trumpet-tongu'd, against
> The deep damnation of his taking-off (1.7.17–20).[1]

For modern commentators such as Wilbur Sanders, however, the source of Duncan's troubles, and of Macbeth's brutality, is obvious. Only look where Shakespeare has set the play, Sanders insists: not in some "cosy, well-hedged and benignly arable" place but in a region "colder, wilder, and more frightening"—not in England, that is, but in Scotland. In the "pagan" Scottish society evoked by *Macbeth*, a "barbarian warrior-culture" "given over to the bloodiness of tribal violence," the wonder for Sanders is not that Duncan should die but that he should live so long.[2]

Such a description of Scottish culture, or rather lack of culture, would have had a familiar ring to Shakespeare's first audiences. Around the time that Shakespeare's play was first performed, the Scottish unionist Sir Thomas Craig (1605) reported that a member of Parliament named Sir Christopher Piggott had entered into a "bitter and scandalous Invective against the Nation of the *Scots,* and *Scottishmen*" that met no opposition among his colleagues:

> He did not scruple to declare in Parliament that Scotland is the barrenest country in the world; that Scotsmen are the most perfidious and barbarous of all nations, devoid of an altar of faith, as the saying is, not to be tolerated in the courts of kings, and of a bloodthirsty and treacherous disposition; that the only possible relation between the two countries [England and Scotland] would be that of judge and thief, the one decreeing, the other undergoing the penalty; and that in public representations of comedy a Scotsman is always treated as a fitting subject of ridicule.[3]

Enraged by this speech and by the Commons's acquiescence to it, the Scottish-born King James I had Piggott committed to the Tower, even though Piggott's views were so widely shared at the time that they were occasionally expressed by no less a figure than James himself. For instance, in a 1602 letter to Sir Robert Cecil that he wrote before leaving Scotland for England, James complained that the Scottish were "a far more barbarous and stiff-necked people" than the subjects of Queen Elizabeth: "Saint George surely rides upon a towardly riding horse where I am daily burstin [*sic*] in daunting a wild unruly colt." In part, James's grievances against the Scots must have stemmed from their ill treatment of kings. Piggott reportedly claimed that the Scottish had "not suffered above two kings to die in their beds, these 200 years. Our king hath hardly escaped them; they have attempted him." In one such assassination attempt shortly before James took the English throne, the earl of Gowrie plotted to murder James, as Macbeth does Duncan, while the king was a guest at his home.[4]

It would be hard to deny that, with its nearly continuous stream of bloodshed and not one but two kings murdered by the end, Shakespeare's play offers plenty of evidence to satisfy Scotland's detractors. But Sanders's claim that the "state of his country" is what makes Macbeth "murderous" sits uneasily with all the Scottish expressions of horror toward murder in the play. A genuine barbarian, one presumes, would not ask his "eye" to "wink" at his murdering "hand" (1.4.52) as Macbeth does, or be "afraid to think what I have done" (2.2.48) once he had committed his crime, or suffer the "affliction" of "terrible dreams" (3.2.18) long afterward. Lady Macbeth famously worries that her husband is "too full o' th' milk of human kindness" (1.5.17) to kill Duncan, and though we hear of Macbeth's martial prowess from the start of the play, the man we actually meet in the first act seems far more the courtier than the warrior. "Kind gentlemen, your pains / Are regist'red where every day I turn / The leaf to read them" (1.3.150–52), he declares to some fellow courtiers who have brought him word from the king, and with similarly exquisite social grace he later assures Duncan himself of "the service and the loyalty" he "owe[s]" the king, which,

> In doing it, pays itself. Your Highness' part
> Is to receive our duties; and our duties
> Are to your throne
> and state children and servants;
> Which do but what they should, by doing every thing
> Safe toward your love and honor. (1.4.22–27)[5]

Where did the savage learn such good manners?

Commentators on Shakespeare have long attributed these and other contradictory signals in his plays to the popular theater for which he wrote. As the dramatist Thomas Heywood put it in 1624, "they that write to all, must strive to please all." From a commercial perspective, it makes sense that Shakespeare would have mixed his messages so that he could appeal to all the segments of his mixed audience: in the case of *Macbeth,* to his pro-Scottish as well as anti-Scottish spectators.[6] But not all theater historians have conceived of Renaissance dramatists as merely catering to their customers. Some, as Richard Helgerson emphasizes in his *Forms of Nationhood* (1992), have assigned the playwright a more active role in *shaping* tastes, especially when writing history plays. For critics such as Alfred Harbage, to dramatize a nation was to help create one. By giving a relatively accidental and heterogeneous assemblage of spectators a sense of their common past, a commercial play as complex and multivalent as *Macbeth* (according to this account) did not merely reflect the ideological differences in its audience: it helped to bridge those differences and thus encourage a "feeling of national solidarity across the classes."[7]

Of all the major Shakespeareans in the past half-century, Helgerson was perhaps the least swayed by this vision of inclusiveness in Shakespeare, and the questions he raised about Shakespeare's supposedly conciliatory relation to his mixed audience are not easily answered. Citing what he claimed was a greater sympathy with commoners found in the history plays of other contemporary dramatists, Helgerson depicted Shakespeare as a social climber whose ambitions led him to identify with the aristocracy in his histories and to dramatize their interests exclusively. In Helgerson's view, the theater public that Shakespeare hoped to forge was a homogeneously elite audience "purged" of the "barbarism" that his plays associated with "popular culture." No small part of this new high society, Helgerson maintained, were the "polished manners" of a nobility who could no longer rely on the "military role" of feudal aristocrats such as Macbeth to show that "they were different from other people." By developing a language of refined civility even for savage Scots, Shakespeare could not only promote this new form of aristocratic distinction but also raise himself and his theater "to the status of gentility and high art" in the process. What should we make, then, of the brutality that continues to appear alongside the courtesy in *Macbeth*? Helgerson concedes that, no matter how much Shakespeare may have "wanted to efface, alienate, even demonize all signs of commoner participation" in his theater as well as his nation, the actual heterogeneity of his audience remained an obstacle he could not afford to overlook: it was the "popular character" of the commercial theater that blocked Shakespeare from purging his stage of barbarism entirely.[8]

In this chapter, I hope to combine the perspectives of Helgerson and the critics he challenges by showing how *Macbeth* registers Shakespeare's deep ambivalence toward his audience even as the play attempts to forge this audience into a consensual public. To begin with the question of consensus, let us suppose that Shakespeare's theater did indeed constitute "a school for social advancement" as Helgerson claims. Why should we conclude that the gentry were the only spectators capable of learning its lessons?[9] The most distinguished historian of manners in the Renaissance, Norbert Elias, shares Helgerson's view that a new interest in manners arose among aristocrats during this period, but Elias maintains that the emergence of new or newly invigorated media such as the commercial theater helped "spread" the gospel of good manners from "the upper class" to "society as a whole." For Elias, the very mixture of refined and barbarous behavior in early modern writings attests to this gradual process of dissemination, which he calls "the advancing internal pacification of society": "It is only to us, in whom everything is more subdued, moderate, and calculated, and in whom social taboos are built much more deeply into the fabric of instinctual life as self-restraints," Elias contends, that the simultaneous display of courtliness and savagery in earlier texts such as *Macbeth* "appears as contradictory."[10]

Macbeth insists on the contradiction. Where Harbage, Helgerson, and Elias each charts a historical process of homogenization—for Harbage, from class division to national unity; for Helgerson, from a mixed to an elite audience; for Elias, from medieval passions to modern pacification—*Macbeth* repeatedly discredits any promise that conflict can be controlled or resolved. "From that spring whence comfort seem'd to come," a bloody soldier observes during the warfare that begins the play, "discomfort swells" (1.2.27–28). The fighting soon ends, peace seems achieved, and the scene shifts in an ostensibly civilizing direction, from the warrior on the battle-field to the courtier at home; but the violence in the play not only persists, it grows. Not even the intervention of civil Englishmen in the final act of *Macbeth* offers any relief from it. Arguably, the most cold-blooded char-acter in the play is an English general, Siward, who, upon learning of his son's death in battle, asks only, "Had he his hurts before?" and when he hears that his son's wounds were indeed "on the front," briskly replies,

> Why then, God's soldier be he!
> Had I as many sons as I have hairs,
> I would not wish them to a fairer death.
> And so his knell is knoll'd.

It is the Scottish Malcolm who adds, "He's worth more sorrow, / And that I'll spend for him," but Siward dismisses the thought: "He's worth no more; They say he parted well, and paid his score, / And so God be with him!" (5.9.12–19).[11] Neither class nor manners nor nation can cordon off the civil from the barbarous in *Macbeth,* because the civilizing process as the play presents it inspires a brutality of its own.

Tragic Civility

What is it that makes the Scottish King Duncan so killable? All we have to go on is his meek and blameless life, which we experience in the play through his continual expressions of regard for his subjects. His first words to his eventual murderer are characteristically effusive courtesies:

> O worthiest cousin!
> The sin of my ingratitude even now
> Was heavy on me. Thou art so far before,
> That swiftest wing of recompense is slow
> To overtake thee. Would thou hadst less deserv'd,
> That the proportion both of thanks and payment
> Might have been mine! Only I have left to say,
> More is thy due than more than all can pay. (1.4.14–21)

According to Sanders, this very gentility is the problem: Duncan's virtues render him an "anomaly" among the "only half-civilized" Scottish and thus constitute "a standing provocation to all that is murderous in Macbeth's nature."[12]

But we have already seen how courteously Macbeth replies to Duncan's speech, and when the king later greets Lady Macbeth at her home, she too matches him politeness for politeness. Duncan exclaims,

> See, see, our honor'd hostess!
> The love that follows us sometime is our trouble,
> Which still we thank as love. Herein I teach you
> How you shall bid God 'ield us for your pains,
> And thank us for your trouble.

To this highly mannered, almost torturous graciousness, Lady Macbeth replies in kind:

> All our service
> In every point twice done, and then done double,
> Were poor and single business to contend
> Against those honors deep and broad wherewith
> Your Majesty loads our house. (1.6.10–18)

Although Sanders ignores such pleasantries, they are the coin of the realm in Shakespeare's Scotland. Even the witches exchange them, in the terse manner of witches: "I'll give thee a wind," says one; "Th' art kind," says the other (1.3.11–12).[13]

Those critics who do acknowledge the politeness of the Scots in *Macbeth* also tend to dismiss their good manners as mere sugarcoating and pretense. The most influential of these critics, Harry Berger, agrees with Sanders that Shakespeare's Scotland is a barbarous "warrior society," but Berger's Scots at least try to hide their "bloody-mindedness" behind a mask of courtesy. A flimsy mask: violence, in Berger's view, is so fundamental, so "deep-structural" to Scottish society that it "diffuses itself throughout all the expressions and relationships in the play." Thus Berger underscores how Lady Macbeth feels she must "contend" with Duncan's politeness, and he portrays the two characters as "struggling to outdo" one another "in the duel of compliments." Similarly, in Duncan's first greeting of Macbeth, Berger allows that the "tone" of Duncan's address may be "courtly and effusive, but the language is that of competition, debt, and payment." In Berger's account, Duncan knows all too well that he can bear himself so meekly because his generals can battle so fiercely; for all his virtues, Duncan is painfully aware that the "natural basis" of the "gentle weal," as Macbeth later insists, is "blood."[14]

And here again it would be hard to deny that the play offers plenty of evidence to support the view that Scottish courtesy is only skin-deep. When Lady Macbeth incites her husband to murder, for instance, she counsels him to "bear welcome in your eye, / Your hand, your tongue; look like th' innocent flower, / But be the serpent under 't" (1.5.64–66). Yet this notion of Macbeth as civil only in appearance is something that Lady Macbeth believes she must persuade her husband to accept about himself: it is the expression of a wish on her part, not a statement of fact. In an earlier soliloquy, she had confessed that she herself might lack the proper bloody-mindedness for the coming murder. Fearing that she was "compunctious" by "nature," she had called upon "spirits" to "unsex" her, "take my milk for gall," and "fill" her top to toe with the "direst cruelty" (1.5.40–48). In the end, as we know, Lady Macbeth finds it easier to kill Duncan than to quash the supposedly shallow fellow feeling to which her civilities give voice: her guilt drives her mad.

By treating the civility in Shakespeare's Scotland as a fiction shot through with the "tension and contention" it tries to dissemble, Berger not only underestimates the reality of such fellow feeling in the play. He also misinterprets the expressions of "competition, debt, and payment" in Scottish civility as pathological symptoms of suppressed rage, when they are in fact endemic to civility and its common themes. In *The Faerie Queene*'s Book of Courtesy, for instance, Spenser defines the noblest version of civility—courtesy—as "yeelding" what you "owe" to others; one of Spenser's main sources, the *Galateo* of Giovanni della Casa, states that the primary aim of courtesy is to behave "not according to thine own mind and fashion: but to please those, with whom thou livest."[15] Duncan's civility may indeed be a provocation to violence in *Macbeth* as Sanders claims, but not because it pretends to stand apart from Scottish tensions. Rather, the courteous language of obligation and self-abnegation in the play continually thematizes civil relations as vexatious burdens. Greeting Lady Macbeth, Duncan apologizes for the "pains" and "trouble" he is causing her (1.6.13–14); when Ross and Angus convey the terms of Duncan's praise to Macbeth, he twice thanks them for their "pains" (1.3.117, 150). Directly after Duncan's murder, Macduff and Lennox enter Macbeth's house and force the now unnerved Macbeth into an almost maddening series of quotidian pleasantries:

> *Lennox.* Good morrow, noble sir.
> *Macbeth.* Good morrow, both.
> *Macduff.* Is the King stirring, worthy thane?
> *Macbeth.* Not yet.
> *Macduff.* He did command me to call timely on him,
>   I have almost slipp'd the hour.
> *Macbeth.* I'll bring you to him.

As Macbeth walks Macduff to Duncan's room, the vacant time seems to demand further expressions of regard from both men:

> *Macduff.* I know this is a joyful trouble to you;
>   But yet 'tis one.
> *Macbeth.* The labor we delight in physics pain.
>   This is the door. (2.3.44–51)

So otherwise gratuitous a prologue to the discovery of Duncan's body makes the pain and trouble of having to act civilly seem the odd tragedy that Shakespeare has set out to represent from the start.

While various characters in *Macbeth* may share Berger's view of civility as merely the superstructure to the base of violence, the play also repeatedly depicts violence as a *response* to civility, a dreamlike release from the social pressures of the "gentle weal" (3.4.75). Before the witches transform Macbeth into a regicide, they first make him rude. "Look how our partner's rapt," Banquo comments as the witches begin to stir "horrible imaginings" in Macbeth. "New honors come upon him, / Like our strange garments," he must add exculpatorily while Macbeth continues daydreaming till finally Banquo is forced to interrupt his fellow warrior's musings—"worthy Macbeth, we stay upon your leisure"—and Macbeth, apologizing, thanks his attendees for their "pains" (1.3.138–50). The first characterization of Macbeth in the play depicts his ferocity in battle as an exhilarating release from the canons of civility. A Scottish soldier recounts to Duncan how Macbeth "carv'd out his passage" through the ranks of the rebels, searching for their leader Macdonwald, "till he fac'd the slave; / Which nev'r shook hands, nor bade farewell to him, / Till he unseam'd him from the nave to th' chops" (1.2.19–22).

Whether Shakespeare sees the good manners in *Macbeth* as disguising or provoking violence, he makes the boundaries between these two categories of behavior disturbingly difficult to draw. The Scots as Shakespeare depicts them are no less courteous for being murderous, while England has its own gentle king in Edward the Confessor and its own battle-hungry general in Siward. Is the point of the play, then, to bridge more than the class divisions in Shakespeare's mixed audience by overcoming the chauvinistic barriers of "civil" and "savage" that separated England from Scotland and promoting instead the union of the nations under James? Now that James ruled England as well as Scotland, one contemporary unionist after another declared, "the Spirit of Division" had been "cast out of the British Body of this Ocean-walled world."[16]

But the breakdown of categorical distinctions in *Macbeth* does not in itself amount to a plea for unity. For most of the play's characters, it represents a horror, embodied by witches with beards who mix chimerical brews and who declare that "foul" and "fair" are one and the same (1.1.11).[17] Conversely, the attempt to escape such intermixtures in the play and be one thing wholly and purely, top to toe, invariably leads to killing.[18] "Who can be wise, amaz'd, temp'rate, and furious, / Loyal, and neutral, in a moment?" (2.3.108–9) Macbeth demands to know, in defense of two murders he has just committed. And yet the play repeatedly suggests that such chaotic multiplicity is a fact of life. In the "world" as Lady Macduff knows it, "to do harm / Is often laudable, to do good sometime / Accounted dangerous folly" (4.2.75–77). The presence of witches in the play makes this discord seem more than the consequence of human frailty and error. To Banquo, the witches "look not like th' inhabitants o' th' earth," even though they "are on't" (1.3.41–42). How can the world itself be whole and one if the otherworldly is a part of it?

Again and again, Shakespeare's Scots frame the boundary crossings that disturb them in terms of civility, as if these perceived contaminations were the ill effects of courteous hospitality in particular. To remain single-mindedly committed to her murderous "purpose," Lady Macbeth feels she must block any "compunctious *visitings* of nature" (1.5.45–46); Malcolm describes the "swoll'n and ulcerous" people whom Edward the Confessor cures as "strangely-*visited*" by their disease (4.3.150–51). In the play's most uncanny mixture of contagion with civility, Banquo, invited as a "guest" to a feast that the Macbeths have arranged, appears instead as a "ghost" there, and it is only when Macbeth courteously decides to "mingle with society, / And play the humble host" (3.4.3–4) at his feast that he discovers this irruption of the supernatural into his world. "Please't your High-ness / To grace us with your royal company?" inquires one polite Scottish lord; "May't please your Highness sit," asks another (3.4.38–44). Thanks to the ghost who also joins the company, these genteel invitations end up generating horror and dismay. "Our duties," the guests pledge to the seated Macbeth, who abruptly responds with the kind of fantasy discourteousness he had earlier displayed on the battlefield: "Avaunt, and quit my sight!" (3.4.91–92).

Tragicomic Civility

Categorical breakdowns or confusions are not peculiar to Shakespeare's representations of civility in *Macbeth:* they arise in Spenser's treatment of courtesy too. How, book 6 of *The Faerie Queene* asks us from the start, can Calidore's "gentlenesse of spright" and "manners mild" coexist with his love of "batteilous affray"? For Spenser, the answer is *controlled* violence: in combat, his courteous warriors typically experience a fellow feeling that encourages them to take pity and exercise restraint. Shakespeare's primary source for *Macbeth,* Holinshed's *Chronicles,* pictures a similar happy medium, but presents it as attainable only through the imaginary fusion of two entirely different people. The woeful subjects of Duncan and Macbeth, writes Holinshed, "wished the inclinations and manners of these two cousins to have been so tempered and interchangeably bestowed betwixt them, that where the one had too much of clemency, and the other of cruelty, the mean virtue betwixt these two extremities might have reigned by indifferent partition in them both, so should Duncan have proved a worthy king, and Macbeth an excellent captain."[19]

In Shakespeare's play, where civility amounts as much to an engine of violence as to a brake on it, even so magical an intermixture of persons would not achieve the result Spenser envisions. Harbage and Helgerson help us to recognize that this difference between the two writers must, to some degree, have derived from the different audiences that Spenser and Shakespeare addressed. The social immediacy of the theater, and the heterogeneity of the audiences there, made the demands of civility weigh far more heavily on theater people than on epic poets. "How hard a thing it is, / Of sundry minds to please the sundry kinds," laments the prologue to *The Contention betweene Libertie and Prodigalitie* (1601), before deciding that the best course is to "crave" the "courtesy" of the audience.[20] "What we are, is by your favor. What we shall be, rests all in your applausive encouragements," adds the epilogue to John Marston's *Antonio and Mellida* (1599–1600), in the abject tones of the Macbeths to their king.[21] The prologue to Ben Jonson's *Epicene* (1609) presents the author and actors as hosts welcoming the audience to their playhouse: "Our wishes, like to those make public feasts / Are not to please the cooks' tastes, but the guests." This conventional sublimation of hired entertainment into gracious hospitality manifests the pressure felt by theater people to delight their customers with good manners as well as good shows.[22] Even the amateur playwright Samuel Brandon in his 1598 *Octavia* speaks of the author's "care" and the actors' "pains to please" their audience.[23]

"Pains to please"—the phrase itself presents a categorical dilemma, suggesting both the obsequiousness of theater people and the potentiality for resentment that such obsequiousness bred in them. When the swindler Face at the end of Jonson's *Alchemist* (1610) promises the audience that he will "feast you often, and invite new guests," he means to insult as well as flatter his spectators by assimilating them to the dupes they have watched him fleece throughout the play.[24] Occasionally, Jonson made an exception for the reigning monarch, particularly in epilogues that claimed the dramatist could expect no greater reward than "t'have pleased the King."

But other playwrights, provoked by having to cater to *any* audience, often entertained the fantasy of thrusting a knife into even the regal paying customer. Early in Thomas Kyd's *Spanish Tragedy* (ca. 1582–92), for example, the Spanish king and the Portuguese ambassador are well "pleased" by a spectacle that Hieronimo has staged for them, and the king expects that his loyal subject will similarly "grace" him with a delightful show at the end; but when Hieronimo takes "pain" a second time as a dramatist, it is to arrange a play in which he can murder the king's nephew. Himself voicing the epilogue to this play, Hieronimo delights in disclosing to his royal spectators that they have witnessed no ordinary drama, where the actors die and then "in a minute, starting up again, / Revive to please tomorrow's audience."[25] For ordinary theater people, of course, it would be suicide to spite one's audience this way, and suicide is what Kyd quickly forces Hieronimo to commit—but not before he gives his authorial surrogate the chance to kill a second member of the royalty.

By portraying Scotland as a bewildering concoction of civil and barbarous behavior, Shakespeare walked a fine line between flattering and offending his own king. Why did he risk offending James at all? Certainly, he had other customers to satisfy, but the dramatization of courtesy in *Macbeth* suggests that Shakespeare viewed his half-expressed belligerence toward James as generated in large part by his own pains to please. In earlier plays of Shakespeare's, the Fool had served as a kind of pressure valve for this catalyzation of subservience into antagonism; by the time of *Hamlet,* however, the figure of the jester had become so powerfully offensive that the character who acts like a fool is the one who kills his king. Yet Shakespeare had also begun to explore the possibility of managing the felt instability of his courtesy in a different way: not so much by exercising greater self-control as by broadening for his audience what it would mean to please them.

Renaissance dramatists often assumed that, to please the "sundry minds" in their audiences, their plays had to be capacious not only in message but in mode: so John Rastell (ca. 1518) maintained that, to engage the playgoer "disposed" to "mirth and sport" as well the more seriously inclined spectator, he had "mixed" his "philosophical" play *The Four Elements* "with merry conceits."[26] Helgerson represents Sir Philip Sidney's famous denunciation of such "mongrel" entertainments as an attack on the social as well as dramaturgical mixture of "high and low" in the Renaissance theater—a "contagion" from which Shakespeare supposedly aimed "to remove" himself "as far as possible." Although Helgerson does not mention it, *A Midsummer Night's Dream* might seem to bear out this claim in exposing to ridicule the piece of "tragical mirth" (5.1.57) that Bottom and his fellow "patches" (3.2.9) offer to an aristocratic audience. But the aristocrats *select* that absurdly mixed play for their entertainment; tragical mirth is in any case what they themselves have performed from the opening lines of the *Dream*.[27] Diverse beliefs and tastes, the *Dream* strongly implies, are not simply the result of social mixture. When, in the prologue to his *Susanna* (ca. 1565), Thomas Garter declares that "nought delights the heart of men on earth, / So much as matters grave and sad, if they be mix'd with mirth," he presents the "sundry minds" that he must please as belonging to each and every playgoer.[28]

The convergence of civility and barbarity in *Macbeth* shows how deeply Shakespeare shared Garter's view of playgoers, and how determinedly he resisted the tendency to regard the ideological conflicts in a play as the results of catering to different segments of a mass audience. For Shakespeare, the mixed audience of the commercial theater encouraged a view of *individuals* as mixed, and the cohesive public that he hoped to make of his disparate spectators were theatergoers who could consistently relish a dramaturgy of heterogeneous effects.[29] His own motives for such consensus building were themselves mixed, as *Macbeth* suggests. Toward the end of his career especially, Shakespeare strove to ease the pains of pleasing by schooling his audience to enjoy his belligerence no less than his courtesy— indeed, to accept his belligerence *as* courtesy. Worse than death itself, for the purist Lady Macbeth, is dwelling "in doubtful joy" (3.2.7), and yet this divided condition is the one to which Shakespeare devotes his final tragicomedies.[30] These plays force their protagonists to accept that events will end happily for them—as they like it—only when they come to find a pleasure in their pain.

The Winter's Tale pursues this paradoxical outcome by first speedily reenacting the tragic conversion of civility into barbarity that Shakespeare dramatized in *Macbeth*. The play begins with a seemingly gratuitous exchange of courtesies between a Bohemian and a Sicilian, in which the Bohemian thanks the Sicilian for having hosted him and the Sicilian insists that the Bohemian think nothing of it. Though their theme is of "loves" (1.1.9) reciprocated, the speakers find themselves resorting, as Duncan and Macbeth do, to a language of debt and shame (5–18). The next scene further highlights the conflicting emotions that good manners arouse, when the visiting Bohemian king, Polixenes, describes himself as a "burthen" to his hosts and despairs of ever repaying the "debt" (1.2.3, 6) he owes them: "I have stay'd / To tire your royalty," he laments to the Sicilian king Leontes, who with equally fraught courtesy replies, "We are tougher, brother, / Than you can put us to't" (1.2.14–16). We soon learn that Leontes's threshold for pain is significantly lower than he claims. Just as the Macbeths decide to kill their guest Duncan rather than continue to entertain him, so Leontes conspires to have the vacationing Polixenes murdered. Like the Macbeths, Leontes suffers terribly for this host rage, yet Shakespeare gives him the second chance he denies Macbeth: in the final act of *The Winter's Tale,* he allows Leontes not only to play the host once more but also to become a courteous guest himself in visiting the "house" of Paulina and apologizing for the "trouble" he causes her there (5.3.6, 9). Paulina promptly makes Leontes pay for her pains. She introduces him to a statue of his dead wife, a sight that Leontes calls "piercing to my soul" (5.3.34), and then assures him that she could "afflict" him even "farther." "Do, Paulina," Leontes surprisingly responds, now embracing the torment that civil society imposes on him, "for this affliction has a taste as sweet / As any cordial comfort" (5.3.75–77).[31]

In *The Tempest,* the central character is a host and playwright combined who prefers to "give . . . pains" (1.2.242) rather than "take" them (1.2.354, 4.1.189).[32] Among the many trials that Prospero devises for the visitors to his island is a show of seemingly "monstrous" creatures who at first surprise with their exceedingly "gentle" and "kind" good "manners" (3.3.31–32), but who then follow these courtesies with derisive "mocks and mows" (3.3.*s.d.*), which produce drawn swords. For his more favored victim Ferdinand, Prospero attempts to conflate these opposing experiences of social interaction by encouraging his future son-in-law to see the "labors" that Prospero imposes upon him as "pleasures" (3.1.7). At the same time, Prospero reports how his spectating of such pains helps him experience his own fellow feeling and consequently accept that he must forego the pleasures of solitude for the "afflictions" of social life (5.1.22). In the epilogue to the play, Prospero tries to pass on this "uneasy" lesson (1.2.452) to his larger audience. Having spent most of the play torturing any- and everyone in sight, including his own daughter, he ends *The Tempest* by protesting that his sole aim has been "to please." How can we credit him? By having Prospero wed an obsequious appeal for pardon with the galling suggestion that we think on our own "crimes" (epilogue 12–13, 19), Shakespeare transfers the trials of courtesy to us.

NOTES

1. William Shakespeare, *Macbeth*, in *The Riverside Shakespeare*, ed. G. Blakemore et al., 2nd ed. (New York: Houghton Mifflin, 1997), 1360–87. The parenthetical dates in the text of this chapter refer to composition for manuscript texts, to first publication for printed texts, and to first performance for plays.

2. Wilbur Sanders, "*Macbeth*: What's Done, Is Done," in Wilbur Sanders and Howard Jacobson, *Shakespeare's Magnanimity: Four Tragic Heroes, Their Friends and Families* (London: Chatto & Windus, 1978), 60, 59, 65–66. Cf. Arthur Kinney, "Scottish History, the Union of the Crowns and the Issue of Right Rule: The Case of Shakespeare's *Macbeth*," in *Renaissance Culture in Context: Theory and Practice*, ed. Jean R. Brink and William F. Gentrup (Aldershot, UK: Scolar Press, 1993): "Reading the entire 1577 *Historie* now, we can see how closely Shakespeare's *Macbeth* captures the character of Scotland portrayed in Holinshed's chronicle and in William Harrison's prefatory description of the country. For Harrison, at the outset, the Highlands . . . as well as the Lowlands and border country are wild, often barren and noted for the cruelty and savagery of geography and human behavior" (28).

3. *Journals of the House of Commons* (London, 1803–), 1:336; Sir Thomas Craig, *De Unione Regnorum Britanniae Tractatus*, MS ca. 1605, ed. Sandford Terry (Edinburgh: Edinburgh University Press, 1909), 112 (for Latin original), 356 (for English translation).

4. G. P. V. Akrigg, ed., *Letters of King James VI and I* (Berkeley: University of California Press, 1984), 201; William Cobbett, ed., *Cobbett's Parliamentary History of England* (London, 1806), 1:1097. For the relationship between the Gowrie plot and *Macbeth*, see Steven Mullaney, *The Place of the Stage: License, Play, and Power in Renaissance England* (Chicago: University of Chicago Press, 1988), 116–34.

5. Sanders, "*Macbeth*," 70.

6. Heywood, *Gunaikeion: or, Nine Bookes of Various History. Concerning Women* (London, 1624), A4v. Cf., e.g., Larry S. Champion, who argues in *"The Noise of Threatening Drum": Dramatic Strategy and Political Ideology in Shakespeare and the English Chronicle Play* (Newark: University of Delaware Press, 1990) that Shakespeare's "chronicle plays are framed to permit—indeed, to encourage—a multiplicity of ideological responses; responses that, in turn, accommodate and stimulate the divergent political views of a socially heterogeneous audience" (13).

7. Richard Helgerson, *Forms of Nationhood: The Elizabethan Writing of England* (Chicago: University of Chicago Press, 1992), 206.

8. Ibid., 241–43, 214, and 243.

9. For further remarks on Helgerson's tendency to narrow Shakespeare's audience as he claims Shakespeare did, see my *Shakespeare's Tribe: Church, Nation and Theater in Renaissance England* (Chicago: University of Chicago Press), 224n48, and *Shakespeare Only* (Chicago: University of Chicago Press), chap. 2.

10. Helgerson, *Forms of Nationhood*, 242; Norbert Elias, *The Civilizing Process*, vol. 1: *The Development of Manners*, trans. Edmund Jephcott (1939; New York: Urzen Books, 1978), 115, 123, 200.

11. Sanders is a great admirer of Siward, whom he calls "the alternative warrior—modest, Christian, invincible" ("*Macbeth*," 93).

12. Ibid., 69, 66, 70.

13. Civility is so ingrained in the Scots that they repeatedly envision even nonhuman interactions with people as courteous: thus Lady Macbeth imagines that Duncan's "hard journey" will "soundly invite him" to sleep (1.7.62–63), and Macbeth thinks that a bell "invites" him to murder Duncan (2.1.62).

14. Harry Berger, Jr., "The Early Scenes of *Macbeth*: Preface to a New Interpretation," *English Literary History* 47.1 (Spring 1980): 1–31; 25, 22, 20, 26.

15. Berger, "Early Scenes," 20; Edmund Spenser, *Faerie Queene,* 1590 and 1596, ed. A. C. Hamilton et al., 2nd ed. (London: Pearson Education, 2001), 6.2.1; Giovanni della Casa, *Galateo* (1558), trans. Robert Peterson (London, 1576), 4.

16. James Maxwell, Prospectus for "Britaines Union in Love," Royal MS 18A.51, 3v.

17. Even when the play evokes the prospect of unity between England and Scotland, the specter of division remains. In a vision Macbeth calls a "horrible sight," he sees the Stuart kings carrying "twofold balls and treble scepters" (4.1.121–22), while Malcolm later refers to the subjects of Macbeth who join the Scottish and English invaders not as newfound friends but rather as "foes that strike beside us" (5.7.28–29).

18. Macbeth twice claims that murder will make him "perfect" (3.1.108 and 3.4.21).

19. Spenser, *Faerie Queene,* 6.1.2; Raphael Holinshed et al., *Second Volumes of Chronicles* (London, 1586), bk. 3 ("The Description of Scotland" and "The Historie of Scotland"), 168.

20. *A Pleasant Comedie, Shewing the Contention betweene Libertie and Prodigalitie, As it was playd before her Maiestie* (acted 1601) (London, 1602), A3r.

21. John Marston, *Antonio and Mellida* (acted 1599–1600), in *The Malcontent and Other Plays,* ed. Keith Sturgess (Oxford: Oxford University Press, 1997), 55.

22. Ben Jonson, *Epicene, or The Silent Woman* (acted 1609), in *English Renaissance Drama: A Norton Anthology,* ed. David Bevington, Lars Engle, Katharine Eisaman Maus, and Eric Rasmussen (New York: Norton, 2002), 775–860, prologue, 8–9. With its continual reference to debt and payment, the talk of courtesy in *Macbeth* similarly mixes good manners and commerce.

23. Samuel Brandon, *Tragicomoedi of the Vertuous Octavia* (London, 1598), I1r. Cf. the prologue to Thomas Lupton's early Elizabethan comedy *All for Money,* published in 1578: "Our Author a pleasant Tragedy with pains hath now made" (A2v).

24. Ben Jonson, *The Alchemist,* in *English Renaissance Drama: A Norton Anthology,* 861–960, 5.5.165. Courtesy breaks down for Spenser at a similar moment of epilogue in book 6, when the book's final stanzas remark on Spenser's own relationship to his audience, and the ideal of courteous self-restraint suddenly becomes an object of bitter sarcasm: "Therefore do you my rimes keep better measure, / And seeke to please, that now is counted wisemens threasure" (Spenser, *Faerie Queene,* 6.12.41).

25. Ben Jonson, *Bartholomew Fair,* in *English Renaissance Drama: A Norton Anthology,* 961–1066, epilogue, 12; Thomas Kyd, *Spanish Tragedy,* in *English Renaissance Drama: A Norton Anthology,* 3–74, 1.4.173, 4.1.62, 4.3.2, 4.4.81–82.

26. John Rastell, *The Nature of the Four Elements, Three Rastell Plays: Four Elements, Calisto and Melebea, Gentleness and Nobility,* ed. Richard Axton (Cambridge: D. S. Brewer, 1979), prologue, 134–37. Cf., e.g., the prologue to Ulpian Fulwell's *Like Will to Like* (London, 1568; ca. 1563–68), A2v. In the prologue to *Perkin Warbeck* (in *'Tis Pity She's a Whore and Other Plays,* ed. Marion Lomax [Oxford: Oxford University Press, 1995], 241–323 (ca. 1624–34), John Ford attests to the continuing persuasiveness of this view that a play should be as mixed as its audience by explicitly refusing to adulterate his high-minded play in deference to the vulgar herd: "nor is here / Unnecessary mirth forced, to endear / A multitude" (23–25).

27. Philip Sidney, *The Defence of Poesie,* in *Defence of Poesie, Astrophil and Stella, and Other Writings,* ed. Elizabeth Porges Watson (London: Everyman, 1997), 122; Helgerson, *Forms of Nationhood,* 201. Commentators regularly note that Shakespeare may have been mocking *A Lamentable Tragedy, Mixed Full of Pleasant Mirth, Conteyning the Life of CAMBISES King of PERCIA . . . By Thomas Preston,* first published ca. 1570 but reprinted around the time that Shakespeare was writing *A Midsummer Night's Dream.* Cf. also R. B.'s *New Tragicall Comedie of Apius and Virginia,* published in 1575.

28. Thomas Garter, *The Commody of the Most Vertuous and Godly Susanna* (London, 1578), A2v.

29. For a more extended demonstration of this claim, see my *Shakespeare Only,* especially chapter 2.

30. In perhaps the first English play to style itself as a "tragical comedy," Richard Edwardes's *Damon and Pythias* (ca. 1565), the prologue states that the "matter" of the play will be "*mixed* with mirth and care" (prologue, 37–38; emphasis added). Mixture is also emphasized on the title page of *Cambyses,* as on the title page of Robert Greene's *Scottish Historie of Iames the Fourth, Slaine at Flodden. Entermixed with a Pleasant Comedie* (London, 1598).

31. William Shakespeare, *The Winter's Tale,* in *The Riverside Shakespeare,* 1617–51.

32. William Shakespeare, *The Tempest,* in *The Riverside Shakespeare,* 1661–86.

CHAPTER FOURTEEN

The Political Fortunes of Robin Hood on the Early Modern Stage

JEAN E. HOWARD

In *Forms of Nationhood,* Richard Helgerson made some characteristically bold statements about Shakespeare's English history plays of the 1590s in relation to those histories produced for companies connected to Richard Henslowe, particularly Worcester's Men and the Admiral's Men. Juxtaposing Shakespeare's histories written after *2 Henry VI* to plays such as *Sir Thomas Wyatt, Sir John Oldcastle, If You Know Not Me You Know Nobody— Part I, Jack Straw,* and *Edward IV,* Helgerson argues that after he wrote the Jack Cade scenes early in his career, Shakespeare turned away from identification with the commons and began to write history from the point of view of the powerful. He sees Shakespeare as banishing the popular voice from his histories and excluding the commons from his vision of the nation, whereas Henslowe's dramatists embraced that popular voice and created a more inclusive national polity. As Helgerson summed up his position: "Shakespeare's history plays are concerned above all with the consolidation and maintenance of royal power. The history plays Henslowe paid for give their attention to the victims of such power."[1]

Forms of Nationhood is a brilliant book, and it is no slight to its greatness to say that in what follows I shall argue against Helgerson's view that there was an absolute divide between history plays written by Shakespeare and those produced for Henslowe's theaters. I am skeptical of claims that Shakespeare and the Henslowe dramatists were drawing on two separate publics arrayed along the axes of popular and elite, inclusive and exclusive, which smacks a bit too much of another kind of gulf posited by critics such as Alfred Harbage who saw a clear divide between the healthy public and the decadent private theater traditions.[2] For instance, in considering Helgerson's thesis, think about Christopher Marlowe, named by Helgerson as one of those who eschewed clownage and "the jigging veins of riming mother-wits."[3] He wrote his early plays for Henslowe. It is hard to think of *Tamburlaine* as composed primarily from the point of view of the victims of monarchical oppression or, to pick a properly English history, even to describe *Edward II* in that way. Moreover, as the work of Roslyn Knutson has made clear, in the 1590s playwrights (Shakespeare after 1594 being the exception) moved readily from one playhouse to another, and plays of particular popularity in one company's repertory could easily spawn a run of similar plays at the other theater. Knutson offers a dense series of examples, including the explosion of history plays about Henry V, Oldcastle, King John, and Edward I (Longshanks) launched by one company and echoed by another, and the rage for Turk plays and Jew plays that spawned imitations and appropriations across company lines.[4]

What Helgerson's chapter on the histories provides is salutary attention to a suite of history plays that extends far beyond Shakespeare and to an overarching framework within which to think with more particularity about the political work done by this broad range of plays. As a result, I will challenge or nuance some of Helgerson's more absolute claims. To focus my observations, I turn to a particular body of received material—namely, the legends of Robin Hood—to explore the different ways in which that material became a resource used and reused by playwrights, to varying political and artistic ends, in the historical drama of the 1590s. Moreover, in examining these plays, I shall argue that their varying politics are conveyed in part by how they construct Robin Hood's masculinity. Although this figure comes down to us in contemporary movies as a swashbuckling heterosexual righter of social wrongs, that is not always the way he was represented in the history plays of the 1590s. This chapter will examine what happened to the medieval ballad figure as he was transported to the stage and appropriated for a quite varied set of political purposes.

I chose the Robin Hood legend, first, because it is notoriously "popular." Helgerson mentions its origins in English ballads in which unrecognized kings encounter common people and a bond of sympathy connects the two, erasing class distinctions.[5] Jeffrey Singman, whose *Robin Hood: The Shaping of the Legend* I have found to be a very good account of the development of the Robin Hood material from the twelfth century to the present, argues that this story in all its manifestations is a distinctively English part of medieval popular culture that has, with many modifications, persisted into the present.[6] In the 1590s no less than seven plays featuring Robin Hood appeared on the commercial stage, not counting works such as *As You Like It,* which refers to Duke Senior in exile in the Forest of

Arden as resembling Robin Hood in Sherwood Forest. Five of these plays are extant; most are tied to companies connected to Henslowe. I will use them to investigate how this popular material was used to tell different stories about masculinity and politics on the commercial stage of the 1590s.

I have also chosen this material because it brings into focus the complexity of theater culture in the 1590s and highlights the various roles played by dramatists, actors, and audiences in creating this culture and forging forms of association through it. The very existence of so many Robin Hood plays suggests that playwrights were aware of what other dramatists were doing and that audiences followed with appreciation and discernment their implicit attempts to respond to and surpass one another. In the London theaters the shared heritage of the Robin Hood materials was transformed by diverse dramatists and acting companies. Part of the pleasure of theatergoing in the 1590s, I suggest, depended on audiences comparing how various theater practitioners modified received stories, generic conventions, or stage traditions. Awareness of these modifications also revealed how the same material could be mobilized for different political ends. Within the theater world of the 1590s, audiences did a lot of the work. They not only paid money to go to the theater, and probably not just to one playhouse, but they also entered into implicit association with other theatergoing Londoners, achieving a shared theatrical literacy and forming communities of appreciation and judgment.

In *Forms of Nationhood*, Helgerson saw dramatists and theater companies as divided into opposing ideological camps. My work on the Robin Hood plays suggests a more fluid and interactive theater culture, one in which the pleasure of playgoing depended in part on observing the different ways in which the familiar could be made strange and new political positions elaborated from within it. Theatergoing, I am suggesting, was less a direct expression of political commitment than a practice through which the discernment of political difference was solicited and made possible. If coterie audiences did evolve around some theaters, in the 1590s and later there was also a shared theater culture the richest navigation of which depended on knowledge of many playwrights, acting companies, and theatrical conventions. To see how this is so, let us now turn to the Robin Hood material, the common inheritance of playwrights and audiences alike.

The Matter of Robin Hood

Scholars believe that ballads and oral accounts of Robin Hood go back to the twelfth century, though the written record begins in the fifteenth.

The earliest materials consist of printed ballads and a long poem, *The Gest of Robin Hood,* published in 1500, that consists of eight fits or segments. The stories collected in these printed sources are those familiar to me from the Children's Classics edition of *Robin Hood* that was one of my prized childhood possessions.[7] There, alongside enticing pictures of Robin Hood in a pageboy and tights with a long bow over his shoulder, were stories in which Robin, disguised as a poor man, sneaks into Nottingham and wins an archery contest against the evil sheriff's men; or tales of Robin ambushing a rich abbot in the middle of the forest and confiscating his riches; or Robin quarreling with his faithful Little John and, as a result of their quarrel, one or the other being captured by the sheriff and then daringly rescued by the other; or Robin fighting with and being bested by a common man, a potter or a pinner, then inviting him to join his forest band.

As scholars have noted, these stories form less a continuous narrative than a collection of episodes that share certain recurring features, including contests of skill and strength usually involving the longbow or quarterstaff; disguise, assumed both by Robin and by his enemies; entrapment and daring rescue, often by ruse; equalitarianism among the men of the band; intense loyalty to an absent king; and resistance to the oppression of institutions like the church and the law—hence the long connection of Robin Hood with popular resistance, carnival, and rebellion. The central locus of these stories is always the greenwood, presented as a place of liberty and freedom, and the narrative begins and ends in the forest. In all the old stories, when Robin eventually goes with the king to court, he grows unhappy there and returns to his life in the forest.[8]

Although Robin Hood has come down to us as a figure who steals from the rich to give to the poor and as someone who fights against the tyranny of abbot and sheriff, the politics of the Robin Hood material is surprisingly malleable because it is built on a series of contradictions. The most notable of these is Robin's piety and loyalty to the monarch as set against his repeated plundering of the wealth of churchmen and killing of the deer in the king's forest, not to speak of his rough treatment of the king's deputies. The contradictions are in theory resolved by the fact that church and state have grown corrupt rather than being inherently bad, which enables Robin to be notionally loyal to both while disrespectful to each in practice. But the contradictions embedded in the material, as will become evident, were an extremely useful resource for dramatists who put Robin on the stage.

By the late medieval period there began to be records of *theatrical* events involving the Robin Hood story. Several very brief plays or play fragments on Robin's encounters with the Sheriff of Nottingham, with a friar, and with a potter are extant from the late fifteenth and sixteenth centuries; but the bulk of the dramatic activity surrounding Robin occurred in largely improvisational dances, games, quasi-theatrical entertainments, and pageants, which were recorded in civic and ecclesiastical records and were sometimes linked to festivals such as Whitsun ales. Often Robin was used as a "gatherer" who collected money for the church during or after the performance.[9] Paul Whitfield White argues that in some instances these games may have played up those parts of the tradition that emphasize a "holy Robin," who venerated the Virgin and insisted on going to Mass in Nottingham despite the danger of doing so.[10] Occasionally, however, such games were organized not by the church or a religious fraternity but by individual groups of young men with the potential for rowdy, violent, and disorderly behavior, and who would use the occasion of their theatrics to extort money from passersby.[11]

It was also in the sixteenth century that Maid Marian was grafted onto the Robin Hood material. Previously, she had been an independent figure in the May Games, where she was played by a woman, and in the morris dance, in which she was often impersonated by a cross-dressed boy and engaged in erotic play with Friar Tuck, with whom she was sexually linked.[12] Gradually, however, Marian became the love interest of Robin Hood, and a number of civic records indicate that the May Games often included "a bower" for their woodland trysts. Collectively, as Stephen Knight argues and as the records of the REED Project show, "the Robin Hood plays and games were *the* most popular form of secular dramatic entertainment in provincial England for most of the sixteenth century."[13]

The ubiquity of the Robin Hood material does not mean that it was uniformly embraced. While Henry VIII, for example, twice took part in Robin Hood theatricals,[14] Hugh Latimore and other reformed clergy took umbrage at the persistence of such popular pastimes as likely to lead to popular disorder and disrespect for established religion and perhaps because of the Catholic resonances of "the holy Robin." Latimore was encouraged in his dim view when, arriving at a church where he was to preach, he found the church locked and everyone gone off to take part in Robin Hood's Day.[15] Others connected Robin to more serious rebellions. Sir Walter Ralegh, at his trial in 1603, specifically disavowed association with Robin Hood, Kett, and Cade. There was, then, an unsettling or potentially subversive edge to the Robin Hood materials. They could be used to criticize kingly or clerical injustice, and they could be used as a rallying point for rebellion against established authority.

Yet even as some of the godly tried to suppress the popular forms of festivity connected with Robin Hood, and others construed him as a dangerous rebel in the tradition of Jack Cade, antiquarians and historians were writing him into the national histories produced in the second half of the sixteenth century. The Scottish historian John Major assigned Robin Hood to the reign of Richard the Lionhearted, a choice echoed by a number of English historians, among them John Stow and especially Richard Grafton, who added many embellishments to the story, including the suggestion that Robin was not of base stock but a nobleman who, because of heavy debts, had been forced into leading the life of an outlaw. Robin Hood's customary behavior he summarized as follows: "he would suffer no woman to be oppresed, violated, or other wise abused. The poorer sort of people he favoured, and would in no wise suffer their goodes to be touched or spoyled, but relieved and ayded them with such goodes as hee gate from the riche, which he spared not, namely the riche priestes, fat Abbotes, and the houses of the riche Carles."[16] In this account, Robin Hood is a spokesman for an economic redistribution plan that favors the rights of the poor and women and is particularly hard on the remnants of a decadent Catholic clergy.

Robin Hood in the Commercial Theater

In the 1590s the extremely popular Robin Hood story was translated to the commercial stage, and the result was an energetic shuffling and transposition of its elements and the addition of some new ones. As a resource to be exploited by entrepreneurial dramatists, it was put to a variety of aesthetic and political purposes. A straightforward example is afforded by the anonymous play *The Comedy of George a Greene,* the pinner of Wakefield. Printed in 1599, it had been entered in the Register of the Stationers' Company in 1595, and Henslowe noted that it was performed at the Rose by Sussex's Men in 1593–94.

Robin Hood in his own person plays a very small part in this quasi-historical comedy. He pops up at the end when Maid Marian complains that George a Greene's beloved, Bettris, is said by everyone to be more beautiful than she. Marian wants Robin to fight with George to prove himself the better man and she the more beautiful beloved. Robin and his men do fight with George, George beating Will Scarlet and Much the Miller's son and battling Robin to a draw. The two then don disguises and bait King Edward and King James, also disguised as common men, into carrying their staves on their shoulders through Wakefield, a custom forbidden by the shoemakers of the town. After a lot of fighting and drinking,

King Edward reveals himself, pardons everyone, tries to knight George, who refuses the honor, and gives the shoemakers the appellation of "the gentle craft."

In this delightful wild farrago of a play, Robin has a walk-on part as a good-hearted fighter with a jealous lover. The big exploits all belong to George, who urges his townspeople to be loyal to King Edward when a usurper, the earl of Kendall, conspires with James of Scotland to seize the crown. George thus plays the part often assigned to Robin: loyal defender of an endangered monarch. He is not awed by rank and won't back down before Kendall and his men or, like a good pinner, let the noblemen pasture their horses in the town's grain fields. Nor will he, in the end, agree to be made a knight. In this populist play, a true man of the people, a commoner, defends the customs of his town and is loyal to his monarch, mixing both deference and easy familiarity in his interactions with his sovereign. The play's novelty, then, lies in the way it transfers to a townsman, a citizen of Wakefield, the physical energy and robust loyalty to the true king previously embodied in the woodland yeoman, Robin Hood. At heart, *George a Greene* is a citizen play, and the play's valorized masculinity embodies citizen values. Both Robin and George are lusty lovers and lusty fighters but are loyal to, rather than disruptive of, monarchical authority.

Another unusual feature of this play is the nature of the rebel, the Earl of Kendall. Robin and his men, though unconnected to the earl in the plot, are nonetheless linked to him by the fact that they are famously said to dress in Kendall green and because the earl has stolen Robin's lines when explaining his rebellion. Several times he asserts, "I rise not against King Edward, / But for the poore that is opprest by wrong."[17] The play shows this to be a blatant lie. The earl rebels to gain a throne for himself, and he is quickly shown appropriating food from poor men like a very Tamburlaine, as he calls himself. Heroism in this play is connected to an actual commoner with a respectable job, not with a forest outlaw, and the traditional justification for outlawry, echoed even by Richard Grafton, is shown to be nothing but a smokescreen for pillage and self-advancement. As Edwin Davenport has argued, this makes the popular understanding of Robin Hood seem a dangerous fiction or a lie.[18]

The play certainly captures some of the energy and feel of the early ballads and *The Gest of Robin Hood* in that it foregrounds contests of strength, features multiple disguises, including cross-dressing, and shows the lasting bond between commoner and king. It has the energy and the optimism that scholars associate with the ballads and the narratives of Robin Hood in Sherwood. This is all true, and yet the elements are scrambled. Most notably, the populist energies of a forest outlaw are transferred to a sturdy citizen, the pinner of Wakefield. It is as if the dual potentialities of the Robin Hood material fissure: the rebellious and dangerous aspects of the story are transferred to the Earl of Kendall and disavowed; the energetic patriotism and physical prowess of the commoner hero are transferred to George and captured for what I would call a populist civic agenda stressing the inviolable bond between citizens (pinners and shoemakers) and the king. Much as Helgerson has suggested, this is a play written from the perspective of the loyal commoner, here closely aligned with the monarch; however, the commoner is not Robin himself but George. The urban context of theatrical playing has left its imprint on received material, making a guildsman the play's true hero and foregrounding his heterosexual prowess as lover, fighter, and loyal supporter of the king.

A second early Robin Hood play treats Robin even more warily and summarily in that he is never onstage at all. George Peele's *The Chronicle of King Edward the First,* first published in 1593 and regularly performed by the Admiral's Men throughout the 1590s, mainly concerns itself with threats to Edward's throne after he returns from a Crusade in the Holy Land.[19] To the north Scottish rebels threaten him; to the west Welsh rebels are in arms. Between battling both, he must deal with the excessive pride of his Spanish queen, Elinor, whom he adores but who enrages his English subjects with her high-handed ways. In this play Robin Hood enters the narrative via Lluellen, Prince of Wales. After a truce is first established between Lluellen and Edward, to while away the time Lluellen asks that the Book of Robin Hood be brought to him from Brecknock, and then, playing Robin Hood himself, he assigns his men the parts of Little John, the potter, and Friar Tuck, while his fiancée, Elinor de Montfort, plays Maid Marian. Various tricks and fights ensue, until Edward himself comes to fight with Lluellen / Robin Hood in hand-to-hand combat. Eventually, game gives way to seriousness, and Edward wars against the Welsh rebels in earnest. Lluellen is killed by a common soldier with a pikestaff, and his head taken to London.

In this play, then, Robin Hood is not a person but a role inscribed in a book. Rather than being the one who uses disguise to fool abbots or the Sheriff of Nottingham, he is now the disguise that others wear. Moreover, the role is performed by a dangerous rebel. Rather than protesting against an unjust king, Lluellen is fighting the noble Edward Longshanks, hero of the Crusades. Never mind that both the Scots and the Welsh might have good reason to slip the English yoke; in this play they are simply those who must be conquered in order for rightful majesty to assume its proper place. And the Robin Hood story, however awkwardly, is appropriated by those who are rebelling against what is represented as a just monarch. No longer in Sherwood Forest, Robin has been transported to Lluellen's redoubt in the Welsh mountains and pressed into service for a rebel cause. When Lluellen/Robin fights Edward, there is no joyful recognition scene at the end in which the mountaineer pledges fidelity to a long-lost master. Rather, the rebels are crushed, and with them the outlaw Robin Hood.

Peele's fiction, though a Henslowe history, is written entirely from the perspective of the English king rather than that of his victims, and any suggestion of kingly tyranny is conveniently displaced onto Edward's proud Spanish queen, who dies confessing her heinous crimes. In this particular work, built around a confrontation between monarch and rebels, there is no place for the traditional understanding of Robin Hood as a "good" outlaw. Here, he embodies a dangerous rogue masculinity, always one of the potentialities lurking in the role, though the fact that this Robin Hood exists as a character in a book means that he could be appropriated elsewhere to serve quite different ends.

The biggest theatrical transformation of Robin Hood, however, came in 1598, when Anthony Munday wrote not one but two plays in which he is the titular character—except this title character's name is now Robert, Earl of Huntington. This Robin comes to embody a masculinity entirely unique in the history of the Robin Hood material. Munday's plays accept Grafton's claim that Robin was a nobleman, and this decision is of a piece with Munday's general evisceration of the popular elements of the story and his transformation of Robin from a yeoman who physically resists church and sheriff to an earl who stoically suffers the adversities of tyranny while demonstrating utter loyalty to the monarchy: Robin Hood's masculinity is no longer the active masculinity of a wrestler, master archer, and trickster but the feminized heroism of a patient Griselda. Munday's transformations of the Robin Hood legend are striking, and although these plays are produced by Henslowe, their overall effect is to consolidate royal power, delegitimate resistance, and attack Catholic corruption—though, as I shall argue, their creation of new kinds of theatrical effects from scenes of prolonged suffering interestingly complicate their apparent political and religious agendas.

The framework for the first play indicates the shift in focus. It opens in the court of Henry VIII, where Sir John Elton and Master Skelton are discussing political developments and preparing to put on a play about Robert, Earl of Huntington, who, Skelton explains, was "your Robin Hoode,"[20] a verbal gesture that distances the popular story from its new courtly setting. A certain self-consciousness has entered the tradition. Robin is again metadramatically discussed *as a role,* and several times in the course of the play these same figures (Elton and Skelton) drop out of character and comment on the action as it unfolds. At one point John asks Skelton why the play contains no jests of Robin Hood, and Skelton replies that everyone knows those stories, and besides the king has approved the "plat" (plot) of his play (1.2.2219).

Munday's drama, then, explicitly unfolds under kingly auspices, purged of most of its familiar wrestling matches and daring raids on the sheriff's forces and the church's strongboxes. Instead, a noble Robert is betrayed by his steward, Warman, on the day he is to marry Maid Marian (here called Matilda); and he flees with Marian to the forest where, insisting on her chastity and his own, he does not sleep with her but mostly repines and laments his downfall. Only once, when he dresses as a blind man and rescues Scarlet and Scatlock from hanging, does he enact one of the traditional stories of Robin Hood. Instead, forgiveness is this Robin's (or Robert's) main activity. He forgives Warman, the steward who betrayed him; he forgives his uncle, the prior of York, who seized his land; he forgives the illegitimate King John when, on the return of his brother, Richard the Lionhearted, John is caught sneaking through Sherwood Forest disguised as an outlaw. What this Robin never does is contest unjust authority. The dangerous potential of the greenwood's yeoman hero has been neutered. No rebellion will come at his instigation.

This play was quickly followed by *The Death of Robert Earl of Huntington,* which Chettle was paid by Henslowe to revise for presentation at court. Again cast as a victim, Robert dies a fourth of the way through this play, poisoned by Doncaster and his uncle the prior of York, who fulfills Protestant stereotypes of devious Catholic villainy. Before he dies, Huntington forgives everyone again (for his uncle this is the second time) and writes a will in which he leaves all he owns to Matilda, who will also acquire the title of countess. Prince John, who has long lusted after Matilda, promises to leave her alone. However, the rest of the play reveals his promise to be a lie as, made king on the death of his brother, John pursues Matilda, who flees to a nunnery to escape him. John also persecutes the Bruce family, occasioning a grotesque martyrdom when he has Bruce's wife and young child walled up in a tower without food until they starve to death. John's henchman then pursues Matilda to her convent and gives her a poison drink, which she willingly imbibes, though as she dies she forgives King John. When news comes that Lewis of France is about to invade England and topple John, however, even Bruce vows to defend king and country rather than be "a stranger's slave."[21] It seems that no kingly evil is too much to be endured by England's suffering nobility.

These two plays' focus on the prolonged suffering and torment of Robert and Matilda, in particular, evokes traditions of Catholic martyrdom even in works marked by overt anti-Catholic sentiment and creates emotional effects that complicate the thematic emphasis on obedience.[22] Robert and Matilda both die by poison; both are hounded by evil men who act under the authority of a corrupt king; and both display a form of saintly heroism in which sheer endurance and stoic self-possession trump active resistance. In fact, the novelty of the plays lies in the way they transform Robin's commoner status and active masculinity into Robert's noble rank and stoical, patient-Griselda masculinity. The extremity of the hero's and heroine's suffering, moreover, has political consequences. It invites a visceral revulsion toward kingly tyranny and clerical treachery despite the overt message that resistance to a sitting monarch is unthinkable. The plays thus experiment with the effects of pathos connected with Michael Drayton's "Heroical Epistles," on which Munday's Marian/Matilda is partly modeled,[23] even as they make Robin a member of the nobility and sever his links to a dangerous rebelliousness.

The plays transfer to a male figure the emotions characteristically assigned to suffering women in Drayton's works. In Munday's plays there is criticism of kingly and clerical abuse but no model of resistance, only powerful identification with the suffering of power's victims. In making Robin a lover rather than a fighter, an earl rather than a commoner, a forgiver rather than a righter of wrongs, Munday thus drastically changes the political valence of the traditional Robin Hood narratives, replacing vigorous swordplay and daring attacks on fat abbots and evil sheriffs with the elegant forbearance of passive martyrs. As a result, the Munday plays both do and do not fit Helgerson's description of Henslowe's history plays and what we imagine to be the dominant masculinity of the history play genre. Although oppressed by the monarch, those sufferers are no longer "commoners," but rather a faction of the nobility alienated from royal favor and, affectively at least, linked to Catholic culture. The political consequence of this very complicated representation seems to be a veiled critique of monarchical tyranny—but a critique coupled with the assurance that the injured parties will not resist the tyrant. Robin Hood, his masculinity redefined, has both been appropriated by a new class and pressed into the service of a Catholicism defined by its loyalty to the monarch who is the agent of its oppression.

Shakespeare's Robin Hood

So how did Shakespeare respond to this outpouring of Robin Hood theatricals? His *As You Like It* has been offered as an answer. Entered in the Stationer's Register in August 1600, it is usually thought to have been written in the period between 1598 and 1600—in short, around the same time as the Munday plays, and commonly taken to be in dialogue with them and the other Robin Hood plays of the decade. In a general way, this has to be right. The Duke is not Robin Hood, Arden is not Sherwood, and yet the Duke is said to "have many merry men with him" in the forest, and "there they live like the old Robin Hood of England. They say that many young gentlemen flock to him every day, and fleet the time carelessly, as they did in the golden world" (1.1.100–103).[24] This description deliberately evokes the Duke as a *kind* of Robin Hood and Arden as a *kind* of Sherwood, and by doing so keeps in play the political undercurrents of this pastoral comedy of love. A usurper sits on Duke senior's throne and has corrupted the world of the court, causing good men (and women) to flee or to be forced out into the forest. The play's politics tend toward peaceful restoration, when the good ruler, like King Richard of the Robin Hood story, will once again ascend his throne.

Nonetheless, the play overtly changes the Robin Hood materials. The Duke is as much Richard as Robin, and in this regard he is elevated in rank like Munday's Robert Earl of Huntington. But Shakespeare's Duke, though he endures wind and rough weather with fortitude, is not a passive sufferer so much as a leader in exile, biding his time until the course of things will bring about his restoration. Not a lover, just surrounded by lovers, his essential role is to use his pastoral retreat for spiritual renewal and then to return to the court and resume his rule. He does not use the forest as a site of active resistance in the form of raids on his brother or his brother's men. He waits, and then he returns. This is quite opposite to the deepest currents of the traditional Robin Hood material, in which going to court is, for Robin, always a deeply unhappy event because his real home is the forest, his essential activity resistance to clerical and monarchical tyranny.

What Shakespeare finds most useful in the Robin Hood legend is the idea of the forest as an equalitarian space, however temporary, within which there can be a kind of release from the cares of the workaday world. Singing, talking, hunting, and loving, the Duke's followers do "fleet the time" pleasantly, and the image of the fellowship of Sherwood hangs over their woodland idyll. Yet Shakespeare imposes a strict pastoralism on the forest, not only by mixing sheep with deer, sheepherding with hunting, and love with more martial concerns, but also by suggesting that such a space offers an interlude to which the disillusioned or the exiled repair and from which they will reemerge, thus restoring the hierarchical order of ordinary society. Even given Jacques' refusal to participate, this is nonetheless the play's spatial movement.

I would argue, however, that Shakespeare creates a much more imaginative and daring engagement with the matter of Robin Hood in another set of plays, namely *1* and *2 Henry IV,* also written in the latter half of the 1590s and much more edgily in touch with the rough energies of the early Robin Hood material and its contestatory possibilities than is *As You Like It.*[25] In these two plays, Hal's masculinity is a strange amalgamation of the tonalities that have variously accrued to the Robin Hood figure in his 1590s stage incarnations. Sometimes Hal is a fighter, as at Shrewsbury, where he becomes the essence of the chivalric hero; at other times, he is the trickster leader of a homosocial band that makes its home in Quickly's Eastcheap tavern; at still others, a philosophical leader in waiting; but above all Hal emerges as a politician, embodying a cold and calculating masculinity that uses disguises, both literal and figurative, for his own advancement more than in the service of the poor.

In these central plays of the Henriad, Shakespeare uses a band of urban outlaws, the gang in Quickly's Eastcheap tavern, to create a world at odds with that of established authority. Here the characters flout the law, flout the demands of time, flout the king's authority. And they live, moreover, in a competitive environment of male camaraderie in which characters fence with words if not with longstaffs, assume disguises, rob rich travelers on the Canterbury highway (some allegedly clad in Kendall green), and abuse the king's power of impressment most damnably. In this world there is not much romantic love, and Maid Marian, aka Mistress Quickly, seems much closer to the lewd wench of the popular tradition that couples her with Friar Tuck, here Falstaff, rather than a fair mate for Hal. Only very late in the tetralogy, at the end of *Henry V,* will Hal refashion himself as the triumphant heterosexual conqueror of the French princess. In the Eastcheap tavern, by contrast, we get a re-creation of the homosocial world of the greenwood, but with the genuine camaraderie of the forest edgily competing with the sense of false companionship that emanates from Hal's careful distance from and wary observation of his mates. Much, of course, goes into the creation of these scenes besides the residue of the Robin Hood material. Carnival and the medieval figure of Vice, for example, play their parts. But present too is the cultural template of an outlaw band of good fellows who provide a refuge for those not in the king's favor, and who trouble the administration of the king's justice and the king's finances.

With this material Shakespeare is doing something iconoclastic and canny. The tavern does provide an alternative world from which to criticize the rigidities and insufficiencies of the court and its troubled monarch. But by having Hal double as both the leader of the outlaw band and the king's son, Shakespeare muddies the division between the two worlds and complicates the choices Hal must make. The question always haunting the Robin Hood material—which is the better life: one of absorption into the world of the court or critical distance from it?—is usually decided in favor of Sherwood Forest; but for Hal the resolution is difficult and long-delayed. When the audience first sees him, he is in Eastcheap, frittering away the time with Falstaff; only later do we see him in Westminster. For ten acts it is not clear whether or not his trajectory will be that of Robin Hood (from outlaw world to court and back to the outlaw world) or that of Duke senior (from court to outlaw band to court). Prince Hal, like Robert Earl of Huntington, is a nobleman—in fact, heir to the throne—but for much of ten acts that fact does not seem to secure either his identity or his ultimate social location. At times, it seems that if he does return to court it will be simply to transform Westminster into a riotous version of the tavern. Shakespeare, then, long refuses to supply a simple resolution to the question of Hal's trajectory, making us feel, queasily, the betrayals on all sides as he slips from one world to the other.

Moreover, if Shakespeare merges Robin Hood and the king's son into one figure, he also merges into one figure the image of the good king and the bad. In the traditional Robin Hood material these are separated into good King Richard and his bad usurping brother, John, which makes it possible for Robin to be loyal to the absent king and disloyal to the present one. In *1* and *2 Henry IV,* all the audience *has* is Henry Bolingbroke, a reigning monarch who is nonetheless demystified by Falstaff's parody of him, by his own shape-shifting at Shrewsbury, by his admission of weariness, and by his circuitous and morally questionable route to the throne. This is the pattern of kingship that Hal must negotiate, assume, deny, or refigure. In short, Shakespeare makes the question of allegiance to a flawed but not clearly illegitimate monarch *difficult,* and especially difficult for his son. The politics of these plays are far less easy to discern than is the easy populism of *George a Greene* or Munday's refusal to embrace popular or aristocratic resistance.

The anti-idealizing tendency in the plays is furthered by the fact of their central transposition of the outlaw's world from the mythical Sherwood

Forest, echoed in *As You Like It*'s Forest of Arden, to the urban world of Eastcheap. The contrast between Nottingham and Sherwood Forest is replaced by the contrast between Westminster and East End London. Whereas most stage appropriations of the Robin Hood material have a nostalgic and idealizing tone, looking backward to a woodland golden age, the outlaw band at Quickly's tavern is the most modern thing, temporally speaking, in *1* and *2 Henry IV*. The Eastcheap world in many respects resembles the late sixteenth-century world of contemporary London more than the early fifteenth-century world represented in the court scenes.[26] Shakespeare uses this fact to question the old paradigm in which commoners automatically are loyal to their monarch and true monarchs are both discernible as such and worthy of that loyalty. In what passes for modernity in these plays, the Eastcheap world, not one of these assumptions holds. From the clear binaries of the Robin Hood story there has been a fall into a much more complex polity, one in which the disguises adopted by the old Robin Hood to effect a rough justice against the true king's enemies have become a permanent tool of rule and a permanent part of political personality, and in which allegiance of the commons has to be won, cannot be assumed. For this world of modernity Shakespeare crafts, from old materials, a new masculinity for Hal—a masculinity that, as in a palimpsest, shows beneath the cool exterior of the modern politician the old constructs of merry trickster, bluff companion to a merry band of men, and monarchical loyalist.

1 and *2 Henry IV* do not, to evoke Helgerson's categories, exactly champion the rights of the oppressed, though neither do they merely take the side of power. The clear villains and heroes, the idealized and corrupt kings of the Robin Hood legend just don't exist in the world of the Henriad. The plays make it hard to love Hal; generations have loved Falstaff/Tuck much more, partly because Falstaff has an air of authenticity paradoxically produced by the fidelity of his character to familiar prototypes such as Friar Tuck and the Vice with the dagger of lath. By contrast, Hal seems insincere, a hollow man, because there is no congruence between the popular materials from which he is constructed—madcap prince and leader of a merry outlaw band—and the realities of the political world he has been created to confront and master.

To account for the complex political valences of these plays, we need a more nuanced story than one that stresses an absolute difference between the Henslowe and the Shakespearean histories. In the 1590s, a theater culture had taken shape in which companies both observed and responded to the offerings of other companies. The amount of intercompany borrowing, comment, and cross-comment was significant. In such a culture, novelty often consisted of reworking familiar material, and it was in those reworkings that political nuance was created, making it impossible to read the politics of a play simply from the company that produced it or from prior uses of popular themes, figures, or genres. Robin Hood pops up repeatedly in the historical drama of the 1590s, an exploitable resource, but one whose political implications shifted and changed as dramatists called on different, often contradictory, aspects of the familiar legend and as they responded to the innovations of fellow dramatists. Nowhere is this more apparent than in the emergence from the figure of the merry woodland outlaw of the saint-like martyr that was Anthony Munday's Robert Earl of Huntington and of the infinitely elusive, coolly calculating politician of Shakespeare's most complex history plays. Judging from the popularity of Robin Hood material on the public stage in the 1590s, the theatergoing public must have enjoyed processing these innovative uses of familiar materials, the theatrical stuff through which varying conjunctions of gender, religion, and politics were elaborated and re-elaborated, and the intersections of a complex theater culture made visible.

NOTES

1. Richard Helgerson, *Forms of Nationhood: The Elizabethan Writing of England* (Chicago: University of Chicago Press, 1992), 234.

2. Alfred Harbage, *Shakespeare and the Rival Traditions* (Bloomington: Indiana University Press, 1952). There has been a similar tendency to see a pronounced difference between the repertory and theater practices of the Admiral's Men and the Chamberlain's Men in the 1590s, with the Admiral's Men's plays portrayed as more populist and more invested in visual spectacle and bombastic speech than those of the Chamberlain's Men. For the latest articulation of this position, see Andrew Gurr, *Shakespeare's Opposites: The Admiral's Company, 1594–1625* (Cambridge: Cambridge University Press, 2009).

3. These words come from the first line of Marlowe's preface to *Tamburlaine, Part I*, quoted in Helgerson, *Forms of Nationhood*, 199–200.

4. Roslyn Lander Knutson, *Playing Companies and Commerce in Shakespeare's Time* (Cambridge: Cambridge University Press, 2001), 48–74.

5. Helgerson, *Forms of Nationhood*, 231–32.

6. Jeffrey Singman, *Robin Hood: The Shaping of the Legend* (Westport, Conn.: Greenwood Press, 1998), 155.

7. *Robin Hood*, intro. George Cockburn Harvey (London: The John C. Winston Company, 1923).

8. Singman, *Robin Hood*, 29–45.

9. If earlier scholarship connected the Robin Hood games to agrarian festivals of the spring and summer and stressed their carnivalesque qualities (see David Wiles, *The Early Plays of Robin Hood* [Cambridge: D. S. Brewer, 1981]), much recent scholarship has stressed the games' links to the fund-raising activities of the Church. See, for example, John

Marshall, "Gathering in the Name of the Outlaw: REED and Robin Hood," in *REED in Review: Essays in Celebration of the First Twenty-five Years,* ed. Audrey Douglas and Sally-Beth MacLean (Toronto: University of Toronto Press, 2006), 65–84. James Stokes, "Robin Hood and the Churchwardens in Yeovil," *Medieval and Renaissance Drama in England* 3 (1986): 1–25, has discovered that in the town of Yeovil the men who played Robin Hood were usually ex-churchwardens and drawn from the town's prosperous guildsmen. Their jobs extended throughout the year and involved various fund-raising activities for the church.

10. Paul Whitfield White, "The Parish Robin Hood and Religious Guilds," in *Drama and Religion in English Provincial Society, 1485–1660* (Cambridge: Cambridge University Press, 2008), 43–65.

11. Edwin Davenport, "The Representation of Robin Hood in Elizabethan Drama: *George a Greene* and *Edward I,*" in *Playing Robin Hood: The Legend as Performance in Five Centuries,* ed. Lois Potter (Newark: University of Delaware Press, 1998), 45–62, at 45–46.

12. Singman, *Robin Hood,* 83–85.

13. Stephen Knight and Thomas Ohlgren, eds., *Robin Hood and Other Outlaw Tales* (Kalamazoo, Mich.: Medieval Institute Publications, 1997), 269.

14. Singman, *Robin Hood,* 69.

15. Ibid., 117.

16. Quoted ibid., 107.

17. *The Comedy of George a Greene,* ed. F. W. Clarke (Oxford: Oxford University Press, The Malone Society Reprints, 1911), C4.

18. Davenport, "The Representation of Robin Hood," 51.

19. George Peele, *Edward I,* ed. Frank S. Hook, in *The Life and Works of George Peele,* gen. ed. Charles Tyler Prouty (New Haven, Conn.: Yale University Press, 1961), 2:1–212.

20. Thomas Munday, *The Downfall of Robert Earl of Huntington* (1601), ed. John Meagher (Oxford: Oxford University Press, Malone Society Reprints, 1964), A3, l. 88.

21. Thomas Munday, *The Death of Robert Earl of Huntington* (1601), ed. John C. Meagher (Oxford: Oxford University Press, The Malone Society Reprints, 1965), Mv, l. 3013.

22. Phebe Jensen, in *Religion and Revelry in Shakespeare's Festive World* (Cambridge: Cambridge University Press, 2008), 126, assumes that Munday's plays make Robin a thoroughly Protestant hero. I, by contrast, find the plays full of contradictions, especially in their religious implications. Attacks on Catholic clerical corruption are, of course, part of the Robin Hood tradition exploited by Munday, but the plays also exploit a Catholic template of aestheticized martyrdom in representing the suffering of their hero and heroine.

23. See *Poems by Michael Drayton,* ed. J. William Hebel (Oxford: Basil Blackwell, 1861), 2:147–59.

24. *As You Like It,* in *The Norton Shakespeare,* ed. Stephen Greenblatt, Katherine Eisaman Maus, Jean E. Howard, and Walter Cohen, 2nd ed. (New York: Norton, 2008), 1627. All further references to Shakespeare's plays will be taken from this edition and referred to by act, scene, and line only.

25. Lois Potter briefly makes a connection between the tavern band of the *Henry IV* plays and Robin Hood's band in "The Elizabethan Robin Hood Plays," in *Playing Robin Hood,* 21–22.

26. Jean E. Howard and Phyllis Rackin, *Engendering a Nation: A Feminist Account of Shakespeare's English Histories* (London: Routledge, 1997), esp. 164.

Afterword

Richard Helgerson and Making Publics

PAUL YACHNIN

So long as men can breathe, or eyes can see,
So long lives this, and this gives life to thee.
SHAKESPEARE, Sonnet 18

IN this afterword, I reflect on Richard Helgerson's scholarship, especially his masterwork, *Forms of Nationhood,* as seen through the multiplex lens of the splendid essays in this volume. I also consider the essays on their own terms, taking particular note of their critical treatment of Helgerson's research, and especially of how their engagement with Helgerson draws his work into ongoing thinking about the social creativity of works of art and intellect. Understanding the public-making capacity of artistic and intellectual works, as well as the social creativity of the people who made and those who partook in plays, poems, maps, law books, paintings, works of religious thinking, and so on, was, of course, the particular business of the Making Publics (MaPs) project (2005–10), an undertaking that Helgerson helped quite centrally to create.

The members of MaPs and those who have come to share our research questions have undertaken to produce this volume in an effort to keep Helgerson among us—not as a talismanic figure of great scholarship (which he could very well be), nor from personal sentiment alone (though he certainly aroused admiration and affection in those who knew him), but rather as a conversation partner. On this account, ours is an ethical as well as a critical enterprise. It is also an enterprise that enacts one of the principal features of publics, which has to do with how works (broadside ballads, antiquarian studies, scurrilous rhymes and pictures, sonnets, etc.)

and practices (playgoing and playing, reading, writing, mapping, etc.) create human—specifically historical—temporality, a quality of being in time that frees humans from their embedment in the cycles of natural birth and death, and thereby provides them with a kind of life after death through the marvelous agency of the things they make and the future-oriented forms of public association they and the works they make call into the world.

Of course, a life after death by way of being lifted into the starry constellation of textual publicity entails certain significant changes to the character of the survivor. This is well captured by Shakespeare's Sonnet 18, where the poet promises eternal life to the addressee by way of poetic composition, scribal and/or print publication, and the long-term attention of a reading public, but where he does not reveal and thus preserve the addressee's actual name or identity—if, in fact, he was a real person (as opposed to an invented one).

In what follows, I discuss the chapters in this volume in relation to three interrelated topics that bear on the theory and history of publics and also on Helgerson's thinking about the social life of literature ("literature" defined broadly) as well as his ideas about the social creativity of theater and painting. The first topic is publics as the building blocks of larger political formations, especially the public sphere and the nation, as well as an account of what publics are. The theory and history of publics can help us understand how a nation that somehow had the spirit of egalitarianism and publicness in its genes, which was Helgerson's view of early modern England, actually came into existence. We might say that publics were the building blocks of the nation.

As the members of MaPs discovered, however—and very much under the prompting of Helgerson's definitional precision—publics are not at all well defined as blocks, or even as building blocks. In her chapter Vera Keller describes publics as scientific objects or categories of thought rather than as things that "exist in concrete reality as the mundane objects of everyday life do." Much of the work of the MaPs project was directed toward the task of defining publics, a task that led to work on the relationship between publics and other forms of association such as networks, circles, spheres, audiences, readerships, professional and amateur organizations, the Church, the court, the public, and the nation-state.

In comparison to most of these other forms of association, publics emerged in our thinking as especially vital sites of artistic and intellectual creation and collective action. Understanding the created, creative, and processual nature of publics was one of the principal leaps forward made by the members of MaPs. It allowed the researchers in the project to think about publics as moving things rather than as hard-shelled, durable entities—instantiations of cultural, intellectual, social, and/or economic initiatives in which human aspirations were interactive with discourses, spaces, and things.

The second topic is the discourses, things, and spaces themselves. This is not a matter of human agency working on the raw matter of the world, as if language, material things, and spatiality were fully subservient to human wishes. Discourses, things, and spaces have their own kind of agency. The mobility of language and things like texts and artifacts and the plasticity of space are key drivers of public making, a process by which people who may well remain strangers to each other, living in different places in a nation or even in different nations, are nevertheless able to become members of a public within a virtual common space.

Third are the domains of private and public, an interrelationship ubiquitous across history, always shifting, and formative of large-scale social change in early modernity. The relationship between private and public became somewhat of a grand obsession for many members of the research team. The two domains collide and interpenetrate across space, language, material life, identity, and so on; the relationship between the two is endlessly interesting; and for many members of the team, the dynamic interaction between the private and the public provided a key way of understanding publics, which, we said, "have the capacity to pass in and out of the state of publicity." Publics, on this account, are private-public hybrids.[1]

What Are Publics?

Consider Lesley Cormack's chapter, "Geography and Its Publics in Early Modern England," which seeks "to situate [Helgerson's] work within a new interpretation of publics and public making" by arguing for the limitations of his landmark study of early modern English chorography (that is, the study of local geography and history) and by developing its own account of the relationship between networks and publics. Helgerson, Cormack says, mistakenly assumes that early modern people could easily make sense of maps. He argues, based on this idea about popular cartographic literacy, that early modern maps were able to drive forward a geographically based democratization of political culture as the English shifted their loyalty from the monarch to the land of England itself. What happens, Cormack asks, if we shift the terms of Helgerson's argument toward publics and public making? To answer this question, she explains how a geographical public was formed in early modern England, how it extended across national borders (more about that later in relation to Sacks and Keller), and how it was able to exert the kind of nation-building force that Helgerson attributed to "discursive communities" (for more about discursive communities, see the Introduction to this volume).[2] The public in this case started life as a different kind of association—what Cormack describes as a network.

Richard Carew was a scholar and a member of the landed gentry. He met William Camden and Philip Sidney, among others, during his university days. He cultivated a life as an amateur translator, chorographer, and antiquary. His exchanges with a number of others, mostly men he knew, and the other exchanges among these men created a network, Cormack says, not a public. What Carew and the others made was a foundation on which a public could then be created.

To describe this public, Cormack shifts her focus from Carew to William Camden, a man from common stock, and shifts also from a loose grouping of friends and associates to a virtual gathering of people that grew over time in relation to the publication of a series of ever-expanding texts of Camden's great work, *Britannia*. Those who contributed to the expansion of the book (it was thousands of pages long by 1786), those who bought and read it, and those who wrote and read other, related books (these groups no doubt overlapping) can properly be described as a public. The membership included those who were strangers to each other, people separated by space, and also people belonging to different generations. Carew's network was served by the circulation of manuscript and print, but that network was not anchored in a radical way by the circulation of texts as was the public that formed around Camden's *Britannia*. Finally, because of its public character—its potentially limitless growth in space, across time, and among thousands of people of all kinds—the geographical public was able to exert a powerful democratizing influence in England. Cormack's analysis therefore supports Helgerson's claim about the effectively oppositional politics of early modern cartography and chorography, but it does so by taking his thinking further, in particular by rerouting his thinking through the theory and history of publics.[3]

Meredith Donaldson Clark takes Helgerson's work on the politics of geography on a similarly revealing journey through the theory of publics. Her chapter tells the story of John Shrimpton, an amateur antiquarian and resident of St. Albans whose circa 1630 compilation, *The Antiquities of Verulam and St. Albans,* provides confirmation of Cormack's ideas about the formation of a chorographical public in early modern England. Shrimpton's work remained unpublished: it nevertheless demonstrates the uptake of published texts like *Britannia,* the circulation of geographical and political commonplaces, the dissemination of ideas and values by way of the circulation of print and written texts, and the consequent formation of what Donaldson Clark calls a "textual public."

We have noted (in the Introduction) that publics are oriented toward futurity; they are bent toward growth in a way that communities are not. Donaldson Clark shows that publics also deepen the pastness of human living and human spatiality. This is not an invariable characteristic of publics, but it is of major importance in early modern public life, and it might be a feature that distinguishes early modern from modern public making.

Donaldson Clark therefore provides a critical supplement to Michael Warner's theorization of public making: "In contrast to the relative immediacy of Warner's model," she comments, "the public which created the idea of Verulamium in the early modern period is diachronic: it was little concerned with the present, and instead was oriented to the past (the source of the people, texts, and artifacts it takes as its interest) and the future (in its desire to restore and preserve the past for posterity)." As she also points out, this idea of how people recruit the past in order to shape forms of public association such as "discursive communities" and nations is a central feature of Helgerson's thinking. In effect, then, his work can help us understand the temporal character of publics as well as how public making changes the early modern experience of time and space.

To review what we have said to this point: the theory of publics serves to critique, confirm, and extend Helgerson's work on the emergence of early modern England. Publics are the building blocks of the nation. It makes good sense to rethink Helgerson in terms of publics because his work is strongly anticipatory of the insights of the MaPs project. He was writing about publics before we, or he, had a name for them or a theory to explain them. Publics themselves, as we have seen, are complex forms of association different from but related to networks (or formal organizations such as the Society of Antiquaries); they are open-ended and tend to be friendly toward strangers of all social kinds; they embody the democratizing tendencies that Helgerson attributes to what he calls discursive communities. Publics are bent toward growth; and they help create a peculiarly human spatiality and temporality.

Patricia Fumerton's chapter can advance our description of publics and can add another element, which has to do with their remarkable dynamism and changeability. Fumerton writes movingly, in light of the "making and unmaking" of her close friend Richard Helgerson, about the mutability of publics—their tendency to appear, expand, and disappear, or to morph into something different. Building on Cormack's argument about how publics emerge out of networks, Fumerton provides an innovative account of publics in the coupled terms of Clifford Geertz's famous study of Balinese cockfighting and Warner's ideas about the necessary self-reflexivity of publics (you and others have to *think* you are in a public to *be* in a public). The mercurial character of publics is of a piece with the changing degree of attention people pay to the things that enable publics and that are enabled by them. So, Fumerton says, "[ballads] were cultural artifacts that circulated in complex reflexive and nuanced ways formative of an expansive, multivalenced, and organic ballad public." As publics might be said to exist just so long as people pay attention to them (and to themselves paying attention), it follows that publics might be organized along the lines of Geertz's cockfight—as a series of circles within circles, with the most engaged at the core and with increasingly more numerous and less attentive groups of people occupying the outer rings. However, because publics depend for their life largely on attention, this proposed concentric organization cannot guarantee their durability: the whole series of circles could shift, massively and suddenly, as an effect of a shift in the content and/or the style of the circulating ballads.

Javier Castro-Ibaseta's chapter, "Sonnets from Carthage, Ballads from Prison," takes us into new territory, that of Helgerson's last two books, *Adulterous Alliances* (2000) and *A Sonnet from Carthage* (2007). Castro-Ibaseta develops a critique of Helgerson's account of the "new poetry," but he also addresses the questions about publics that Helgerson had put to the MaPs team.

Helgerson's subject in *A Sonnet from Carthage* is the Spanish importation of Italian poetic models between around 1530 and 1580—a poetic revolution, according to Helgerson, of considerable ideological consequence. Castro-Ibaseta challenges this argument. It is true, he says, that Garcilaso's sonnet, the subject of Helgerson's last book, registers resistance to the idea and language of empire, but that ideological complexity is eclipsed by the social creativity of a second Spanish literary revolution that started around 1580. That second revolution included the rise of the *comedia nueva* (a commercial theater that spotlighted issues of social justice and represented the peasantry as well as the higher classes) and of popular, printed literary forms such as romances (equivalent to English folk ballads) and *jácaras* (comic romances often featuring bandits and prostitutes). The new, Italianate poetry achieved very little from the point of view of public making. "[The poets] Garcilaso and Boscán did not want to create a new social group," Castro-Ibaseta says, "but to transform an old one. Their project presumed the preexistence of a community of peers, and their poetry simply addressed that community." In contrast to the courtly setting of the first, the second revolution took place in a marketplace. Commercial relations between writers and readers/playgoers changed everything, opened participation (in principle) in literary and theatrical culture to all, and created an authentic public, which was a space for playful discourse and debate and also generative of new forms of association among people of different social ranks. As it happens, this argument about the public making of literature and theater draws on Helgerson's book, *Adulterous Alliances,* particularly on chapter 5, "The Liberty of Spanish Towns." Where Helgerson admits to being a bit stymied in his attempts to explain the huge popularity of the *comedia nueva* in terms of class affiliation (after all, as a class, the mostly bourgeois audience should not have flocked to drama about peasant life), Castro-Ibaseta argues for a new understanding in terms of publics.

The transformative influence of the market is part of this understanding. Added to that is a brilliant analysis of audiences, classes, communities, and publics. Publics are revealed to be new social creatures, ones able to draw people together, even from different classes and communities. A public is like an audience in its relationship to recreational pleasure and its social heterogeneity but unlike an audience in its capacity to create new social identities and bonds among participants. A bourgeois in an audience remains a bourgeois, her responses conditioned by her class habitus; a bourgeois in a theatrical public is able mostly to leave aside that habitus in a collective act of social transformation: "we should never underestimate the degree to which art creates its own publics—publics whose members are relatively unencumbered by . . . preexisting social identities."

Public making disrupts how audiences and readerships might be expected to respond to works of art precisely because artistic practices enable spectators and readers to re-create themselves. They are not the same people they were raised to be, at least not so long as they are watching or reading (or listening to music or looking at visual art).

The explanatory force of this insight into the social creativity of early modern, market-based artistic practice is powerfully demonstrated by Jean Howard's chapter, "The Political Fortunes of Robin Hood on the Early Modern Stage." Howard undertakes a critique of Helgerson's most controversial work, "Staging Exclusion" (in *Forms of Nationhood*), where he argues that Shakespeare, as opposed to the dramatists who wrote for Henslowe's companies, was a social climber whose history plays are conservative and royalist, to the point that the England his plays offer us seems a space reserved for the interests and stories of social elites, an England that excludes the life experiences and historical and political agency of the commons.

As Howard points out, Helgerson's argument depends on the idea that there were different audiences—one for Shakespeare and another for Henslowe, one elitist and the other populist. The facts, she argues, do not bear this out very readily. The playwrights (with Shakespeare after 1594 as the exception) moved from company to company as opportunities arose. The plays themselves are more various and harder to categorize than Helgerson suggests. The Robin Hood plays (including, in Howard's argument, *As You Like It* and the *Henry IV* plays) are exemplary of this complexity. The matter of Robin Hood is a particularly good test case because it has deep roots in English folk and popular traditions. The Robin Hood stories often bring king and commoners together, to the exclusion of the social elite, in a shared project of social reform that includes the restoration of traditional justice and the redistribution of wealth and power.

The commercial theater complicated the political orientation of the Robin Hood stories. George Peele's *The Chronicle of King Edward the First*, to take one example from Howard's rich archive, was staged by the Admiral's Men throughout the 1590s, but it is nevertheless a play "written," Howard tells us, "entirely from perspective of the English king rather than that of his victims." It is not populist, not in line with the Robin Hood tradition, but rather a provocatively royalist rewriting of the tradition. On the other side, in Shakespeare's *Henry IV* plays, where we might have expected to find conservatism, we encounter instead an "iconoclastic and canny" (Howard's phrase) engagement with the tradition that recaptures the antiauthoritarian masculinity of the Sherwood Forest outlaws and that merges the bad king John and the good king Richard of the tradition into the single figure of Henry Bolingbroke. "Shakespeare makes difficult the question of allegiance to a flawed but not clearly illegitimate monarch," Howard says. "The politics of the play are far less easy to discern than is the easy populism of George a Greene or Munday's refusal to embrace popular or aristocratic resistance."

How are we to account for the apparent inconsistency in the political orientation of these plays, with the Henslowe play advocating for obedience to the ruler even in the face of the unjust treatment of the people and the King's Company's play reviving the tradition of antiauthoritarian camaraderie? Though Helgerson's argument has much merit and is able to marshal telling evidence, especially about how Shakespeare's plays tend to feature kings, queens, and dukes over members of the lower social orders, it seems nevertheless to have got the angle of view a bit wrong. The resolution to this problem of focus lies in part in Howard's account of the contradictions internal to the Robin Hood material, especially the conflict between the principle of loyalty to the king and the equally strong and opposing principle of resistance to the unjust distribution of wealth and power. That contradiction is also operative in the printed and performed histories as well as in the political culture of early modern England, and it can help us understand the ideological complexity of writers like Shakespeare.

Also important is Howard's argument that there were not two theater audiences in early London but rather one theatrical public. In early modern London, the playwrights were able to move from one playing company to another; so could the playgoers; and so also did the various stories and differing ways of representing the matter of Robin Hood. Howard explains here how those intersecting movements of people and ideas, coupled with a growing self-reflexivity, created a public:

> [The] playwrights were aware of what other dramatists were doing and . . . audiences followed with appreciation and discernment their implicit attempts at responding to and surpassing one another. . . . Part of the pleasure of theatergoing in the 1590s . . . depended on audiences comparing how different theater practitioners modified received stories, generic conventions, or stage traditions. Awareness of these modifications also revealed how the same given material could be marshaled for different political ends. Within the theater world of the 1590s, audiences did a lot of the work. They not only paid money to go to the theater, and probably not just to one playhouse, but they also entered into implicit association with other theatergoing Londoners, achieving a shared theatrical literacy and forming communities of appreciation and judgment.

So far in our work, as also in Howard's chapter, we have tended to ascribe to publics a democratic ethos. In some measure, ironically enough, this characterization of publics derives from Helgerson's work (not to mention Habermas and others). Publics on this account are forms of association that enable individuals to be recognized and valued for who they are apart from their socially assigned identity and worth. The last two chapters I will consider in the section, by Jeffrey Knapp and Anne Lake Prescott, raise important questions about the political and ethical character of publics. By doing so, they open the way toward a possible reconsideration of Helgerson's controversial assessment of Shakespeare.

Like Jean Howard, Jeffrey Knapp is interested in how contradiction plays out in Shakespeare. Where Howard focuses on contradiction internal to the matter of Robin Hood, Knapp looks at the contradictory situation of the commercial dramatist. His chapter engages with Helgerson's argument about Shakespeare's social elitism, not by attempting to rebut it, but rather by embracing and blending it into an analysis of the social conditions of early modern playwriting, an analysis that also issues in a provocative new reading of *Macbeth*. Together, these two sides of Knapp's chapter suggest something important about the ethical character of the public that Shakespeare's theater helped to make.

Shakespeare wrote for a predominately commoner audience. At the same time, as Knapp tells us (following Helgerson), he sought to associate his drama with the social elite. Shakespeare's work was thus vexed by an ethical and commercial requirement to please the audience and by an opposite drive to disassociate from that audience. To understand the conflict-ridden conditions of playwriting is to begin to grasp the fusion of barbarism and civility in *Macbeth,* especially the ways in which politeness and hospitality are inseparable from violence. Other critics, Knapp says, have simply misread Shakespeare's Scotland as a savage nation. It is no such thing. Rather, it is a culture marked by painstaking civility, a place where even the witches have exquisite manners. An insightful reader such as Harry Berger might see Scottish politeness and hospitality as curiously distorted forms of violence (the core principle of a warrior society), but Knapp nevertheless insists that we take both the civility and the violence as authentic and incommensurable components of Scottish life and also of Shakespeare's work in the theater. A certain aggressiveness toward the audience on the part of Shakespeare and other playwrights is of a piece with how careful the dramatists and players were to please the playgoers. But they, Shakespeare especially, also wanted to make their playgoers suffer. Shakespeare, as Helgerson argued, wanted to excel and outshine the commoners who filled his playhouse.

Building on Helgerson's argument about Shakespearean exclusivity, Knapp invites us to consider how major ethical components of early modern social life such as deference, hospitality, hierarchy, and aspiration affected the character of the newly forming publics, especially perhaps the theatrical public. Such a reconsideration might find itself grappling, for instance, with the persistence of ideas about intrinsic hierarchical differences between people (gentry better than commoners, men than women, Christians than Jews, and so on) in the formation of early modern publics, forms of association that we usually take to be precursors to the democratic political culture of modernity.

Anne Lake Prescott also invites us to rethink the ethical character of

publics. She offers her wonderfully learned and witty chapter as "an addendum to Helgerson's work." It is that: it supplements Helgerson by way
of a study of printed news pamphlets that flooded early modern England
with satire and slander against the French and against Catholics and that
thereby helped create a public for political debate and discussion.

Prescott's chapter also contributes provocatively to publics theory by
pointing to gaps in Helgerson's (and other scholars') thinking about publics. For one thing, she is interested in marginal genres that trade not in
Habermasian "rational-critical debate" but rather in the cultivation of
scorn and laughter. Her chapter thus joins a small body of recent work,
by members of the MaPs project and others (including Michael Warner),
that seeks to understand the place of nonrational, nondiscursive practices
(weeping, laughing, dressing up, playing, dancing, etc.) in the formation
of public life.[4] In addition, Helgerson's account of how discourse creates
the nation (in *Forms of Nationhood*) or lower-class resistance to tyranny
(in *Adulterous Alliances*) or even the profession of poetry (in *Self-Crowned
Laureates*) has little to say about how solidarity among groups of people is
often built on the fear, derision, and exclusion of others—what Prescott
calls "the muddy social cement of scandal and even slime." What would
happen if we were to rethink publics in terms of the powerful human capacity for collective hate and fear?

Of course, Prescott's chapter leavens this way of looking at publics as
the pamphlets she studies must have struck even early modern readers
as uproarious and over-the-top. But the main question remains; and it
represents a challenge that we can only take note of here. With the significant exception of the chapter on Shakespeare in *Forms of Nationhood*,
Helgerson's "discursive communities" as well as the "publics" described in
this volume take very little account of unfriendliness to strangers as a salient feature of public making. In light of Prescott's argument, however, we
might want to look again at Helgerson's "theater of exclusion" as arguably
a sound foundation for the study of an early modern public, one made
of the "social cement of scandal and even slime," where the playgoers (including even commoners), players, and the playwright found themselves
forming a socially influential association around an entertainingly derisive
antipopulist history of the nation.

Discourses, Things, Spaces

It is not people alone who make publics. We make publics together with
discourses, things, and spaces; they have lives of their own, so to speak, and

their lives are interactive with the lives of people. Publics, Warner says, "are created by the reflexive circulation of discourse."[5] Discourse and things are overlapping but distinctive categories. Things like written or printed texts facilitate the mobility and social creativity of discourse, but some made things that are participant in public making (paintings, works of music, maps, globes, etc.) are not exactly discursive.[6] In his important work on what he calls Actor-Network-Theory, Bruno Latour comments that "any thing that does modify a state of affairs by making a difference is an actor."[7] Finally, thinkers such as Henri Lefebvre, Michel Foucault, Gaston Bachelard, a number of human geographers, and Richard Helgerson himself have taught us that space is not a neutral container, but rather something made by and able in turn to influence social relations and practices as well as individual and collective actions and innovations.[8]

We can return briefly to Donaldson Clark. Her chapter demonstrates above all the "thingness" of publics—how they are enabled by the interactivity of people and of things like chorographies and commonplaces. Things are themselves agents of publicity and public making. In part, this is on account of their mobility and reproducibility: the multiplication, movement, and interpretive openness of texts can stitch people together across great physical and social distances. Things can connect people across time too.

Hannah Arendt has argued that the things we make transform bare nature into an authentically human world possessed of a deep historical temporality. "[T]he reality and reliability of the human world," she says, "rest primarily on the fact that we are surrounded by things more permanent than the activity by which they were produced, and potentially more permanent than the lives of their authors."[9] The world's thing character also provides a common objective reality: "Only where things can be seen by many in a variety of aspects without changing their identity, so that those who are gathered around them know they see sameness in utter diversity, can worldly reality truly and reliably appear."[10] Might the particular character of the things around which people gather and the specific nature of the gathering process influence what Arendt calls "worldly reality"?[11]

Vera Keller's chapter on "The Album Amicorum and the Popularity of John Owen" studies things and modes of associating markedly different from those in Helgerson's *Forms of Nationhood*. He is interested in how large-scale publications fostered national and individual identity in early modernity: "The unified self of the Englishman or Frenchman, the Italian or German, is founded on the political and cultural unity of the nation to which each belongs. The denial of nationhood is experienced as a denial of integrated selfhood."[12] Keller's is a study of people and texts in motion. The people are "methodical travelers," men who traveled internationally in order to "observe forms and places of association, especially the markets, universities, gardens, libraries, and art collections found in urban spaces." The texts include "books of friends" in which travelers collected souvenirs, engravings, descriptions, inscriptions, commonplaces, and so on, and also manuscript and printed books of Neo-Latin epigrams by writers such as George Buchanan and John Owen. These publications were hugely popular, printed many times and in different nations. The epigrams, commonplaces, citations, and images were themselves in constant motion from person to person and text to text. Owen's epigrams are "a convenient currency of cosmopolitan sociability." The mobile network of texts and persons suggests the development of an international rather than a national public life. Keller suggests that the nation building studied by Helgerson might be seen not as opposed to medieval feudalism but rather as a response to a "disturbingly new internationalism." Significant also, early modern subjectivity and spatiality are very different in Keller and Helgerson. His persons develop a strongly unified selfhood rooted in the land of the nation. The men she describes are public and politic, connected to each other and the world by a tissue of epigrammatic and commonplace textuality. For Keller, finally, these various kinds of public-making texts and different sorts of personhood and spatiality are not mutually exclusive but mutually constitutive. How they constitute each other is another matter.

One area of work ahead might be to formulate the relationship between national and international forms of public making. Keller shows us how texts and people in motion create a certain kind of public space, person, and collectivity. In his discussion of Shakespeare's *Julius Caesar*, David Lee Miller illuminates Shakespeare's creation of a compound, public-making space in the playhouse, a space that is at once Caesarian Rome, Judea at the time of Christ, and the stage of the Globe Playhouse in around 1600. Miller explains how Shakespeare fashioned this transhistorical, intercultural, and interconfessional space. For one thing, his drama is highly metatheatrical. Just after Caesar's assassination, Cassius says, "How many ages hence / Shall this our lofty scene be acted over / In states unborn and accents yet unknown!"[13] The moment intermixes ancient Rome and circa 1600 England and also enfolds ancient Roman republicans and English players. In addition to this metatheatrical capacity to create spaces within spaces, the play, as Miller shows, interweaves biblical, classical, and modern texts, practices, and spaces in order to deepen the transhistorical panorama. Consider the complex effect of Antony's display of Caesar's body:

> When Antony descends from the "pulpit" (3.1.236) to display Caesar's body, Shakespeare is effectively superimposing on his Roman marketplace two other settings familiar to an Elizabethan audience. The first would be the area at the front of the church called the chancel or sanctuary, where services are performed and the altar is placed. The second is the stage itself, evoked again here as it was earlier, when Brutus and Cassius imagined the assassination as being performed by players.

Miller argues brilliantly that the tendency of Shakespearean syncretism is toward the secularism of modern public life. And while the theater does afford the playgoers something like an agnostic view of intensely controversial matters (such as the meaning of the Eucharist), it does not by any means empty these controversies of their affective force. In the play the figure of the process that creates this transhistorical space for feeling and thinking together through questions of public concern is Antony speaking for the wounds of the dead Caesar—indeed, Antony speaking *as* the wounds, the gashes in Caesar's body that "like dumb mouths do ope their ruby lips / To beg the voice and utterance of my tongue" (3.1.60–61). In *Julius Caesar*, on this account, the players create a deeply historical public (like the one described by Donaldson Clark) wherein the movement of discourse between ages and cultures is driven by the ethical requirement to speak on behalf of the suffering subjects of classical, biblical, and modern narrative.

It is important to note also that although the arguments of Miller and Howard about the English theater have some significant differences, they share an understanding of the political character of the theatrical public. *Julius Caesar* creates a kind of historical distance internal to the spaces it represents and so enables a critical perspective on Rome, Judea, and England. The *Henry IV* plays coax out the ideological contradictions in early modern ideals of community and rule that earlier versions of the Robin Hood stories tended to suppress. In both cases, the theater fosters discussion among people of all ranks rather than promulgating a particular class ideology or an aristocratic history of the nation. In the discussions of both Miller and Howard, the drama begins to look like a "people's theater" rather than the theater of exclusion described by Helgerson.

When we are thinking about how discourse, things, and spaces create publics, the key question is: How do they move? For Keller's epigrammatic public, texts as well as people move through geopolitical space but not historical time, so their motions remain remarkably light-footed. Miller's theatrical public is founded in transhistorically resonant, performed spaces and is therefore moving in an emotional sense as well as in the sense of locomotion. The juristic public that is the subject of Stephen Deng's chapter is created by the translation, so to speak, of texts from the exclusive possession of the legal community into the open space of a potentially innumerable readership.

The differences between Deng's "Translating the Law: Sir Edward Coke and the Formation of a Juristic Public" and Helgerson's "Writing the Law" (chapter 2 in *Forms of Nationhood*) are particularly illuminating in regard to the basic theme of this volume as well as the MaPs project itself. Helgerson unfurls a remarkable history of struggle over the law in early modern England. The main points of contention between King James and others (like Francis Bacon) on one side and Sir Edward Coke and the common lawyers on the other had to do with the character and modality of English law. Common law, the dominant kind of jurisprudence in England, is case law—a matter of tradition and accumulated principle and practice, rather than a law of written statutes like the Institutes composed by the Emperor Justinian. James argued for the importance of having a written and widely promulgated law in English rather than a mostly unwritten law of custom belonging to the lawyers and judges. Indeed, the written adjuncts of the common law were promulgated in law French, a professional idiom incomprehensible to outsiders.

From the king's point of view, Coke's defense of the common law was an attack on royal prerogative and power; from Coke's, the king was using an argument for jurisprudential transparency as a way of arrogating to himself the power to make law and so to elevate the monarchy above the law. Helgerson presents this struggle quite dramatically, almost as if it were going on between two powerful personalities, which to a degree it was. It unfolds against the background of a public sphere that is assumed to exist but whose operations are left unexplained. In Helgerson's account, Coke's campaign for the common law, including his authorship of the massively learned work the *Institutes,* which was written in English, is of a piece with the writing of the nation. But the mechanisms by which his struggle and his publications contributed to the formation of the nation-state are left mostly unexamined.

Deng's chapter is a powerful critical supplement to Helgerson. He argues, first of all, that Coke's decision to write the *Institutes* in English rather than Latin or law French puts in question Helgerson's claim that Coke was bent on keeping legal knowledge and authority within a common law "arcana that would exclude the king even from the judgment seat in his own

Court of Star Chamber . . . and empower rather a professional community of learned lawyers."[14] The public-making orientation of Coke's work is also indicated in many passages in the *Institutes,* cited by Deng, that describe a far broader readership than the lawyers and the king. His work, Coke says, "concerneth all the subjects of the realm." Drawing on work by Warner, historians Peter Lake and Steve Pincus, and the MaPs project, Deng is able to show how the struggle between the king and Coke did not just take place against the background of an already constituted public sphere. The exchanges among these powerful adversaries tended to call on address-ees like "the people," "the commonwealth," and "the nation"; and by that rhetorical summoning, they helped to call these entities into existence. The welter of controversial English publications about the source of legal authority, the modalities of the law, and the relationship between ruler and judge created a public space for discussion and debate that became increas-ingly well populated, even by ordinary people.[15] Deng shows us, therefore, how the translation, publication, circulation, and uptake of legal discourse created a public, an inclusive juristic public that joined with others and thus contributed to the making of a democratically grounded nation-state.

Before addressing questions about the private and the public (in the last section of this overview), I want to turn to the chapters by Torrance Kirby and David Sacks, which are also featured at the start of the Introduction. Kirby counters Helgerson's argument in the last chapter of *Forms of Na-tionhood* about a deep divide in early modern England between apocalyp-tic and apologetic kinds of religious identity. On one side is Foxe's radical, story-filled *Book of Martyrs;* on the other, Hooker's conservative and philo-sophical *Lawes of Ecclesiastical Polity.* The nation-defining argument that unfolds between these two great texts, and a number of others that line up on one or the other side, takes place (as also in Deng's chapter "Writing the Law") in what is imagined as an already fully formed public sphere. Kirby is a historian of religion and here a historian of hermeneutics rather than a historian of cultural practices, but his approach shares with the other chapters in this volume a focus, not on what works of art and intellect say (as if they could speak to an already existing public world), but rather on what they do, especially how they are able to create the public world they address precisely by addressing it.

Kirby argues that Foxe and Hooker, for all the differences enumerated by Helgerson, are involved together in a sea change about what counts as real knowledge, a change that issues in what Kirby has called a "culture of persuasion." To grasp the "dynamic interplay between these two distinct modes of [Foxian and Hookerian] religious self-understanding," he says, is to begin to understand how religion itself created the conditions of possibility for public making. The Protestant argument against Catholicism, that there must be a difference between the body and blood of Christ and the signification of that body and blood, meant that the effectiveness of the Eucharist depended, not on the sheer magical power of the transformed bread and wine, but on the inward capacity of each communicant to undergo salvific transformation. The reformed sacrament in effect opened a field where the truth could not simply be taken for granted but where truth must always be the outcome of discussion and debate among conscientious people. This is how Kirby explains the effect:

> It is precisely in the definition of this liminal space between the internal and the external forums and of their interaction with one another that the conditions for a radical transformation of the forms of civil association are revealed. It is specifically through re-formation of the terms of the relation between the forum of the conscience and the external political forum that the hermeneutics of the sacrament sheds light on the conditions for the emergence of new forms of civil association, that is, "publics."

If we ask what kind of movement, what thing in motion, is able to create a public in this case, Kirby might tell us that it is the principle of sacramental movement itself—from the bread and wine as able to transubstantiate, to the receiver of the sacrament herself who changes (or does not change). If Foxe is one of the principal Elizabethan historians of "the inner private realm of individual conscience," Hooker is the leading theorist of "the external public realm of institutional order and political community." Far from being the irreconcilable rivals described by Helgerson, they were, in Kirby's account, partners in a project of public making in early modern religious culture.

Sacks's chapter, "States, Nations, and Publics: The Politics of Language Reform in Renaissance England," focuses on the local history of a single word in order to develop an important argument about the internationalism of early modern publics. The chapter bears critically on Helgerson's work and on ongoing work on publics in general. The word in question is "Greekes." The sentence in which the word appears is from Spenser's 1580 letter to Gabriel Harvey: "For why a God's name may not we, as else the Greekes, haue the kingdome of our owne Language?" Of course, this is the sentence with which Helgerson begins *Forms of Nationhood;* what Helgerson construes as Spenser's patriotic, England-centered mission of language reform sets the direction for the whole book. Sacks argues that the word "Greekes," as Spenser meant it, refers not only to the ancient founders of Western philosophy, politics, and letters, but also to a group of sixteenth-century Cambridge-based language reformers that included luminaries such as Thomas Smith and John Cheke, and that was inspired by Erasmus's program of reform of Greek pronunciation. Because of their commitment to the reform of Latin and especially Greek, they were known variously as "the Athenian tribe," "the Grecians," or "the Greeks."

This seems a small point, but it is in fact a gateway to a much larger argument about the nature of early modern publics. That argument is that Spenser's thinking and his membership in a public was not parochially English but characterized by a sense of nationality coupled with active participation in the pan-European Republic of Letters:

> when [Spenser] uttered his wish for the English to emulate the Greeks in having the kingdom of their own language, he was not only engaged in the "writing of England," but also participating as a member of England's community of humanist scholars and poets in a discussion about the role of language in culture that, under the influence of Erasmus and his followers, had since circa 1530, if not earlier, engaged the interests of an international scholarly public.

Sacks's case for the internationalism and universal values of the Republic of Letters reminds us that publics, as we have seen repeatedly in this volume, are by definition bent on growth. Publics are sectoral, but they give expression to their expansionist aspirations in the way they address themselves to the commonwealth, the nation, or the world. Sacks's chapter makes more specific the pertinence of this capacity for growth. Insofar as it makes sense to re-describe Helgerson's "discursive communities" as publics, it is also possible to see how his account of the discursive fashioning of the English nation could be reconceived in terms of a much larger process of national and international public making. Keller, Cormack, and Sacks himself, as well as a number of other "publics" essays, have begun that task.[16] There is clearly more work to do toward achieving a fuller understanding of how the movement of discourses, things, spaces, and people created publics that crossed the borders of the very nation-states they helped to create.

The Private and the Public

The members of the MaPs team discovered early in their work that the categories of the private and public are mutually exclusive and also mutually constituting. We learned we could not understand public life without also understanding privacy. We came to see the categories themselves and the relationship between them as remarkably changeful. And, as I already noted, we moved toward an understanding of publics as private-public hybrids able to rework the relationship between and the relative value of privacy and publicity. Bear in mind that in early modernity "private" and "public" were social categories: "public" people were members of the social elite, a very small group that took up most of the social and political space, while "private" people, who comprised the great majority, were excluded from public life in any strong sense.

Helgerson's account of the private and public in *Forms of Nationhood,* and especially in *Adulterous Alliances* was at the forefront of work on this crucial interrelationship. As the chapters by Lena Cowen Orlin and Angela Vanhaelen suggest, however, his work, as ground-breaking as it was, nevertheless calls for some critical rethinking, largely in terms of the theory of publics. Orlin's "Making Public the Private" looks at windows in English drama and Dutch painting. She rethinks what Helgerson has to say about the growth of the private sphere and its role in changing the social landscape of early modern Europe. The private, Helgerson tells us, is represented in plays and paintings as vulnerable to invasion by the public, an invasion usually figured as the violation of women in the home by outsiders like English kings or Dutch soldiers. Indeed, Helgerson argues, the private coalesces as a distinctive zone of activity and value as an effect of state formation. "The private sphere," Orlin says, recounting Helgerson's argument, "achieved its public character in 'response to a new organization of public power,' in 'conflicted relation to the competing cult of monarchy,' and in 'competition with the state and its history.'" "In such a figuration," she says, "the private is always already secondary, subsumed, disempowered, reactive, and vulnerable." What happens, she asks, if we think of windows not as thresholds across which the public penetrates the private but rather as instruments of display where the private impinges on the public. Looked at this way, fenestration empowers the private, giving it control over the exchanges of looks that pass between the two zones. In many plays and paintings, figures look out from windows and/or are seen in them. The fenestrated figures set the terms of visual engagement and are able to appear before the public gaze or to disappear into what we apprehend as an impenetrable interior space—a zone of privacy in itself and for itself.

Although it is true that the private became a distinct sphere in part because of the political and religious scrutiny of domestic and spiritual life, it is also the case, Orlin says, that the drama, particularly the newly invented domestic drama, contributed to the formation of a coherent private

sphere. The values of the domestic, the private, the familial, and the inward, staged in common playhouses before public audiences, engendered
a populace less compliant to public authority than victimized homebound
women such as the character Jane Shore in Heywood's *Edward IV* or the
many compromised young women in Dutch paintings.

One way to understand the changeful relationship between the private
and public is to consider that the works of art around which publics gathered were themselves public-private hybrids. Shakespeare's *Hamlet* represented in the public playhouse a struggle between private knowledge and
feeling and public discourse and political power. The painting by Gerard
ter Borch known as *Paternal Admonition,* which hung in a private home,
could be read, as Helgerson shows, either as an image of domestic order or
as a scene from a brothel.[17] The outpouring of public-private works of art,
which were integral to the growth of publics, suggests how artists, thinkers, and ordinary people were able to mobilize a wide range of nonpolitical
practices and recreational pleasures in order to rethink and redesign the
social world.

Angela Vanhaelen's chapter, with which I conclude, illuminates how
works of art could be both sources of pleasure and agents of significant
social change. She takes off from Helgerson's discussion of Dutch genre
painting, especially his argument that put history and politics back into a
genre from which it had been expelled by generations of art critics; however, she reconsiders his thinking about the politics of painting in terms
of the theory of publics. Where he sees, as Orlin has told us, a predatory
rivalry between the public and private, Vanhaelen finds something still
mindful of difference but far more creative, experimental, and socially
effective.

One example from her rich archive of hybrid works of art is the painting
Leaving for the Walk by Pieter de Hooch. It depicts a young woman and a
soldier passing directly from a private room into the Citizen's Hall in Amsterdam, a public building that was not in fact directly accessible from any
private dwelling. "It is as if every home has a door that opens directly into
the Citizen's Hall," she says, "and the many doors of the Town Hall lead directly right back into the home, so that the stock figures of genre painting
can move easily between private and civic life." *Leaving for the Walk* is mas-
terful and playful, but it is also a work that thinks creatively about gender,
domesticity, and war as well as about the intersecting spaces of privacy and
publicity. It also leads Vanhaelen to a striking reconsideration of the paintings that are at the heart of Helgerson's "Soldiers and Enigmatic Girls." He
says that the pictures can be read (characteristically, he does not insist on

his reading) as representations of the violation of private, domestic life (the young women) by public state power (the soldiers) and as expressions of an anxiety on the part of Dutch householders that their authority was being supplanted by a militaristic monarchy.[18] Vanhaelen points out that rape as an allegory of tyranny is a common feature in history paintings, but that in the genre paintings Helgerson discusses, the soldiers are not rapists and the girls not victims of sexual violence:

> History painting . . . produced multiple images of the forceful subjection of female bodies by violent male soldiers. Genre paintings—pictures made of and for the domestic interior—consciously alter this well-established pictorial tradition by wittily replacing violation with conversation. The brutal soldier and the victimized woman become the peaceful soldier and the enigmatic woman. With this strikingly new motif of intercourse between a soldier and a woman, these self-aware paintings signal their own capacity to bring about a new kind of reciprocity between public and private life.

Vanhaelen also considers a second painting by de Hooch, *Council Chamber of the Burgomasters in the Amsterdam Town Hall.* This small painting, which was made to hang in a private home, depicts people looking at a large history painting in a public hall. A male figure in sober attire is standing in front of the inset painting, lecturing a woman, no doubt his wife, about what the painting means. *Council Chamber of the Burgomasters* tells us something important about the forms of association that grew up around different genres of art. History painting is for the grand public, the expansive space where men of the upper ranks stand and discourse about matters of great consequence. Genre paintings foster a new way for people of all stripes to be together, and they open an altogether different kind of space where people sit and converse with one another. They are what Vanhaelen calls "conversation pieces," and they change the character of domestic space and private talk. "[T]hey transform the home," she says, "into a discursive realm, and thus a new kind of public realm."

Vanhaelen's chapter is exemplary of our engagement with Helgerson's scholarship. Publics theory makes possible an account of the social creativity of art and literature that is perhaps more cogent than the multifaceted version he produced over the course of writing his six books and numerous essays. It is a fine irony that his work has enabled so much of the scholarship in this volume, provided so much of the political and ethical foundation of our readings, allowed us to see the history and politics in works where it might not have previously been evident, and focused our attention on collective agency, creativity, and action rather than on the victories or tragedies of the individual in the face of society. It is also ironic, but not at all a bad thing, that Helgerson did so much of the original hard thinking about publics. Our debt to him cannot be repaid, but that too is just as it should be.

Toward the end of the disease that claimed his life, Richard Helgerson decided to take himself off life support and let nature take its course. When, however, the lawyers discovered a problem with his will and he was roused from semiconsciousness, he had the IV restarted and came back to his sound mind in order to take care of this one important piece of unfinished business. His willingness to endure suffering for the welfare of his survivors is one instance of his remarkable courage and goodness.

We have lost Richard Helgerson the man, but we still have his wonderful books and essays; and we also have the unfinished business of the historical, critical explorations to which he devoted his scholarly life. As we hope we have demonstrated, the public-making work of art and scholarship is always unfinished business. In this volume we have engaged with most of Helgerson's publications, but by no means all of them. We have undertaken to rethink his contributions to our understanding of how early modern people and the things they made changed the world, and how the new forms of association they created have issued in the political culture of modernity. We hope that this volume will prove valuable in its own right. We also hope it will confirm—by virtue of its engagement with books such as *Forms of Nationhood*—that Richard Helgerson's historical and theoretical work is assured to continue to incite and inform our understanding of art, change, and the social world—"so long as men can breathe, or eyes can see."

NOTES

1. Bronwen Wilson and Paul Yachnin, eds., *Making Publics in Early Modern Europe: People, Things, Forms of Knowledge* (New York: Routledge, 2010), 8.

2. For "discursive communities," see Richard Helgerson, *Forms of Nationhood: The Elizabethan Writing of England* (Chicago: University of Chicago Press, 1992), 13.

3. Cormack also briefly discusses the Society of Antiquaries, which flourished from around 1586 to 1608. This formal organization of mostly gentlemen scholars provides another useful way of understanding what publics are not.

4. See, for example, Kate Welch, "Making Mourning Show: Hamlet and Affective Public-making," *Performance Research* 16 (2011): 74–82; and my "Performing Publicity," *Shakespeare Bulletin* 28 (2010): 201–20.

5. Michael Warner, *Publics and Counterpublics* (New York: Zone Books, 2002), 90.

6. For paintings and maps, see Vanhaelen and Donaldson Clark in this volume; for mu-

sic and globes, see the chapters by Julie Cumming and Lesley Cormack in *Making Publics,* ed. Wilson and Yachnin.

7. Bruno Latour, *Reassembling the Social: An Introduction to Actor-Network-Theory* (Oxford: Oxford University Press, 2005), 71. Italics in original.

8. Henri Lefebvre, *The Production of Space,* trans. Donald Nicholson-Smith (Oxford: Blackwell, 1991); Michel Foucault, *Power/Knowledge: Selected Interviews and Other Writings, 1972–1977,* ed. and trans. Colin Gordon (New York: Pantheon, 1980); Gaston Bachelard, *The Poetics of Space,* trans. Maria Jolas (Boston: Beacon Press, 1969). Other notable work includes David Harvey, *Cosmopolitanism and the Geographies of Freedom* (New York: Columbia University Press, 2009); Michel de Certeau, *The Practice of Everyday Life,* trans. Steven Rendall (Berkeley: University of California Press, 1984); and Edward W. Soja, *Postmodern Geographies: The Reassertion of Space in Critical Social Theory* (London: Verso, 1989).

9. Hannah Arendt, *The Human Condition,* 2nd ed. (Chicago: University of Chicago Press, 1998), 95–96.

10. Ibid., 57.

11. Of course, Arendt might object that the character of the thing and the process of gathering make no difference as what she has in mind is how reality emerges from the structure of relationship rather than from a particular relationship between the evident self-sameness of the thing and the different views of it.

12. Helgerson, *Forms of Nationhood,* 22.

13. *Julius Caesar,* ed. Arthur Humphries (Oxford: Oxford University Press, 1984), 3.1.111–13.

14. Helgerson, *Forms of Nationhood,* 100.

15. Deng does not have space to discuss it, but the engagement with issues of private and public law everywhere in early modern English drama provides substantial support for his argument for the formation of a "juristic public." See, to take one example, Lorna Hutson, *The Invention of Suspicion: Law and Mimesis in Shakespeare and Renaissance Drama* (Oxford: Oxford University Press, 2007).

16. See a number of the essays in *Making Space Public in Early Modern Europe: Performance, Geography, Privacy,* ed. Angela Vanhaelen and Joseph P. Ward (New York: Routledge, 2013).

17. Richard Helgerson, *Adulterous Alliances: Home, State, and History in Early Modern Drama and Painting* (Chicago: University of Chicago Press, 2000), 79–81.

18. Ibid., 84.

About the Contributors

JAVIER CASTRO-IBASETA is Lecturer III in the Romance Languages and Literatures department at the University of Michigan. His work focuses on the interconnections between political life and literature in early modern Spain, and particularly on the way in which the emergence of public forms of literature affected the feudal dynamics of government and protest. He is currently finishing a book titled *Beware the Poetry: Political Satire and the Emergence of the Public Sphere in Spain, 1600–1645*. He has a PhD, a Spanish Diploma de Estudios Avanzados, and a BA from the Universidad Autónoma de Madrid.

MEREDITH DONALDSON CLARK currently holds a postdoctoral fellowship at the University of Toronto (English) from the Social Sciences and Humanities Research Council of Canada (SSHRC). She received her PhD in English literature from McGill University and has taught courses on early modern literature at McGill University and Nipissing University. She recently published "'Now through You Made Public for Everyone': John Ogilby's *Britannia* (1675), the 1598 Peutinger Map Facsimile and the Shaping of Public Space," in *Making Space Public in Early Modern Europe* (2013) and "Hymnic Epic and *The Faerie Queene*'s Original Printed Format: Canto-Canticles and Psalmic Arguments" (coauthored with Kenneth Borris, *Renaissance Quarterly,* 2011). Current projects include articles on the rhetorical underpinnings of Renaissance ekphrasis, on John Milton's engagement with contemporary theories of decay and progress, and her postdoctoral research, which focuses on monuments and the writing of early modern English nationhood.

LESLEY B. CORMACK is a historian of early modern science, specializing in geography and mathematics in sixteenth-century England. She received her PhD from the University of Toronto in 1988 and taught at the University of Alberta in the Department of History and Classics for seventeen years. From 2007 to 2010, she was the dean of the Faculty of Arts and Social Sciences at Simon Fraser University. In July 2010, she became the dean of the Faculty of Arts at the University of Alberta. Her publications include *Charting an Empire: Geography at the English Universities 1580–1620* (1997); (with Andrew Ede) *A History of Science in Society: From Philosophy to Utility* (2004; 2nd ed., substantially revised, 2012); and *Making*

Contact: Maps, Identity, and Travel, coedited with Glenn Burger, Jonathan Hart, and Natalia Pylypiuk (2003); as well as a number of articles on early modern geography, cartography, and universities. She has been a team member of a SSHRC-funded MCRI project, *Making Publics,* and a coinvestigator for a SSHRC-funded Cluster, *Situating Science,* and is past president of the Canadian Society for the History and Philosophy of Science. Lesley is presently working on a monograph-length study, funded by SSHRC, entitled *The Molyneux Globes and Mathematical Culture: Instruments, Practitioners and Scholars in an Age of Discovery,* and an edited volume, *Mathematical Practitioners and the Transformation of Natural Knowledge in Early Modern Europe.*

STEPHEN DENG is an associate professor of English at Michigan State University. He is the author of *Coinage and State Formation in Early Modern English Literature* (2011) and coeditor of *Global Traffic: Discourses and Practices of Trade in English Literature and Culture from 1550 to 1700* (2008). He is currently writing a book on *Hamlet* and accountability.

MARLENE EBERHART teaches music history and ear training at Vanier College in Montreal. She was the project manager and a postdoctoral researcher for the Making Publics (MaPs) Project from 2005 to 2011. A former orchestral flutist, she studied at Baldwin-Wallace College (Ohio), the Royal Conservatory in Liège, Belgium, and the Jacobs School of Music at Indiana University–Bloomington. Her research brings into collaboration the history of the senses, the public (and private) life of the performing and visual arts, and early modern Venice. She has published articles on Titian, Aretino, and the evolving sensory spaces of early modern public life, including an essay in *Making Space Public in Early Modern Europe: Performance, Geography, Privacy,* and continues to investigate the sensory dynamics of early modern publics. She is currently coediting (with Matthew Milner) an interdisciplinary collection on the senses in sixteenth-century Europe.

PATRICIA FUMERTON is a professor of English at the University of California, Santa Barbara, and director of UCSB's NEH-funded online English Broadside Ballad Archive (EBBA). In addition to numerous articles, she is author of the monographs *Unsettled: The Culture of Mobility and the Working Poor in Early Modern England* (2006) and *Cultural Aesthetics: Renaissance Literature and the Practice of Social Ornament* (1991). She is also the editor of *Broadside Ballads from the Pepys Collection: A Selection of Texts, Approaches, and Recordings* (2012) as well as coeditor of *Ballads and Broadsides in Britain, 1500–1800* (2010) and *Renaissance Culture and the Everyday* (1999). She is currently adding to EBBA the pre-1701 broadside ballads from the Houghton Library, Harvard University, and working on her new book, *Moving Media, Tactical Publics: English Broadside Ballads in the Early Modern Period.*

JEAN E. HOWARD is George Delacorte Professor in the Humanities at Columbia University, where she teaches early modern and contemporary drama and feminist studies. An editor of *The Norton Shakespeare,* she is the author of *Shakespeare's Art of Orchestration: Stage Technique and Audience Response* (1984); *The Stage and Social Struggle in Early Modern England* (1994); (with Phyllis Rackin) *Engendering a Nation: A Feminist Account of Shakespeare's English Histories* (1997); *Theater of a City: The Places of London Comedy, 1579–1642* (2007); and, most recently (with Crystal Bartolovich), *Marx and Shakespeare* (2012). She is presently completing a book on uses of history in contemporary theater that focuses on Caryl Churchill and Tony Kushner.

VERA KELLER is an assistant professor of history at the Robert D. Clark Honors College of the University of Oregon. A historian of science, Keller is interested in the theories and practices of sociability in the study of nature. She is the author of articles in *Ambix, British Journal for the History of Science, Configurations, Early Science and Medicine, History of Science, Isis, Journal for the History of Ideas, Nuncius,* and *William and Mary Quarterly.* Her first book project (forthcoming, Cambridge) explores the coproduction of science and politics via a history of desiderata, or collective, epistemic wish lists.

TORRANCE KIRBY is a professor of ecclesiastical history and director of the Centre for Research on Religion, McGill University. His recent books include *Persuasion and Conversion: Religion, Politics, and the Public Sphere in Early Modern England* (2013), *The Zurich Connection and Tudor Political Theology* (2007), and *Richard Hooker, Reformer and Platonist* (2005). He also edited *A Companion to Richard Hooker* (2008) and *A Companion to Peter Martyr Vermigli* (2009) and is coeditor with Paul Stanwood of *Paul's Cross and the Culture of Persuasion in England, 1520–1640* (2014).

JEFFREY KNAPP is Chancellor's Professor of English at the University of California, Berkeley. The author of *An Empire Nowhere* (1992), *Shakespeare's Tribe* (2002), and *Shakespeare Only* (2009), Knapp is currently completing a book titled *Pleasing Everyone: Mass Entertainment in Renaissance London and Golden-Age Hollywood.*

DAVID LEE MILLER is Carolina Distinguished Professor of English and Comparative Literature at the University of South Carolina, where he directs the Center for Digital Humanities. He is the author of two books, *The Poem's Two Bodies: The Poetics of the 1590* Faerie Queene (1988), and *Dreams of the Burning Child: Sacrificial Sons and the Father's Witness* (2003); the coeditor of several collections; and one of five general editors of "The Collected Works of Edmund Spenser," under contract to Oxford University Press.

LENA COWEN ORLIN is a professor of English at Georgetown University, executive director of the Shakespeare Association of America, and one of many who are grateful for the personal and intellectual exemplarity of Richard Helgerson. She is the author of *Private Matters and Public Culture in Post-Reformation England* (1994) and *Locating Privacy in Tudor London* (2007). Her edited collections include

Othello: The State of Play (2014); *Center or Margin: Revisions of the English Renaissance in Honor of Leeds Barroll* (2006); (with Stanley Wells) *Shakespeare: An Oxford Guide* (2003); and *Material London, ca. 1600* (2000). She has also coedited (with Russ McDonald) *The Bedford Shakespeare* (2014).

ANNE LAKE PRESCOTT, Helen Goodhart Altschul Professor of English Emerita at Barnard College, is the former president of the Sixteenth Century Society, John Donne Society, and Spenser Society. Author of *French Poets and the English Renaissance* and *Imagining Rabelais in Renaissance England,* she is the coeditor of *Spenser Studies* and the Norton edition of Spenser, as well as, with Betty Travitsky, an Ashgate series of texts by early modern women. She has recently written on Renaissance jest books, some Neo-Latin translations of Ronsard, the Renaissance David and images of upward mobility, and Thomas More's role in a sci-fi novel by R. A. Lafferty.

DAVID HARRIS SACKS, Richard F. Scholz Professor of History and Humanities at Reed College, holds a BA degree in history from Brooklyn College and an AM and PhD in history from Harvard University, where he taught before moving in 1986 to Reed College, Portland, Oregon. His published works include *The Widening Gate: Bristol and the Atlantic Economy, 1450–1700* (1991); an edition of Thomas More's *Utopia* (1999); and a collection of essays, edited with Donald R. Kelley, on *The Historical Imagination in Early Modern Britain: History, Rhetoric, and Fiction, 1500–1800* (1997); plus more than thirty articles and essays in early modern British and Atlantic history.

AMY SCOTT completed a PhD at McGill University in 2010 under the supervision of Paul Yachnin. Her dissertation, "Finding Faith between Infidelities: Historiography as Mourning in Shakespeare," was awarded the McGill Arts Insights Dissertation Award in 2010 (given to the best dissertation in the Faculty of Arts). Thinking about the ethics of history in her dissertation has led her to work on early modern funeral practices, including the rituals of dressing, waking, burying, and elegizing the dead. Her current research focuses on how religious practices both before and after the Reformation influenced early modern historiography, theater, and historical drama. She is currently preparing a monograph based on her dissertation.

ANGELA VANHAELEN is associate professor of art history in the Department of Art History and Communication Studies at McGill University. She is the author of *The Wake of Iconoclasm: Painting the Church in the Dutch Republic* (2012), which was awarded the 2013 Roland H. Bainton Book Prize by the Sixteenth Century Society and Conference. She is also author of *Comic Print and Theatre in Early Modern Amsterdam: Gender, Childhood and the City* (2003). She has recently coedited (with Joseph Ward) the volume *Making Space Public in Early Modern Europe: Performance, Geography, Privacy* (2012). She is coeditor (with Bronwen Wilson) of a special issue of the journal *Art History,* "The Erotics of Looking: Materiality, Solicitation and Netherlandish Visual Culture" (November 2012), and has published articles in journals such as *Art Bulletin, Oxford Art Journal, De Zeventiende Eeuw, Art History,* and *RES: Journal of Anthropology and Aesthetics.*

PAUL YACHNIN was born in Montreal and educated at McGill, Edinburgh, and the University of Toronto. He is Tomlinson Professor of Shakespeare Studies and Director of the Institute for the Public Life of Arts and Ideas at McGill. He directed the Making Publics (MaPs) project (2005–10) and now directs the project Early Modern Conversions (2012–18). He is past president of the Shakespeare Association of America. Among his publications are the books *Stage-Wrights* and *The Culture of Playgoing in Early Modern England* (with Anthony Dawson); coedited editions of *Richard II* and *The Tempest;* and four coedited books, including *Making Publics in Early Modern Europe.* His book-in-progress is *Making Theatrical Publics in Shakespeare's England.* His ideas about the social life of art, and those of his MaPs collaborators, were featured on the fourteen-part CBC Radio IDEAS series *The Origins of the Modern Public.*

Index